THE
BIBLE WAR
IN IRELAND

THE BIBLE WAR IN IRELAND

The 'Second Reformation'
and the Polarization of Protestant-
Catholic Relations, 1800–1840

IRENE WHELAN

The Lilliput Press | Dublin

First published 2005 by
THE LILLIPUT PRESS
62–63 Sitric Road, Arbour Hill,
Dublin 7, Ireland
www.lilliputpress.ie

Copyright © Irene Whelan, 2005

All rights reserved. No part of this publication may
be reproduced in any form or by any means
without the prior permission of the publisher.

A CIP record for this title is available from
The British Library.

ISBN 1 84351 004 9

1 3 5 7 9 10 8 6 4 2

Set in 10.5pt on 14.5pt Caslon
Printed by MPG Books, Bodmin, Cornwall

*For my mother, Esther Roche Whelan,
and for Daniel Ezergailis*

Contents

List of Illustrations	IX
Acknowledgments	XI
Introduction	XV
Abbreviations	XX

One: Eighteenth-Century Antecedents
Religious Revival and International Awakening	3
Cultural Revival and National Awakening	19
Renewal and Reaction: A Tale of Two Irelands	37

Two: The Age of Moral Reform
Religious Revival in the Church of Ireland	53
Agents and Agencies of Moral Reform	62
The Grand Design	76

Three: The Mission to the Catholic Population
The Methodist Example	86
The Challenge of Dissent: The London Hibernian and Baptist Societies	92
The 'Quiet Progress' of the Church of Ireland	108
The Popular Response to the Evangelical Mission	118

Four: The Politics of Catholic Emancipation
Ambitions and Frustrations	125
The Bible Society Crisis of 1819–20	131
Millenarianism and Popular Sectarianism	141

FIVE: THE 'SECOND REFORMATION' 1822–7
    Archbishop Magee and the Church Militant   153
    Moral Ascendancy and the Landed Elite   161
    Conversions and Controversy: Kingscourt and Askeaton   172
    Conversions and Social Conflict   187

SIX: THE CATHOLIC COUNTER-ATTACK
    The Vindication of Catholic Ireland: Bishop Doyle and
        Prince Hohenlohe   193
    The Bible War of 1824   204
    Propaganda and Counter-Propaganda   209
    Controversial Sermons and Monster Debates   224

SEVEN: NEW DIRECTIONS, 1828–40
    Retrenchment and Redefinition   232
    Archbishop Trench and the Evangelical Movement in the West   238
    The Idea of Protestant Colonies: The Achill and Dingle
        Experiments   251

Conclusion   266
Appendix A: Tracts on the Popish Controversy   275
Appendix B: Richard Lalor Shiel's Account of a Contest between
    Doyle and Magee   276
Notes   279
Bibliography   320
Index   339

List of Illustrations

(between pages 156 and 157)

Selina Hastings, countess of Huntingdon (1707–91).

Gideon Ouseley (1762–1839).

Methodist Meeting House, The Mall, Castlebar, County Mayo. Built by the earl of Lucan. The foundation stone was laid by John Wesley in 1785. Courtesy of Deirdre Hopkins, Ross East, Castlebar, County Mayo.

Robert Jocelyn (1788–1870), 1st Viscount Jocelyn (later Lord Roden). Artist: George Harlow, 1817. Courtesy of Robert Jocelyn, 10th earl of Roden, Doon House, Cashel, County Galway.

James Warren Doyle (1786–1834), bishop of Kildare and Leighlin (1819–34). Courtesy of the Cathedral of the Assumption, Carlow.

Tollymore House, Castlewellan, County Down. Courtesy of Robert Jocelyn, 10th earl of Roden, Doon House, Cashel, County Galway.

Robert Edward King (1773–1881), 1st Viscount Lorton. Courtesy of King House, Boyle, County Roscommon.

View of Rockingham House and Lough Key, Boyle, County Roscommon, from John D'Alton's *Annals of Boyle* (Dublin 1845).

Dr William Magee (1766–1831), archbishop of Dublin (1822–31). Courtesy of Trinity College Dublin.

Dr John MacHale (1791–1881), archbishop of Tuam (1834–81). Courtesy of St Patrick's College, Maynooth.

Frontispiece of Archbishop Magee's sermon in St Patrick's Cathedral, Dublin, 24 October 1822.

Frontispiece of Bishop Doyle's *Vindication of the Rights and Civil Principles of the Irish Catholics* (Dublin 1823).

Memorial to Bishop Doyle by John Hogan in Carlow Cathedral. Courtesy of the Cathedral of the Assumption, Carlow.

Memorial to John Jebb (1775–1833), bishop of Limerick (1822–33), in St Mary's Cathedral, Limerick.

View of the Church of Ireland, Ardcarne, County Roscommon, from John D'Alton's *Annals of Boyle* (Dublin 1845).

Postcard of the Achill Mission from the early twentieth century.

Acknowledgments

I have received much support during the years it took to complete this work, and it is a pleasure now to acknowledge it. I would like to thank Queen's University, Belfast, for a Riddel Bursary during the initial stages of my research, and for a Junior Research Fellowship at the Institute of Irish Studies. I would also like to thank the Woodrow Wilson National Fellowship Foundation of Princeton, New Jersey, for a Charlotte W. Newcombe Doctoral Dissertation Fellowship.

I am grateful to the following libraries and record depositories for allowing me to consult material in their possession: the British Library; the Cavan County Library; the Church of Ireland College of Education, Rathmines; the Dublin Diocesan Archives; Galway County Library; the Linen Hall Library; the Memorial Library of the University of Wisconsin-Madison; the National Archives of Ireland; the National Library of Ireland; the New York Public Library; the Public Record Office of Northern Ireland; the library of Queen's University, Belfast; the library of the Representative Church Body, Dublin; the School of Oriental and African Studies, London; the library of Trinity College Dublin; the library of Westminster College, Cambridge, for access to the Cheshunt Foundation papers; and the Zentralbibliothek, Zurich, for access to the Pestalozzi papers. Finally, a special thanks to Rhonna Goodman and the staff of Manhattanville College Library, particularly Susan Majdak of interlibrary loans who facilitated my every need with efficiency and patience.

This project was begun when I was a graduate student at the University of Wisconsin–Madison, and it is to my supervisor, James S. Donnelly, that I owe

Acknowledgments

the greatest debt. His conscientiousness helped to keep me on track over what was often a rocky and turbulent road, and the standard of scholarship he upheld was always inspirational. If this book lives up to his expectations I will be well satisfied. I would also like to acknowledge the kindness and support of Dr Ronnie Buchanan who was Director of the Institute of Irish Studies during my time in Belfast, as well as the friendship and advice of David Hempton, Myrtle Hill and Joseph Liechty, scholars whose knowledge of evangelical history was far superior to mine. They pointed me in directions I might not otherwise have considered, and without their input this book would have been much diminished. Needless to add, any errors are solely the responsibility of the author.

In the United States I have benefited greatly from the community of scholars engaged in Irish studies. From the very beginning of my ventures into Irish religious history, Kerby Miller has been a bulwark of support, always ready to share his knowledge and enthusiasm. Bill Kelleher and Jo Thomas, Gearóid Ó hAllmhuráin and Cecilia McDonnell, and Nancy J. Curtin have provided fellowship as well as practical help. In Madison Dineen Grow shared her wonderful friendship as well as her love of Irish culture. Likewise, my Irish-American relatives have contributed enormously to my sense of community and belonging in my adoptive homeland. Maureen Barrett and Bill Verdier of Nashville, Kathleen Jennings of Seattle, Bobby Ryan and his family of Staten Island, Maura Ryan Tier and her family of Brielle, New Jersey, and the various outposts of the Roche family in Pittsburgh and Los Angeles, have all personified the ties that bind the inhabitants of the Irish diaspora.

In New York there are many who have enhanced my life with their friendship and kindness. Maureen Faherty of New Rochelle and her late husband, Marty, made me a part of their family in a way that only emigrants from Ireland could, and Marty's premature death left a void in my life that will never be filled. Frank and Monica Durkan were a constant source of reassurance and support. Phil and Ruth D'Antoni provided friendship and hospitality in New York as well as Connemara, and Jacqueline Sareil helped me to organize my life around keeping a foothold on both sides of the Atlantic.

I wish to express my gratitude to my colleagues at Manhattanville College for providing intellectual stimulation and a supportive work environment. Gillian Greenhill and Randy Hannum deserve special thanks for never failing to be on hand when help was needed, and for their most gracious and generous hospitality. Cecilia Winters has been a model of courage and dedication to her academic community and her family, and not least a wonderful friend to me.

Acknowledgments

My colleagues in the History Department, Lawson Bowling, Mohammed Mbodg and Colin Morris, have helped to make my work environment collegial and intellectually challenging. Finally, a special thanks is due to the technology staff. Tom Joyner's understated graciousness and gentle humour always made the most difficult computing task seem like child's play, and Gale Justin was an artist as well as a teacher in guiding me through the mysteries of incorporating visual images and organizing text. They both taught me how technology can serve the needs of scholarship, and it is something I will forever appreciate.

In Ireland there are many people who have made the exigencies of my transatlantic journeyings not only bearable but enjoyable. A special place is reserved for Josephine Griffin who shared the challenges of graduate-student life at the University of Wisconsin and whose friendship has been one of the greatest blessings of my life. In recent years she and her husband, Colm Luibhéid, have made their lovely home in Claregalway a haven of repose and hospitality during my visits home. In Galway and Clare my friends Eileen Mannion and Alan Brannelly, Anne Brew and Daithi Scanlon, and Fidelma O'Neill have proved that distance is no impediment to bonds that seem to grow stronger and more precious with time.

In Dublin, Jackie Hill has been a source of kindness and support beyond what I could ever hope to repay. She provided friendship and accommodation in good times and bad, and kept me in touch with the Irish scholarly and intellectual world. Also in Dublin, Linda Kellicut and Chris Foley, and John Hegarty and Neasa Ní Chinnéide provided wonderful hospitality and helped me to accommodate and to make sense of the breakneck pace of change in contemporary Ireland. To Neasa, whose love of the Irish language has always been inspiring, and who gave most generously of her time and hospitality to introduce me to the Dingle Peninsula, I wish to register a special thanks. To my cousin Jack Whelan of Dundalk and his wife Agnes I would like to express gratitude for a lifetime of care and concern as well as shared memories.

In Clifden it is not just individuals but an entire community whose support I feel compelled to acknowledge. Nevertheless, a number of people deserve to be thanked individually, among them Brendan Flynn, Anne and John Marshall, and Sr Immacula, formerly of the Mercy Convent and Anne Lee Ueltschi of Streamstown. Mrs Mary Whelan and her family of Castle Demesne and my uncle Thomas Roche and his family of Fahy, have always provided that indefinable sense of home so precious to the returning exile. In a similar vein, Bernadette Gavin Flynn, Freddie Gibbons, Bríd Clancy McLoughlin, Mary

Acknowledgments

O'Malley, Laura Kelly, Kathleen Villiers Tuthill, Carmel Lyden and Mary O'Connor de Brún have sustained friendships that are continually renewed and refreshed with each visit.

There are a number of people without whose help this book would never have become a reality. Cormac Ó Gráda and David Dickson played a key role in putting me in touch with The Lilliput Press. Brendan Barrington shepherded the project through the vital early stages of acceptance, and edited the text with a skilful and sensitive hand. Marsha Swan and Aedín Mac Devitt completed the editing process with patience and efficiency, and in record time. Finally, Antony Farrell has been a publisher *sans pareil* who never skimped on time or energy when I needed assistance and advice. To all of them I owe an enormous debt of gratitude for bringing this project to completion. Robert Jocelyn of Doon House, Cashel, Connemara, read and commented on an earlier version of this work. He also allowed me to consult the Roden family papers in his library and provided the photographs of Viscount Jocelyn and Tollymore House for the illustrations. To him and his wife, Ann Henning, I wish to express heartfelt thanks for having shared their scholarly and literary interests, as well as their great love for Connemara and its people.

No accounting of gratitude owed would be complete without mention of my extended family in Ireland and abroad. The support of my brothers, Tommy and Paddy, and my sisters, Margaret Ann, Mary, Regina and Philomena, and their families has been so great that, simply put, I do not believe I would have prevailed in its absence. My father, Joe Whelan, did not live to see this book completed, but I hope he would have approved of the result. My mother's generosity and constancy over the years would be impossible either to measure or repay. Her kindness and love, and not least her good humour, ensured that our home on the Sky Road always had a central place in our hearts. In recognition of her devotion to me and to all of our family, I dedicate this book to her. I also dedicate it to Daniel Ezergailis, whose creative spirit and dedication to his art has been the greatest inspiration of my life.

Introduction

This is a study of the role of evangelical religion in shaping the attitudes of Irish Protestants in the great age of revolution and counter-revolution between 1750 and 1840. My purpose in writing it has been twofold. First, to examine how the religious enthusiasm associated with the international awakening of the eighteenth century took root and flourished in Ireland. Second, to illustrate how this movement affected relations between Protestants and Catholics during a period in which existing political establishments throughout the European and colonial worlds were challenged, and in some cases overturned and destroyed, by the rise of democratic nationalism and the demand for representative government.

Religious safety had been an abiding preoccupation for Ireland's Protestant community since the sixteenth century, and religion continued to define the identity of colonial Ireland in the eighteenth century. It was only to be expected, as the new winds of revivalism swept through the international Protestant world, that Ireland would be among the countries caught up in the excitement. The main focus of the opening chapter of this book is therefore to locate Ireland's place in the 'international community of the saints', to establish the social class of those who first rallied to the evangelical standard, to chart the cultural and political forces that were driving certain well-defined groups to embrace the principle of 'Protestant ascendancy' (the exclusion of Catholics from the political process) and to explain why the turmoil of the 1790s caused these trends to converge into a powerful expression of counter-revolutionary zeal.

The challenges facing Irish society in the last quarter of the eighteenth century were a consequence of economic and political change reflective of the country's position in the dynamic world of Britain's Atlantic empire. Rapid economic growth, population increase, class conflict and a volatile political climate were all familiar components of Irish life in the decades after 1750. By the 1790s, failure to achieve political reform had brought the country to a condition of civil war, and the catastrophic experience of rebellion and reaction left a dangerous political vacuum in its wake. For many this was filled by a conservative piety, inspired by the belief that moral reform grounded in biblical Christianity was the most effective guarantor of social and political stability.

In the years immediately following the Union, the belief gained widespread currency that the native population of Ireland, like that of Wales and Scotland, could be made peaceful, industrious and loyal through scripture-based education designed to wean them from their traditional allegiance to Catholicism, preparing them for integration into the Protestant establishment of Church and State. The route through which this ideology gained ascendancy in Ireland, the emergence of an evangelical elite of moral reformers in business and the professions as well as clerical life, and the strategies used to extend the moral revolution to the Catholic population are examined in chapters two and three. Among the issues addressed in this part of the book is the degree to which this movement was part of the evangelization of the Celtic fringe, in which the native populations of Wales and Scotland were brought within the orbit of 'awakened Christianity' by preachers and instructors fluent in the native languages. This process, it is argued, was part of a broader movement in which the Celtic periphery was subjected to an economic and cultural transformation, through which it was acclimatized to the new political and economic realities of the nineteenth century.

The full implications of the moral revolution in Ireland pointed ultimately to the Protestant establishment claiming authority over the direction in which the consciousness of the Catholic population would develop. It was an ambition that would make a battleground of the area marked out by the evangelicals as their primary territory of advancement, namely popular education. During a period in which the Catholic Church was itself experiencing a powerful surge of growth and renewal and the ambitions of Catholics generally were invested in obtaining political equality, this challenge was bound to cause friction. In the combustible atmosphere that followed the ending of the Napoleonic Wars, it proved to be explosive. Conscious of the threat both to the institutional Church and the political ambitions of Catholics generally, two of the most outspoken leaders, Rev. John MacHale and Daniel O'Connell, publicly condemned the policies of evangelical agencies whom they accused of perverting the ideals of education in order to subvert the political ambitions of the Catholic population. Chapter four examines the Emancipation movement against this background of cultural and political conflict and seeks to explain why the evangelical challenge drew the Catholic clergy into the political arena, where they staked out their own claim for authority over the hearts and minds of their congregations.

Catholic resistance to the evangelical vision for a 'new reformation' in Ireland greatly increased the political and sectarian tension of the early 1820s. A new avenue of hostile public debate was opened up with the famous 'antithetical' sermon delivered by the archbishop of Dublin, William Magee, at his inauguration in St Patrick's Cathedral in October of 1822. Magee claimed that the Church of Ireland was the only legitimate ecclesiastical body in the country and called on its followers to embrace the evangelical vision and work towards bringing the entire population, including Catholics and Dissenters, into its fold. His charge revealed the degree to which the Church of Ireland was ready to take the lead in the moral crusade, and the symbiotic relationship between the Church and a core of great landed families who now began a serious campaign to implement the reformation at the local level. Chapter five addresses the political background to Magee's charge, the role of the 'Bible gentry' in furthering the drive for converts, and the effect of these events on denominational relations and popular sectarianism.

More immediate and more dynamic in its impact on political events was the response Magee's sermon drew from the Catholic quarter, particularly from the youthful and articulate bishop of Kildare and Leighlin, James Warren Doyle. The context of Bishop Doyle's political debut in responding to the evangelical challenge, the role played by rhetoric and propaganda in the Emancipation campaign, and the forging of political links between Catholic clergy and lay political leaders is examined in chapter six. The primary focus of this chapter is on the importance of print culture and propaganda, most particularly on Doyle's role as the leading theorist and propagandist of the Catholic cause, and the revolution in consciousness that accompanied the Catholic response to the challenge of the evangelical crusade.

Even as the prospect of a new reformation at the national level began to recede, the evangelical movement did not evaporate, but continued to increase in scope and influence among the Protestant population. The final chapter deals with the emergence of rival religious-based national identities in the period after Emancipation and the redirection of the evangelical movement to the

Introduction

impoverished, Irish-speaking west, where it would set the scene for another, more acrimonious phase of missionary activity during and immediately after the years of the Great Famine.

The scope of the present work was determined by its focus on the origins and growth of the Irish evangelical movement in the eighteenth and early nineteenth centuries, and the concrete historical circumstances that made the decade of the 1820s the crucible in which the lines of denominational rivalry and political polarization were redrawn and redefined. While the term 'Second Reformation' is usually associated with the period 1822–7, and more specifically with the events on the Farnham Estate in County Cavan in 1826–7, I use it in the more general sense to apply to the movement to evangelize the Catholic population that had its origins in the years immediately after 1798.

One advantage of this approach is that it allows for a consideration of the movement's international origins in the eighteenth century. Historiography of the 'Second Reformation' has tended to focus on the 1820s and the uproar occasioned by Archbishop Magee's famous sermon. In his pioneering study, *The Protestant Crusade in Ireland, 1800–70* (1978), Desmond Bowen was certainly correct in highlighting 1822 as a watershed in Protestant–Catholic relations. But his description of the conflict as '… beginning abruptly in 1822 with a declaration of war by a Protestant prelate'[1] at a time when denominational relations were otherwise congenial, ignores forces that had been in motion for a long time, certainly since the tumultuous 1790s and arguably since Bishop Woodward's assertion of the need for Protestant 'ascendancy' in 1787. If clerical leaders embraced tolerance and conciliation in the early 1820s, it was precisely because they feared the implications of the approaching storm.

Bowen's *Protestant Crusade* is, to date, the only full-length study of the denominational conflict generated by the 'Second Reformation', although the event is dealt with in several other important works on Irish religious history. David Hempton and Myrtle Hill's landmark study *Evangelical Protestantism in Ulster Society, 1740–1890* (1992) offers an especially valuable account of its impact in Ulster, where evangelicalism eventually came to dominate political culture. Stewart J. Brown's *The National Churches of England, Ireland and Scotland, 1801–1846* (2002) examines the movement as the Irish dimension of an attempt to create a Protestant United Kingdom through the imposition of religious orthodoxy. Finally, the influence of the reformation crusade on Catholic politics and public opinion during the crucial years 1824–7 is dealt with in *Politics, Interdenominational Relations and Education in the Public Ministry of Bishop James*

Introduction

Doyle of Kildare and Leighlin, 1786–1834 (1999), the first of Thomas McGrath's magisterial two-volume work on the career of Bishop Doyle. I have benefited enormously from the work of these scholars and I hope that the present work will build upon what they have accomplished. My main objective in this study is to locate the 'Second Reformation' in a broader cultural and historical context and to evaluate its contribution to the growth of rival religious and political traditions in Ireland.

In spite of Catholic victory in the Emancipation campaign and the introduction of a national system of elementary education in 1831, the evangelical crusade to win converts from Catholicism did not cease. In one form or another, either in the colonies of the west or in the slums of Dublin, the reformation movement and the sectarian hostility that accompanied it endured throughout a good part of the nineteenth century. By the 1840s its impetus had spread into the Presbyterian community and was being exported along with the great migration of the Catholic Irish into Britain, the United States and the colonies of Canada and Australia. At the national level, however, in spite of the attempts that were being made on the western seaboard, the battle for the minds and hearts of the Catholic population had been decidedly lost. On the eve of the Famine the Catholic Church was in a stronger position than it ever might have been had evangelicals not issued their challenge of moral and religious supremacy during the crucial decade of the 1820s. The hardened antagonism that had come to define relations between Protestant and Catholic during that turbulent decade would carry over to become a permanent feature of the Irish political landscape.

IRENE WHELAN
Sky Road, Clifden
August 2005

Abbreviations

ADV   Association for Discountenancing Vice and Promoting the Knowledge and Practice of the Christian Religion

BFBS   British and Foreign Bible Society

CMS   Church Missionary Society

HBS   Hibernian Bible Society

KPS   Kildare Place Society (The Society for the Education of the Poor in Ireland)

LHS   London Hibernian Society (Originally the London Hibernian Society for the Diffusion of Religious Knowledge in Ireland, in 1814 the name was changed to the London Hibernian Society for Establishing Schools and Circulating the Holy Scriptures in Ireland)

LMS   London Missionary Society

THE
BIBLE WAR
IN IRELAND

—ONE—
Eighteenth-Century Antecedents

These New Lights have arisen in Ireland also. They are nicknamed Swadlers [*sic*]. As far as I have been able to learn, their religion is a monster in spirituals, begotten by Jacob Beman upon Mrs. Hutchinson—Count Zinzendorf rocked its cradle—Mrs. Law was its nurse—Messrs. Whitefield and Wesley were its sponsors—and the Devil was the midwife that ushered the brat into existence.

ATTRIBUTED TO JONATHAN SWIFT[1]

Poor wretched Ireland ... shall yet have a Gospel day. I can't yet see how or when, but it must be, and till then, my eye is only waiting darkily [*sic*] for its accomplishment.

SELINA HASTINGS, COUNTESS OF HUNTINGDON[2]

The British muse is not yet informed that she has an elder sister in this isle; let us introduce them to each other. Together let them walk abroad from their bowers, sweet ambassadresses of cordial union between two countries that seem formed by nature to be joined by every bond of interest and of amity. Let them entreat of Britain to cultivate a nearer acquaintance with her neighbouring isle. Let them conciliate for us her esteem and her affection will follow of course. Let them tell her that the portion of her blood which flows in our veins is rather ennobled than disgraced by the mingling tides that descended from our heroic ancestors.

CHARLOTTE BROOKE[3]

RELIGIOUS REVIVAL AND INTERNATIONAL AWAKENING

It is clear from the characteristically acerbic account of Dean Swift quoted above that, by the middle of the eighteenth century, the hybrid product we have come to know as 'religious enthusiasm' or 'vital religion' had found a footing in Ireland. A decoding of the terms and personalities referred to by Swift indicates that Irish revivalism was being fed through several international channels that spanned the entire Protestant world, from central Europe to North America.[4] Thanks to a rich flowering of scholarship in the history of the evangelical movement in the eighteenth century, we now have a more complete understanding of its dimensions as well as its role as a catalyst in the development of the Protestant missionary awakening.[5] In the light of modern historiography, therefore, Swift's encapsulated account of the origins of evangelicalism may be seen to have stood the test of time. It also provides an obvious and welcome starting point from which to assess the place of Ireland in what Susan O'Brien has called a 'transatlantic community of saints'.

The wellspring of missionary evangelism in the early eighteenth century was to be found among the oppressed Protestant minorities of central Europe whose geographic location had placed them outside the ring-fence secured by the Peace of Westphalia in 1648 for those countries with Protestant Church establishments. Such communities were to be found mainly in Silesia, Moravia and Bohemia. Under threat from the confessional absolutism of the Hapsburg state, they developed a new awareness of how spiritual needs could be accommodated outside the formal structure of a Church establishment. This awareness found expression in the movement known as pietism (essentially a return to the regenerative essence of basic Christianity), and many of the characteristic features of revivalism, such as field-preachers and camp meetings, owe their origin to this period.[6] The most influential feature of all, however, was the missionary impulse that often accompanied the forced migration of these minorities, both within Europe and to the New World. It was one such settlement that produced the first Protestant missionary church with a worldwide vision. This was the reconstituted Church of the United Brethren, which came into being among a community of Moravian and Bohemian Protestant refugees who had been given asylum on the estate of Count Nicholas Zinzendorf in Upper Lusatia in 1727.[7] Named Herrnhut (literally 'The House of the Lord'), this community was the point from which the beams of the new awakening radiated all over Europe and across the Atlantic.

Nicholas Zinzendorf was a Lutheran nobleman who had been educated at the University of Halle, the centre of the Protestant Enlightenment in Germany. In his association with the exiled Moravians, he discovered the radical power of popular Protestantism and committed himself to 'religion as the means and way to a better life', an ideal that lay at the heart of the German Enlightenment.[8] Distinguished in the first place by the catholicity of his religious views, he was willing to converse with representatives of every denomination, 'his one concern being that a man's heart should beat true to the love of Christ'.[9] Beginning in 1727, the Herrnhut settlement under Zinzendorf's leadership developed as a religious commune organized on the basis of the revealed truth of the scriptures. During the first twenty years of its existence it experienced repeated outbreaks of religious revival that drew attention from several quarters. Deputations were sent abroad in response to enquiries from Protestant communities in other countries such as Denmark, Switzerland and England, and visitors in search of inspiration came to see for themselves what the awakening was about. Herrnhut also attracted the attention of the Court of Saxony, which observed developments with growing unease because of the continuing arrival of refugees from Moravia. Following a commission of inquiry in 1732, the settlement was granted a licence to continue, provided that the flow of refugees from Moravia was stopped. Perceiving this as a threat to their collective safety, the descendants of the Moravians decided to disperse and form safe colonies in whatever Christian countries would welcome them. The strongest justification for adopting this policy was the biblical directive to spread the Gospel. Those members of the settlement who were native to the area, and mostly Lutheran in origin, decided to stay on and continue the work at Herrnhut, which increasingly assumed the character of a missionary centre.[10]

Among those influenced by Moravian religious enthusiasm and missionary idealism were John and Charles Wesley, who first came into contact with Count Zinzendorf at a North American missionary colony in Georgia in 1738. This encounter with the Moravians provoked a religious crisis that resulted in the conversion of the Wesley brothers to the new spirit of 'awakened' Christianity. Shortly after his return from Georgia, John Wesley went to Herrnhut, where he observed the workings of Zinzendorf's commune at first hand. Deeply inspired by the experience, he adopted many features of the Herrnhut experiment for the Methodist movement that he founded and led in England, not least of which was the missionary impulse to bring the unenlightened into the fold.[11] By the middle of the eighteenth century, therefore, the foundation of the modern Protestant missionary movement was in place, though another fifty years were to pass before the acceleration began that would carry the Bible to every quarter of the globe. During that period, roughly 1740 to 1790, 'vital religion' became a powerful force on the fringes of mainstream denominations in Britain and the North American colonies.

The defining feature of eighteenth-century evangelicalism was its emphasis on the personal. Above all else, religious enthusiasm implied a personal and emotional response to the demands of biblical truth. After about 1740 the type of experience that transformed the Wesleys following their meeting with Zinzendorf—the spiritual flooding that brought about a total surrender of the individual will, followed by an intense and unwavering commitment to a particular ideal—multiplied in a way that suggests a movement. Adherents were united across boundaries of geography and denomination in pursuit of a common vision of a society perfected by the serious practice of Christianity. The international evangelical community at this stage can best be seen as one large pen club whose members exchanged views and aspirations across continents and oceans, a religious counterpart to the secular world of the *philosophes* and freemasons, in which passionate idealists considered the ways religion could and should be adapted to the needs of a changing world. It was also a community characterized by remarkable mobility. The latter part of the eighteenth century was the age of the travelling religious enthusiast, and nothing but revolutionary fervour can explain the number of miles travelled and countries visited by evangelical missionaries and itinerant preachers.

Insofar as it was Protestant, Ireland was part of this world of the international awakening, with similar internal and external forces fostering the growth of the 'enthusiasm' that drew the ire of Jonathan Swift. The appearance of revivalist preachers in Dublin in the 1740s was a clear indication that Ireland had fallen within the ambit of those countries touched by the international awakening. Before the arrival of John and Charles Wesley in 1747, the most significant missionary work was undertaken by a Moravian preacher, Rev. John Cennick, an Englishman of Czech origin whose ancestors had fled Bohemia after the Battle of the White Mountain in 1620. Originally connected with the Wesleys and George Whitefield, Cennick had a disagreement with them that caused him to join the Moravians in 1745. In the following year, at the invitation of a Baptist student named Benjamin Latrobe, he arrived in Dublin and began to preach in the Old Baptist Hall.[12] His sermons were received with applause in some quarters and hostility in others, and often with outright derision. The apocryphal tale of how Irish Methodists came to be known as 'swaddlers' is associated with an occasion when he made use of the text, 'Ye shall find the babe wrapped in swaddling clothes and lying in a manger' (Luke, 11, 12). The term 'swaddling' was employed so often that it was taken up by a drunkard who ran through the streets calling Cennick and his congregation 'swaddlers'.[13] The name became synonymous with the promoters of the new religion and was ever afterwards used as a derisive term for Methodists; it was eventually applied to evangelicals of every persuasion and even found its way into the Irish language.

Cennick's stay in Dublin was unfortunately destined to be short-lived. When the Wesleys arrived in 1747, they took over the Old Baptist Hall meeting house. Cennick thereupon left for County Antrim in Ulster and founded a famous Moravian colony at Gracehill, about a mile outside Ballymena.[14] The movement spread rapidly to the surrounding counties, especially the area around Lough Neagh, and enjoyed a vigorous though brief existence in the 1750s. A combination of bad management and Cennick's early death in 1755 contributed to its rapid decline. Apart from providing an inspirational model for evangelicals connected with other denominations, the Moravians made little impact on mainstream religious life in Ireland. Nevertheless, as David Hempton and Myrtle Hill have emphasized in their study of Ulster evangelicalism, the response they evoked in the northern counties indicated that 'in an area formerly settled by Puritans, the traditions of a strict and self-denying religious culture had by no means died out'.[15]

In contrast to the experience of Cennick and the Moravians, the Methodists established deep roots in Irish soil and played a central role in pioneering the evangelical cause. From the record of John Wesley's involvement in the practical operations of Irish Methodism, it is clear that from the beginning he considered Ireland to be part of his spiritual empire. His ambition was not only to inject new zeal into a complacent Protestant Church establishment but also to bid for the allegiance of the Catholic population. In this, as in many other areas of endeavour, he was to pioneer a cause later to be taken up with great zeal by evangelicals of the Church of Ireland. Between his first visit to Dublin in 1747 and his death in 1790, Wesley made a remarkable total of twenty-one visits to Ireland.[16] During that period Irish Methodism shifted from the 'enthusiastic' fringe to a position, if not of outright acceptance, then certainly of influence and respectability in the country's religious life.

Undoubtedly, the decisive factor in its successful growth was its leader's personal commitment and energy. Dissuaded neither by the contempt of the Protestant establishment nor by the hostility of Catholics, Wesley persevered in gathering together the loose ends of Irish Protestantism—artisans in newly industrialized areas, soldiers in garrison towns, and the occasional disaffected aristocrat—and created a challenge to existing traditions that none of the major denominations, whether Catholic, Protestant or Dissenting, could afford to ignore.[17] The Wesley brothers' first experiment with itinerant preaching in Ireland was less than auspicious. Frequently scoffed at by the rakehelly elements of the Protestant upper classes and physically assaulted by hostile Catholics, initially they could not even depend on the forces of law to defend them. In 1749 in Cork city a small group of Methodists came under attack from a crowd led by a ballad-singer named Nicholas Butler, resulting in the worst case of rioting that Methodism had ever encountered. When charges were laid against Butler and his followers, the grand jury threw out the case and demanded instead that the Methodists be punished, adding that 'we find Charles Wesley to be a person of ill-fame, a vagabond, and a common disturber of his majesty's peace, and we pray that he may be transported'.[18]

The reaction of the authorities and of polite society was not altogether at variance with the treatment frequently accorded the Wesleys in England during the early days of the Methodist movement.[19] John Wesley reserved his indignation for fellow Protestants whom he saw as not only allowing Catholic tormentors a free hand in harassing preachers but also in some cases providing active encouragement. Following a visit to Cork shortly after the notorious Butler episode, he penned a censorious letter to the lord mayor, commenting on the lack of hospitality he had found in that city:

> I fear God and honour the king. I earnestly desire to be at peace with all men. I have not willingly given offence either to the magistrates, the clergy, or any of the inhabitants of the city of Cork; neither do I desire anything of them but to be treated (I will not say as a clergyman, a gentleman, or a Christian) but with such justice as are due to a Jew, a Turk, or a pagan.[20]

Despite these early embarrassments, Wesley did succeed in advancing the Methodist cause in Ireland, though as Hempton observes, what he established was 'not so much a cohesive movement as a motley band of military personnel, Palatine settlers (in the south-east), some lapsed Presbyterians, and a much larger number of enthusiastic Anglicans'. Early successes at winning followers in the garrison towns and among the Palatine settlers suggest that Wesley was following a pattern, already adopted in England, of appealing to those sections of society most likely to be neglected by the Established Church. This was especially true in areas where industrialization was underway. Irish Methodism in the late eighteenth century registered its greatest successes in those areas of Ulster associated with the development of the linen industry and the growth of a commercial economy.[21]

Although there is some evidence that influential noblemen approved of John Wesley's vision of revitalized Christianity—the fine meeting house built by the earl of Lucan in Castlebar is one example of the support coming from this quarter—it was rare for individuals from well-to-do backgrounds to involve themselves in the work of evangelization. The most famous case is that of Gideon Ouseley, who was for many years the chief spokesman for Methodism in Ireland, especially in connection with its mission to the Irish-speaking Catholic population. Ouseley came from a wealthy family from Dunmore in east Galway, and as a youth he had been greatly influenced by Wesley's preaching. To assist him in his work among the peasantry he learned fluent Irish, a skill which served him well during his career as a preacher in rural areas. His long and colourful career as both circuit preacher and polemicist spanned the heyday of the Irish evangelical movement in the early nineteenth century and testifies to the special influence and position occupied by the Methodist community.[22]

If Ouseley's espousal of Methodism was symptomatic of revivalist stirrings among the Irish Protestant community in the mid- and late eighteenth century, he was certainly not alone. Dissatisfaction and disillusionment with the complacency of the Church of Ireland was being expressed in several quarters, and manifestations of this unease throughout the latter half of the century brought Irish Protestantism firmly within the boundaries of the international awakening. The popularity of itinerant preachers from England and Scotland indicates a desire for a more effective form of spiritual nourishment than that available through the usual channels. George Whitefield, who was probably the most important figure in the international evangelical world at this time, visited Ireland several times and was particularly welcome in Ulster, where his toleration of Dissent ensured his popularity with the Presbyterian community.[23]

In the 1760s and 1770s preachers associated with the countess of Huntingdon's Connexion also became familiar and often highly controversial figures in Ireland. Lady Huntingdon, who along with Wesley and Whitefield was among the most influential evangelicals of her day, especially among the aristocracy, took a keen interest in the promotion of the movement in Ireland.[24] Her family connections there included her daughter, Lady Moira, the Rev. Walter Shirley of Loughrea and Lady Mountcashell, all of whom kept her informed on Irish religious affairs, and acted as liaisons for her travelling preachers. Lady Moira was an influential figure in Dublin society, particularly with the group of philanthropists whose ranks included the well-known families of Guinness and La Touche, Alderman Henry Hutton, and Lady Arabella Denny. The Rev. Walter Shirley was an English aristocrat (the son of Earl Ferrers) and beneficed clergyman who had been associated with the Wesleys and the Holy Club during his student days at Oxford.[25] His ministry at Loughrea was characterized by deep unhappiness and disillusionment over the apathy of his congregation. 'Surely my God hath not placed me here to no purpose,' he commented despairingly to Lady Huntingdon in 1760; 'if I may not be for the salvation of their souls, the truths I have uttered will be for their condemnation and rise in judgment against them on the last day ... I would that it had pleased the Lord that I had been driven to the outermost parts of the earth rather than have come hither.'[26]

Lady Huntingdon's attempts at remedying the type of spiritual apathy that Shirley described involved not only deploying itinerant preachers but also paying the cost of maintaining a resident minister of her Connexion in Dublin. In 1771 one of these ministers, Henry Mead, was in a position to complain that he was in need of an assistant because of the pressures of work.[27] This is one measure of the degree of interest that revivalist religion was capable of arousing in the metropolis. Progress in the provinces was more dependent upon individual initiative. This is illustrated by the case of Albert Blest of Sligo, worth considering in some detail not merely because of the important consequences it had in the early nineteenth century but also for the light that it sheds on the social class of those who first responded to the evangelical message. Along with his father-in-law, Andrew Maiben, Blest was responsible for establishing a strong tradition of evangelical Dissent in County Sligo.

The emergence of Sligo as a base for evangelical Independents was a direct result of its importance as a crossroads of trade between Ulster and Connaught. Up to the middle of the eighteenth century the bulk of the trade of Sligo was with the northern counties, a consequence of the spread of the linen industry introduced by Scottish entrepreneurs who came to play a dominant role in business and commerce in Sligo town.[28] Andrew Maiben belonged to this class. By birth a Scotsman and a strict Calvinist, he was 'an extensive and opulent merchant' much given to a serious consideration of his religious duties. Disappointed with the apathy of the local Church of Ireland congregation, he took an interest in Methodism. Having found Wesley's Arminian theology to be at odds with his own Calvinist beliefs, he began his own prayer-meetings, which attracted the attention of the young Albert Blest. Originally from a Church of Ireland background, Blest's character and temperament were particularly conducive to the spirit of religious awakening. Described as a riotous and dissolute youth, with a mind 'ardently attached to poetry', he turned to vital religion following a near-fatal illness and thereafter lived a life of complete dedication to the evangelical cause, a commitment strengthened by his marriage to one of Maiben's daughters in 1780.[29]

Blest was especially important for establishing links with English and Scottish evangelicals, and he arranged for the preachers of Lady Huntingdon's Connexion to visit Sligo in the 1790s. He was also in close contact with the Haldane brothers of Edinburgh and cooperated with them in arranging venues for the preachers they sent to Ireland. Soon after 1800 he was instrumental in setting up the London Hibernian Society's (LHS) school system in County Sligo and in securing the patronage of the local gentry for its work among the Catholic population. Though he remained a Nonconformist all his life, he kept close links with the Church of Ireland and always maintained that it was the practice rather than the tenets of its faith that caused him to separate from it in the first place.[30] He provided inspiration and support for the revival that began in the Established Church in the early nineteenth century, and in fact he had partially laid the foundation for this through his active commitment to the evangelical principle that all who belonged to the 'Bible world' were working towards the same goal of transforming the world according to the designs of its maker.[31]

The ecumenical or pan-evangelical outlook expressed by Blest was fairly typical of the relationship that came to exist among denominational advocates of the evangelical movement in the early nineteenth century. But this had not always been the case. Having begun in the spirit of catholicity advocated by Count Zinzendorf, evangelicalism went through a kind of honeymoon phase between 1740 and 1760, when all followers of the revival actively supported each other in the grand design of spreading Gospel truth. More an attitude to life than a matter of denominational allegiance, it was characterized by an open and spontaneous approach to religion; as John Wesley described it, 'all controversial points were left alone and Christ alone was preached'.[32] But the optimism and fellowship that characterized this first evangelical spring camouflaged the serious theological differences that distinguished the followers of John Wesley from those of Whitefield and Lady Huntingdon, and which are usually interpreted by historians of the movement as reflecting a class bias. Wesley's theological position was based on the Arminian principles that held that Christ died to save all mankind. Individual salvation depended on the acceptance of this saving grace—faith, in other words—reinforced by a commitment to the development of a moral perfection that Wesley believed should be the goal of every Christian. The element of free will inherent in this doctrine was particularly attractive to the neglected fringe groups among whom Wesley found his most ardent followers—artisans and craftworkers aspiring to improve their status in society through hard work, self-discipline and rigorous attention to religious duties. But Arminianism found little favour with some of his fellow evangelists, who were more accepting of the Calvinist doctrine of predestination.

George Whitefield was by far the most significant figure among the Calvinist-oriented evangelicals, and Lady Huntingdon was one of his most faithful and influential supporters. In comparison with the Arminian doctrine that personal salvation was the responsibility of the individual person, Calvinistic Methodists believed that it was preordained by God. Those who were to be saved were the 'elect' upon whom grace was bestowed, regardless of merit. Knowledge that one was of the elect came when one was 'called' to grace, usually accompanied by some sign or indication that this had taken place. Because there was not the same degree of emphasis on personal piety, Wesleyan Methodists feared that the Calvinist-inspired group tended towards a toleration of immorality. Calvinistic Methodists in turn felt that the Wesleyan stress on good works was not far short of Roman Catholicism.[33] Despite Wesley's 'accommodating silence' on the subject of predestination, the seeds of division were deeply embedded in the foundations of eighteenth-century revivalism and sprouted into open conflict in the 1770s.[34]

The 'Calvinistic controversy', as it was known, extended to Ireland and for a time was the cause of a bitter dispute among Dublin evangelicals, with the aristocratic circle of Lady Moira and her husband closing ranks against the Wesleyan Methodists. One of the consequences of this conflict was the forging of stronger links between the Calvinistic Methodists and the Irish Independent evangelicals, especially Albert Blest. Preaching tours by itinerant ministers of Lady Huntingdon's Connexion became commonplace in Ireland in the 1780s and '90s, and well-known controversialists like Rowland Hill and Henry Peckwell attracted large audiences in Dublin and Sligo.[35] The problem of obtaining pulpits for these preachers was remedied by the use of 'free' or 'proprietory' chapels—private places of worship attached to aristocratic households as allowed for by the Conventicle Act, where a peer might have his own chapel and private chaplain provided that it was not open to the public. Lady Huntingdon had used this system to great effect to expand the chapels of her Connexion in England. In 1773 the Plunkett Street Chapel in Dublin was opened under the auspices of her Connexion. Several other chapels of this type sprang up in the capital around the same time, patronized not only by evangelicals of the Independent churches but more significantly by a growing number of Church of Ireland adherents who wished to hear the doctrine of the revival preached without jeopardizing clerical orthodoxy or their allegiance to the episcopal faith. The emergence of an evangelical party within the Church of Ireland had the effect of softening theological differences between Calvinists and Wesleyans, and helped to pave the way for the cooperation and mutual respect that characterized Protestant interdenominational relations in the early nineteenth century.

The revival that took root in the Church of Ireland in the 1780s was the product of two interconnected trends: the initiative and influence of Methodists and evangelicals of the Independent churches, and the growth of spiritual piety and social responsibility among the aristocracy and business classes that had turned eighteenth-century Dublin into a showcase of Protestant philanthropy.[36] The eighteenth-century concept of philanthropy was predicated on the improvement of State and society along rational lines, with a built-in acceptance that limitations were a fact of life: as one historian has described it, it was 'limited in scope, its doctrine of charity expressed without emotional fuss, commended by rational argument and set at practicable and immediate objectives'.[37] It was not possessed of a visionary or apocalyptic urge to build a new Jerusalem or remake the world in God's image, which was the hallmark of the evangelical approach. This is not to suggest that men like Jonathan Swift or Bartholomew Mosse (the founder of the Rotunda Hospital) were uninfluenced by the ideal of Christian charity; on the contrary, this was the basis of their philosophy. Objectively, however, this approach was cast in a temporal rather than a spiritual mould. With the evangelicals the emphasis was reversed. Good works were to be done in the first place for the love of God; the redemption of the individual soul and the general improvement of society would follow. This renaissance of the Calvinistic spirit was imbued with a certain revolutionary fervour, the full implications of which would not become apparent until well into the nineteenth century, when its effects would be felt not only in the British Isles but also throughout the world. For our purposes, however, what is important was the manner in which evangelicalism took root in the Church of Ireland and grafted itself onto a tradition of philanthropy already in existence.

Among the community of people who supported private philanthropy in Dublin in the late eighteenth century, the names that stand out as having exerted a lasting influence are those of Alderman Henry Hutton and Lady Arabella Denny. Hutton was associated with Mary's Abbey Presbyterian church, and his home on St Stephen's Green was famous as a meeting place for visiting preachers and lay people interested in religion and philanthropy, particularly students from Trinity College.[38] Lady Arabella Denny was famous as the benefactress of the Magdalen Asylum, which she founded for 'unfortunate females abandoned by their seducers'.[39] She was also involved in the running of several other charitable institutions, including the Foundling Hospital. Her close association with Lady Moira suggests that she was part of a circle of wealthy aristocratic women who eschewed the glamour and vanities of the age in favour of a more serious and conscientious commitment to Christianity.[40]

The most prominent supporters of the charitable works of aristocratic female philanthropists like Lady Arabella were the great brewing and banking families of Dublin, represented by the names of Guinness and La Touche respectively. The appeal of the evangelical message, particularly its emphasis on moral and social reform, to this section of the Dublin *haute bourgeoisie* bears a striking resemblance to the trend that was concurrently being set in London under the leadership of William Wilberforce and his colleagues in the Clapham Sect. In fact, the route by which the evangelical ethos made inroads into the Church establishment in Ireland is so similar to what took place in the Church of England that one can hardly see it as a separate or distinct development. This is understandable, considering Ireland's colonial status; as R.B. McDowell has expressed it, 'during the eighteenth century Ireland could be taken as forming part of the British cultural, intellectual, and social world'.[41] However questionable this statement might be when applied to the Catholic population, there can be no doubting its validity with respect to the Protestant community. Both culturally and economically, Irish Protestants were intimately linked to Britain. The symbiotic relationship fostered by strong economic and political ties was reflected in the religious sphere. Similar charges were levelled against the Church establishments in both countries by disaffected idealists, many of whom in the late eighteenth century began to coalesce into an energetic and vocal minority providing both the foundation and leadership for an episcopal evangelical movement.

Such was the influence of the first generation of evangelicals in the Church of England that it has been common ever since the mid-nineteenth century to credit them with having 'transformed the whole character of English society' and with having imparted to the Victorian age 'that moral earnestness that was its distinguishing characteristic'.[42] The connection between the growth of evangelicalism in England and the pattern of social change in the late eighteenth and early nineteenth centuries has provided historians with a unique opportunity to study the links between religious movements and general social trends. But the theories that serve to explain what social transformations were fuelling the spectacular growth of the evangelical revival in England, or 'the broadening of a sectarian cult into something like a national faith'[43] are not easily transferred to Ireland. The problem is compounded by the fact that all the evidence of the nineteenth century suggests that the appeal of the evangelical ethos in Ireland, particularly among the upper classes, was even more intense than that of Britain.

The traditional explanation of evangelical revival is that it was the religious counterpart of the Romantic movement, the turning away from reason as the basis of belief to revelation and 'religion of the heart'. The noun 'evangelical' denotes one who has heard the word of God and who accepts the Bible as the supreme ordinance of His will on earth, with particular emphasis on the command to evangelize or bring the saving grace of 'true religion' to those outside the fold, which included Christians of all denominations as well as non-Christians or 'heathens'. The committed evangelical was therefore concerned not only with his own moral and religious conduct but with securing a social and political environment conducive to the propagation of the evangelical way of life. Earlier scholars such as Harold Perkin, E.P. Thompson and V. Kiernan have interpreted the resurgence of this fundamental tenet of the reformed faith in the late eighteenth century as an indication of the manner in which English society responded to the twin challenges of political and social revolution. Perkin identifies the movement as an expression of the moral ascendancy of the middle classes, a phenomenon he describes as 'a new morality designed to support a new society'.[44] According to this theory, evangelicalism was the offspring of seventeenth-century Puritanism 'shorn of its political radicalism', which took the form of moral imperialism as the middle classes rose to ascendancy in the wake of the industrial revolution. Thompson and Kiernan are essentially in agreement with this view, except that where Kiernan sees the revival as a progressive trend leading to the development of nineteenth-century liberalism, Thompson emphasizes its potential as an anti-revolutionary force.[45] These starkly contrasting views are muted somewhat by later historians who, while not denying the conservative ramifications of the evangelical movement, nevertheless come down heavily in favour of perceiving it as the optimistic creed of those who stood to gain the most from the social and economic changes consequent upon industrialization. The 'upper working classes' as described by Stuart Piggin, and the businessmen and factory masters whom Paul Johnson identifies as the driving force behind the revival led by Charles Grandison Finney in western New York during the 1830s, are the two most identifiable groups that fall into this category.[46]

The most radical and forceful argument in favour of the moral ascendancy theory, however, comes from a cultural and intellectual historian, Gerald Newman, who identifies the evangelical movement as the catalyst that brought together the various currents of English nationalism that had developed in the eighteenth century, providing the ideological fuel for England's rise to world dominance in the nineteenth century. Newman argues that eighteenth-century England must be seen as part of a general European crisis centred on the conflict that resulted when the political and economic aspirations of an increasingly ambitious bourgeoisie were resisted by an equally ambitious aristocracy bent on preserving exclusivity and privilege. Unlike France, where the battle was fought along political lines, bourgeois ascendancy in England was based upon industrial and technological progress. The revolution that took place was moral and ideological in character (before it assumed explicitly political dimensions in the reform acts of the nineteenth century) and was inspired by a vision of the uniqueness of English national character and society created by artists, writers and intellectuals of the eighteenth century—notably Defoe, Hogarth and Johnson. This vision promoted the virtues of honesty, sincerity and fair play at the expense of the dissipated habits, extravagant lifestyle and arrogant manners of the aristocracy. Rooted in the 'aesthetic revolution', or the flowering of interest in antiquities, popular folk culture, music and national character, it was first and foremost anti-French in tone. It strove to assert English national identity over and against the cosmopolitan supremacist doctrine upheld by the French *ancien régime* to which English aristocrats in almost every aspect of material and intellectual culture were held to be in thrall.[47]

What secured the moral revolution, according to Newman, was the timely outbreak of revolution in France. The awful consequences of the conflict between bourgeois radicalism and aristocratic reaction in France put the necessary ammunition into the hands of England's moral reformers to effect a bloodless ideological revolution. The storm troopers of its first campaign according to Newman were those Low Church evangelicals and Methodists whose piety and respectability provided a perfect camouflage for the radical process on which they were about to embark:

> seizing the initiative, they cunningly fitted the dreadful vision of France to their own ambitions, and, to the increasingly horrified realization of the aristocracy, began to fight what must be regarded as one of the most remarkable moral and social battles of modern times.[48]

Over the course of the following four decades, roughly between 1790 and 1830, the evangelicals, having established themselves as watchdogs on national morality, effected a moral revolution that secured the ideological dominance of the bourgeois or Victorian ethos.[49] The ease with which all this was accomplished is explained by the deceptive or subversive nature of the process. Behind this pious and respectable front of the 'Saints', as Newman claims, 'an extremely radical process was now working under cover of an extremely conservative one'.[50] Exacting standards of conduct in personal and domestic affairs became the order of the day, as did rigid adherence to duty and conscience in the operation of government and the world of business and commerce. In the words of Ian Bradley, 'the pastimes of the aristocracy became the professions of the middle classes'.[51] A levelling process took place whereby the offices of Church, State and the armed services—hitherto the preserve of aristocratic privileges and sinecures—now became the career goals of ambitious and upwardly mobile bourgeois possessed of the necessary virtues of honesty, dependability and serious attention to duty. It was a world in which each man knew his duty, and his exercise of it was open to the scrutiny of his peers. This moral earnestness, when applied to every aspect of business and personal life, made English industry and banking in the Victorian period the envy of the world. In the political arena the concern for a society based on Christian morality was translated into demands for government intervention in the reform of social issues which, in an era of rapid and often destabilizing economic development, managed to keep at bay the more serious class conflicts that bedeviled other countries in Europe.

Newman's bracing argument on behalf of the radical and far-reaching implications of the moral revolution spearheaded by the evangelicals goes further than those of previous participants in the debate as to who sided with the 'optimistic' or progressive school. It builds upon the work of Kiernan, Perkin and Bradley, and handsomely complements Johnson's pioneering interpretation of the revival of the 1830s in North America. Taken together, all of these historians put forward an understanding of the new religious enthusiasm as the cement that bound social relationships and produced a set of ethics congruent with the demands of a society experiencing the critical transition from a small-scale, family-based economy to one that was highly integrated and complex, based on wage labour and mass production. This 'moral ascendancy' explanation rests on the premise that it was industrialization and free-market capitalism that produced the conditions whereby the middle classes were able to impose Puritan moral values on the aristocracy and the lower classes. But what of the success of the evangelical movement in Ireland, where such conditions existed, if they existed at all, within a social and economic framework largely dictated by a system of colonialism unique in Europe, yet without exact parallel in the New World. If, as David Hempton has suggested, the character of evangelicalism in any given society reveals a symbiosis with the surrounding culture, then it is only to be expected that the movement in Ireland would reflect the highly complex and volatile interface between religion and politics that characterized Irish society in the late eighteenth and early nineteenth centuries.[52]

The key to the ascendancy of evangelical religion (especially the reform of manners and morals that was its chief by-product) among Ireland's Protestant population is to be found in that section of the community that first responded to its appeal in the 1780s. Impressed with the message and example of the Methodists and Lady Huntingdon's preachers, certain people connected with the Church of Ireland opted to build a church where they could attend revivalist services without jeopardizing their denominational loyalty. In 1784 the foundation was laid for the Bethesda Chapel in Dorset Street, which has rightfully been described as 'the only place of worship in connection with the Church of Ireland where men could hear preached the doctrines of the revival with which so many were in sympathy'.[53] The importance of the Bethesda Chapel in the history of Irish evangelicalism cannot be overestimated; it provides an obvious point from which to begin a more detailed analysis of the movement.

The Bethesda was built at the personal expense of William Smyth, a protégé of Lady Huntingdon and a nephew of the former archbishop of Dublin. Smyth's brother, Edward, became the first chaplain on its opening in 1786. From the beginning the Bethesda was characterized by an uncompromising allegiance to the Established Church and by a close association with Trinity College. The display of loyalty to the Church of Ireland may at first appear curious in view of the archbishop of Dublin's refusal to grant the chapel a licence, thereby obliging its founders to register it as a Dissenting place of worship. According to one historian, however, the Bethesda 'gave to those who preferred allegiance to the church to Methodist separation from it the opportunity to maintain their principles'.[54] In connection with developments in English evangelicalism at about this time, this can be more readily understood. The rise of the Bethesda marked the emergence of a cohesive evangelical party within the Church of Ireland in precisely the same manner that the Clapham Sect signalled the arrival of evangelicalism in the Church of England. Although in some ways the differences between the two are easier to point out than the similarities, there was nevertheless an underlying foundation of clerical orthodoxy and episcopal allegiance that united the Irish experience with that of Clapham Common. In both cases there was manifest a respect and sympathy for the voice of evangelical Dissent. At the same time, and often in spite of severe opposition from the episcopal bench, the possibility of stepping outside the bounds of the Church establishment was never considered. In the case of the Bethesda, the chaplains and trustees were all ordained ministers of the Church of Ireland. Regardless of the ecumenical spirit that existed between them and the evangelicals of the Dissenting sects, no one who was not episcopally ordained was ever allowed to preach at the Bethesda.

In its firm advocacy of nonschismatic evangelicalism, the Bethesda quickly became a home for those members of the Church of Ireland who sought to pursue the new spirit of enquiry associated with vital religion without putting either their ecclesiastical allegiance or social respectability at risk. Its location in Dorset Street in the neighbourhood of the fashionable Rutland (now Parnell) and Mountjoy Squares—the doorstep, literally, of Dublin high society—was no doubt an added advantage. In 1787, John Wesley noted the presence of seven or eight hundred communicants at the chapel on Easter Sunday, and two years later he remarked that the congregation was liberally sprinkled with 'honorable and right-honorable persons'. During the following half-century several other free or proprietory chapels were built to accommodate evangelical preachers, but none achieved the status of the Bethesda. Under the chaplaincy of the Rev. Benjamin William Mathias from 1805 to 1835, it became a focal point for Irish evangelicals in general and was particularly influential in moulding future generations of clergymen. It was finally granted a licence in 1828 by the archbishop of Dublin, Dr William Magee, a powerful advocate of the cause. By 1838, as Alan Acheson attests, 'the evangelicals were the most powerful single force in the Church of Ireland'.[55]

The involvement of the Guinness and La Touche families with moral reform mirrored the representation of banking and trade (Thornton and Wilberforce) and brewing (Fowell-Buxton) at Clapham Common. But the unique character of Irish evangelicalism, in particular the appeal of the evangelical ethos to the young generation, was betokened by the role of Trinity College as a nursery of the revival in the Church of Ireland. As many of the students were destined for careers in the ministry, their importance in spreading the new spirit of moral reform and religious renewal throughout the provinces was to be crucial. When the revival in the Church of Ireland began to manifest itself during the first two decades of the nineteenth century, the common factor shared by its most prominent representatives was attendance at Trinity between 1775 and 1800.

Unlike Cambridge, where the Rev. Charles Simeon presided as the spiritual fountainhead of the revival in the Church of England, there was no dominant figure at Trinity who served as the guiding light for the students who worshipped at the Bethesda. It seems futile, in retrospect, to seek for some distinguishing feature that might have made Trinity a hospitable environment for the gestation of the new ideas on religion and society in circulation around this time. Trinity was the training ground for the great majority of Church of Ireland clergymen. If spiritual and social reform were strong components in the intellectual atmosphere to which the generation of 1775–1800 was exposed, a certain proportion were bound to be sufficiently influenced to carry the spores that would bear fruit wherever they chanced to deposit them.

CULTURAL REVIVAL AND NATIONAL AWAKENING

During the first half of the eighteenth century the spirit of the Enlightenment had taken effective root in Ireland as it had throughout Europe, with many of the same consequences. A critical mentality fostered by the ascendancy of reason and science was disseminated through new channels of exchange such as learned societies, clubs and coffee-houses, and above all through the growing popularity of newspapers, journals and pamphlet literature. The result was the emergence of 'public opinion' as a new and dynamic element in political life, and a corresponding trend towards debate and criticism of many aspects of government policy. Inspired by the belief that reason could liberate humanity from the restrictions of an earlier age dominated by ignorance and superstition, advocates of the Enlightenment were characterized by self-confidence in their ability to fashion the world according to a rational vision. Religious tolerance, education and economic progress were among the areas seen to hold the key to this new, more rational and more humane society. But advances like religious tolerance and education carried particular implications in a country like Ireland whose identity as both 'kingdom and colony' was at best ambiguous, and where the overwhelming majority of the population was not simply outside the boundaries of the religious and political establishment, but also subject to discriminatory laws designed to ensure the permanence of their degraded status. Advocates of reason, tolerance, and scepticism were to meet formidable challenges in eighteenth-century Ireland.

The peace that Ireland enjoyed between 1700 and 1760 was characterized by rapid economic development and the consolidation of a classic *ancien régime* tiered society consisting of a colonial aristocracy, an expansionist middle class that included Catholic as well as Protestant merchants and industrialists, and a peasantry rapidly increasing in numbers.[56] While the experience of conquest and colonization in the seventeenth century had brought about change and upheaval unequalled in any other European country, the eighteenth century saw a remarkably smooth transition to a modern commercial economy. This can be accounted for in part by the country's increasing integration into a dynamic imperial economy driven by the trade of the north Atlantic. Under the leadership of a self-confident and ambitious colonial aristocracy, great landed estates were developed and gracious new 'big houses' and planned estate villages transformed the countryside. The systematic development of fairs and markets in the provinces, and the building of a modern network of roads and canals all bore witness to the sophistication of a growing integrated economy. The city of Dublin was perhaps the most obvious symbol of Protestant self-confidence, with its handsome squares and classical architecture, illustrative, as Cullen suggests, of the 'elegant, serene, and mellowed atmosphere' that the contemporary establishment felt was a reflection of its social and political environment.[57]

The sense of security enjoyed by Protestants, though temporary, was not illusory. Despite fears of a papist plot in 1715, again in 1745, and an isolated outbreak of agrarian discontent in the west in 1711–12, S.J. Connolly concludes that 'the rulers of early eighteenth century Ireland appear to have had few fears concerning the security of their position'.[58] Economic prosperity and Catholic quiescence ensured the continuation of this situation up to the 1750s. But Catholic quiescence did not imply either stagnation or acceptance of the status quo. As Kevin Whelan, Thomas P. Power and others have shown, Catholic Ireland was remarkably resilient in adapting to the catastrophic implications of the Williamite victory and the Penal Code.[59] The condition of the poor was always a concern, increasingly as economic growth resulted in a sharp rise in population at the lower end of the social scale. Yet, while the prospect of converting Catholics was always paid lip service to, it was never pursued with any meaningful purpose.[60] A campaign of evangelization proposed by Rev. John Richardson during the first decade of the eighteenth century revealed how lukewarm was the establishment's opinion on the prospect of integrating Catholics through a policy of conversion. Richardson's proposals included a radical scheme of compulsory school attendance, free Bible distribution and the use of Irish-speaking missionary preachers. Even though the scheme was discussed in parliament in 1710 and a resolution passed for the training of Irish-speaking preachers, progress became impossible because of the fear that support of any kind for the Irish language would strengthen the native Catholic interest.[61] This was a fear that future evangelists, as we shall see, would never be able to lay to rest.

To a certain extent Richardson may be seen as an inheritor of the seventeenth-century Puritan tradition, which may in part account for the lacklustre response to his far-sighted proposals. When the question of assimilating the native Irish was again considered, it was in a markedly different climate of opinion, with the state itself willing to take the initiative. The appearance in 1733 of the Incorporated Society in Dublin for Promoting English Protestant Schools in Ireland marked the first move towards government involvement in the education and integration of the Catholic population. The spirit that motivated the founders of the Charter Schools (so called because of the society's incorporated status) was a mixture of the older but still vibrant fear of popery, and the newer optimistic spirit of enlightenment and benevolence. The subsequent reputation of the Charter Schools, and the hatred they aroused among Catholics, ought not to obscure the original vision of the founders (who included Berkeley and Swift) that they should function as vehicles to educate and improve the children of poorer Catholics in order to equip them to earn their living in commerce, industry and agriculture.[62]

The Incorporated Society was only one manifestation in Ireland of the ascendancy of Enlightenment ideas. An organization of much greater significance and influence, the Dublin Society, was founded in 1731 for the express purpose of promoting and improving agriculture, industry and 'useful arts' such as architecture and glass-making. Behind the promotion of manufacturing (especially the linen industry) lay an attempt at economic diversification prompted by the need to create employment and lessen the country's dependence on imported goods—a clear enough indicator of the link between the advocates of progress and improvement and the defenders of constitutional liberty. The people most likely to respond to the appeal of a body like the Dublin Society—improving landlords and lesser gentry anxious to increase their wealth through efficient agriculture and industrial innovation—were precisely those who were most likely to support and sponsor Charter Schools in the vicinity of their residences.

Implicit in the philosophy of the Enlightenment was a view of the world that presupposed man was a rational being, and that society could be ordered, indeed perfected, according to rational laws. This view gathered momentum during the middle decades of the century, when Cartesian logic confronted philosophers with the uncomfortable truth that the existence of God could not be established with certainty. The realization that Reason was unable to answer any of the fundamental questions about religion, morality and the meaning of life caused philosophers to turn to the study of 'useful subjects' in order to achieve the human perfectibility they believed was possible. As a result, the study of history and society, or what was called 'the experience of mankind', took on a new importance and replaced abstract speculation as a more effective instrument for understanding the nature of man. The search began in earnest for a universal natural order that might be understood in the light of experience—history, in other words—in order that philosophers might determine which human qualities were desirable for the perfect society. Their task, in Carl Becker's words, was 'to go up and down the wide world with the lamp of Enlightenment looking, as Montaigne did before them, for "man in general" and to identify and enumerate and describe the qualities that were common to all men in order to determine what ideas and customs and institutions in their own time were out of harmony with the universal natural order'.[63] This change in the intellectual climate lay at the heart of the demand for a 'new history' that was loudly voiced in the mid-eighteenth century, and that radically altered perceptions of the past as well as attitudes towards it. It was also to have profound consequences for Ireland.

To a much greater degree than her European neighbours at this time, Ireland was subjected to remarkable scrutiny and speculation regarding the nature of her past. Even more remarkable was the fact that this development had little to do with events within the country itself, instead stemming from a combination of the intellectual turbulence described above and the reverberations from the imperial expansion that was every year bringing France and England into contact with vastly different societies and cultures at the far end of the globe, notably China and India. Inspired by the belief that Europe had once shared a universal Celtic culture, a wave of Celtomania swept through the Continent, sending artists and scholars to the remotest western fringes in search of Fingal and Ossian, and securing the myths and legends of the Celtic past as one of the cornerstones of the Romantic movement. Those of a mind to cast their nets wider in the search for a broader cultural basis for all mankind began to look for comparisons between the Celtic languages and Sanskrit, Hebrew and Arabic, and even those tongues spoken by native tribes in North and Central America.[64] Scholars in search of Britain's Celtic past found their task facilitated and enriched by a study of Irish antiquities and the Irish language. The net result was a heightened awareness that Ireland had once been possessed of a great civilization, and a debate was opened up as to how, and by whom, this past might be appropriated. Among the major class and ethnic strata in Ireland at this time—an aristocratic Anglican establishment, upwardly mobile middle-class Protestants, cautiously optimistic aristocratic Catholics, and the newly emergent and ambitious Catholic middle class—there were strong vested interests in respective versions of the past that might be employed to vindicate the claims and objectives of the present. From about 1750 onwards the debate over which version of the Irish past was going to prevail was carried on against a backdrop of growing crisis in the country's economic and political life. This did much to ensure that the battle would be a lively one.

From about the middle of the eighteenth century, developments in the Irish economy brought about social change and political instability that starkly revealed how fragile the consensus of earlier decades had been. The underlying tension was a reflection of the degree to which political reform had failed to keep pace with the aspirations stimulated by economic progress. Pressure for change originated with three major social groups: ambitious, well-to-do Catholics eager to secure political influence in order to back up the economic clout that they already possessed; a peasantry willing to resort to violence in order to restore the 'moral economy' upset by economic rationalization, and a broad stratum of middle-level Protestants, including the Presbyterians of the north-east, who looked to parliamentary reform as the most effective way to obtain the political and economic security that would realize their claims for leadership of the emergent Irish nation. All three groups were united in their opposition to the contemporary political and religious establishment represented by the great landed magnates and the Church of Ireland respectively. But the ability of this establishment to hold the line on political reform (a stand greatly facilitated by the combustible blend of sectarian interests among the opposition) ensured that no consensus would emerge regarding political strategy or the probable character of the future state. As a result of this failure, during the 1790s the country would be torn apart by political instability and military insurrection verging on civil war.

The chief factor governing the health of the Irish economy in the late eighteenth century was the demand in Britain, Europe and the Atlantic colonies for its staple commodities: namely beef, butter, and linen. After about 1750, in harness with the demand generated by industrial take-off in Britain and the expansion of the colonial trade, the Irish economy entered a period of accelerated growth that lasted until the 1770s. The chief beneficiaries of this upturn were the farming classes, especially the beef and dairy farmers of the great river basins of Munster, and the weavers and merchants of the north-east, where a thriving proto-industrial economy had grown up on the foundation of a cottage-based linen industry. Population growth, social stratification, and political turmoil were the necessary by-products of this trend, and all were endemic in both of these regions in the latter part of the eighteenth century.[65]

In Munster the first indicator of change on the horizon was the appearance of a Catholic political interest in County Tipperary in the 1750s. Among the southern counties Tipperary was unique for its combination of a strong Catholic gentry class and an equally powerful Protestant landed interest. The chief representatives of the liberal Catholic cause were the Mathew family of Annfield and Thomastown, a classic example of the model advanced by Kevin Whelan of a clan who had survived and prospered in the 'shelter belt' of the Butler lands in Tipperary and Kilkenny. Though nominal converts to the establishment by the 1750s, the Mathews were connected by marriage to the leading Catholic families in the county and, according to Whelan, 'were seldom far from the centre of the Tipperary political stage'.[66] When Thomas Mathew stood for a parliamentary seat in the election of 1761, the rival Protestants saw his candidacy as a front for Catholic ambitions in the country and dredged up rumours of a 'Popish plot'.

Such fears were not entirely without foundation, as Tipperary Catholics by mid-century had become openly assertive both in the practice of their religion and in the founding of teaching establishments. Many who had made their fortune in trade began to increase their influence as creditors and also to re-invest in landed property.[67] It was the truculent spirit of these *nouveau riche* Catholics that enraged the opposition and made a sectarian flashpoint of the 1761 election. Mathew won the election, but was later unseated as a result of an election petition.[68] But Protestant fears were not so readily appeased, and the sectarian hostility aroused by competition from the Catholic gentry soon found an outlet as a result of developments lower down the social ladder.

Forces that were drawing the Catholic gentry of Tipperary into political and economic competition with their Protestant counterparts were also pushing their poorer co-religionists in the direction of clandestine agrarian protest. The appearance of the agrarian combinations known as 'Whiteboys' in south Tipperary in the 1760s was a symptom of the growing desperation of the rural poor as marginal common pasture land fell prey to an enclosure movement fuelled by the contemporary demand for the beef and butter of the valleys of the Suir and the Blackwater.[69] The rapid spread of the movement terrified the authorities and lent additional weight to Protestant fears that a Popish plot was indeed being hatched. Not the least of the factors contributing to the scare was the grievance expressed by the peasantry over the tithes that they were obliged to pay for the upkeep of the Established Church. There were many who sympathized with the poor, including Fr Nicholas Sheehy, the popular and outspoken parish priest of Clogheen, in whose vicinity the disturbances had originated. Sheehy came from a well-to-do background and was therefore an ideal target for the venom of conservative Protestants driven by social jealousy and sectarian fear. Determined to suppress the Catholic challenge at all levels, they sought to make an example of him on grounds of a conspiracy theory that he was involved in Whiteboy activities. After an infamous show trial in which the heavy hand of Protestant military and political supremacy was only too apparent, Sheehy was convicted on the flimsiest of evidence and executed in Clonmel on 15 March, 1766.[70] Sheehy's execution was followed by the rounding up of substantial Catholic farmers who were also implicated in the Whiteboy activities, three of whom were executed the following May. Those alleged accomplices revealingly were not from the Whiteboy rabble but respectable Catholic *arrivisti*, recently possessed of land and ideal targets of jealousy because of their new-found gentry status.[71]

The fate of Sheehy and his companions was designed to strike terror into the hearts of Tipperary Catholics, both at the level of the ambitious gentry and among the poor. The witch-hunt was accompanied by the appearance of traditional works on the perilous situation of Protestants in Ireland, chief among which was Sir John Temple's *History of the General Rebellion of 1641*, reissued by Bagnell's of Cork and sold openly in Clonmel in 1766.[72] The exemplary effect that the campaign was designed to achieve was soon apparent in the number of Catholic gentry who converted to the Church of Ireland and in the virtual disappearance of the Whiteboys for several years. The significance of the 1760s in Tipperary was the manner in which Protestant fears had been ignited by the concurrent appearance of Catholic political ambition and social protest. The lesson of the episode was that while Catholic political ambition and social protest were only remotely linked (indeed wealthy Catholic farmers had been the object of Whiteboy protest as much as Protestant landlords), the temptation to play the 'sectarian card' was increasingly attractive to those who would resist social and economic change. But in the 1760s the dispute remained regional in character, and Protestants in most of the country outside Munster judiciously remained uninvolved.[73]

During the 1770s and 1780s, the 'Catholic question', though by no means a dead letter in Irish political life, was eclipsed by the constitutional struggle led by Protestant 'Patriots' for the legislative independence of the Irish parliament. This was a further consequence of the economic and social upheaval of the times. Like the anti-popery spirit that surfaced during periods of threat to Protestant safety, real or imagined, the defensive nationalism of patriotic-minded Protestants tended to appear whenever the effects of a downturn in the British economy were felt in Ireland. During the 1770s the trading relationship between the two countries, having developed in accord with the classic colonial or mercantilist model, was exposed in all its weakness when the English economy went into a recession as a result of the American war. The impact of the crisis in Ireland was all the more intense for having followed on the heels of a quarter-century of rapid development accompanied by rising expectations among the gentry and aristocracy and by population growth among the peasantry. Dependence on the English market, which had formerly acted as a spur to economic growth, came to be seen as the main cause of Ireland's economic woes when the country found itself on the brink of financial bankruptcy towards the end of the decade.

The political consequences of the economic downturn were immediately manifest in the growth of a colonial nationalism similar in kind to that which had inspired the American revolutionaries, with whom the Protestants of Ireland had ties both by kinship and through a sense of solidarity in the pursuit of a common political cause. Inspired by the American example, progressive members of the Dublin parliament pressed for a greater degree of economic freedom by means of non-importation agreements, and demanded free trade and ultimately legislative independence. The British were forced to make concessions, including the granting of legislative independence in 1782, mainly because they could not afford a second theatre of war in Ireland. This was certainly a possibility since behind the demands of the Patriots stood an armed volunteer force of 40,000 men, organized in the first place to defend the country in the event of a French invasion, but 'no less ready to defend the rights of Ireland'.[74]

The question that arises here is: to which 'Ireland' were the Patriots referring? Obviously, it was not the hidden Ireland of the peasantry, nor yet that of their wealthier co-religionists. But if the traditionally disenfranchised Catholics were not to have a representative voice in the nation, whose political identity was forged by the 'Constitution of 1782', neither, as it turned out, were the Protestant middle classes, either Anglican or Dissenting, whose support for the Volunteer movement had provided the military muscle behind the campaign for constitutional reform. Throughout the 1780s there were signs of a widening cleavage among the Protestant population, and disillusionment with the unrepresentative and corrupt character of the Dublin parliament rapidly escalated into a demand for parliamentary reform in the years following 1782.

The reform spirit had taken root most effectively in Ulster, the most advanced quarter of the island economically by virtue of its thriving linen industry, and radically different from the other provinces in its denominational character. The self-confidence of its mercantile and textile elite derived not only from economic prosperity but also from the absence of any significant rivalry from the local Catholic populace, few of whom, unlike their countrymen in Leinster and Munster, were to be found in the ranks of the bourgeoisie. More significantly, the Presbyterian community, to which most of this elite belonged, had suffered equally with the Catholics from political discrimination. Their alienation from the centre of power politics in Dublin was deepened by close links with lowland Scotland—the home of the British Enlightenment—from whence most of them had migrated in the seventeenth century, and where future aspirants to the ministry and the professions were educated at the great universities of Edinburgh and Glasgow. Ties of kinship as well as political sympathy also linked them to the American colonies, where many of their persuasion had emigrated in the course of the eighteenth century and had contributed powerfully to the cause of political liberty. All of these factors combined to make Ulster, and particularly Belfast, the 'Athens of the North', a natural crucible for the fermentation of a uniquely radical blend of reform politics in the 1780s. The range of the debate was extended to include the questions of political rights for Catholics and the immutable character of the 1688 constitution. Even the prospect of separation from Britain was openly debated.[75] The real threat to the government, however, lay in the possibility of an alliance between the advanced radicals and the disaffected Catholics. Something of a prelude to this nightmare had already been experienced in Munster during the Rightboy disturbances of 1785–7. Conservative reaction on this occasion, as we shall see, left little doubt as to what might transpire should Protestant radicals translate their concern to include Catholics in the political process from theory into practice.

Clearly, the growth of the reform movement in Ulster, with its emphasis on liberty and equality, its demand for the abolition of Church privileges and State sinecures, and its concept of popular democracy marked a challenge to aristocratic hegemony similar in kind to that experienced in many other parts of western Europe in the 1780s. It was not initially in this province, however, that the authorities of Church and State reacted with alarm to the prospect of the Protestant middle class breaking ranks, but in Munster, where a further outbreak of agrarian protest erupted in 1785. The Rightboy movement—so called because its followers styled themselves the followers of 'Captain Right'—was different in many significant ways from others of its kind. In its geographical scope it was wider than anything that had yet been seen in Ireland, and it cut across class boundaries in a manner completely uncharacteristic of either previous or subsequent waves of agrarian protest. It was also characterized by novel methods of mobilization, a high degree of effectiveness in securing objectives, a low level of serious violence, and comparatively moderate treatment at the hands of the authorities. All of these factors suggest that, in addition to the traditional grievances of the poor over high rents and tithes, there were other issues involved that combined to make the Rightboy movement what James S. Donnelly has called 'a remarkably aberrant variety of agrarian rebellion'.[76]

The singular aspect of the Rightboy movement was the involvement of Protestant gentlemen who joined forces with the peasantry in a general attack on the tithe system. Their support for the anti-tithe movement was less an expression of solidarity with the oppressed poor, however, than an assault on the establishment through its most vulnerable flank, namely, the Church of Ireland. The animosity that drove these 'Gentlemen Whiteboys' into such a remarkable alliance had been many years in the making. As early as 1775, a group of Protestant gentlemen in the Blarney area of Cork had banded together in an association they called the Cork Farmers' Club—the very name redolent of the group's rejection of gentility and aristocratic pretension. Its chief motto was that the burden of tithe was an unnecessary and restrictive barrier to the industry of the farming classes and the general improvement of agriculture. This was a remarkably explicit acknowledgment of class interests by these provincial representatives of the fledgling third estate, and their involvement in the Rightboy movement was one manifestation of this frustration.[77] Contemporary evidence lends much weight to this theory, particularly in light of the electoral contest of 1783, in which the ringleader of the Cork Farmers' Club, Sir John Conway Colthurst of Ardrum, representing 'independent virtue and spirit', went down to ignominious defeat at the hands of the 'aristocratic combination' of Lord Shannon, one of the greatest boroughmongers in the country. Frustrated political ambition was thus added to the other ingredients propelling Colthurst and his friends into a clandestine and anti-aristocratic alliance with the popular classes.

Remarkable testimony regarding the motivation of the Gentlemen Whiteboys came from the pen of a Cork city apothecary, John Barter Bennett, who as the author of the *Shopkeeper's Letters* had strongly defended the Established Church against contemporary critics. Unwilling at the time to publicly condemn the conspirators, he was nevertheless anxious to preserve his information and opinions for posterity, and thus consigned them to a private manuscript.[78] His collective portrait of the Gentlemen Whiteboys reveals a company of aspiring businessmen–farmers whose social and commercial dealings were governed by a tough-minded concern to increase their own wealth and influence. The ringleader of the group, John Conway Colthurst, was the very model of yeoman ambition heightened by a class-conscious pique, the symptom perhaps of an inferiority complex in the face of aristocratic polish and pretension. According to Barter Bennett, he had all the attributes to cut a dashing figure when he thought it proper to dress like a gentleman, 'which was but seldom, choosing rather generally to appear like a farmer, by which title he affected to distinguish himself'. Despite his comfortable background he was badly educated, his written work flawed by bad spelling and grammar and his public address impaired by a confused manner of expressing himself in debate. Badly equipped to handle himself in a world dominated by aristocratic manners and fashion in the first place, it is small wonder that he took refuge in the pose of the 'honest farmer' governed by 'virtue and independence', those hallmarks of middle-class identity and righteousness.[79]

As Barter Bennett willingly conceded, Colthurst was a true friend to those whom he favoured and he provided free medical care for the sick poor in his neighbourhood. If he had a reputation for ruthlessly extracting rent payments as they fell due, he was also just in his dealings and punctual in meeting his own financial obligations—'a virtue little known to the generality of country gentlemen' (a truism to which Barter Bennett, dependent on their custom, could no doubt ruefully testify). As someone who had little use for the fashion and manners of the aristocracy, Colthurst had even less for the comforts of religion. He considered the clergymen of the Established Church to be little better than parasitical sycophants: 'If people will be weak enough to send for them when they are sick, let them be dismissed with their fee like the doctor,' was his comment on their social and spiritual utility.[80] A man of such opinions was well placed to give vent to his anti-clerical sentiments in Munster during the 1780s. Along with some of his associates in the Farmers' Club (whom Barter Bennett described as equally grasping and opportunistic Protestant gentlemen) he had already established the practice of distressing clergymen by refusing to pay tithes on his substantial estates in Cork and Kerry. When the opposition to tithes emerged as a central feature of the agrarian protest that became widespread in Munster in 1785–6, these men were prepared to exploit the crisis in order to achieve their own objective of having tithes reduced and possibly abolished completely.[81]

According to contemporary critics, the sophisticated strategy and tactics of the Rightboy movement stemmed directly from the influence of Colthurst and his friends, the 'internal cabinet of the Whiteboy republic,' as they were caustically described by the barrister Dominic Trant, one of their leading opponents.[82] Trant and others saw the hand of Colthurst and his accomplices at work behind the increasingly sophisticated techniques employed by the Rightboys to advance the anti-tithe campaign. These techniques included an emphasis on nonviolence, the swearing-in of great numbers of sympathizers outside Catholic chapels after Sunday Mass, and the coordinated design by which the movement was spread from parish to parish. But the most remarkable feature of the Rightboy campaign (even when the participation of Protestant gentry among the leadership is taken into account) was the inclusion of the dues paid to the Catholic clergy as one of the popular grievances that needed to be remedied. Trant and Barter Bennett saw this as nothing more than a ploy by the Gentlemen Whiteboys to dupe unsuspecting Protestants about the true nature of their motives, namely, the abolition of the tithes paid to the Established Church.[83]

There may well have been some truth in this suspicion, but it does not alter the fact that irritation at the demands of the Catholic clergy was on the increase among the popular classes at this time. Nothing indicated more clearly the security that the Catholic Church was beginning to enjoy following the relaxation of the more odious of the Penal Laws than the growing distance between priests and people that was now becoming a feature of life in rural Ireland. The solidarity that had characterized relations between the two in penal times was showing signs of strain as toleration enabled the hierarchy and clergy to build up a more institutionalized diocesan structure. Financing was naturally a key element in this process, and the peasantry, already burdened with the support of the Established Church, now found that they were confronted with ever-increasing demands from their own Church.[84] This friction within Catholic ranks provided the Gentlemen Whiteboys with an opportunity to carry their anti-clerical campaign one step further. By opposing priests' dues as well as tithes, they could profess the nonsectarian and secular nature of their ambitions and further their own self-interest under the guise of championing the cause of the oppressed poor.

The alliance between Colthurst and his accomplices and the Munster peasantry in 1785 and 1786—the 'extraordinary marriage of the Padderreen [rosary beads] and the Common Prayer Book'[85] as it was called by a contemporary—presented the Catholic authorities with a quandary. Considering the leadership role of the Catholic clergy at both the local and national levels, and the fact that their Church had only recently emerged from the shadow of the Penal Laws, they were forced to tread a delicate line between the watchful eye of the government and the grievances and needs of their flock. Acutely sensitive that they were held responsible by the government for the good behaviour of their followers, Catholic priests and bishops as a consequence were implacably opposed to the Rightboy movement.[86] The formidable organization and sophistication of the agrarian rebels threatened not only the incomes of the clergy but also their authority at the local level, their social respectability, and even their political security. Not surprisingly, during the height of the disturbances in 1786 several priests in Munster took drastic measures to curb the influence of the Rightboys. These included refusals to say Mass or to administer the sacraments, as well as public condemnation of agrarian outrages through that most effective weapon of social control in rural Ireland, the 'priest's curse'. The Rightboys' answer to this display of clerical censure was novel, to say the least. At the behest and sometimes under the blatant leadership of the Gentlemen Whiteboys, they deserted the Catholic chapels and marched *en masse* to the Protestant churches.[87]

The most influential of the Protestant leaders in this latest technique of distressing the Catholic clergy, besides the ubiquitous Colthurst, was no 'gentleman' but the colourful Arabella Jefferies of Blarney Castle, *doyenne* of the advanced radicals and self-styled feminine activist. If anything served to illustrate the potentially destabilizing threat to the social order implicit in the rise of this new politics, it was the spectacle of 'Lady' Arabella, 'the modern Zenobia' as she was labelled by a caustic Catholic opponent, championing the rights of the poor against the exactions of both priests and parsons. Her Orléaniste tendency to cast off the mantle of aristocratic privilege in sympathy with the grievances of the popular classes is a significant reflection of the crisis that was overtaking the Protestant community at this time. It is all the more significant considering that she was the sister of the Irish attorney general, John Fitzgibbon, the most intransigent defender of Protestant supremacy in government circles and notoriously hostile to political reform.[88]

The combination represented by Arabella Jefferies, Colthurst, and the Rightboys, localized though it might have been, carried an implicit threat of anarchy that could topple both the entrenched Protestant clerical establishment and its fledgling Catholic counterpart. The reaction of the Catholic clergy to this unholy alliance was judicious. Opting for concession rather than condemnation, which was certain to lead to further conflict, the Munster bishops capitulated to Rightboy demands concerning the regulation of priests' dues, and they also took the unprecedented step of removing from office two priests who had been particularly notorious for their anti-Rightboy activity. Some bishops went so far as to engage in friendly association with Colthurst, the agent of so much of their recent distress. This spectacle filled the sober-minded Barter Bennett with disgust, convincing him that 'Sir John and the Roman Catholics ... had no further regard for each other than each endeavouring to make the other instruments of their schemes'. The prelates had assessed the situation correctly, it would appear, as their formerly alienated flocks began to return to the chapels in the latter part of 1786, and Colthurst engaged no further in his unorthodox methods of securing proselytes for the Church of Ireland.[89]

The ease with which this potentially turbulent situation had been defused, and the leniency of the Munster bishops in dealing with their rebellious congregations, owed much to the influence of Fr Arthur O'Leary, the Capuchin friar who had a national reputation at this time as a pamphleteer on behalf of the rights of the Catholic poor. In the spring of 1786 Fr O'Leary had personally led an investigative committee to examine the grievances of tithes and priests' dues in the diocese of Cloyne and Ross. His findings convinced him that the complaints of the poor were indeed justified and the need for reform urgent. The bishops wisely heeded his counsel when they met in provincial synod in the following June, and it was shortly after this that they agreed to the Rightboy demands. The question of priests' dues soon ceased to be an issue for the agrarian rebels.[90] But the criticisms of Fr O'Leary, which had included the exaction of tithes as well as priests' dues, were not allowed to slip so comfortably into the grave where the major combatants on the Catholic side had buried their differences. Outspoken defenders of the Church of Ireland made profitable use of O'Leary's sympathy for the Catholic poor to stir the hornet's nest of no-popery and thus added a vital ingredient to the intransigence of the anti-reform lobby.

If the anarchistic spectacle of the Gentlemen Whiteboys in league with agrarian rebels caused such tremors among the clergy and hierarchy of the Catholic Church, it need hardly be emphasized that their counterparts in the Church of Ireland were shaken to a much greater degree. Several concerned defenders, Barter Bennett included, rushed to the defence of the Established Church, but none did so with more effect than Dr Richard Woodward, bishop of Cloyne and Ross, in whose diocese the Gentlemen Whiteboys had plied their dangerous trade. Woodward's famous pamphlet, *The Present State of the Church of Ireland* (1787) carried the debate about tithes far beyond the boundaries of Cork and even of Munster. His argument on behalf of the Church of Ireland and the legitimacy of the tithe system was the cornerstone on which the implacable opposition to political reform for Catholics would be erected. With the possible exception of Wolfe Tone's *An Argument on Behalf of the Catholics of Ireland* (1791)—which may indeed be most effectively understood as a response to the arguments advanced by Woodward—no political tract of the late eighteenth century carried greater weight among contemporaries or was invested with such influential and far-reaching implications.

There was nothing complex or novel about Woodward's argument concerning the danger to the Church of Ireland. Indeed, it was the essence of simplicity. His uncompromising logic hammered out the principle that the security of Irish Protestants depended upon the maintenance of what he called 'the Protestant ascendancy' (he was the first to give popular expression to the term), that is, the exclusive control of the Irish parliament by Protestants of the Established Church.[91] It was his firm conviction that the abolition of tithes would result in the collapse of the Church of Ireland, which would inevitably open the way to the ascendancy of the Catholic religion and the consequent subversion of the social and economic status not only of the Anglican community but of all Protestant denominations in Ireland. This reality, if allowed to transpire, would be followed as a matter of course by the separation of Ireland from Britain. Woodward was equally firm in his conviction that the current threat to the Established Church was extremely serious, and he considered himself to be fulfilling his official duty by spreading the alarm to 'the inhabitants of the most distant parts of the kingdom, who were taught to think these disturbances *of little moment*' (my emphasis).[92]

The remarkable element in Bishop Woodward's pamphlet was the clarity with which he seized upon the implications of Protestant gentry involvement in the Rightboy disturbances. If it were not for the existence of a 'dark and deep laid scheme, planned by men skilled in law', he claimed, the Rightboy episode would have blown over in much the same fashion as the Steelboy outbreak in Ulster, where 'the popular fury, not being stirred or afterwards kept up by designing men ... soon died away'. Clearly, it was those 'enemies of the public peace' whom he described as 'nominal Protestants' who raised the Rightboy outbreak from the realm of a localized agrarian protest to the level where it posed an immediate and formidable threat to both Church and State.[93]

In retrospect, it is possible to see that the influence and potential of the Gentlemen Whiteboys were perhaps exaggerated. But Woodward's fears and his sense of responsibility must be considered in the context of the turbulent 1780s, when the cause of constitutional reform had already triumphed in the North American colonies and was making rapid strides in much of western Europe. In Ireland, if such reform were to include the Catholic population (and this was the direction in which the opinion of liberal and radical Protestants seemed to be headed), the inevitable outcome, according to Woodward's logic, would be the collapse of the Church of Ireland and the erosion of Protestants' religious and political freedom and economic security. What gave Woodward and others, notably Patrick Duigenan, a pretext for transforming a regional crisis of a mainly socio-economic character into an emotionally charged national debate on the persecuting and intolerant tendencies of the Catholic Church was Fr O'Leary's vindication of the poor in their struggle against the tithe system.

Woodward, Duigenan and, to a lesser extent, Barter Bennett interpreted

O'Leary's commentary on the injustice of the tithe system as evidence that the Catholic Church was once again involved in a conspiracy to overthrow the Protestant establishment. There was very little to support this suspicion. Indeed, Catholic leaders, Fr O'Leary included, were remarkable for the conservative, if not downright obsequious, character of their dealings with the authorities in Dublin and London. Unlike the Gentlemen Whiteboys, O'Leary had not espoused the total abolition of tithes, but merely the reform of the system in order to distribute the burden more equitably across the social scale. His strongest complaints were reserved for the agents and proctors who made a living out of tithe collection, not the clergymen of the Church of Ireland.

The grounds for building a 'popish conspiracy' theory on the strength of the Rightboy episode and Fr O'Leary's defence of the Catholic poor were therefore flimsy in the extreme. The chief worry that Bishop Woodward had expressed in the main body of his pamphlet had been the danger to Church and State implicit in the politicization of the Rightboy movement by seditious middle-class Protestants. It was Patrick Duigenan, a fellow of Trinity College and an employee of the Church of Ireland's ecclesiastical court, who had asserted that the Rightboys were 'a popish banditti, spirited up by agitating friars and Romish missionaries, sent hither on purpose to sow sedition'.[94] A spirited rebuttal of this claim by Fr O'Leary was the spur that caused Woodward to take up the issue of Catholic influence in the anti-tithe agitation in a postscript to his original pamphlet, which had already been sent to press. Woodward could find no conspiracy to expose, but he seized upon the tone of O'Leary's address, especially the language used to condemn the tithe system, as deliberately calculated to arouse anger among the peasantry, and to excite rebellion against tithes and ministers of the Church of Ireland generally.[95]

In pouncing upon O'Leary's writings as evidence of the subversive inclinations of the Catholic clergy Woodward and Duignan provided the anti-reform lobby with a pretext to focus more exclusively on the implications of voting rights for Catholics as the stumbling block in the debate for political reform. The Woodward–Duigenan–O'Leary exchange soon assumed the character of a 'paper war' as others joined in the argument over the legitimacy of tithes and the prospect of sharing power with Catholics.[96]

It was no surprise that the most staunch defence of the establishment was raised by associates of Trinity College, the nursery for Church of Ireland personnel, who would be the first to suffer if tithe-based revenue were interfered with. Nor was it surprising that the strongest criticisms against tithes and in favour of political reform should have originated in the Presbyterian north, where the debate on constitutional reform was in full spate.[97] What is revealing is how rapidly the subject of 'Protestant ascendancy' took centre stage, to the exclusion of almost every other aspect of the crisis that the Protestant community was now facing. Apart from Woodward's famous pamphlet, little or nothing further was heard from or about the Gentlemen Whiteboys. Early in 1787, Colthurst met his death in a duel with his old enemy, Dominic Trant. The remaining members of the Cork Farmers' Club lost their taste for clandestine activity in the course of the same year, when the Rightboys added rents and hearth money to their list of grievances.[98]

The debate about tithes and political representation for Catholics, however, retained a life of its own in the world of parliamentary opinion and public debate long after the Rightboys had been coerced into submission. Except for the conscientious John Barter Bennett, the identity of Colthurst and his accomplices, the threat that they posed to the Church of Ireland, and the backlash that issued from the same source would have been largely lost to posterity. What Barter Bennett's motives were in recording what he knew about the Gentlemen Whiteboys must remain a matter of conjecture. But in an 1803 postscript to the main manuscript (written in 1787) he claimed that he had recorded events that had 'in a great measure since contributed to the calamities of the kingdom'.[99] The reader is thus left in no doubt as to his understanding of the connection between the conservative backlash occasioned by the Rightboy movement and the revolutionary and counter-revolutionary terror of the 1790s.

The debate about 'Protestant ascendancy' that took place in pamphlet literature, on public platforms, and in private correspondence between 1788 and 1792 makes it clear that Woodward's pamphlet was much more than an expedient salvo set off in the Church of Ireland's hour of danger in 1785–6.[100] In the face of the rising tide of revolutionary democracy that had recently swept the American colonies and would soon envelop France, it functioned as a clarion call to Ireland's Protestant population to consider what would be their future if current trends were to continue to accelerate. Above all, it was the admission of Catholics to political power that was held up as the great danger. This was hardly an unfamiliar theme at the time. Among reform-hungry Protestants no question was debated more heatedly, or gave rise to so much division within the ranks, as that of sharing power with Catholics. Although there was no consensus on the subject, most reformers agreed that only those Catholics who could be trusted, that is those who possessed property and education sufficient to warrant their support for the status quo, should be allowed a voice in the political process. The remainder might be considered after they had been improved and enlightened to such a degree that they could assume the civic responsibilities fundamental to the modern nation–state.[101]

While Woodward and his supporters were in full agreement as to the necessity for moral reform, they imposed the *ne plus ultra* when it came to Catholic political rights. To justify their position they adverted to the teaching of the Catholic Church regarding the treatment of heretics, and above all the fate of Irish Protestants during Catholic uprisings in the previous century, especially in 1641 and 1690. The only way to assure the future safety of the Irish Protestants was therefore to secure exclusive control of political power in Protestant hands. The obvious advantage of this position was that reform of any kind could be opposed or dismissed on grounds of possible Catholic subversion. It placed an effective block in the way not only of Catholic aspirations but of reform-oriented Protestants as well. As W.J. McCormack has claimed, the advocates of the Woodward–Duigenan school 'were remarkable for the manner in which they substituted the single concept or slogan of Protestant Ascendancy for the complexity of a society in crisis'.[102]

That the conservative Protestant retrenchment spearheaded by Woodward and Duigenan amounted to more than just a temporary girding of the loins while the winds of democracy blew through western Europe is evident from the manner in which the offensive against reform was launched against its intellectual foundations as well as its contemporary political expression. From about the middle of the eighteenth century onwards, developments in the cultural and historical awareness of the Irish past had been moving in the direction of constructing a comprehensive theory of nationality, based on an accommodation between the Protestant and the Catholic traditions. This process now came under attack from the conservative flank. The battle for the past, as it were, was almost as important as the battle for the present.

RENEWAL AND REACTION: A TALE OF TWO IRELANDS

Interest in the cultural legacy of Gaelic Ireland had been growing steadily since the middle of the eighteenth century. By the 1780s a cultural renaissance was clearly underway, and it was unquestionably an integral part of the patriotic impulse that lay at the root of the movement for constitutional freedom and political reform. Embracing the study of antiquities, history, language, literature, and music, it involved members of the business and professional classes as well as the landed elite, and Catholics as well as Protestants. A movement of this kind was not by any means unique to Ireland. All over Europe similar forces were at work as ideas on democracy in the interests of the 'people' or the 'nation' began to gain ascendancy over concepts of monarchy, aristocratic privilege and established State religion.

A positive assessment of the Gaelic past was a natural corollary of the Anglophobia that fuelled the growth of Irish Protestant nationalism. It was no coincidence that the great advocate of Irish economic freedom in the late seventeenth century, William Molyneux, had also been a patron of antiquarian research.[103] His successors, who assumed the reform mantle during the middle decades of the eighteenth century, were equally anxious to integrate the Gaelic tradition as a fundamental and distinguishing characteristic of the nation that they were in the process of creating. The cultural and ideological bedrock of the new entity would be laid by uniting an ancient and honorable Gaelic past with a rational and progressive Protestant present. The route towards such reconciliation, however, was strewn with pitfalls. In the first instance, its ideologues and propagandists were faced with the daunting task of competing with an inherited colonial view of the native Irish that was highly prejudicial and often blatantly racist in tone.[104] Secondly, a rehabilitation of the Gaelic past carried an implicit assumption that the inheritors of this tradition would inevitably be elevated to a position of respect and equality in political and economic affairs. This truth was not lost on the more astute and politically conscious Catholics. Indeed, Catholics like Charles O'Conor, Sylvester O'Halloran and John Curry were already following their own initiative in the area of historical scholarship and, if anything, were ahead of their Protestant countrymen.

During the first phase of the cultural renaissance in the 1740s, the debate about the Celtic past was characterized by tolerance and cooperation between 'enlightened' Catholics and 'moderate' Protestants. This was nowhere more apparent than in the friendship between the playwright and historian Henry Brooke and Charles O'Conor of Belnagare. O'Conor was a leading representative of the Catholic gentry, one of the few whose family had survived the seventeenth century with its estates partially intact and its religion unaltered. A prototypical 'tame' Catholic, he sought to further the Catholic cause from within rather than to plot the destruction of the system from without, as many of his compatriots had done through their support for Louis XIV and the restoration of the Stuart pretenders. The quiescence of the Catholic Irish during the Jacobite rising of 1745 and the ultimate failure of that ill-fated venture left O'Conor in a particularly strong position to win acceptance among the Enlightenment-inspired circle of Protestant intellectuals in Dublin.[105]

Antiquarian research was the avenue through which O'Conor personally sought to elevate the reputation of his Catholic countrymen, and in this he found an ally in Henry Brooke, a well-known dramatist who had already established his reputation on the London stage. From the scholarly investigations of these two men there emerged a synthesis of the ancient Gaelic past that could be used as a foundation for a new or 'philosophical' history of Ireland. Briefly, this upheld the view that Irish society before the Norman conquest had been characterized by a high degree of literacy and civilization, including an early form of 'parliamentary' government. According to Jacqueline Hill, who has identified the O'Conor–Brooke thesis as the cornerstone of the 'patriotic' view of Irish history, its purpose was clear: it was 'to integrate past and present, to reconcile the Gaelic and Catholic past with the Williamite revolution and its political and religious legacy in England, Scotland, and Ireland'.[106]

The 'patriot' version of the ancient past, then, had obvious potential as an ideological poultice to heal the division between native and colonial. This potential would be increased immeasurably if its lesson could be applied to the divisive and bloody events of the recent past—the terrible catalogue of conquest, rebellion, massacre, and confiscation that was the legacy of the seventeenth century. It was readily appreciated, not only by the patriotic Protestant elements but equally by reform-oriented Catholics, that a complete overhaul of the recent as well as the ancient past was necessary before a political accommodation based on mutual toleration could be established. No one understood this more effectively than Edmund Burke, himself the product of a Protestant–Catholic union. Throughout his political career his position on the Irish question was shaped by his desire to see a complete restoration of Catholic rights, coupled with the full integration of Ireland as a peaceful and prosperous member of the British imperial union. Burke's influence was such that his machinations were considered by that most outspoken defender of Protestant supremacy, Patrick Duigenan, to lie at the very heart of the newly awakened political consciousness among Catholics.[107]

By the 1760s Burke was an active promoter of the idea that the time was now ripe for a 'philosophical' history of Ireland that would help clear the air for a new departure in contemporary political affairs. The scholar upon whom he prevailed to undertake this formidable task was the Rev. Thomas Leland, a fellow of Trinity College who already enjoyed an established reputation as a historical scholar. High hopes were invested in the enterprise, and Leland received gracious assistance and support not only from the ubiquitous Charles O'Conor, but also from such Patriot stalwarts as the earl of Charlemont and Sir George Macartney.[108]

Leland's projected great work on Irish history was carried on in a political and intellectual atmosphere charged with the dynamic of Enlightenment thought. Eventually published in 1773, it was designed in part to be the Irish equivalent of the recent 'philosophical' histories of England and Scotland by David Hume and William Robertson respectively. It was also hoped that it would rescue Ireland's reputation from the treatment that it was continuing to receive from these 'new' historians, Hume in particular. Hume's opinion of Ireland and especially of the role of the Catholic religion in the lives of the native population was influential in the debate concerning the dangers of allowing political freedom to Catholics. His position was essentially the old-fashioned colonial view of the native Irish as an inferior and ungovernable race, tempered by an Enlightenment philosopher's condemnation of religious bigotry as the great obstacle in the path of progress and civilized government. The event that he and other opponents of the Catholic Irish seized upon as the clearest evidence of barbarity and bigotry was the great rebellion of 1641, in which it was alleged that, driven by their priests into a bloodthirsty crusade for revenge, they massacred innocent Protestants guilty of no other crime than introducing prosperity and civilized government into a wild and hitherto ungovernable country.[109]

The rebellion of 1641, of course, had functioned as the 'Blood River' of Protestant colonists in Ireland long before it appeared in this light in the pages of Hume's *History of England*. Its importance in the mythology of Protestant resistance and martyrdom was clearly recognized for what it was by politically aware Catholics like the physician John Curry, who had already in 1758 produced his own attempt at rehabilitating the Catholic record in connection with the infamous rebellion.[110] Dr Curry was a close friend of Charles O'Conor, with whom he cooperated, on both scholarly work and the promotion of the contemporary campaign for Catholic political rights. In the guise of 'moderate Protestants' they had produced a number of anonymous pamphlets in support of the Catholic cause with which they hoped to influence members of the Irish parliament.[111]

For Curry and O'Conor and the body of progressive Catholic opinion that they represented, the manner in which the seventeenth-century record of the Catholic Irish would be dealt with in Leland's *History* was of vital importance. A vindication of the Catholics on grounds that they had been provoked into rebellion would undermine the position of Hume and others who promoted the belief that they were barbarous and priest-driven, and no more to be trusted in the present than in the past. A dismissal of this interpretation, meanwhile, would lend weight to Hume's case. It was the fervent hope of O'Conor and Curry that Leland would prove to be the first Protestant historian to liberate the Catholics from the ideological straitjacket in which they were bound as a consequence of the Protestant version of the events of 1641.[112]

Their hopes were not fulfilled. Leland was an ordained minister of the Church of Ireland, which hardly left him in a strong position to undermine an interpretation of history upon which many of his Protestant contemporaries (especially those in clerical orders) believed that the safety of their position rested. Even the usually generous-minded O'Conor suspected that the *History of Ireland* was written with a view towards clerical preferment. Whatever the truth of this, there was no denying Leland's dedication to upholding the Protestant line on 1641; indeed, he even went so far as to subject Curry's earlier account to an extended scrutiny and to attack every detail that attempted to establish the innocence of Catholics.[113] The sense of betrayal felt by O'Conor and Curry was total. Of the two, Curry was the less surprised, as he had never placed the same faith in Protestant scholarship as O'Conor, nor had he enjoyed the same ease of access among the upper echelons of the Protestant intellectual world as his more aristocratic comrade-in-arms. Now, upon the appearance in print of Leland's work, he felt justified in adopting a self-righteous attitude towards the usefulness to the Catholic cause of O'Conor's dalliance with the Protestant world.[114] His attitude implied a grim future for Protestant–Catholic cooperation in the field of historical inquiry. Henceforth, Catholics would write their own history, according to their own interpretation of events and to suit their own needs.[115]

The single most important aspect of Leland's *History*, according to Jacqueline Hill, was its failure to build upon the O'Conor–Brooke thesis, or to extend the patriotic view of the ancient past into the modern period.[116] In the decade that saw the founding of the Volunteer movement and the beginnings of the campaign for legislative independence, the chief scholarly representative of the Protestant community in Ireland had failed to produce the historical synthesis out of which a genuine political accommodation between native and colonial might have emerged. Such a failure, in retrospect, may therefore be seen both as foreshadowing and as having contributed to the actual political breakdown of the 1790s.

It did not herald an end of scholarly interest in the Gaelic past, however. Patriotic Protestants, anxious to put cultural flesh on the political skeleton of their infant nation, continued in their ardent support of the Gaelic heritage. The founding of the Royal Irish Academy in 1786 was the clearest expression of this trend. But there was a pronounced shift away from the politically charged subject of relations between Gael and Saxon in recent times, and towards less controversial areas such as language and antiquities, literature and music. This shift would probably have taken place in any event, since Ireland at this time was no different from many other parts of Europe where, in the first flush of the early Romantic movement, the 'volk' was in the process of being discovered by Enlightenment intellectuals.[117] The unique political conditions in Ireland lent a particular urgency to the quest, however. The necessity of discovering a holy grail that would unite the opposing parties in Ireland, and the unlikelihood of finding it in the realms of empirical scholarship, accentuated the role in Irish political life of culture, and literary culture in particular, since this was seen as the area in which Gaelic Ireland could lay claim to indisputable greatness.

The uniquely talented Charlotte Brooke was among the first to appreciate the importance of providing Irish literature in translation for an educated, English-speaking public, and the first to possess the literary and linguistic skills equal to the task. As the only surviving member of Henry Brooke's offspring, she was, one might say, almost raised for the purpose of bridging the gap between Protestant patriots and the Gaelic world. The publication of her *Reliques of Irish Poetry* in 1789 was a milestone in the evolution of Irish cultural nationalism. The task she set herself, in essence, was to harness the literary legacy of ancient Ireland as well as its contemporary popular counterpart (the songs of O'Carolan, for example) in support of the patriotic view of Irish history. In this her work must be seen as part of the European movement of cultural renewal grounded in the search for the 'genius of the people' and fuelled by the same forces that were propelling the growth of political nationalism. The concept of race was central to this development, particularly the notion that inherently just forms of government developed in some former golden age in accordance with the needs of the indigenous race—the Saxons in England and the Gauls in France, for example—had been suppressed and uprooted by a 'foreign aggressor'.[118]

The successful application of this model to Ireland, it need hardly be said, was inhibited by certain glaring realities. What were Irish Protestants, after all, if not the descendants of the foreign aggressor who had stripped the native Catholics of their cultural and political birthright? Charlotte Brooke's answer to this dilemma was to appeal to the literary remains of ancient Ireland as evidence of the culture and nobility, the *racial equality*, in other words, of the Gaelic race, and to suggest that amity between the two communities in Ireland and good relations between the 'sister kingdoms' could best be achieved through racial and cultural integration.[119]

Charlotte Brooke was not overtly political, and nowhere in her work is there a hint of the necessity of allowing Catholics a voice in the political process. But this was equally true of the larger scholarly and intellectual world to which she belonged. Despite the patriotic ardour inspired by the growing body of information on ancient Ireland in the 1780s, and despite the popularity of such works as Joseph Cooper Walker's *Bardic Remains*, there was no consensus as to how modern political structures might accommodate the 'cultural fusion' deemed so attractive by scholars of the ancient past, in any case, until the programme of radical reform espoused by the Society of the United Irishmen in the 1790s. The cultural legitimacy the first Celtic revival conferred on the idea of the Irish 'nation' was a necessary prelude to its evolution as a political ideal. As Gerald Newman reminds us:

> Nationalism is something larger than mere politics; it enters the political domain from a sphere outside it. Nationalism is a phenomenon of feeling and consciousness, an intellectual phenomenon, which originates in certain stressful cultural and psychological conditions, which typically manifests itself in literature, which may very well spawn a social movement which not infrequently spills over into politics as well, but which nevertheless aspires to a state of affairs so idyllic as to make politics, literature, and social movements irrelevant. That is, its ultimate goals, like its roots, are cultural and psychological: its goals are personal wholeness and fraternal solidarity within a completely united and free community of the future to match the mythical one of the past.[120]

The radical ideologues who founded the Society of the United Irishmen in 1791 looked forward to the setting up of a secular liberal democracy, in which the sectarian divisions of the past would be swept away and replaced by an organic State capable of embracing all its citizens under the common name of Irishman. The connection of which Newman writes between the world of politics and that of the writers and intellectuals could hardly have been more obvious.

The link between the concept of an organic nation based on cultural and racial integration and the increasingly strident demands of the political reformers did not go unnoticed in the conservative quarter. It was the Rev. Edward Ledwich, perceiving in the trend 'a dangerous association of Gaelic, Catholic, and radical political views', who, according to Oliver MacDonagh, began the counter-offensive with his *Antiquities of Ireland* published in 1790. Ledwich's self-appointed task was to debunk the notion that ancient Ireland had ever been possessed of a great culture, thereby undercutting the case for cultural fusion and racial integration. Though Ledwich was by no means the first scholar to question the existence of a great civilization in pre-Christian Ireland, the polemical tone of his work nevertheless represented such a departure from established and accepted norms that he has been described by MacDonagh as the father of modern Irish historiography.[121] What he unquestionably set in motion was the process whereby a 'developmental' view of the Irish past (in which the native population was seen as capable of evolving towards a higher state of development and therefore towards peaceful coexistence and eventual integration with the colonial stock) was superseded by a 'timeless' version, with 'beleaguered' Protestants forever on their guard, on the one hand, and 'long-suffering Catholics' assured that God was on their side and that their day would eventually come, on the other. With no shortage of dedicated and enthusiastic advocates to further develop and advance these models, the result was the evolution of two completely polarized versions of the Irish past that would provide the ideological ballast for the growing chasm between Catholic and Protestant, and which, in the words of Jacqueline Hill 'would prove to have great coherence, adaptability, and persistence in the nineteenth and twentieth centuries'.[122]

Even the most idealistic and committed of those who espoused the cause of political reform based on the unity of Gael and Saxon, however, had obvious difficulties in reconciling the glory and chivalry of the ancient Irish (as reflected in Celtic mythology) with the level of degradation to which their modern descendants had fallen. Throughout the 1780s, as the debate on political reform grew more intense, one of the central preoccupations of its advocates was the necessity of effecting a 'moral transformation' among the Catholic population that would enable them to throw off the superstition and ignorance accumulated through centuries of abuse and neglect and to rise to a level of moral and intellectual freedom congruent with the needs of a political system based on parliamentary constitutionalism. For radical ideologues like

Dr William Drennan and Thomas Russell, 'moral regeneration' took its place alongside political reform and cultural renewal to form the intellectual tripod on which their secular democracy would be erected.

The appeal of moral reform, however, extended to a far wider expanse of public opinion than that occupied by the radicals. If anything, it was taken up with even greater fervour by the conservatives, particularly by the intellectual network centred on Trinity College, which was closely in tune with the political opinions of Bishop Woodward and the defence of the Church of Ireland. Although this latter group was to some degree interested in reform at the popular level, particularly educational reform, it was the condition of religion and morality among the upper classes, especially the dreadful apathy that seemed to have overtaken the Church of Ireland, that engaged their immediate attention and energies in the 1780s and 1790s.

Fears concerning the health of the Church of Ireland were well justified during the last quarter of the eighteenth century. Faced with criticism on every side simultaneously, the Church establishment was overtaken by a sense of crisis. By far the most serious threat was that launched against tithes, which provided the economic lifeblood of the entire structure. During the years of the Rightboy disturbances and the paper war, the combined assault launched by an aggrieved peasantry and their increasingly articulate clerical leaders, the even more articulate and outspoken representatives of the Presbyterian community, and lastly the shadowy manoeuvrings of the Gentlemen Whiteboys, had shaken the Church of Ireland to its foundations. Furthermore the spirit of social reform associated with the Enlightenment had taken root *within* the political establishment and was asserting its influence through conscientious bureaucrats such as the chief secretary, Thomas Orde, and the great advocate of penal reform, Jeremiah Fitzpatrick. Among the institutions that came in for stinging criticism from this quarter was the Charter School system, which was found to be inefficient, corrupt, and grossly abusive of both the government's funds and the children entrusted to its care.[123]

The radical overhaul of the educational system proposed by Thomas Orde in 1787, which was designed in part to accommodate Catholic needs at the secondary and tertiary levels, was considered wholly inimical to the interests of the Church of Ireland because of its recommendation to abolish the Charter Schools. Bishop Woodward was again in the front line of the defence on this occasion, and another of his allies, Sir James Hutchinson, MP for Jamestown, County Leitrim, denounced the idea of abolishing the Charter Schools as 'the most fatal blow to the Protestant religion in Ireland ...; nothing would be more grateful to the Society de Propaganda Fidei in Rome'.[124] Hutchinson's comment on the Charter Schools pinpointed yet another worrying prospect for the Church of Ireland: the resurgence of the Catholic Church and its implicit claims to the loyalty of the great majority of the population, particularly in educational matters.

It was a recognition of this very reality that lay behind the support for educational reform in the first place, since it was believed that Catholics educated in Ireland and dependent to some degree on government assistance would be more easily assimilated into the social and political establishment and would likely display greater loyalty to a Protestant government than those educated in Europe. Also implicit in this view was the Enlightenment belief that education and rational thought would triumph over ignorance and superstition, and that Catholics, thus enlightened, would begin to appreciate and inevitably to adopt the doctrines of the reformed faith. When the opinions of the Catholic hierarchy on the proposed educational reforms were solicited, however, there was no disguising their hostility to any form of state intervention in the education of Catholics, which they clearly considered the exclusive preserve of their own Church. The Catholic bishop of Kildare, Daniel Delany, thought that Orde's scheme was aimed at 'the utter extirpation of our holy religion, together with the property of its possessors'. Most of his colleagues among the hierarchy shared this view and felt that the reforms were designed to strengthen the Protestant and weaken the Catholic interest.[125] It is easy to suggest that it might have been obvious to Protestant contemporaries that any attempt to lay claim to the allegiance of Catholics in spiritual or educational matters would be met with resistance by the Catholic clergy. At the time, however, it was assumed that Catholics, once educated and enlightened and granted access to civic and political power, would transfer their denominational allegiance to the reformed faith. As Ian McBride put it, it was the Protestant element that would absorb.[126]

A final source of anxiety for the Church of Ireland was the challenge to episcopal orthodoxy represented by the growth of the evangelical movement. There was a double irony here, for however much the 'enthusiasm' and independent ways of the evangelicals might be regarded with apprehension and contempt by the episcopate, it was precisely they who would provide the energy and initiative that gave the Church of Ireland a new sense of purpose and mission. The evangelical ideal of personal religion implied commitment, challenge and innovation—a combination of virtues perfectly suited to an institution recently shocked into recognizing that it must take itself and its mission seriously or risk being engulfed by the treacherous currents of the contemporary political crisis. Not surprisingly, the cause of 'serious' religion gained ground in Ireland in the 1780s and '90s, particularly in Dublin.

The rise of the Bethesda Chapel was the clearest indicator that the laity of the Church of Ireland were beginning to experience the first stirrings of religious enthusiasm. Of even greater importance was the emergence of Trinity College as the centre for a reform movement within the Church. Though not originally evangelical in the fundamental sense of the term, this movement gradually absorbed, or was absorbed by, the spirit of revivalism that had been gestating for decades on the denominational fringes of the Irish Protestant world. The fusion took place against a background of national and indeed international crisis in the late 1780s and '90s. As the evangelical movement was absorbed into the mainstream of Irish life in the second and third decades of the nineteenth century, the close interweave between religion and politics, already so apparent in the early stages, would become even more pronounced. In his study of the role of Trinity College in the rise of Irish evangelicalism Joseph Liechty claims that it was the atmosphere of defensive intransigence generated by the political crisis of the late eighteenth century that paved the way for the ascendancy of serious religion among the Trinity-based ideologues and defenders of the Church of Ireland. Given that what was at stake was the very existence of their Church as a national institution, it was hardly surprising that Trinity men should rally in support of the campaign launched by Bishop Woodward to forestall any threats to the tithe system and to thwart any claims for the political independence of Catholics.[127]

According to an informed observer in 1789, fully two-thirds of the student body at Trinity were destined for a career in the ministry.[128] Of the fellows who, according to Liechty, dominated intellectual life at the college and determined its ethos, only four were not in clerical orders. It was the influence of the junior fellows in their role as tutors to future generations of clergymen that Liechty has isolated as the fountainhead of the ideas on reform and renewal that were to cross-fertilize so effectively with the spirit of vital religion wafting into the establishment from the fringe areas occupied by the Methodists and Lady Huntingdon's Connexion.[129] The direction in which this movement for conservative reform would proceed was already evident in the late 1780s, but it was the cataclysmic events of the 1790s that really shaped its future character.

In the aftermath of the French Revolution political events in Ireland moved with terrifying speed. In 1791, inspired by the French example, a group of Belfast radicals founded the Society of United Irishmen with the express purpose of securing radical parliamentary reform, including the right of Catholics to vote and to take seats in parliament. Within four years this organization would be driven underground into a revolutionary alliance with the Defenders, a mass-based agrarian secret society.[130] The hopes of middle- and upper-class Catholics, meanwhile, had been given a tremendous boost by the outbreak of war between Britain and France in 1793. The desire of the British government to keep the peace in Ireland was a key element in reducing parliamentary opposition to Catholic demands, for no government could afford to allow such a large and disaffected body as the Catholics of Ireland to fall prey to the doctrines of liberty and equality that were then beginning to sweep all before them on the Continent.[131] Fully conscious of their position of strength in this regard, the more radical of the Catholic leaders strove to drive a hard bargain with the government. In this, they first had to overcome opposition in their own ranks, which came mainly from the conservative episcopate and the remnants of the old Gaelic aristocracy represented by lords Fingal and Kenmare. Their success in this matter was an indication that the locus of power was shifting towards members of the progressive middle class, who had risen, as their chief spokesman Richard Burke (the son of Edmund Burke) put it, 'by their industry, their abilities, and their good fortune to considerable opulence and of course to an independent spirit'.[132]

The net result of the Catholic agitation of the early 1790s was the passing of Hobart's Relief Act of 1793. This piece of legislation granted Catholics the right to vote on the same terms as Protestants and several other concessions, including the right to bear arms, to act as grand jurors, to sit on town corporations, to take degrees from Trinity College, and to occupy all but the chief offices in the army and civil service.[133] Nevertheless, the prize apple in the barrel—the right of Catholics to sit in parliament—was still withheld. This above all indicated the limitations of the government in the face of the Irish Protestant establishment's opposition to Catholic demands. A statement made by a member of the Dublin parliament, Sir John Parnell, in connection with the concessions under review in 1792 could be applied with equal force to the measures eventually passed. Parnell remarked that while concessions might be unpalatable to Protestants, they 'might keep the country quiet until the frenzy of reform had passed over Europe'.[134]

This observation helps to illustrate the predicament that faced any government seeking to introduce political reform in Ireland. Essentially, the authorities stood to be damned by radicals and Catholics for giving too little and by loyalist Protestants for giving too much. The dilemma became especially marked in 1794–5, when Earl Fitzwilliam, the recently appointed viceroy, committed the government, without first securing its full consent, to supporting a bill that proposed to admit Catholics to parliament. This had the effect of crystallizing the attitudes of conservatives, many of whom agreed with Alexander Knox's conclusion that the passage of such a bill would open the door to Catholic ascendancy and lead to a situation in which Protestants would be 'bound to do suit and service for their very existence'.[135]

These fears were allayed when Fitzwilliam was recalled to London and replaced by the more reliable Earl Camden. If this peremptory action by the government appeased conservative opinion in Ireland, however, it had the opposite effect on liberals and radicals, the former being reduced as a result to an ineffective opposition and the latter being pushed further along the road to revolution. Over the next three years events moved inexorably in this direction and rebellion broke out in several areas in 1798. For a variety of reasons, primarily because the revolt was badly coordinated, while the government was well prepared and ready to act, and because meaningful French help failed to materialize, the Rebellion was effectively put down. In a development that had dangerous portents, however, the spread of radical politics among the Catholic population had produced a reaction among the Protestant community that was expressed in the rise of popular loyalist defensive organizations. After 1795 these quickly coalesced into the Orange Order, a populist movement with gentry leadership that mobilized loyalists, particularly in the inflamed border areas of south Ulster, into a powerful bulwark against the radical ambitions of the United Irish movement.[136]

It goes almost without saying that the events of the 1790s caused Protestants in general to confront their own vulnerability in the face of a hostile and overwhelmingly Catholic majority. But it is less clear by what process the self-confident Protestant 'nation' of the 1780s evolved into the garrison-minded and fear-ridden community of the 1820s. While the Union represented a commitment by the government to the integration of Ireland into a united kingdom, the issue of how Catholics were to be culturally and politically accommodated within this entity was the great challenge facing the architects of the measure. What becomes immediately apparent in the early decades of the new century is the growth in Ireland of what Ian d'Alton has called a 'distinctly Protestant political culture'[137] and a preoccupation on the part of the Protestant establishment with controlling the direction of Catholic political consciousness. It is in connection with this trend that evangelical opinions on education and moral reform assume a pre-eminent role. One purpose of this study is to demonstrate the manner in which evangelicalism provided an ideological base for the section of the population in Ireland most concerned with protecting the 'Protestant interest'. Although certain clear parallels can be drawn between the rise of the evangelical ethos in Ireland and the concurrent development of a similar phenomenon across the Irish Sea, the outstanding difference is that whereas for a brief period the Irish movement, like its English equivalent, was directed against the 'infidelity' of revolutionary France, it soon became clear that the full force of its energies was aimed at blocking the political ambitions of the Catholic population, and particularly at undermining the leadership role of Catholic Church.

The passing of the Act of Union in 1800 was by no means accepted with equanimity by all Irish Protestants, despite the shock of the recent insurrection and the proof thus afforded that without the military support of England the Protestant regime in Ireland could not withstand a popular national rebellion. Conservative opposition was grounded in the belief that Westminster's desire to placate the Catholics of Ireland would make of the Union 'a constitutional Trojan horse which would lead to the overthrow of the Protestant ascendancy in Ireland'.[138] This fear was not without substance. Traditionally, Catholic leaders had looked to London rather than to Dublin for redress of their grievances, and appeasement of the Catholic population was foremost in the minds of the chief architects of the Union. Though unable to include full political equality for Catholics as part of the Union settlement, Prime Minister Pitt gave them to understand that such a measure would follow as a matter of course once the war with France was over and the threat of Catholic subversion removed. Though this promise won the approval of the conservative Catholic hierarchy, it aroused the ire of extreme Protestants, who feared that their interests would by no means be as secure when they were governed by London as when they had possessed their own parliament in Dublin.

Such opposition notwithstanding, the Union was enacted and political life in Ireland entered a relatively stable period. For Protestants and especially for the landed classes, it was a period of introspection and sobriety during which the carefree and profligate ways of the eighteenth century were cast aside in favour of a more serious approach to life in general and to religion in particular. Elizabeth Bowen observed that there occurred at Bowen's Court in County Cork from about 1817 onwards a 'kind of spiritual flooding', a development that she attributed to a relative of French–Huguenot extraction, but that was far more indicative of the winds of change blowing through the ranks of the Protestant gentry than she realized.[139] By 1817 the age of 'moral force' in Ireland had not only arrived but was on the point of full flowering.

–TWO–
THE AGE OF MORAL REFORM

A political revolution was effected in America through the agency, it is said, of Benjamin Franklin, George Washington, and J. Arnold; a bookseller, a farmer, and a horse-dealer. In Ireland a more difficult moral revolution was attempted, and in many instances effected, by a country clergyman, a Dublin curate, and a bookseller.

WARBURTON ET AL., *City of Dublin*[1]

The French Revolutionists ... rising amidst the awful devastation which marked their progress, sought to involve in one common ruin every political edifice, which the wisdom of ages had erected in surrounding nations, and to introduce that anarchy, of which they had given so woeful an example. To accomplish their dire purpose, they laboured to snatch the Sacred Scriptures from the hands of man, and sent forward their heralds, the missionaries of their infidelity; thus when it is our anxious wish to establish civil order and political stability, is it not our wisest policy, deeply to infuse into the minds of our countrymen, by the early study of the Word of God, those happy principles ... which incline every soul to be subject to the higher powers, and to submit to every ordinance of man for the Lord's sake. Thus will Ireland be blessed with a wise and an understanding people, taught by the wholesome discipline of judicious instruction, that Liberty consists not in an unrestrained indulgence of unbridled desires, but in the prudent regulations of well digested, and equally well executed laws; at once protecting the meanest from oppression, and controlling the power of the most exalted.

Fourth Report of the HBS, 1814[2]

Yet I do believe our savages resemble the mountains in which they live. Under a rugged surface there lurks a rich vein of ore, which one day may enrich the British empire.

JOHN JEBB[3]

RELIGIOUS REVIVAL IN THE CHURCH OF IRELAND

The decades that followed the outbreak of the French Revolution were remarkable throughout the British Isles for a massive swing towards social and political conservatism. Many contemporary observers believed that they had witnessed the collapse of civilized society as they knew it, and took refuge in a closer adherence to the teachings of Christianity, particularly those pertaining to individual morality and the maintenance of the social order.[4] It was a perfect opportunity for the promoters of serious religion to assert their claims to moral leadership in social, political and ecclesiastical affairs, and they lacked neither the will nor the resources to exploit it. In a campaign that involved completely new methods of influencing and mobilizing public opinion, the moral reformers succeeded in imposing their own particular hegemony over social and political life. Under the leadership of William Wilberforce and the Clapham Sect, the English, as Harold Perkin has claimed, 'ceased to be one of the most aggressive, brutal, rowdy, outspoken, riotous, cruel and bloodthirsty nations in the world and became one of the most inhibited, polite, orderly, tenderminded, prudish and hypocritical'.[5] The triumph of moral reform among the Protestant population in Ireland was no less pronounced. If anything, the process was intensified by the stark political implications of the turbulent 1790s and the passage of the Act of Union.

In the years immediately following the Union, the political mood in Ireland was characterized by a nervous calm that scarcely camouflaged the fears and animosities reanimated during the 1790s. Referring to the impact of the Orange outrages in the aftermath of the 1798 Rebellion, Peter Burrowes spoke of the 'determined and desperate spirit of counteraction' that had been aroused among Catholics of every description. If Catholic sentiment were to settle against the government at the commencement of the Union, he warned, the connection between the two countries would be 'as unstable as the winds and waves upon which it must depend'.[6] A similar mixture of guilt and fear caused many conscientious Protestants to embrace the belief that Christian morality afforded the soundest foundation for the regulation of human affairs, both public and private. The concept of 'atonement' was of particular importance in this context. Because it emphasized personal accountability, forgiveness, reconciliation and spiritual rebirth, it proved to be enormously attractive to those who were torn between the need to account for the vengeance and hatred unleashed during the 1790s and a concern for the safety of their own future.

Few exemplified this tradition of enlightened Christianity as powerfully as Whitley Stokes, whose passion for justice, freedom and the cause of his Catholic countrymen had taken him into radical circles in the early 1790s. By 1798 the extremism of the United Irishmen and the threat of expulsion from Trinity College combined to bring him back into the fold of the establishment. But he lost none of his faith in religion as the great motivating force behind social justice, political equality, and ultimate reconciliation between native and colonial in Ireland. He believed passionately that exposure to the moral precepts of the Gospel would lead both groups to realize how far they had strayed from the original teachings of Christ. Even if agreement in matters of religious belief were to be impossible, the basic Christian message of love and forgiveness might teach them to tolerate each other's opinions with charity and indulgence. Stokes urged that Protestant ministers and Catholic priests alike rally to the standard and instruct their followers in the Christian faith. Of the Protestant clergymen, he believed that many 'would hazard their lives for the diffusion of pure Christianity', while Catholic priests might be prevailed upon both to preach in the vernacular and to make use of the scriptures in the Irish language.[7]

Among contemporary fellows of Trinity College, Whitley Stokes's blend of political radicalism and religious enthusiasm was highly unusual. Most of his evangelical colleagues, though no less passionate in their desire to reform moral and religious standards, were staunchly on the side of the establishment during and after the crisis of the late eighteenth century. Throughout the 1790s the cause of moral reform and the evangelical spirit generally had gained strong momentum in Trinity College. Closely identified with those who were concerned with the security of the Church of Ireland, the reform ethos was especially popular among the fellows, who accounted for most of the teaching staff, and the majority of whom were in clerical orders. Galvanized by the outspoken defence of their Church by Bishop Woodward in the late 1780s, they were imbued with a new sense of responsibility regarding the mission of their Church in the rapidly changing world of the late eighteenth century.

In the general assault on Protestant ascendancy and privilege that had started in the 1780s, the Church of Ireland found its legitimacy called into question. Its apologists and defenders were solidly behind Bishop Woodward in their belief that the admission of Catholics to political equality would be followed by Catholic ascendancy, dissolution of the Church of Ireland and the downfall of the Protestant community. From the very beginning, therefore, the movement for reform in the Church of Ireland was driven by a deep-seated fear of Catholicism coupled with an adherence to episcopal orthodoxy, and by an abiding distaste for 'enthusiasm' that was tempered by an urgent need to improve religious life at every level of society. This last objective was in line with the trend emerging in England, where the newly acquired religiosity of the upper classes was driving episcopal reform in the shape of new church buildings, new livings and a general increase in the role of religion in society.

There were many areas of common ground between episcopal evangelicalism in the Dublin metropolitan area and its counterpart in London. The most important of these were the agencies through which the reform spirit was propagated—in the private sphere through personal and professional connections, and publicly through voluntary organizations. For example, many of those who went on to play leading roles in the evangelical movement in the early nineteenth century, were the direct products of an identifiable Trinity network composed of fellows, students, and graduates.[8] Among the clergymen who held fellowships during this period, six went on to become bishops of the Church of Ireland and two out of this number, Charles Elrington of Meath and William Magee of Dublin, would earn lasting reputations as champions of renewal and expansion.[9]

The organization that became a rallying point for Trinity evangelicals and eventually became the flagship of the moral reform movement in the Church of Ireland was the Association for Discountenancing Vice (ADV). Its founders were the Rev. Singleton Harpur, Dr O'Connor of Castleknock, and a Dublin bookseller, William Watson of Capel Street. In 1788 Singleton Harpur had published a pamphlet on temperance in which he showed himself to be clearly in line with the new stridency of the movement for moral reform in England led by William Wilberforce and Hannah More.[10] Wilberforce and his circle had succeeded in 1787 in persuading George III to issue a proclamation to improve piety and morality and to 'discountenance and punish all manner of vice, profaneness and immorality, in all persons of whatsoever degree or quality within this our realm'. The proclamation was sent to every magistrate in the country and ordered to be read from every pulpit in the land four times a year. Shortly afterwards, Wilberforce founded the Proclamation Society for the Suppression of Vice, a voluntary organization dedicated to attacking every manifestation of vice and immorality in public life: drunkenness, cursing and swearing, immoral literature, prostitution, and the popular blood sports of the lower classes, such as cock-fighting and bear-baiting.[11]

The Association for Discountenancing Vice, more popularly known as the Dublin Association, was the Irish equivalent of the Proclamation Society.[12] Its objectives regarding moral reform were, if anything, more all-embracing than its English progenitor, and, as its full name suggested, it stressed education as the most effective way to instill morality. Its explicit aim was, on the one hand, to check the spread of immorality and infidelity by promoting the type of scriptural education sanctioned by the Established Church, and, on the other, 'to guard against the dangers of enthusiasm'—a clear indicator of the cautious and conservative road it planned to follow. During the 1790s the ADV pursued its campaign for moral reform on many different fronts. Among the sources of 'immoral influence' that came under immediate attack were many staple institutions of leisure and entertainment among the lower classes, including drinking, gambling and popular literature. Under pressure from the Association the Dublin lottery was suppressed and the sale of liquor on Sunday prohibited. Likewise, Sunday promenades at the Rotunda were forbidden, and steps were taken to substitute moral tracts of the kind made famous in England by Sarah Trimmer and Hannah More for the more colourful and often bawdy tales of pirates and highwaymen sold by pedlars and hawkers. As cheap moral tracts were not as yet being produced locally, the bookseller Watson imported an English edition of Hannah More's tales and had them republished in Dublin. In 1795–6, 120,000 copies of these tracts were printed and distributed to the poor at reduced prices.[13]

It was to the upper middle classes and aristocracy, however, that the Association directed its strongest pitch for support. Again, in the fashion of Wilberforce and the Claphamites, the power and influence of 'those who count' was consciously sought out and extolled as the most important lever by which the principles of moral reform might be spread throughout the whole of society.[14] As in England, the wealthy and powerful were urged to set the standard for manners and morality in the private sphere through exemplary conduct, and in public life and politics through philanthropy and legislative reform. The success of the ADV in winning the support of the influential and powerful in the metropolitan area was impressive. By 1795 the membership list had risen to 500 and the society could boast of the most powerful man in the country, the viceroy, as its president, and the archbishops of Armagh, Cashel, Dublin and Tuam as honorary members.[15] The Association generally functioned as an umbrella group under whose auspices many different shades of opinion were accommodated, from the strictly orthodox viewpoint of the episcopal bench to the zeal and energy of committed evangelical clergymen like the Rev. Joseph Stopford and the Rev. Thomas Tighe. Intellectually, it was a clearing house for ideas and debates about how to improve religious life generally among the clergy and to upgrade church attendance and domestic piety among the laity. Ideas were disseminated through monthly meetings, printed pamphlets and personal correspondence, and especially through what was becoming the most vital of all forms of public address during this period, the sermon.

Radiating from the capital city, the reform spirit was carried to the provinces by clergymen who had absorbed the message of renewal and reform during their student days at Trinity. Many of these individuals would function as driving forces behind Church reform on a local or provincial basis, and they would also continue to maintain their communication with the Association in Dublin as well as with each other. The clearest example of the links that were fostered between the advocates of spiritual and moral reform in Dublin and the provinces is that afforded by the Rev. Peter Roe and the Ossory Clerical Association (OCA). Ossory was unique among Irish dioceses at this time for its concentration of reform-minded clergymen. Before his transfer to Meath in 1798, Bishop Thomas Lewis O'Beirne had initiated regular meetings for his diocesan clergy in the hope of improving their knowledge of the scriptures and their duties of office. Upon O'Beirne's departure, however, this custom was brought to an end. The clergymen responsible for beginning anew were Peter Roe and Hans Hamilton, a son of Bishop Hugh Hamilton, O'Beirne's successor.[16] Hans Hamilton is credited with the inspiration for the new plan, the idea having occurred to him as he was riding home one night from a meeting concerned with agricultural improvement. If people could convene to advance the cause of agriculture, it seemed to him logical that spiritual husbandry, or the care of souls, could be advanced in the same manner.[17] This story is reminiscent of the experience of the great English abolitionist, Thomas Clarkson, who was overtaken by a similar flash of inspiration as he was riding from Cambridge to London in 1787, and who went on to become one of the most important propagandists in the campaign to arouse public opinion against the slave trade. Experiences of this kind typified the capacity of evangelicals to utilize spiritual inspiration as a means to pursue practical and often very political and material ends.

Hans Hamilton's suggestion of holding meetings on a regular basis was welcomed by the Rev. Robert Shaw of Fiddown, who had complained that when he first settled in the diocese in the early 1790s 'he did not know a brother minister whom he could invite to join with him in prayer'. Within a short period the Rev. Edward Pidgeon, rector of St Mary's in Kilkenny, was persuaded to join Hamilton and Shaw in their evangelical beliefs and objectives.[18] By the time Roe was appointed as his curate in 1799, Pidgeon was already a committed advocate, though undoubtedly the arrival of a young clergyman fresh from the metropolis and imbued with the activist ethos of the Trinity establishment was an enormous boost to morale. These four clergymen—Roe, Shaw, Hamilton and Pidgeon—formed the nucleus of the OCA, formally instituted in 1800, and they went on to enlist other clergymen from different parts of the county. The OCA was never very large, amounting to no more than fifteen or sixteen members in 1804. In characteristic evangelical fashion, however, this collective wielded an influence that belied its small membership.

The first aim of the OCA was to foster the improvement of spiritual and pastoral care among the clergy and piety and religious practice among the laity. The approval of the local bishop, Dr Hugh Hamilton, was a distinct advantage, as episcopal support for the idea of a revival within the Established Church at this time was not something that could always be relied upon. At a time when sympathy for the evangelical insistence on the Bible as the fundamental source of spiritual and moral authority could well be construed as a threat to episcopal power, Hamilton judiciously remained within the boundaries of orthodoxy on all matters of Church policy. His personal sympathies, however, are revealed by the fact that his five sons and two daughters were all identified with the evangelical movement, and by the tolerance and approval he showed to the clerical association of which his son Hans was a founder. Hamilton had no objection to the groups' convening once a month for a public meeting in Kilkenny town. In fact, he tacitly approved of the practice and considered the evangelicals to be the most efficient and progressive of the diocesan clergy.[19]

The monthly conferences on spiritual and pastoral care proved to be a most satisfactory vehicle for stimulating the enthusiasm of the members of the Association. Besides liturgy and doctrine, the more practical question of spreading the revivalist spirit throughout the country was addressed. An entry taken from the minute book of 1802 indicates the kinds of matters discussed:

> October 6th, 1802.—Had a long conversation arising from prayer-meetings in awakening the unconcerned and in building up 'in our most holy faith' those who have begun to see the value of salvation. Several testimonies were borne to the excellent effects produced by them in all those parishes where they have been adopted; and it is the opinion of this association that speedy and effectual means ought to be used to introduce and

establish prayer-meetings in our respective parishes; and also to insist on the great necessity of family prayer and on the expediency of adopting it universally.[20]

While the doctrine of justification by faith was the principal tenet of evangelical Protestantism, the emphasis on the interdependency of faith and good works was no less marked. Visiting the sick, the poor and the imprisoned, collecting funds to provide food and clothing for the needy, and supporting an institution for the relief of destitute females were among the regular duties of Peter Roe's ministry in Kilkenny. The effectiveness of his combined spiritual and temporal campaign was almost immediately evident in the increase in attendance at church on Sundays and holy days, in the numbers presenting themselves for the sacraments of communion and confirmation, and above all in the interest shown in prayer-meetings, lectures on the interpretation of the Bible and catechism classes for children. The commitment to active catechizing and preaching was the outstanding feature that set the Ossory reformers apart from their fellow ministers of the Established Church. Not only did they organize sermons, lectures and discussions in their own districts, but they also exchanged visits with each other for much the same purposes, and eventually extended these visits into preaching tours of the adjoining counties.[21]

During the early years of the century the preaching tour, previously the hallmark of Methodists and Independent evangelicals, now began to be a regular feature of clerical life in the Church of Ireland. In this area, as in many others, the OCA was clearly in the forefront. Roe was an active itinerant in his native Kilkenny and also in the counties of Waterford, Cork and Tipperary. On a tour conducted in March 1804, during which he visited Thomastown, Ross, Waterford, Fiddown and Piltown, he was pleased to note that 'religion is spreading fast and the ministers increasing in number'.[22] He was also a frequent visitor to the capital, where his ability as a preacher made an enormous impact, as witnessed by his biographer:

> The interest excited by his preaching was of the most extraordinary description, and only exceeded by that called forth by Dean Kirwan. Bride's Church used to be crowded to such excess that the very windows were filled even outside and not one spot in the whole church left unoccupied. St. Peter's Church also, and St. Catherine were likewise overflowing. When he was in Dublin, his father's servant was obliged constantly to stand the whole day in the hall to answer the never-ceasing inquiries of where he was to preach.[23]

The delivery of charity sermons on behalf of such institutions as the Royal Hospital School and the Meath Hospital became a regular feature of Roe's visits to the capital. By the time he preached his last such sermon in 1837, it was estimated that the total sum collected over the years had amounted to £7300.[24] His frequent visits to Dublin strengthened his acquaintance with the advocates of religious revival and moral reform, many of whom he had known since his student days. Of these, the most influential undoubtedly were the Rev. Benjamin William Mathias and James Digges La Touche. Like Roe, these men were young (in their mid-twenties), dedicated evangelicals, and firm in their commitment to the Church of Ireland. In character and outlook they likewise represented the manner and form that Irish episcopal evangelicalism was beginning to assume.

Mathias had been orphaned at an early age and had imbibed his religious principles from the man who had taken him as a ward, a Presbyterian minister named Dr Benjamin McDowell, who was known as 'an earnest advocate of the Calvinistic theology'.[25]

Between 1791 and 1796 Mathias attended Trinity College, where his evangelical beliefs were strengthened but his institutional preference was channelled away from Dissent and towards the Church of Ireland. In 1798 he was ordained and took up an appointment in Rathfriland, County Down, and served as curate to the Rev. Thomas Tighe of Drumgooland where his commitment to evangelicalism was further reinforced. He returned to Dublin in 1805 to assume a position as chaplain to the Bethesda, which he held until 1835, when he was obliged to retire because of ill health. Throughout this period Mathias dominated the evangelical movement in the capital and was considered by many to have rendered more service to the ministry of the Church of Ireland than the professor of divinity in Trinity College. Preaching was his forte and the source of his great popularity and influence:

> His voice, his appearance, his fluid address, his deep fervour, and the excellence of his matter all contributed to promote his popularity; and at length not a few of the elite of the metropolis became his constant auditors. Students of Trinity College, lawyers, physicians, gentry and nobility, as well as many of the humbler classes flocked to the Bethesda.[26]

Mathias's popularity was a measure of how the evangelical spirit was moving from the fringe to the centre of religious life in the Church of Ireland. Originally the victim of censure and disapproval by both the archbishop of Dublin, who refused to allow him to preach in any licenced churches, and the provost of

Trinity, who commanded students not to attend his sermons, Mathias went on to enjoy undisputed popularity in the 1820s as a leader of the most vital reform movement ever experienced by the Established Church.

Among the lay community, the involvement of several members of the La Touche family in the moral reform movement provides an equally illuminating picture of the ascendancy of the evangelical ethos. The La Touches were among the most famous of the Huguenot families who had set down roots in Ireland after the Williamite wars. By the end of the eighteenth century they were one of the most socially prominent families in Dublin with several townhouses in fashionable residential areas such as St Stephen's Green and Ely Place, and substantial properties in land and mining throughout the provinces.[27] Like the Guinness family they were a highly visible presence in the capital city's many charitable and philanthropic enterprises.

By the turn of the century, the dynamic influence of evangelical morality was easily distinguishable in the opinions of John David La Touche, who confessed that he was 'willing to spend and be spent in the service of the Lord', even if it meant becoming a preacher of the gospel, on behalf of the spiritual and temporal welfare of his friends and relatives and mankind in general.[28] Clearly an Enlightenment-inspired advocate of social reform, by his own admission he had made the transition from deism to 'true religion' as a result of conversations with Methodist friends.[29] It was his youthful nephew, however, in whom the impulse for reforming zeal found its clearest expression. James Digges La Touche was a student at Trinity College between 1803 and 1808, during which time he became a regular worshipper at the Bethesda and involved himself in the founding and running of new organizations such as the Sunday School Society and the Hibernian Bible Society (HBS).[30] In his private life his conscience was dominated by the struggle between the vanities and pleasures of the world and the demands of religion and morality, preoccupations he revealed and discussed in a remarkable series of letters written between 1808 and 1810 to his dearest friend and confidant, John Synge. Like many contemporaries who expressed the passions of the age through a religious idiom, La Touche was an ardent Romantic. He professed to love poetry (particularly Cowper), astronomy and the intimacy of close friendships.[31] His friendship with Synge was especially prized because, as he claimed: 'let the world think as it may, there is no stronger bond which cements friendships than joining to their other coincident affections that of fellow warriors in Christ'.[32]

This sense of a shared identity based upon allegiance to a common cause was a particular characteristic of the first generation of Irish evangelicals. Cutting across the boundaries of class, gender and denominational allegiance, it united people from all walks of life—laymen in business and the professions, clergymen, landlords, women, and politicians—into a cohesive movement aimed at effecting the transformation of society, which they believed was their gospel-based directive. Though he never wavered in his loyalty to the Church of Ireland, James Digges La Touche was at all times willing to cooperate with Nonconformists in order to further the evangelical cause. In later years his biographer and fellow evangelical, the Rev. William Urwick, described him as a man 'who, had he lived on the south side of London instead of the south side of Dublin', would have 'belonged to that party in the Church of England which of late has been called the Clapham Sect'.[33] Contrary to the impression given by his biographer, however, La Touche was not an isolated figure in Dublin, but part of a group of activists who made up the high command of the evangelical movement and dictated its character and progress throughout the first part of the nineteenth century.

AGENTS AND AGENCIES OF MORAL REFORM

From about 1805 onwards, Irish evangelicalism began to assume the character of an identifiable movement with explicit social and political aims. Voluntary societies organized on a national basis and designed to cater to special-interest areas such as Bible distribution or Sunday Schools provided the backbone of the system, and these were accompanied by a myriad of smaller, more local or experimental efforts, with such objectives as prison reform, the education of the deaf and dumb and the relief of destitute widows. The massive growth of private philanthropy heralded the involvement of the lay community on a large scale, and it also contributed to a growing spirit of goodwill and cooperation between evangelicals of the Church of Ireland and the Methodists and Independents. From the nature of the work undertaken by the voluntary societies, and the character of the men who provided the leadership and organizational skills necessary for their operation, it is possible to identify lay evangelicals as a distinct community and to mark the progress and eventual ascendancy of their particular views on religion, society and politics. By tracing the careers of a group of the most influential of these evangelical laymen, I shall attempt to show how their outlook and way of life, and their complementary and often interconnected efforts in the cause of moral reform, all contributed to the growth of an effective evangelical party whose influence in Ireland paralleled that of William Wilberforce and the Clapham Sect in England.

James Digges La Touche was the eldest son of William George Digges La Touche, one of the chief partners in the family's banking firm. A diligent and serious student, following his graduation from Trinity College he assumed his father's position as chief partner in the bank. He actively supported many of the new evangelical interdenominational concerns, particularly those connected with popular education. He was instrumental in launching the Hibernian Bible Society (HBS) in 1806 and was chiefly responsible for the founding of the Sunday School Society for Ireland in 1809. The accounts of almost all the evangelical societies were handled by his bank, and he gave liberally of his energy and his wealth in the cause of education and moral reform. Much of the success of the Sunday School Society in its formative years was attributed to his energy and dedication. In the opinion of his biographer, the Congregationalist minister Rev. William Urwick, 'the service rendered by him as a "layman" to the cause of scriptural education in his native land could hardly have been exceeded'.[34] After his untimely death in 1827 the Society that he had done so much to promote became a permanent appendage of the Church of Ireland in much the same manner as the Sunday School Union in Britain.

John Synge was the intimate friend and confidant of the young La Touche, and like him hailed from one of the most prominent gentry families of County Wicklow. A great-uncle of John Millington Synge, in his own lifetime he was known as 'Pestalozzi John' because of his admiration for the educational philosophy of the Swiss educator Heinrich Pestalozzi and his efforts to introduce Pestalozzian methods to Ireland. Following an extended visit to Pestalozzi's famous institute in Yverdon in 1815, Synge returned to Ireland and set up a system of experimental schools at Roundwood, County Wicklow. The 'Roundwood experiment' included a printing press that produced textbooks for use in the schools as well as accounts of Synge's experiences on the Continent. The 'Pestalozzi method' of instruction advocated by Synge was deemed more suitable than either the Bell or Lancastrian models then in vogue in England. It was adopted for use in a model school set up by the influential Viscount de Vesci in Abbeyleix and recommended for adoption by the Kildare Place Society (KPS), whose schools had spread across the entire country by the 1820s. Synge's preoccupation with 'serious religion' took him into the more extreme wing of Irish evangelicalism that was centred on the Powerscourt family and led by Theodosia

Howard, Viscountess Powerscourt. In the 1820s, under the leadership of John Nelson Darby, this group separated from the Church of Ireland and went on to form the splinter group known as the Plymouth Brethren. Synge was a prominent member of the group and eventually moved to the English West Country where the Brethren were particularly concentrated.[35]

Charles Edward Orpen was the youngest son of a Church of Ireland clergyman of Dungourney in West Cork. He was first introduced to vital religion as a way of life through the preaching of the Rev. John Quarry of Lower Shandon in Cork city, considered by many as one of the brightest stars of the revival in the Church of Ireland. A qualified medical doctor, Orpen was a prototypical evangelical in his unwavering commitment to use his skills in the service of God and humanity. Like his contemporaries he was deeply interested in the education of the poor. While recovering from a bout of typhoid fever in 1816 he used his time to give lessons to a deaf and dumb child, and from this point on made the education of the deaf and dumb his particular concern. He started a school for this purpose in Dublin in 1816 and three years later founded the Claremount Institute for the Education of the Deaf and Dumb, which enjoyed the distinction of being the first school of its kind in the British Isles. In 1817–18 he toured the Continent with his brother and made a point of visiting every educational institution he knew of, spending three months with Pestalozzi in Yverdon. Even more than John Synge, he was overawed by the influence of the famous educator, and he thought that the simplicity of the Pestalozzian method was ideal for use in the education of the handicapped. Orpen was also a leading figure in the wing of the evangelical movement that took up the cause of educating the Catholic Irish in their native language, becoming in the process a passionate and outspoken defender of Irish language and culture. Widely respected for his integrity and patriotism by people on both sides of the religious divide, he is easily distinguishable as a harbinger of the cultural nationalism of Thomas Davis and the Young Ireland movement of the 1840s.[36]

Henry Joseph Monck Mason, a barrister and antiquarian, graduated from Trinity College as a gold medal winner in 1798. He never practised law but was appointed chief librarian at King's Inns in 1815. He made a reputation as a champion of prison reform, but the guiding passion of his life was the culture and language of ancient Ireland. A friend of the poet Thomas Moore at Trinity during the 1790s, he went on to become a member of the short-lived Iberno-Celtic Society (founded 1810) dedicated to promoting Celtic literature. Monck Mason was also a close friend of the English poet, Robert Southey, and espoused the same brand of conservative nationalism as the Lake poets. He combined his passion for the Irish language and his evangelical commitments by founding the Irish Society for the Education of the Native Irish through the Medium of Their Own Language (commonly known as the Irish Society) in 1818. A jealous partisan of Protestant ascendancy, he probably did more than any of his contemporaries to advance the theory that the Church of Ireland claimed legitimate descent from the ancient Celtic Church that had split with Rome in 684 AD and was thus considered as having set a precedent for the Church of England in the sixteenth century.[37] Monck Mason was an active member of the Royal Irish Academy and his bigotry notwithstanding, his legacy in the area of Celtic studies is beyond question. He was the chief force behind the setting up of the Bedell scholarship and premiums for the study of Irish at Trinity College and was also instrumental in establishing the first professorship of Irish there in 1844.[38]

Thomas Langlois Lefroy was the eldest son of Anthony Lefroy of Carraiglass, County Longford, a Trinity-educated barrister who enjoyed a lengthy and very public career in law and politics and typified the moral reformer in public life.[39] There was hardly an organization on whose committee his name did not appear. He was involved with the running of KPS from its foundation in 1811 and sat on the original committee of the Hibernian Church Missionary Society in 1814, becoming a vice-president of the same Society in 1822; he was a life member of the Sunday School Society for Ireland, and of the Irish Auxiliary to the Jews Society. He was also a life member and vice-president of the Irish Society and the founder of its appendage, the Scripture Readers' Society, in 1822. As a judge on the Munster circuit in the 1820s, his experiences left an enduring impression of the need for the moral improvement of the peasantry. He was mortified by their disdain for law and the authority of the courts (which he contrasted unfavourably with the attitude of the common people of England), and their adoration of his personal nemesis on the circuit, Daniel O'Connell. A lifelong foe of O'Connell and Catholic claims generally, he was part of the Orange plutocracy that dominated the legal profession, and that Lord Cloncurry (during the uproar over the use of the Bible in the schools of the KPS in 1819) with merciless accuracy described as 'professional fanatics who in that day were in the habit of seeking, through Protestantism and piety, a ready road to the bench'.[40] Lefroy was indeed appointed to the bench at King's Inns in 1819. He became an MP as a member for Trinity College in 1831 and continued his career in law and politics well into his old age. He died in 1869 at the age of ninety-three, having resigned his position as lord chief justice of the Queen's

Bench only three years earlier.[41]

The most visible element uniting this group of men was the homogeneity of their backgrounds and their public occupations. All were Trinity-educated professionals of landed or upper-middle-class backgrounds, possessed of that self-conscious awareness of having been called upon to answer to the demands of 'true Christianity' that was the hallmark of the saved Christian. In the first instance this required an admission that man was born a sinner, and could be redeemed only through faith in the atoning death of Christ. Redemption was attained through a process of regeneration or conversion in which the true Christian would be 'born again' in his awareness of the infinite gift of God's mercy. Such conversion often followed an experience that jolted the individual into a sense of his own mortality, such as the death of a beloved friend or family member or a life-threatening illness. Providence was also a key element in the evangelical's awareness of his place in the world. The timing of one's life on earth was understood to have been dictated by divine will or 'providence' in order to fulfil the Creator's designs for the human race. Once these designs were established, the test of the true Christian was an unwavering commitment to their realization, regardless of obstacles and setbacks. This is what lay behind the relentless dedication of the evangelicals in whatever cause they chose to espouse, what Roger Anstey (in accounting for the persistence of the evangelical leadership of the movement to abolish slavery) has described as the 'sheer dogged determination in the task to which they unfailingly believed God had called them'.[42]

The regenerate Christian could never rest content in the knowledge that he was saved, but was forever obliged to question his conscience regarding his behaviour in order to be accountable on the Day of Judgment. Commitment to the ideals of evangelical Christianity therefore involved not only intense self-examination and self-criticism, but also a sense that one had to account for one's time, energy, and whatever gifts of intellect or personality one happened to be endowed with. Accountability was not simply an individual or personal affair, as the typical evangelical felt obliged not only to answer for himself but for his neighbour and indeed society at large. Evangelicals in consequence tended to be extremely hard-working, introspective and emotional at one level, and heavily involved in public life and politics at the other. They believed that if mankind in general could be brought, through a process of 'willing submission', to live according to the great principles of Christianity, that peace and harmony would universally prevail. It was their duty to work towards this end by promoting the

Christian way of life through example and conviction and, above all, through leading 'useful' lives dedicated to the welfare of mankind and the glory of God. This was as true for those members of the evangelical community in Dublin whose careers I have used for representative purposes as it was for their fellow travellers in Clapham Common.

One of the major differences separating the 'vital religion' of the evangelical revival from the rational Christianity or Deism that had dominated religious outlook in the eighteenth century was the admission of passion into the religious experience. Evangelicalism, after all, professed to be 'religion of the heart' and its appeal was first and foremost to the emotions. The heart was seen as the true source of all that was natural and sincere in humanity, and evangelicals considered the cultivation of a 'good heart' as a far more worthy objective than high intellectual achievement. Heartfelt sincerity employed in the relief of human misery was also a powerful means of attracting converts to the fold. A Dublin Catholic who had converted to Methodism in 1773 after hearing John Wesley preach admitted that 'what endeared him still more to me was seeing him stop to kiss a little child that stood on the stairs'.[43]

The emotional intensity that lay at the heart of the evangelical religious experience was carried over into every aspect of life. The expression of tenderness in human relations was a standard feature of the domestic life of evangelicals, and in this they were advocates of the cult of sensibility as much as the most ardent disciple of Rousseau.[44] In many other areas of cultural expression and political aspiration it is possible to see the evangelical movement as the stream that absorbed the ideals of the late Enlightenment in the British Isles. The emphasis on virtue, sincerity and truth, the importance of expressing heartfelt emotions, the wholehearted desire for a new moral order and the impassioned commitment to achieve it through such pragmatic means as education and social and political reform—these constituted the psychological and social demands of the evangelical blueprint for the ideal society. In many respects it was the expression through a religious medium of what Rousseau and his disciples had called for in secular language. Indeed, some evangelicals like John Synge and Charles Edward Orpen went directly to the source of the continental Enlightenment for inspiration as well as practical methodology. Predictably they ran into trouble when they were faced with reconciling the Rousseau-inspired educational philosophy of Pestalozzi with the demands of an educational experiment centred on Christian teaching.[45]

The common objective shared by followers of the evangelical movement and the Enlightenment was to provide a system of belief and code of conduct that could accommodate the needs and aspirations of the individual in a mass society. The 'willing submission' to divine authority that formed the basis of a society governed on Christian principles was similar in many ways to the theory of the 'general will' formulated by Rousseau. Both systems aspired to accommodate the individual, whatever his rank or station, within the corporate whole, and both underlined education as the most vital instrument through which individuals would be prepared for membership in the new moral order. But while the extremities of the French Revolution had the effect of severely undermining the ideals of the secular Enlightenment on the Continent, they strengthened the hand of the moral reformers in the British Isles, particularly from the point of view of calling the upper classes to account for their lack of morals and ignorance of religion. Besides, secular philosophy suffered for being just that— the product of man's attempts to provide his own understanding of the world and its ways—whereas teachings rooted in a system of religious belief based upon the written word were enormously more powerful and effective, especially during a time of great change and uncertainty. To be sure, there were contemporary interpretations of Christianity that professed to instruct people in the demands of the new moral order. William Wilberforce's *A Practical View of the Prevailing Religious System of Preofessed Christians in the Higher and Middle Classes in this Country Contrasted with Real Christianity* (1797) became the behaviour manual of evangelicals for most of the nineteenth century. Hannah More's tales taught the poor how to be satisfied with their situation in life and how to behave towards their social superiors. But it was the true source of the word, the Bible, that no one who called themselves a Christian could be without. The Bible was not only the chief source from which evangelicals drew their instruction and inspiration, it was equally powerful as an icon and symbol of the righteousness and superiority of the Protestant way of life. Not surprisingly, the dynamic with which the evangelical movement 'took off' within the religious establishments of both Britain and Ireland in the decade between 1795 and 1805 was characterized chiefly through the demand for the mass availability of the Bible.

The initial demand for the widespread production of bibles arose in connection with the Sunday School movement, which had been underway since the 1780s, and the rise of the foreign missionary societies in the 1790s. During this period two trends had combined to make British evangelicals conscious of their responsibility to convert the heathen or non-Christian peoples of the world. One was the knowledge of and interest in such people that had resulted from the enormous popularity of Captain Cook's *Voyages* in the 1780s,[46] and the scandal associated with the East India Company that was brought to light by the famous trial of Warren Hastings that had dragged on from 1788 to 1795. The second was the upsurge in millenarian expectation arising from the political upheavals of the time. The alarming events in France and especially the attack on the Catholic Church and the papacy caused many evangelicals to believe that the thousand-year reign of the Saints was at hand, which would be followed by the Second Coming of Christ. Certain conditions needed to be fulfilled before this would come to pass. For the Baptist preacher William Carey, the most important of these conditions was the conversion of the heathens? Carey's famous *An Enquiry into the Obligations of Christians To Use Means for the Conversion of the Heathen* (1792) was the manifesto that initiated the modern Protestant missionary movement in the British Isles.[47] In the same year the Baptist Missionary Society was founded, followed three years later by the London Missionary Society, another Dissenting organization that, although based in London, was heavily Scottish in character and influence and reflected the 'common sense' school of the Scottish Enlightenment. These two societies' first experiences of missionary operations in India and Africa were marked by mutual support and cooperation. 'Pan-evangelicalism' or the coming together of evangelicals of different denominations on certain basic points of theology was a feature of the 1790s and prepared the ground for the cooperation and mutual support that governed interdenominational relations after the turn of the century.[48]

The Clapham Sect in particular were very favourably disposed to the work of the Baptists and Nonconformists in the foreign missions, and followed their example in 1799 with the founding of the Church Missionary Society (CMS), which quickly became a major force in the overseas missions. With far more access to funds and manpower than its predecessors, the CMS quickly took the lead and made the foreign missions and the conversion of the heathen a national cause in the early years of the new century. It was partly in response to the demand for bibles raised by these societies and partly because the Religious Tract Society (an Anglican body founded in 1799 to provide religious reading material for the domestic market) had drawn attention to the need for Bible distribution on the home front that the British and Foreign Bible Society (BFBS) was founded in 1804. The interdenominational character of the BFBS had been formulated well before its foundation and was responsible for the enormous success it enjoyed both at home and abroad.[49] Although it was directed almost exclusively by members of the Clapham Sect, including William Wilberforce, Henry Thornton, Zachary Macaulay, Charles Grant and Sir John Shore (Lord Teignmouth), membership of the BFBS was open to people of every denomination, and its bibles were made available to Christians of every persuasion, including Catholics. The Bible Society was the quintessential expression of evangelical ecumenism and its auxiliaries and associations were soon to be found all over the British Isles and eventually all over the globe. Its basic objectives were twofold: to provide bibles in foreign languages wherever the ground had been cultivated for this purpose, and to supply the home market wherever the demand existed, whether it was in Sunday schools or the other innumerable philanthropic societies, or for distribution to the public through its own network of auxiliaries.

The demand for bibles in Ireland was accelerated by developments similar to those described above. Initially raised in connection with Sunday schools in the late 1780s, it was voiced even more emphatically in the 1790s by the ADV.[50] In 1800 the ADV directed an appeal to 'Irish absentees and particularly to the proprietors of landed estates who answered to that description', describing the Bible as:

> The irrefragible manifestation of God's will to His rational creatures, [a quality which] raises it, with respect to practical efficacy, infinitely above all that ever came from the pen of man, and makes it a means of working on the public mind, of such invaluable importance as to render it doubtful whether they who neglect to give it the utmost possible circulation are more impious and impolitic, more insensitive to their own interest, or more ungrateful to their God.[51]

This bears the unmistakable stamp of Wilberforce's *Practical View*, which was at this time beginning to make its influence felt in Ireland.[52] The dangers inherent in the mass propagation of secular political philosophy, or 'infidelity' as professed Christians preferred to call it, were underscored by Peter Roe in 1799, in tones that were soon to become familiar throughout the country:

> Be always on your guard against unbelievers. Nothing can prove their depravity more than their circulating, among the weak and half-learned, multitudes of their books, the principles of which destroy their comforts and happiness; and, while affecting to pity the humble and poor, strike at the best and sometimes, alas, their only refuge and consolation amidst the distresses and afflictions of the world—THE BIBLE.[53]

It was Peter Roe's comrade-in-arms in the OCA, the Rev. Robert Shaw of Fiddown, County Kilkenny, who functioned as liaison between the Irish evangelicals and the leaders of the movement in England. During the 1798 Rebellion he had been active as a magistrate in his native county and had suffered a physical breakdown because of his exertions. When he was medically advised to cease parochial duties and to spend a period of time in travel, he used the opportunity to visit England in order to investigate tracts and bibles for the Irish market.[54] He had already established contact with the CMS through its secretary, Josiah Pratt, but had cautioned somewhat apologetically that it was unlikely that Ireland would be able to contribute much to the cause of the foreign missions as it was the custom of the country to 'promise much and never pay up', but more especially because of the enormous want at home:

> ... for here we have no poor rates, and the poor have been so miserably neglected with respect to education, schools of industry etc. that the active clergy here have been obliged to apply themselves first to these purposes, and find that all the money they can make is insufficient to carry them on in any satisfactory manner ... when I look around me here I feel much inclined to say 'come over help us' as the Indian might.[55]

This appeal was prescient. The connections Shaw established ensured that Ireland was kept informed about developments in the foreign missions and, more importantly, that the evangelical circle in London was made aware of the existence and needs of their Irish colleagues.[56]

In the early years of the century Shaw continued to operate independently as a collector of bibles and tracts for distribution in Ireland. Travelling from town to town by horse and cart and collecting bibles along the way, he returned to Ireland whenever his store was abundant and deposited his acquisitions in rural post offices. The postmasters, being Protestant, could be relied upon to see to it that they were properly disposed of. Between 1800 and 1810 Shaw made this pilgrimage annually and is said to have been responsible for the introduction of almost 100,000 copies of the scriptures to Ireland.[57] He attended meetings in London whenever the opportunity afforded and was present at the founding of the BFBS. His colleagues in the OCA were also in contact with evangelical leaders in London and kept them informed of developments in Ireland. In 1804 Peter Roe was advising Josiah Pratt to have the existence and background of the OCA mentioned in the *Christian Observer*, the organ of the evangelical wing of the Church of England. He also assured Pratt that the

Association would contribute its mite to the cause of the foreign missions.[58] A year later another member of the OCA, Rev. George Carr, professed that the interest of the Association in the work of both the CMS and the BFBS was greater than ever, and they wished to know how they might transfer funds collected in Ireland. He recommended that they set up an account with the La Touche bank in Dublin and suggested that John David La Touche would probably be an active supporter. Carr suggested that it would be a highly edifying experience for Ireland if a representation was sent over by the CMS, as the spirit of the revival was spreading rapidly in the Church of Ireland 'and a spirit of love and zeal increasing among many of our clergy'.[59]

It was several years before the CMS applied itself to the task of organizing an Irish auxiliary, however, and the cause of the foreign missions would never achieve the kind of popular support in Ireland that it enjoyed in Britain. But rapid strides were made in the direction of establishing a national Bible society on the model of the BFBS. The organizers included Peter Roe, B.W. Mathias and James Digges La Touche, and the Dublin Bible Society, as it was initially known, was set up in 1806 as an Irish auxiliary of the BFBS.[60] By 1808, however, the bishops of Dublin, Kildare, Derry, Limerick and Cork had come out in support of the Society and the committee recommended 'that one extensive institution pervading the whole country, having one grand fund, and acting on one plan, would contribute more to the general circulation of the scriptures in Ireland than the partial efforts of individuals or even of local and isolated societies'.[61] Thus the Hibernian Bible Society came into being. From the beginning it was the largest and most prestigious of the Irish evangelical societies, fulfilling the same role as the BFBS in meeting the needs of different denominational elements within Irish evangelicalism. Its purpose was to provide bibles and tracts wherever they were needed, whether for use in schools, for sale to the public, or for gratuitous distribution. In structure it was modelled on the BFBS, but while there were strong connections between the two organizations, the operations of the HBS were confined strictly to the Irish sphere. The demands of the domestic mission were so great that there was nothing left to contribute to foreign endeavours. This situation ensured that the relationship between the HBS and the BFBS remained, as one commentator put it, 'one of dependence or at best mutual goodwill'.[62] This assessment is confirmed by the frequency with which donations of bibles to Ireland, free or at greatly reduced prices, are noted in the annual reports of the BFBS.

The HBS adopted the organizational model established by the CMS and

BFBS, based on a network of branches and auxiliaries scattered throughout the provinces 'in order to render a wider circulation of the scriptures more easily attainable by means of a systematic division of labour'.[63] Where possible, the county associations or auxiliaries were located in cities or county towns and had under their immediate control the subordinate branches of the surrounding area. The associations were under the direction of local managers, who maintained close links with central headquarters in Dublin in order to ensure an adequate supply of material for distribution, to report on progress, and to contribute any surplus funds for use in the extension of the system. Free distribution of tracts and bibles was not permitted in the first instance, but those members with sufficient means could purchase various quantities and then distribute them without charge. This appears to have been a common practice, as was the sale of bibles to children attending scripture schools, with the payment often collected in installments.

The growth of the HBS reflected the fortunes of the Irish evangelical movement in general. There was a steady increase from the time of its foundation up to about 1820, followed by a period of intense activity and rapid expansion that lasted throughout the 1820s. In 1822 the Society had a total of 147 contributory institutions, and by 1834 this number had risen to 630.[64] During the early days, however, the growth rate was modest. In the year 1812/13 there were still only eight associated institutions in the country, but in the following year this number increased to thirty-five after a preaching tour by three representatives from the CMS, Josiah Pratt and his colleagues Rev. Jowett and Wilson. This tour was part of a massive campaign launched in 1813 by the CMS to muster popular support for its mission in India, following the decision by parliament to allow missionaries to work freely there. The campaign for 'missions to India' sparked off a general revitalization of missionary endeavours of every kind throughout the British Isles, and events in Ireland were part of an overall pattern. Certainly, the BFBS expanded its domestic operations on an unprecedented scale, especially in extending its home mission, prompting the *Christian Observer* to comment that it was witnessing 'one of the great epochs in the history of religion'.[65]

The rise of the Bible societies and the evangelical ethos in general was especially visible among the aristocracy. The earl of Bristol, at an anniversary meeting of the Suffolk Auxiliary of the BFBS in 1815, probably expressed the sentiments of the majority of his fellow Bible society supporters when he declared that

> in an age when the most tremendous revolution ever known had desolated the fairest portion of the world and shaken to its foundations the

whole fabric of civil society, mankind, roused by the awful vicissitudes of the scene, had risen superior to the paltry objects of worldly anxiety and taken refuge in the consolations of Christianity.[66]

In Ireland, however, the combined efforts of evangelicals, whether they were Methodist, Dissenting or Church of Ireland, were no longer directed against the infidelity of revolutionary France but focused instead on extending the moral reformation to the native Catholic population. This explains in part why, with the exception of the HBS, all of the major societies founded between 1805 and 1825 were in one way or another connected with popular education.

The evangelization of the Catholic Irish did not initially assume the apocalyptic urgency that characterized evangelical thinking with regard to the heathens and the Jews, whose conversion was considered a necessary prelude to the millennium. Guilt and an abiding sense of fear for the security of the kingdom during the Napoleonic Wars appear to have been the sentiments that informed evangelical opinion on the Catholic question on both sides of the Irish Sea during the early years of the nineteenth century. English evangelicals were generally quite sympathetic to Catholic claims, and prominent members of the Clapham Sect, including William Wilberforce and Charles Grant, actually favoured outright Emancipation.[67] As the following extract from the *Christian Observer* in 1814 suggests, their main concern was for national security, in the face of the threat posed by Napoleon, as opposed to specific anti-Catholic bias:

> Our own security as a nation is far more intimately blessed with the moral and religious improvement of the Irish, and with their advancement in civil light, than many would suppose. And if we do not attach them to our cause by benefit of the strong bonds of affection, they will prove, it is feared a sword in the hands of our enemy which will pierce us to the heart.[68]

In Ireland this blend of paternalistic benevolence and political calculation was espoused not only by committed evangelicals, such as Peter Roe and his colleagues in the OCA, but equally by many who supported moral and spiritual reform but who would not have subscribed to the independent tendencies and interdenominational activities of the more passionate revivalists. Indeed, by the first decade of the new century it was clear that the Church of Ireland had embarked on its own version of a revival and that while it drew from the example and competitive challenge of the Independents, it was resolved to plough its own furrow. This trend was most apparent in the appointment of able and ambitious men to episcopal office and their determination to provide sound leadership for both spiritual renewal and the expansion of the Church's role in national affairs.

Among the new breed of Church of Ireland reformers were the archbishop of Cashel, Charles Brodrick, and his lifelong correspondent Rev. John Jebb of Abingdon Glebe, who would succeed to the bishopric of Limerick in 1819. Both were fervent supporters of a moral crusade directed exclusively by the Church of Ireland that aimed to embrace the Catholic population. In the outline of a sermon that was being prepared for the ADV in 1802, Jebb addressed the task of 'bringing over' the Catholics to the side of the establishment in a genuine spirit of Christian charity. If the Protestant establishment, particularly the landholders and the clergymen of the Church of Ireland, could be persuaded to conduct their lives according to the Biblical directive, he believed that their benevolence and sincerity would induce the Catholic poor to receive the Bible 'without suspicion of any sinister view'. The latter would quickly learn to establish the difference between those who would 'hold them in, like brute beasts, with bit and bridle' and those who would 'draw them with the cords of a man, with the bonds of love'. The result would be a country where scripture would 'rule the life and regulate the heart, preparing the way for the glorious time when Christ's kingdom of universal piety shall be established on earth, and for the still more glorious consummation of all things in heaven'.[69]

In the case of both Jebb and Brodrick, there was more than a hint of sympathy for the condition of the Catholic poor and a corresponding criticism of the callousness of the landlord class.[70] But they were keenly aware that if the economic and political order were restructured to accommodate the grievances of the Catholics, the Church of Ireland would be the first institution to be sacrificed. Jebb was in favour of a system of national education that would be financed in part by government funds and directed by ministers of the Established Church.[71] As early as 1800 this idea was being actively promoted by the ADV (Jebb and Brodrick were both ardent supporters of the organization), which conducted a national survey to investigate how such a system might be implemented and the likelihood of its success among the Catholic population. This was not the first instance in which the education of the Catholic Irish had been addressed by the Protestant establishment, but it did represent a new departure in addressing this challenge in the spirit of the dedication and pragmatic innovation of the evangelical revival. As such it inaugurated a period of intense activity and bitter disputation over the control of popular education that inevitably spilled over into the political arena.

THE GRAND DESIGN

If there was an idea to which everyone in Ireland regardless of class, creed, or ethnic background could subscribe in the traumatic years following 1798, it was the desirability of providing for the education of the Catholic poor. In England during the 1790s, the fear of revolution had merged with the rationalism of the Enlightenment to produce a virtual orthodoxy on the need for the education of the lower classes.[72] In Ireland this opinion had an even older pedigree, going back to the 1780s, and it was enhanced by a tradition of state support for education that dated from the time of Henry VIII. Evangelical supporters of popular education in Ireland kept up the tradition and were equally insistent on the need for government money to finance their schools. This was to have profound implications for both their initial successes and their ultimate failure.

Historically, education in Ireland differed greatly from the system that had developed in England. The difference can best be explained by the hopes and fears of the colonial administration that governed its progress. Since the sixteenth century, education had taken its place in Ireland alongside religion as a key area through which the social cleavage between native and colonial could be maintained, and also as an avenue whereby those of the native Irish who desired it, and possessed the necessary means, might rid themselves of the trappings of their native culture and assume those of the colonial power. As a result, education came to play a critical role in the social and political framework of the country, a role that had no equivalent in contemporary England.

The distinguishing feature of the Irish system was the allocation of government aid. Ever since the time of Henry VIII the government had enacted legislation that provided for the establishment of schools, and state subsidies were allocated for their continuing support. The three types of institutions brought into being in this manner were known as 'parish', 'diocesan', and 'royal' schools, and together they catered for the children of the nobility and the middle classes.[73] English and Protestant in orientation, these schools complemented the concurrent attempt to suppress the native culture and the Catholic religion. The education of Catholics did not become a serious issue for the government until the end of the eighteenth century, despite the exhortations of individuals like the Rev. Hugh Boulter, the Protestant archbishop of Armagh, who had advised the government in a petition in 1730 that the only way in which the native Irish might be civilized would be that a sufficient number of English Protestant schools be erected and established, wherein the children of the Irish natives might be instructed in the English tongue and the fundamental principles of true religion, to both of which they are generally great strangers.[74]

This appeal was repeated by the founders of the Charter Schools, and government aid was provided when the Society was incorporated by an act of the Irish legislature in 1733. An annual subsidy begun in 1745, averaged £11,850 by the last decade of the century.[75] And yet the Charter Schools had little to show for their efforts because of the inertia of the managers and the general hostility of the Catholic population to the overtly proselytizing character of the schools. When the education of Catholics was again considered, it was in a markedly different climate of opinion.

The decade of the 1780s, which witnessed the flowering of the Patriot parliament and the implementation of relief measures for Catholics, also saw a reconsideration of educational reform. Initiated by John Hely-Hutchinson, the liberal provost of Trinity College, the question was taken up by Thomas Orde, an MP both at Westminster (1780–90) and in Dublin (as a representative for Rathcormack, 1784–90), as well as chief secretary for Ireland under the duke of Rutland (1784–7).[76] Orde's proposals extended to the whole system then in operation in Ireland and included an appeal that the education of the peasantry be taken into account because, in his view, 'all the violent and atrocious acts which have too often disgraced this nation' were the results of a want of education, which in its turn produced a want of obedience to the law. His proposal was revolutionary in its implications and has rightly been described as a 'touchstone in the evolution of the core of ideas from which the national system of education was eventually to be fashioned'. It achieved little in the immediate sense, except to act as a spur to a study conducted during the administration of Alleyne Fitzherbert, Orde's successor as chief secretary, begun in 1788 and presented in 1791. Like its predecessor it called for novel and revolutionary changes in the system, but it was likewise consigned to the archives, partly because its findings, especially those concerning the Charter Schools, were too disturbing to be made public, and partly because parliament was at this time becoming absorbed in matters of greater urgency.[77]

The question of educating the Catholic Irish nevertheless intensified as a subject of serious debate throughout the 1790s. Around 1800 the ADV began to commission reports on the state of education among the poor, from the point of view of what was already being provided for and how the demand might effectively be exploited by moral reformers in clerical and political life, as well as by landed aristocrats. In a separate appeal to absentees among the latter group, the 'vulgar Irish' were described (no doubt in light of the atrocities of the Wexford rebellion) as

> bloody and ferocious, retaining the habits and feelings of savages, devoid of lasting gratitude, and ready at the impulse of any groundless resentment to exercise the most unrelenting cruelty where shortly before they had proffered the most affectionate attachment.[78]

In what was to become one of the most popular slogans of the campaign it was stressed that the inhabitants of Wales and Scotland, who had once been as primitive and uncivilized as the Irish, had been made peaceful and industrious by virtue of their exposure to the scriptures.[79] Clearly the duty of landlords was to foster the development of scripture-based education, such as was promoted by the ADV, among their tenants.

In the first flush of enthusiasm the ADV commissioners were optimistic about the prospect of success. The presence of popery was mentioned as the grand obstacle, but only insofar as it was connected with ignorance and not a source of animosity.[80] Attention was drawn to the cooperation and goodwill that was known to exist between the rival denominations: Catholics often attended schools run by Protestants, and Protestant children were instructed in the catechism of the Church of England by Catholic masters when no other alternative was available to them.[81] But what was emphasized as the most important indicator of future success was the insatiable demand for schooling among Catholics of every social class, and especially among the rural poor. The peasantry of the south and west, it was reported, despite their impoverished state and the fact that what was being imbibed was often 'imperfect and objectionable', were nevertheless managing to educate their children in far greater numbers than their more prosperous Protestant neighbours in the northern counties.[82] What enabled them to do this were the so-called 'hedge schools': an informal (but no longer illegal) system devised by the poor to provide as best they could for their own education. In tandem with the spread of the market economy and the growth of population in the late eighteenth century, these schools had proliferated, causing every commentator of the Irish scene to marvel at the 'thirst for knowledge' exhibited even by the most wretched of the peasantry.[83] The ADV committee described the system they saw in operation near Castleisland in

County Kerry, where an itinerant master would open his school at the head of the ploughland under a ditch covered with heath and furze; to this abode the wretched inhabitants would send their naked, starving children to learn reading, writing and accounts. At the approach of winter the school would close and the master would be accommodated by local people.[84] 'If the habits of the people are now unfettered and irregular,' they claimed, 'they at the same time manifest a spirit of inquiry and enterprise, which, when well directed, would be found to furnish a powerful principle of national improvement.' It was the decided opinion of the committee that the desire for education that prevailed to such an extraordinary degree afforded the government 'the most favourable opportunity of effecting an important change in the manners of the lower classes'.[85]

The ADV was the first organization to encourage the attendance of Catholic children at schools where the scriptures formed the basis of instruction. When the Association was incorporated in 1801, it was awarded an annual stipend for educational purposes and began operations by attempting to reform and restructure the parish-school system. Provision had been made for these schools by statutes enacted during the reigns of Henry VIII and William III, but by 1800, except for a small number of schools conducted by the Established Church, they existed only on paper.[86] What the ADV sought to achieve was the creation of a whole new system based on these ancient statutes. In the main, the projected scheme was closely based upon the work of Orde and of the commissioners, whose inquiry was reported on in 1791. It provided the basic design for a national system under the control of the Church of Ireland. The schools were to be open to all qualified applicants, regardless of their religion, but management was to remain strictly in the hands of the Church authorities. The leading object of the schools, as reported to a famous inquiry of 1825, was to provide 'an extended system of catechetical instruction' specifically suited to the requirements of the established religion.[87] Only the authorized version of the Bible and the catechism of the Church of England were to be employed for such instruction. Catholic children, however, were exempted from attending catechism classes, although they were obliged to read the scriptures.[88] Once the schools conformed to the main demands of the ADV, i.e. when the managers and teachers were of the established religion and the rules concerning the Bible and catechism were adhered to, the curriculum appears to have been devised by the individual schools and teachers.

All accounts agree that for the first two decades of the century, Catholic children attended these schools in almost the same numbers as Protestants.

Although scriptural education was the avowed aim of the ADV in its attempted rehabilitation of the parish school system, it relied on enticements rather than on obligatory conditions to influence the religious inclinations of the pupils. It was assumed, correctly, that Catholic parents in some cases might conclude that the reading of the Protestant Bible was a small price for their children to pay in exchange for the three Rs. This was especially true when there was no opposition from the local priest, and when the conversion of Catholic children was not attempted. It was hoped or assumed by the directors of the system that exposure to the Bible without note or comment would go some way towards enlightening Catholic pupils about the spiritual darkness of the Church of Rome. This was the basic strategy of all the evangelical agencies involved with the education of the Catholic Irish. The principle of scriptural instruction was so firmly entrenched as the cornerstone of popular education that it eventually assumed an ideological dominance that held sway even with the promoters of a professedly nonsectarian system such as the KPS.

Outside of the immediate circle represented by the ADV and the Church of Ireland, the debate on popular education became a matter of national urgency in the early years of the nineteenth century. The anger and alienation of the peasantry following the bloody suppression of the 1798 Rebellion, and the impending prospect of Emancipation consequent upon the passing of the Union, caused every serious observer of the Irish scene to ponder the future with alarm. With his unerring sensitivity to the realities of Irish politics, Peter Burrowes went to the heart of the dilemma when he confessed that he

> knew no case of modern times ... more calculated to puzzle future statesmen than to account for the stability of Protestant Ascendancy in Ireland since the Revolution. To continue it after the Union would be infinitely more difficult. Now that by a relaxation of the Penal Laws they [the Catholics] have been suffered to outgrow that bondage, and with republican France eager to avail itself of their discomforts, and *wanting only some cement to keep their friends together*, is it possible that the Catholics of Ireland can be permanently alienated and the two countries permanently united? [my emphasis][89]

Education came to be seen not only as the most acceptable but also in many cases as the *only* possible solution. The bishop of Durham, writing to the new lord chancellor, Lord Redesdale, emphatically asserted that

> till means are adopted to render education and its consequences, moral and industrious habits, more general among the lower class of Irish

Catholics, till they are humanized, civilized, and Christianized, even in the erroneous opinions of their own Church, they will continue what they have been, thorns in the sides of both countries.[90]

The setting up of a statutory commission of inquiry on Irish education in 1806 is one measure of the importance the government placed on the issue. The commission sat for six years and produced no less than fourteen reports on the various educational institutions then operating in Ireland. In the Fourteenth Report the commissioners recommended State intervention in Irish education to a degree that had no historical precedent either in England or Ireland. A permanent body of education commissioners was established to administer an integrated system of education for the poor, including the building of schools, the professionalization of the teaching profession and the inspectorate, and the development of a suitable curriculum. This in itself was a revolutionary departure and pointed towards the future of educational developments in Ireland.[91] Of equal importance was the emphasis the commissioners placed on the absolute necessity of respecting religious differences:

> We conceive this to be of central importance in any new establishments for the education of the lower classes in Ireland, and we venture to express our unanimous opinion, that no such plan however wisely and unexceptionally contrived in other respects, can be carried into effectual execution in this country, unless it be explicitly avowed, and clearly understood, as its leading principle, that no attempt shall be made to influence or disturb the peculiar religious tenets of any sect or description of Christians.[92]

The board of education created in 1813, however, was not designed to cater for the massive effort needed to extend general education to the poor, but concerned itself exclusively with the state-aided schools already in existence. The organization that exploited the government's promise to fund schools that operated according to the recommendations of the Fourteenth Report was the Society for the Education of the Poor in Ireland, otherwise known as the Kildare Place Society. As the most successful of all the educational agencies that operated in Ireland prior to the establishment of the National Board in 1831, the Society had an interesting pedigree that was rooted in the blending of Quaker philanthropy and the Sunday School movement dating from 1786. In that year a group of Dublin philanthropists that included Arthur Guinness, of the famous brewing family, and Samuel Bewley, a prominent businessman and spokesman for the Society of Friends, drew up plans for the foundation of a

Sunday school in St Catherine's parish. One of the first tasks undertaken by its committee was to compose a statement of purpose for distribution to parents who wished to send their children to the school. It was stated explicitly that after each class 'children belonging to the Established Church were to be taken to divine service, and the Roman Catholic children, in charge of a discreet person, to their own place of worship'. The school was opened on 22 January 1786 and proved so popular that within a few years it could no longer accommodate the number of children who wished to attend. This situation led the directors, chief among them Samuel Bewley, to consider purchasing separate premises for the provision of a more general education for the children of Dublin's poor. A building capable of accommodating 1500 children was erected in a place known as Crawley's Yard, which was ever afterwards called School Street. The cost of the building was met by voluntary contributions, including 'some large ones from Roman Catholics' secured largely through Bewley's initiatives. Catholic support may be explained by the express provision of the trustees that the premises 'should not be occupied for any sectarian education'.[93]

The Society for Promoting the Education of the Poor in Ireland was formally inaugurated in December of 1811. According to its First Report, its leading principle was 'to afford the same advantages for education to all classes of professing Christians without interfering with the religious principles of any'.[94] At the same time it was stated unequivocally that the scriptures without note or comment (as opposed to catechisms or books on religious controversy) should be used for religious instruction, 'as all denominations of Christians profess that the Sacred Scriptures are the criterion by which they desire to have their peculiar tenets examined'.[95] The Second Report, however, made it clear that the ambitions of the Society went far beyond the classroom. Discipline, cleanliness and industrious habits were all underlined as obvious benefits of a well-regulated educational system.[96] The ideological content of the reading matter was seized upon as the most crucial instrument of change. The provision of reading material that would impart morality in public and private conduct became one of the Society's immediate objectives and a special sub-committee eventually laid out plans for a Cheap Book Society with lending libraries in the main provincial centres.[97]

The all-embracing character of the Society's aims were stipulated from the very beginning. What the directors had in mind was nothing less than a complete revolution in the *mentalité* of the Irish poor through the medium of education and popular literature. But this was no imposition from the top down, along the lines of what had been accomplished in Prussia, for example, during the previous century. By the time the KPS made its appearance, the revolution in popular education in Ireland was already in full spate. In a particularly revealing passage from its Second Report, the committee willingly acknowledged, albeit in a strongly pejorative tone, the influence of village or hedge schools and itinerant masters, which they claimed were general throughout the country:

> for such education as has been objected to, under the idea of its leading to evil rather than to good, they are actually obtaining for themselves; and though we conceive it practicable to correct it, to check its progress appears impossible—*it may be improved, but it cannot be impeded* [my emphasis][98]

The task facing the Society was therefore clearly perceived as the harnessing and redirecting of a popular movement that was considered haphazard, uncontrolled, and a potential threat to social and political stability. The enormity of the challenge demanded innovative, even revolutionary measures, and this accounts in part for its turbulent history over the following twenty years.

In its organizational structure and basic policy towards the sensitive question of religious differences, the KPS borrowed heavily from the recommendations set forth by the government commissioners in their Fourteenth Report. Teaching as a career was to be established on a modern professional basis with a training college, decent schoolhouses, regular salaries and an inspectorate. Curriculum needs were to be supplied by the books and primers produced by the Society itself, which would be careful to avoid any possible sources of controversy or insult to the Catholic religion. In theory it appeared that the Society was at this time poised to establish itself as the chief agency of the moral revolution that so many looked to as the salvation of the country.

There were two major obstacles that stood in the way of its ambitious programme, however. The first was the question of how the system would be funded. The second was the likely response from the Catholic poor, the object of the enterprise, or more particularly from the priesthood who oversaw their moral and spiritual affairs. The initial outlook of the Society's directors was not optimistic. Like many others engaged in the business of philanthropy in Ireland, they found that it was the custom of the country to promise much and pay little, and that while the education of the poor had become 'the subject of discussion among the enlightened, and even the theme of conversation among the fashionable', there was 'a lamentable apathy on the subject whenever such persons are invited to realize their theories and carry them into execution'.[99]

Because they adhered so closely to the commissioners' recommendations, however, they were in a particularly strong position to petition for public funds, although even this strategy was not adopted without caution.[100] This may have been the result of fears that such assistance would damage their reputation among Catholics. From the very beginning the Society was anxious to promote itself as a specifically *Irish* concern and vehemently resisted any attempts by the British and Foreign School Society to promote it as one of its auxiliaries.[101] In 1816, however, the KPS successfully petitioned parliament for a grant of £10,000, which was increased substantially over the following ten years.[102] This was what allowed it to make such rapid progress in constructing the rudiments of a truly national system of education in Ireland.

The question of Catholic support was even more complicated than that of securing government funds. Because of its sensitivity to sectarian differences, the KPS had issued a clear declaration of neutrality in religious affairs aimed at appeasing Catholic public opinion. Prominent laymen, notably Daniel O'Connell and some leading members of what was left of the old Catholic aristocracy, were invited to sit on the board of directors and were thus involved in policy-making at the highest level. Similarly, at the parish level the Society was always careful to consider local needs and prejudices when it came to the selection of teachers and school managers, who were often Catholic priests. Even so, it was uncertain whether the enterprise upon which the KPS had embarked would be perceived as an agency working in the national (i.e. mainly Catholic) interest or as a cloak for the imposition of a new moral order geared towards the maintenance of Protestant power and the English connection.

In the event, its chances of weathering the stormy waters of Irish political life in the early nineteenth century were lessened considerably by trends that were taking shape within the broader world of the international awakening. By the second decade of the new century the evangelization of the Catholic Irish had been added to the list of what needed to be accomplished in order to remake the world in God's image, and the countryside was awash with missionary agents and itinerant preachers, all working towards this goal. In a period of intense social and political change this made for a highly inflammable situation. The KPS, with its carefully thought-out strategies and sensible objectives, would be the first major victim of the flames.

—THREE—
The Mission to the Catholic Population

Ye British disciples of Him who came to seek and to save that which was lost, hear the cries of perishing souls, souls whose misery is the more affecting in proportion to their own ignorance of its true nature! A Nation; a brave, grateful and most interesting Nation; a Nation attached to you by the ties of strongest interest and closest relationship, now calls for your aid. Reflect that the great majority of your brethren in Ireland are still the vassals of papal tyranny, and languishing in the lowest intellectual debasement. If any bosom is not warmed by pure benevolence, let it call in the calculations of interest, and contemplate the terrible consequences of continued neglect ... Providence provides great and powerful instruments of good. They lie at your hand. It is yours to grasp them, and fly to the glorious work, with the patriotism of Britons and the compassion of Christians.

An Address ... on the Moral and Religious State of Ireland (1805)[1]

Your Grace [Charles Brodrick] has, doubtless, seen the bishop's [Dr Mant of Killaloe] charge, breathing theological warfare against the papists. To the National School System he is clearly looking as an instrument of proselytism: and I fear he may involve the South of Ireland in flames, and at the same time stop any quiet progress that has been making towards our unsuspected influence over the minds of our Roman Catholic population ... I wish people would have the discretion, and the modesty to acquaint themselves with the circumstances of this country, before they practise upon it. Of all sorts of quackery, theological quackery is the most desperate and deadly.

JOHN JEBB[2]

THE METHODIST EXAMPLE

The conversion of the Catholic Irish to the Protestant faith, as previously noted, was not a high priority on the evangelical agenda of the late eighteenth century. The opinion popular in the eighteenth century was that Catholics, once raised to the same level of education and civilization as Protestants, would transfer their religious allegiance to the reformed faith and be absorbed into the existing social and political order. Between 1800 and 1820, however, this attitude was drastically altered in favour of the belief that a fully fledged missionary offensive was needed to bring Catholics into the fold. The dynamism that accompanied this shift was symptomatic of the coalescence of the many different tributaries feeding into the evangelical mainstream in Britain as well as in Ireland. Whether it was directed at the heathen in foreign lands or at Jews and Catholics at home, the Protestant crusade of the early nineteenth century was a pan-evangelical affair, and the pattern that emerged in England, where the pace was set by Methodists and evangelicals of the Independent churches, was followed in Ireland almost to the letter.

During the tumultuous last decade of the eighteenth century there was a marked increase in the religious activity of Ireland's Protestant community at every social level. There was more itinerant preaching, higher rates of church attendance, and more serious interest in clerical reform than had ever been the case previously. The reform-minded element in the Church of Ireland manifested itself through clerical associations and especially through the ADV. But it was on the fringes occupied by Methodists and Nonconformists that the really dynamic activity was taking place. In each case external influence (from Wales and Scotland in particular) can be readily pointed to as a determining factor.

By the 1790s Methodism had established itself as a permanent presence in the Irish religious landscape. Up to this time it had won its followers mainly from the Protestant population, although it was always clear that the leadership also considered Catholics as being equally within the fold and in need of redemption. Methodist circuit riders preached to crowds without much regard for their religious composition, however, and no specific measures were taken to cater exclusively to Catholics. This situation changed in 1799 when a mission to the native population was begun. After the death of John Wesley in 1791, the Methodist body as a whole had become much more missionary-minded and joined in the growing fervour among evangelicals in Britain to bring Christianity to foreign lands. The cause of the foreign missions was especially dear to Dr Thomas Coke, president of the Methodist Conference in London, and the redemption of Ireland even more so. Under Coke's direction a nationwide mission to the Catholic population was begun in 1799 and greatly expanded over the following twenty years.

The man chosen by the Methodist Conference as its chief itinerant missionary in Ireland was Gideon Ouseley, whose experience as a circuit rider and fluency in the native language were ideally suited to the demands of the job. His two associates, James McQuigg and Charles Graham, were likewise proficient in Irish. McQuigg was a scholarly figure whose health soon failed under the strenuous exertions of circuit preaching, but Graham, 'the Apostle of Kerry', went on to become famous, along with Ouseley, as a 'cavalry preacher' or 'black cap', so called after the close-fitting skull-caps they wore to protect their heads from stones and brickbats.[3]

By 1816 there were twenty-one missionaries working from fourteen stations throughout the country, twelve of whom were able to preach in Irish. The mission was financed and administered by the Wesleyan Missionary Committee in London, to which the preachers submitted quarterly accounts of their experiences and progress.[4] These detailed and sometimes exhaustive letters are important not only for their information on the state of the country and the mentality of the people, but equally for what they reveal about the purpose of the Methodist mission and the attitude of the preachers, and above all for their effect in influencing the opinion of the leaders of the Methodist movement in England on the Irish question and Roman Catholicism generally.

The unequivocal aim of the Methodist Irish-speaking mission was to launch a frontal assault on what was considered the chief source of the ignorance, superstition and bigotry of the native Irish, namely the Catholic religion and the influence of the priests. The impact of the 1798 Rebellion was undoubtedly a factor in rekindling fears of the persecuting and intolerant tendencies of Catholics and in strengthening Methodist loyalty to the king and the rule of law. Throughout the Methodist community around the turn of the century there was a pervasive sense that providence had decreed the hour and the opportunity for moral regeneration and spiritual rebirth, and this was particularly true among those involved in the mission to the Irish Catholics. As David Hempton has observed, the commitment and enthusiasm that the Methodists involved in the Irish mission brought to their particular vocation showed strong parallels with secular Romanticism:

> There is the existence of a 'deluded' and morally corrupt people to whom the Gospel must be taken as the only means of true enlightenment. There is a strong feeling of divine fervour inasmuch as 'divine providence' provided the opportunity. There is the appeal of grand heroic adventure to those who have 'entered upon one of the most arduous undertakings that have been attempted since the primitive times'.[5]

During his early years on the circuit Charles Graham spoke repeatedly of how Catholics listened to his preaching 'with flowing tears and throbbing breasts', and gave the clear impression that the prospects for conversion looked very positive. Writing from the northern circuit in 1803, he described one incident of remarkable tolerance and generosity:

> I find the Catholics are ready to hear us in every public place and many of them bathed in tears ... In the market of Stuartstown [sic] we could hardly restrain the poor Catholics from making a public collection. We told them we made no collections. They answered they would not put us to the trouble of making it, they would make it themselves. Nor did they seem pleased we would not accept it for they said we were worthy of it.[6]

Such displays of the traditional courtesy that the Irish peasantry were famous for made a strong impression on men who were already passionately disposed to believe in the natural goodness of mankind. Gideon Ouseley's sympathies may be illustrated by his description of the native Irish as a

> smart, keen, intelligent [race], and when not exasperated and inflamed by their clergy and by such as they deem to know is fit to be done, they are a generous, kind, good-natured people and rather inclined to be pious and to respect religion more than any of the other orders, if not perverted and corrupted, which alas is easily done.[7]

Sympathy of this kind, coupled with the austerity of their lives and the hazards of working in all weather conditions and in the most desolate and isolated regions of the country, made the Irish-speaking Methodist preachers highly unusual figures in the countryside in the early years of the century. Many of their reports suggest that they were a novelty to which the uneducated peasantry responded with curiosity and enthusiasm, not knowing which denomination they represented or even their class or national origin. William Cornwall described a scene in 1817 in Ballina, County Mayo, where, greatly respected by all present, he led the neighbours in prayer at the house of a woman whose son had drowned that morning. As he left, the mother enquired, 'Are you one of the servants of God?'—which he took to mean a Catholic priest—and fell on her knees, praying that God might prosper and speed him.[8]

The ability to preach in Irish was another feature of the Methodist mission that 'seldom [failed] to draw their attention', as the veteran preacher and fluent-Irish speaker James Bell reported from Castlewellan, County Down, in 1818.[9] His evidence was supported by William Cornwall, working at the opposite end of the country in County Clare, who reported that Catholics in the village of Cross 'were so convinced of the truth of the doctrine I advanced that they raised their responsive voices all round, exclaiming, "is fíor sin, is fíor sin" ' (that's true, that's true).[10] Cornwall, whose circuit covered the counties of Galway, Mayo and Clare, was a man whose already ardent religious spirit was intensified by the romantic scenery of the west and the innocence and enthusiasm of the local population. Describing a scene in 1819 in Connemara, where people had come for miles across moors and mountains to hear him preach in Irish, he confessed:

> When I beheld them coming down the side of a mountain and wading barelegged through the flood, I was moved with compassion towards them and did not regret my coming to seek after them … were they once convinced of the truth as it is in Jesus, they would be as firm as a rock. This observation has been borne out by Catholics already converted.[11]

In reality the number of converts was never very large. The reports make incessant references to the opposition of the Catholic priests who chastised their flocks merely for listening to open-air sermons and threatened with damnation anyone who refused to deliver up the bibles and testaments distributed for free by the preachers.[12] Nevertheless, there is no evidence that the Catholic clergy or hierarchy ever took concerted action, even at the diocesan or parish level, to shield their flocks from Methodist preachers. Certainly, they were not considered as great a danger as the various societies involved with Bible-based education that began to proliferate around this time. The reasons are not difficult to find. Itinerant open-air preaching modelled on the system that had proved so successful in England was totally unsuited to conditions in Ireland, certainly in areas where the population was predominantly Catholic. Designed to revive religious consciousness rather than to bring about formal adhesion to a church, it was virtually useless unless reinforced by a network of scripture schools and the active involvement of local organizers. Methodist missionaries relied on little besides the ardour of their preaching as a means of attracting followers, although as early as 1806 they were already thinking in terms of a national system of Sunday schools. As had happened with so many of the innovations for which they had been responsible, such as preaching in the Irish language, the Sunday School movement was developed to a far greater degree by other denominations with more power and resources at their disposal.

In the case of the Sunday School Society, it was the evangelical wing of the Church of Ireland represented by James Digges La Touche that took its inspiration from the Methodist example. His uncle, John David La Touche, who had been so deeply impressed by the dedication and piety of the Methodist community in Dublin in the 1790s, was in frequent contact with the close-knit circle of Church of Ireland reformers represented particularly by the Woodward–Brodrick family connection. In 1804 Mathias Joyce related to Dr Coke how he and 'old John Pryce' had spent an evening in the company of Dr Henry Woodward and his wife and Woodward's 'good friend' John David La Touche:

> Our conversation was truly edifying and Dr Woodward and his lady were so impressed with old John that she presented him with a ten pound note. A few nights later the Dr had John to drink tea with him and a rap was heard at the door ... [it was] the Bishop of Cashel who had just arrived from Holyhead.[13]

This certainly represented a departure from the attitudes of the eighteenth century, when Methodists had been dismissed as religious enthusiasts and were often despised by the more aristocratic elements for lowering the tone of the Protestant religion in Ireland.[14] And it was a sign of things to come. Increasingly, the circuit preachers found the provincial gentry willing to provide venues for their sermons and even to guarantee an audience. They were particularly welcome in garrison towns and in areas where it was feared that the poorer class of Protestants had lapsed into the habits and practices of their Catholic neighbours. In 1802 during a visit to County Clare, an Irish scholar named Lawrence Kean recounted how he was warmly received by a Colonel Burton who allowed him to preach to full audiences in the Session house and the barracks. As a result Kean enlisted fourteen new recruits for the Methodist cause.[15] In 1806 William Hamilton reported a similarly enthusiastic response to Methodist initiatives in County Mayo:

> These two years since, Brother Ouseley and I have made out a circuit in the Co. Mayo, which will hold two preachers, [we] have 30 members, many of whom are very happy in the Lord. Eighteen of those have been Papists, four of whom will be able to go out as missionaries next year. We

have scattered those two years 1,000 testaments and about 400 bibles, and [have gained] about 40 subscribers for our magazine and sold these about £30 worth of our own books. We have also built a large preaching house and a good lodging for a preacher's family. This country was very dark and full of superstition. Many of the Protestants used to perform penance at wells with their Papist neighbours and would be anointed by the priest at their death. The scene is now changed, to the very great satisfaction of the leading men of that country.[16]

The opposition of the Church of Ireland to the independent tendencies of the Methodists did not disappear overnight, however. In Donegal town in 1804, James Bell and William Hamilton were refused permission to preach in public by the local minister, who was a son of the bishop of Raphoe. 'It was grievous to see people coming in from the country and the greater part of the town flocking' the preachers lamented, adding that what helped to soothe their grief respecting the treatment they had received on this occasion was 'the poor Roman Catholics [who] heard in their own tongue, and as Mr Hamilton preached next morning, about ten of them came to inquire what they should do to be saved'.[17] Denominational rivalry was almost certainly at issue in this case, since east Donegal was heavily Protestant and formed part of the geographical fringe of the Ulster plantation so conducive to the growth of Methodism during this period.

Between 1780 and 1810 Irish Methodism increased its membership from 6109 to 26,323, with most of the growth occurring among the Protestant population in the counties of Armagh, Tyrone and Fermanagh.[18] Such progress undoubtedly fuelled expectations that the mission to the Catholic population might yield equally fruitful results. Important representatives of public opinion in Ireland certainly thought that this was possible. In 1807 a leading advocate of moral reform and a prominent member of the County Wicklow gentry, William Parnell, expressed his opinion that 'if the Catholic clergy were paid by the government, and if the practice and principle of religious restriction were abandoned, in the course of a few years a large portion of the Irish peasantry would be converted to Methodism'.[19] The missionaries' reports to the London headquarters overflowed with optimism of this kind, balanced by an equally stark and despairing picture of a people enslaved by the tyranny of Catholic priests. As the years advanced and the great struggle between the religious and the secular was played out on the Continent by Napoleon and his adversaries, Ireland began to occupy a position of remarkable importance in the minds of Methodist leaders in England. In a report to the Missionary Committee in 1806, Dr Coke described it as the most important mission in which the Methodists were engaged, if all the facts of the contemporary situation were taken into account:

> Three millions of the people of this land are plunged in the deepest ignorance and superstition. The ten men who are employed in bearing the testimony of Jesus to this benighted people run the greatest hazards of any of our missionaries, and were it not for the universal protection they receive under God from the magistracy and military of the country, they must humanly speaking long ago have fallen victims to the violence of bigotry and superstition.[20]

The tone of Dr Coke's report was a signal that Methodist leadership in England was rapidly falling into line with the opinion of Tory conservatives, whose opposition to political reform was beginning to galvanize around the issue of Catholic Emancipation. This trend would become even more pronounced as the demand for Emancipation intensified. Prominent representatives like Joseph Butterworth and Joseph Allan used the correspondence of the Irish missionaries to influence parliament and inflame public opinion about the dangers of resurgent Catholicism.[21] The net result was to bring Methodism to the forefront of the rising tide of conservatism and anti-Catholicism, far from its populist roots in the eighteenth century, and equally far from a genuine appraisal of the condition of the 'poor Roman Catholics' of Ireland. Gideon Ouseley ended his career as a member of the Orange Order.[22]

In the mission field in Ireland, meanwhile, the Methodist missionaries gradually began to lose their unique character as evangelical pioneers as the major Bible and Sunday school societies founded between 1806 and 1825 began to operate. This may be one reason why so little was heard of them in denunciations from the Catholic quarter, which tended to focus on the Established Church as the main perpetrator of the anti-Catholic activity that caused such uproar in the 1820s.

THE CHALLENGE OF DISSENT:
THE LONDON HIBERNIAN AND BAPTIST SOCIETIES

The Methodist missionary initiative had an important influence on the reform wing of the Church of Ireland, which between 1806 and 1818 took a decisive lead in the moral crusade to rescue Catholics from ignorance and spiritual slavery. The leading national organizations in which Church of Ireland personnel were involved included those run exclusively according to their own principles, such as the ADV and the Sunday School Society, as well as those described as interdenominational, such as the HBS, the Religious Tract and Book Society, and the KPS. To these must be added the Irish Society for the Education of the Native Irish through the Medium of Their Own Language (1818), and the Scripture Readers' Society (1822), which, as their names suggest, were aimed particularly at the Irish-speaking peasantry. Before the growth and influence of the Church of Ireland affiliates can be properly discussed, however, it is necessary to assess the work of two Independent evangelical organizations that were also involved in the mission to the Catholic Irish. These were the London Hibernian Society for the Diffusion of Religious Knowledge in Ireland, founded by Congregationalists in 1806, and the Baptist Society for Promoting the Gospel in Ireland, founded in 1814.

Although neither the Congregationalists nor the Baptists were well represented in Ireland, these two British evangelical societies were influential in cultivating the denominational rivalry that brought the evangelical wing of the Church of England into the race to set up missionary enterprises at home and abroad. Both groups had already launched missions to India, Africa and the South Seas, and they were the originators of the policy of translating the scriptures into vernacular languages, which more than any other factor accounted for the global spread of the Protestant missionary movement in the nineteenth century. An additional characteristic shared by these two societies was a strong Scottish influence among the directors. The London Missionary Society was largely a Scottish organization, and the LHS, to a significant degree, was its Irish offshoot. Similarly, the Baptists were heavily involved in the evangelization of the Gaelic-speaking Highlands, and their organization in Ireland borrowed heavily from the experience gained in Scotland.

Some additional characteristics common to both the London Hibernian and Baptist societies are worthy of comment. The first is the goodwill that existed between them and the other societies mentioned above. This was demonstrated by the provision of tracts and bibles by the HBS and the Religious Tract and Book Society, and even more remarkably by the channelling of government funds to the LHS by the ostensibly nonsectarian KPS—all of which corroborates Peter Roe's claim made as early as 1802 about the 'union of spirit prevailing among those who are professedly travelling the same road'.[23] The second is the unequivocal way in which they proclaimed and pursued their objectives. Their statements and reports were generally more candid than those of the Irish-based societies, which were obliged to keep a guarded eye on episcopal censure from within their own ranks as well as on Catholic public opinion.

Were a gold medal for candour to be awarded to one of the innumerable commentaries on the influence of popery in Ireland that began to flow from the printing presses early in the nineteenth century, it would surely go to a study conducted for the LHS in 1807/8. This Society was a natural outgrowth of the mutual interests of evangelicals of the Independent churches on both sides of the Irish Sea. Albert Blest of Sligo was the moving force behind the initiative in Ireland, and his British connections included English, Scottish and Welsh evangelicals with substantial experience in missionary activity at home and abroad. The deputation who visited Ireland on behalf of the Society in 1807 included the Rev. David Bogue of Gosport and Samuel Mills of Finsbury Place, London, both of whom were leading figures in the London Missionary Society. Even more significant was the presence of two Welshmen, Rev. Thomas Charles and Rev. Thomas Hughes, both of whom had an impressive record of involvement in the home mission among the native-speaking population in Wales.[24]

In keeping with the quantitative approach that was the hallmark of the Scottish Enlightenment, the LHS deputation launched the most thorough investigative effort that had yet been attempted to determine the possibilities for a campaign of evangelization among the Catholic Irish. A complete appraisal was made of all the elements that could be turned to advantage, such as the support of the gentry and the desire of the people for education. This was balanced by a sober consideration of the enormous obstacles represented above all by the power of the Catholic clergy, and to a lesser degree by the existence of a language barrier. The deputies pointed to the existence of hedge schools run by Protestants, to which Catholic parents often entrusted their children purely for the benefit of the education provided. Because of this trust the schoolmasters allegedly refrained from condemning the Catholic faith, a precaution the deputies thought fit to be adopted once their own system was in operation. But they also remarked:

> There will be frequent opportunities for disclosing to the Catholic youth the systems of both churches in their amplest extent. And may it not be hoped, with the divine blessing, the clear avowal of inspired doctrine, in opposition to the traditions of men, will induce some who are not as confirmed by Jesuitical sophisms to examine the faith of their forefathers and thus lead them to detect its falsehood and folly.[25]

The newly awakened political consciousness of the Catholic population was appraised in ominous terms:

> The public events of the last twenty years have resulted, it is thought, in arraying them [the Catholics] with fresh consequence. Nor is it merely what may be called political success that has promoted the cause of the Catholics; even failure, by reminding them that they are oppressed, rouses them and unites them to each other with a firmer cement. Local oppression, too, and misguided zeal produce dangerous irritation among a people fond of representing themselves as a persecuted majority.[26]

The influence of the priests was singled out as the greatest obstacle in the path of evangelization, and the Irish were considered the dupes of their clerical leaders: 'Ignorance is the mother of their devotion, and they are the blind followers of those whom it requires a stretch of the imagination to pronounce merely blind.'[27] Besides the power of the priests and the ignorance of their followers, the deputies were concerned about the rate at which the Catholic population was increasing:

> On the whole, popery appears to be exhibited and inculcated there ... with such a decided partiality in favour of its most fantastic and anti-Christian features—the manoeuvres of its priests are so various, so subtle, and alas so efficient—that the moral aspect from these and other causes is so discouraging that the deputation, confining themselves to this view of Ireland, see nothing but formidable barriers erected against every attempt to bless her inhabitants with the light of life; *nor must it be concealed that the numerical predominance of the Roman Catholics is itself a prolific seed of disunion. The hope, therefore, that the Irish will ever be a tranquil and loyal people must be built on the anticipated reduction of popery.* [my emphasis][28]

The optimism with which the LHS set about its appointed task in Ireland was rooted in the successful evangelization of Wales and the Scottish Highlands. In the eighteenth century the Welsh-speaking areas of Wales had been thoroughly evangelized through a combination of itinerant preaching, tract distribution, and an innovative system of 'circulating' or 'ambulatory' schools (an improvised system not altogether different from the hedge schools of Ireland) in which children and adults were taught to read in their own language.[29] By the early years of the nineteenth century this process was being repeated in the Gaelic-speaking areas of Scotland.[30]

Of the elements common to the movement in both areas, by far the most significant was the most basic principle of the Protestant faith, i.e. the insistence on the right, indeed the necessity, for individuals to read and interpret the scriptures for themselves. This immediately raised the question of literacy in the native languages, a challenge that up to this time had never been addressed with any real effectiveness in either Wales or Ireland, and with only limited success in Scotland. The Anglican hierarchy of Wales and Ireland and the Presbyterian Kirk, the State Church of Scotland, were hostile to the idea of catering to the educational needs of native speakers in the vernacular languages. Because of the threat from Catholic missionaries in the Highlands and islands during the years of the Jacobite danger, however, the Scottish Kirk was forced to educate Gaelic-speaking ministers and to provide religious literature in the vernacular. When it came to education, however, the Kirk showed its ambivalence by insisting on English as the medium of instruction in the charity schools. The result was that while Gaelic retained its hold as the 'spiritual' language of prayer and religious literature, English became the language of 'improvement' or practical affairs.[31]

The main consequence of the failure of Church establishments to cater to the linguistic particularities of the Celtic fringe was that the field was left open to the Independent churches, particularly the Congregationalists and also the Calvinistic Methodists of Lady Huntingdon's Connexion. These groups had also acted as magnets for the more committed and missionary-minded elements of the mainstream establishments, such as the Rev. Thomas Charles, who broke ranks and joined the Calvinistic Methodists because his ambitions to evangelize in the Welsh language could not be accommodated by the Church of England. A similar frustration drove the famous Edinburgh philanthropists James and Robert Haldane into an intensive drive to evangelize the Highlands after their ambition to launch a mission to India under the auspices of the Congregationalist Church had been effectively blocked by the East India Company.[32]

The personnel associated with the launching of the LHS were heavily involved with the evangelization of the native-speaking districts of Wales and Scotland. Albert Blest of Sligo was a well-known personality in these circles, and Sligo a familiar preaching venue for itinerant preachers dispatched by the Haldanes as well as Lady Huntingdon.[33] The community of evangelical Dissent in Ireland at this time consisted of small but active groups in Belfast and Dublin who had come together in the aftermath of the 1798 Rebellion to form the General Evangelical Society. In Dublin the activity of these groups centred on the York Street Chapel, which had been built under the sponsorship of Alderman Henry Hutton and was opened by the famous itinerant preacher Rowland

Hill.[34] It was at the home of Alderman Hutton that Albert Blest met the LHS delegation in 1807. Two years later, in 1809, he was formally appointed as the Irish agent of the Society and immediately set about establishing Sligo as their Irish headquarters.[35]

The initial plan was to launch what amounted to an evangelistic blitzkrieg whereby itinerant missionaries through preaching and tract distribution would whet the appetites of their hearers for religious material in print. The desire to read such material would provide the incentive necessary to get adults as well as children into schools where literacy skills would be developed through the medium of religious literature. Literacy in the native language was seen as a natural spur to literacy in English and, it was hoped, the cultivation of closer ties with the laws and institutions of the English world. This was the working model of evangelization that had been developed in Wales and Scotland and it made perfect sense to attempt to repeat it in Ireland.

The original plan of the LHS directors was a three-point offensive based on itinerant preaching, tract distribution, and education.[36] After the first four years, however, they were obliged to admit that little was to be expected from itinerancy: 'So deeply rooted, so habitually prevalent, were the prejudices of the people in general that very few would attend upon the preaching of any individual who came in the character of a Protestant missionary.'[37] In consequence, it was decided to concentrate resources on the education of the young, and the development of a system of day schools became the principal objective, with the society changing its name accordingly to the Hibernian Society for Establishing Schools and Circulating the Holy Scriptures in Ireland.

Despite its avowed aim of securing the conversion of Catholic children to the reformed faith, the LHS did not hesitate to appeal to the needs and sympathies of the Catholic Irish in order to attract their children into its schools. Almost from the beginning the committee adopted a policy of employing Catholic schoolmasters, preferably local people who would be known and respected by the parents.[38] They also worked with Catholic priests who did not feel threatened by their activities and in many cases allowed them to act as managers in the schools. In at least one case where the education of the district was already in the hands of the Carmelite order, they provided free spelling books and testaments.[39] The backbone of the system, however, was the support of the Protestant land-owning class, to whom LHS appealed for the provision of sites, schoolhouses and masters' dwellings. With the cost of the teacher's salary and the teaching materials provided by the Society, a landlord could participate in the fashionable trend for improvement at very little cost.

The directors of the LHS were clearly willing to co-opt hedge-school teachers by providing them with a settled living in the form of a decent salary and a cottage with a plot of land for a garden and a cow. They were also willing to cater to the demand for the teaching of 'useful subjects' as opposed to the strict concentration on scriptural material.[40] The most innovative and controversial of their policies, however, was the use of the Irish language as a medium of instruction. This was copied directly from the experience of evangelical missionaries in Wales and Scotland. The same conditions did not apply in Ireland, however, and the application of the policy involved an altogether more complicated path, with some curious and unanticipated consequences.

The obstacles that confronted the promoters of the scheme to evangelize and educate Irish-speaking Catholics in their native language were enormous. In the first instance there was the fear and prejudice of the landlord class concerning a process over which they would have little or no control. These fears were not without substance, as evidence surfaced repeatedly in the Society's reports that their schools fared much better, and enjoyed much more support from the local Catholic clergy, in areas where there was *no* resident landlord.[41] To placate landlords' fear that the language might be restored because of its efforts, the Society placed great emphasis on an observation that was now commonplace in the Highlands and islands of Scotland. In brief, this was that literacy in the native language was prized and sought after precisely because it quickly opened the door to literacy in English and all that this implied—not only the ability to read tracts and testaments (a far greater variety of which were naturally available in English) but also to participate in the anglophone economy through the use of paper money to buy and sell in the marketplace, to travel to English-speaking regions in search of work, and above all to have access to the knowledge of economic improvement that was available only in English. Albert Blest took great pains to reassure Charles King O'Hara, on whose estate in County Sligo the LHS commenced its operations, about the policy that the Society had developed regarding the teaching of Irish:

> With respect to the Irish, our object in instructing our pupils to read it being only to qualify them for reading the Scriptures in that language for the benefit of their parents or the adults in their neighbourhood who may not be capable of understanding a narration or continued discourse in the English. Our process is very simple and requires neither grammar nor elementary book of any kind. We instruct none but such as speak the

Irish and can read English, and these, with the help of the English Testament and the master's instructions, make a considerable progress in a few months. In this way your postillion can immediately commence the office of preceptor to his young fellow servants, and indeed to any of your domestics who can read English and speak Irish, and I will have great pleasure in sending you as many Irish testaments as they require.[42]

The reluctance of landlords to sponsor education in Irish was matched by that of the Church of Ireland clergy. Even a professedly sympathetic and enlightened figure like John Jebb shared the opinion dominant among the upper classes that Irish was a barbarous language, and welcomed its demise:

> For English order, habit, and language now universally obtain amongst us; it is scarcely imaginable that this country can again relapse into her ancient barbarism ... There is now manifestly no manner of necessity for looking exclusively to the clergy as agents of popular instruction. Teachers skilled in the English language abound; they are daily multiplying and will continue to multiply with the increasing demand; *for after all, the grand security which places the permanent anglicization of this country beyond all reasonable doubt is the anxiety to hear their children instructed which pervades the very lowest of our peasantry.*[my emphasis][43]

In this last observation Jebb had underlined a far greater obstacle in the path of the education-in-Irish enthusiasts than either the hostility of landlords or the indifference of the Church of Ireland. The evidence of practically every commentator who investigated and reported on the state of the Irish language during this period, especially on its use as a medium of instruction, suggests that Irish-speakers were willing to bypass literacy in their native language altogether in their drive for education and economic opportunity. Indeed, so frequently did supporters and opponents alike comment upon this phenomenon that it strongly suggests that the very idea of literacy in the native language was a concept that country people were unable to grasp. For whatever sociocultural or psychological reasons, reading and writing were with few exceptions seen as skills that could only be acquired through English.[44]

Not the least of the challenges undertaken by the LHS was to study the structure of the Irish language in order to produce schoolbooks for instruction in grammar and syntax, a task that demanded the skill of teachers fluent in English and Irish, with some knowledge of linguistics and a willingness to put their services at the society's disposal. Incredibly, during the first decade of its existence the Society was able to show progress in the face of all these difficulties, to such a degree that its example was an immediate influence behind the founding of the Baptist Society in 1814. Together these two organizations placed the issue of education-in-Irish solidly on the evangelical agenda. By 1820 the cause had been taken up by the KPS and the Sunday School Society, and the Irish Society for the Instruction of the Native Irish through the Medium of Their Own Language had been established under the auspices of the Church of Ireland to cater exclusively for the subject.

Much of the credit for the momentum that sustained the LHS in its formative years must go to the energetic and imaginative leadership of men who were already well known for their missionary work in Wales and Scotland. The Rev. Thomas Charles of Bala, for example, was known throughout Britain as the inspiration behind the BFBS and its famous motto on translating the scriptures into vernacular languages: 'If for Wales, why not for the world?'[45] Charles was the driving force behind the LHS's policy on the Irish language. Even when the Society's representatives in Ireland could not reach a consensus regarding the capacity in which the language might be employed for educational purposes, Charles went ahead and ordered the BFBS to publish testaments in Irish.[46] More significant for the growth of literacy in Irish, however, was the influence of two Scottish clergymen associated with the evangelical mission in the Highlands; they visited Ireland between 1810 and 1815 and published their observations in works that were really impassioned appeals on behalf of the Irish language and those who spoke it, and which reportedly drew attention to the subject from all parts of the kingdom. The first to appear was the Rev. Daniel Dewar's *Observations on the Character, Customs, and Superstitions of the Irish and on Some of the Causes Which Have Retarded the Moral and Political Improvement of Ireland* (1812); this was followed by Dr Christopher Anderson's *Memorial on Behalf of the Native Irish with a View to Their Improvement in Moral and Religious Knowledge through the Medium of Their Own Language* (1815).[47]

The strongest point made by both authors was that Irish-speakers were much more numerous than was commonly supposed. Anderson made a valuable and detailed survey of the state of the language in all four provinces, asserting that except for the counties of Dublin, Kildare and Wicklow in the east, and Antrim, Armagh, Derry, Down and Fermanagh in the north, Irish was the everyday language of the majority of the common people. This was true, he claimed, even of urban areas such as Cork city and Youghal. Connaught was reputedly the most thoroughly Irish-speaking of the provinces, where even the resident gentry were obliged to use Irish in conducting business with the lower orders. The contemporary belief that Irish was losing ground as the use of English increased was contradicted; instead, Anderson asserted, the rapid rise in population in Irish-speaking areas was serving to offset numerically any increase in the numbers who spoke English.[48] As to the threat that education through Irish might pose to the English language and culture, Anderson and Dewar both strongly underlined the connection, by now well established in the Highlands, of literacy in Gaelic and the acquisition of English.

The key element in the usefulness of the scheme for educating through Irish—a point emphasized especially by Dewar, who had travelled extensively in Irish-speaking areas and conversed freely with the inhabitants—was the remarkable cultural affinity of the people for their native language. Dewar was keenly aware of the political and cultural divisions in Irish society, maintained by the boundaries of religion:

> A religious designation is here the name of a political party as well as of a religious body; and it is no unusual thing to meet with a ruffian who would fight for that sect whose name he bears whilst he is totally ignorant of the tenets of every sect.[49]

What he was shrewd enough and sympathetic enough to realize, however, was that the quickest way to win the affections of the native Irish was to assume a friendly disposition towards their language:

> So fond are they of their native country and of everything connected with it that he who will talk to them in the tongue of their fathers, which they regard as sacred, and who seems not displeased with their customs, will be considered as their countryman and friend.[50]

What Dewar, Anderson and Charles all shared was a deep and passionate appreciation for the indigenous language and culture of their Celtic homelands, underpinned by a Christian humanism strongly tempered by the Romantic.[51] They were at one with Irish evangelicals like Whitley Stokes, who tended to put the welfare of their native land, particularly its most neglected inhabitants, before everything else, and to look to religion to inspire people to work for the common good. The LHS was to some degree influenced by this mentality. No matter what abuse its agents levelled against Catholic priests, they were seldom disrespectful of the ordinary people. They also had to walk a tightrope between pandering to the prejudices of those who wanted to see the language die out, and the sympathies of the directors and their supporters (especially in Edinburgh and London) who had come to look upon it as a primary instrument for making common cause with the peasantry.

The Irish agents of the LHS were also more familiar than visiting deputies with the real situation concerning the state of the language. There is a certain poignant honesty in the following account submitted by an agent shortly after the appearance of the works by Dewar and Anderson:

> While I acknowledge with you the great importance of attending to the Irish language, I am happy that the Committee are convinced that I have never lost sight of promoting the reading of it in our schools, or of taking advantage of it to communicate the knowledge of divine truth, where it appeared necessary from ignorance of the English language or the early prejudices of the people. The Irish language of this country is rapidly on the decline. The extension of commerce, and the great demand for the produce of the most remote districts of the country, which the late long-continued war occasioned, did more for the cultivation of the English language and its introduction into every part of the land than the exertions of government for centuries. Exaggerated statements have been given of the proportion of the population of the country who cannot speak or understand English, but truth would reduce these calculations, even as they respect the adults, more than three-fourths, and would exclude, with very little reductions, the rising generation altogether; nevertheless, while districts or individuals can be found to whom the Scriptures in Irish may be serviceable or more acceptable than in English, it is a duty to teach it in our schools and to send it to every place where it may be useful and acceptable.[52]

It is doubtful whether the contribution of the LHS did much to hold back this swelling tide of English. What cannot be denied, however, is the Society's role in having introduced to Ireland the dynamic that bound religious revivalism to the development of popular literacy in Wales and the Scottish highlands, and that ensured the survival of Welsh and Gaelic as living languages into the twentieth century. In Ireland this impulse found concrete expression in the production of the first textbooks and primers exclusively for the use of Irish speakers. The LHS was the first organization to produce schoolbooks in Irish for instruction in spelling and grammar, and this measure in itself represented a turning point in the fortunes of the Irish language.

What was of infinitely greater significance, though, was the opening up of the debate over the utility of vernacular Irish in the modern world. The question of how the language and culture of the native Irish might be employed in the creation of a coherent national identity had been around for many decades, but there were few, if any, among its admirers at the upper levels of society who wished to see it rehabilitated and accommodated to the modern world. With the example of what had been accomplished in Scotland by the Edinburgh Gaelic School Society, and with talented men like Thomas Charles and Christopher Anderson making the case for its preservation, the debate over the utility of the Irish language took on an entirely new character from this point onwards.

Even more than the LHS, the Baptist Society for the Promotion of the Gospel in Ireland embraced the Irish language as an instrument of evangelization. This was a direct consequence of the influence of Scottish Baptists, who by now were leading the drive to evangelize the Highlands through the Edinburgh Gaelic School Society. Christopher Anderson had been a founding member of that organization and what he had witnessed of conditions in Ireland during his tour of 1813–14 convinced him of the possibilities that existed for an Irish agency based on similar principles. On his return to Edinburgh in August 1814 he persuaded a number of his colleagues, principally the Rev. Andrew Fuller, to undertake the challenge and the Baptist Society came into being.[53]

From the beginning the Baptist Society consciously sought to imitate the model of evangelization developed in the Highlands and so concentrated their resources on itinerant preaching and 'ambulatory' schools. In doing this the directors hoped not only to keep out of the way of other organizations, but also to elicit their cooperation and goodwill. In the first report Christopher Anderson spoke highly of the work currently being accomplished by the Sunday School Society and the KPS, and expressed the hope that these societies would also see the benefit of taking on the Irish language challenge.[54] Because the schools of the LHS were concentrated in Sligo and the counties immediately to the north and east, the Baptists targeted the western parts of Mayo and Clare as a base to begin operations.

More than any of the other agencies involved in the evangelical mission to the Catholic Irish, the Baptist Society was remarkable for the goodwill that characterized its relations with the Catholic population. Intimacy based on knowledge of the native language and sympathy for the desperate poverty of the Irish poor became the hallmarks of the Baptist mission. These virtues would appear to have been returned in kind by the people among whom the itinerant preachers moved. The Rev. Edmund Rogers, a Welshman who had been appointed minister at the Baptist meeting house in Portarlington, along with his fellow itinerant, the Rev. Isaac McCarthy, repeatedly spoke of the goodwill of the Catholic population. In 1816, Rogers gave an account of his recent itineraries:

> In my late journey I was greatly pleased with the disposition of the Irish: they are a generous and hospitable people; and many of them very desirous of hearing the Gospel, even in the rebellious county of Tipperary, where I preached in several of the most popish towns, and to my great astonishment was not once insulted or disturbed, which should be told much to the honour of the Irish nation.[55]

One year later, despite worsening economic conditions, McCarthy had much the same story to tell:

> I must say, to the honour of the Irish Catholics, that although I have preached out of doors often and baptized people so frequently in our public way, I cannot remember one single rude offence given me at any time. I may say more; I have travelled night and day through the country and have not received any insult from them.[56]

Practical innovations such as the use of 'scripture readers' were also characteristic of the Baptist mission. Scripture readers were local men selected for their ability to move among the peasantry without arousing suspicion. Naturally, they were to have a ready command of Irish and an ability to read but, as a contemporary directive stated, 'they must not be learned or refined, nor must they be ministers', and 'their language, their manners, their customs, and (where they are known) their object will ensure them the warmest corner, the pipe, and the potato'.[57] Another innovative policy of the Baptist Society was the custom of having their schools in Ireland twinned or 'adopted' by Baptist congregations in England, in the hope that 'the criminal alienation of affection which has too long subsisted between the people of the two countries, will be progressively removed and suspicion and apathy ultimately cease'.[58] In 1820 there were twelve such schools in the west of Ireland—because of their associations known as 'Norwich Schools', 'Hammersmith Schools', and so on—located mostly in counties Mayo, Sligo and Clare.[59]

Overall, the scope of the Baptist Society's educational activities was never as broad as that of other agencies in the field, particularly those that had access to public funds. In 1820 the Society reported sixty schools in Connaught catering to 5000 children and 150 adults, and a further ten in County Clare with 880 pupils.[60] Besides founding schools and employing scripture readers, the Baptist Society sponsored the labours of seven itinerant ministers from England and Wales whose circuits covered the central Midlands area, north as far as Newry in County Armagh and west as far as Sligo and Ballina in County

Mayo.[61] They do not appear to have had any more success than the Methodists and Congregationalists in winning converts from Catholicism; by their own account the improvement of the character of Catholic children, as opposed to conversion, was the sole purpose of their schools.[62]

Much of the hostility aroused by the work of the LHS was a consequence of its being the recipient of public funds. Although it started out as a voluntary agency, the Society was enormously successful in acquiring government funds, some of which were channelled through the KPS. Other monies, such as the £19,000 awarded from the Lord Lieutenant's Fund in 1819, were given with open state approval. By 1820, as a result, the schools of the LHS could be found in all four provinces. The heavy concentration in the west and north-west is probably a reflection of the numerical strength of Protestants in the Sligo–Roscommon area.[63]

DISTRIBUTION OF LHS SCHOOLS IN 1818[64]

County	Schools	Scholars
Leitrim	58	4712
Fermanagh	53	3671
Mayo	52	4188
Donegal	47	4202
Sligo	47	4140
Monaghan	38	3596
Cavan	35	2817
Galway	23	1699
Tyrone	21	2087
Roscommon	9	799
Longford	6	457
Waterford	2	100
Cork	1	46
Total	392	32,514

In 1822 the *Christian Observer* reported that the total number of schools had increased to 624 and furnished a breakdown of the religious and social backgrounds of those employed as supervisors:

OCCUPATIONS OF LHS SCHOOL SUPERVISORS, 1822[65]

Minister of the Established Church	175
Noblemen and gentlemen	123
Roman Catholic priests	85
Ladies	25
Dissenting ministers	7
No visitor resident in the vicinity	209
Total	624

The prominence of Church of Ireland clergy, noblemen and ladies is not surprising, but the scarcity of Dissenting ministers raises some questions since the LHS was a Nonconformist organization. It is possible that Irish Dissenters objected to the interdenominational activity of the Society, but it is more likely that Presbyterians, who constituted the largest Dissenting body in Ireland, were at this time still influenced by the Unitarian beliefs that had been influential in their community during the eighteenth century. In general, Irish Presbyterians did not succumb to evangelical influences until the 1830s and 1840s, a trend strongly associated with the ascendancy of the Rev. Henry Cooke. Up until the late 1820s even the most committed of the Presbyterian evangelicals favoured Emancipation in the belief that Catholics, once 'emancipated' in politics would seek freedom in religious affairs as well.

The most surprising feature of all is the presence of eighty-five Catholic priests, especially since the Society's reports consistently referred to priestly opposition. On the other hand, the prominence of priests as school supervisors does validate claims made by other societies during the early years of the evangelical crusade that the Catholic clergy had sometimes been willing to cooperate with the evangelicals, particularly in matters having to do with education. In the case of the LHS, the principle of non-interference with a pupil's religion was apparently written into the rules, though its due observance depended on the vigilance of the school supervisor. In this way a priest could avail of the funds offered by the Society and conduct a school perfectly acceptable to the Catholic community, while an evangelical minister could use funds from the same source to pursue the ultimate conversion of his pupils. Also, until the early 1820s, the Catholic hierarchy's attitudes towards the evangelical crusade were inconsistent and not clearly defined. The arguments used against the movement were based not on charges of proselytism but on the perceived dangers of unrestricted Bible distribution among an ignorant populace.

This attitude changed dramatically between 1820 and 1824, however, and it is surely significant that by 1825 the number of priests acting as supervisors in LHS schools had dropped to twenty-five.[66] During the first half of 1824 the Catholic clergy launched a united effort to have Catholic children withdrawn from the LHS's schools, as a result of which the Society experienced a sharp drop in both teachers and pupils. By 1826 many of the schools had been incorporated into the Kildare Place system, mainly because this body had more funds at its disposal. This reversal of fortune undoubtedly stemmed from Catholic opposition, but the LHS was also discredited by a condemnation issued against it by the commission of inquiry for education of 1825–7. When interviewed before the commission in 1825, the Society's representatives freely admitted that their objectives involved a change of religious allegiance, and they stoutly defended their position while at the same time denying allegations of proselytism. What the Society sought, claimed those who were interviewed, was 'a religious and moral transformation', as opposed to

> exchanging the mere ceremonial of one church for that of another. Instances of such conversion [would always] be found to be a consequence of the unrestricted use of the scriptures; as they owe their reality to the divine efficacy of that word, so will the society be indebted for their number to the extent of its full circulation. Such conversions as these the committee unequivocally associate with the plan and design of the society, and if the question should be asked, as it not infrequently is, *whether such conversions involve an abandonment of the Roman Catholic church, the committee, in speaking from experience, will candidly avow their conviction that they do.* [my emphasis][67]

In the light of this comment it is small wonder that the LHS was considered the most actively proselytizing of all the evangelical educational agencies.[68]

After 1825 the Society became involved in the notorious activities taking place on the Farnham Estate in County Cavan, in connection with which the term 'Second Reformation' first entered into common usage. On the national scene, however, the LHS schools met the same fate as those of the KPS and the ADV. Very little was heard of them after the setting up of the National Board of Education in 1831 and it appears that many of their more successful schools simply applied for funding to the board and were thus integrated into the national system.

THE 'QUIET PROGRESS' OF THE CHURCH OF IRELAND

The response of the Church of Ireland to the energy and commitment of the Methodists and Nonconformists in pioneering the cause of evangelical religion in Ireland was ambivalent. While some clergymen of the Established Church welcomed the spirit of interdenominational cooperation, others feared that the spread of Bible societies and the accommodation of itinerant preachers would inevitably pose a threat to ecclesiastical authority. A sense of denominational and even national rivalry sometimes provoked otherwise complacent churchmen into tightening the ranks against outside competition. The archbishop of Armagh, William Stewart, captured this spirit perfectly when he expressed his desire to set up a branch of the Society for Promoting Christian Knowledge in his diocese 'as the clergy cannot become members of the London [Hibernian] Society and we now want something to unite them and to strengthen ourselves against these various associations *formed by laymen and conducted by Methodists and Englishmen*' [my emphasis].[69]

With regard to the mission to the Catholic population, the Established Church was initially content to pursue moral reform through the more gradual means of education and popular literature. With the appearance of the Religious Tract and Book Society (1807), the Sunday School Society (1809), and the KPS (1811), in addition to the ADV and the HBS, there was no shortage of outlets for members of the Church establishment, either lay or clerical, to express their commitment to the cause. The objective of effecting a wholesale change in the religious allegiance of Catholics was seldom voiced, however, and the general attitude was one of paternalism, benevolence and quiet expectation.[70]

Nevertheless, the sense that battle would inevitably be joined with the Catholic clergy was there from the beginning. As early as 1803 John Jebb had drawn up a list of books concerned with the 'Romish Controversy' that he recommended for distribution among the members of the ADV (see appendix A). Several years would pass, however, before the Church of Ireland would raise the banner of reformation on a national scale. In the meantime the committed advocates of evangelical religion and moral reform within its ranks would pursue an extraordinarily successful campaign to win support for their cause.

Among the first of the voluntary agencies to win widespread popular support among the clergy and laity of the Church of Ireland was the Hibernian Sunday School Society, founded after a meeting at the La Touche bank in

Dublin in 1809. Alone among the educational agencies begun during this period, it could justify its existence without recourse to the Catholic population. It was founded by and for Protestants, and while this did not preclude the acceptance, or indeed the active recruitment, of Catholic children, nevertheless it was not dependent on their presence. During the first decade or so Catholic children did attend the Society's schools, and occasionally priests applied to the Society for funds to set up their own Sunday schools on principles approved by the organizing committee.

Whatever good feeling may earlier have existed between the parties, however, disappeared during the general sectarian animosity of the early 1820s, and the Sunday school movement throughout the remainder of the century may be said to have been a purely Protestant concern. The movement made rapid progress in Ulster, where the effects of the recent Rebellion were still in evidence and 'infidelity' continued to exercise a strong hold on the popular classes, as the following commentary suggests:

> In the year 1810, when I became a Sunday-school teacher, a dark cloud hung over Belfast. The rebellion of 1798, following up the French revolution, opened the floodgates of infidelity, and a number of Deistical characters actually commenced a Sunday school about 1808–9 to inculcate their pernicious views and to ridicule the Bible. This gave the alarm to the Christian community and hence the opening of the Smithfield Sunday School ... From the very first the Sunday School Society for Ireland gave us help.[71]

Within twenty years of the Society's foundation the overwhelming majority of Sunday schools were in Ulster. This was so despite the fact that Presbyterians were in the majority in the province, while the directors and patrons of the Society belonged to the landed and business elites of Dublin and the provinces and were mostly affiliated with the Church of Ireland. This feature was one of the first indications of a trend that was later to characterize the Irish evangelical movement, in which the Protestant upper classes provided the leadership and ideology necessary to weld their own interest to that of the Protestant rank and file. Among the patrons of the Society were the earls of Meath and Bandon, Count de Salis, Bishop Thomas Elrington of Ferns and Leighlin, and the countesses of Bandon, Charleville, Kingston, Meath, Portarlington, and Powerscourt.[72] According to one contemporary source, the schools were popular among the largely Protestant 'middle ranks and strong farmers'.[73] The number of schools increased dramatically between 1816 and 1819:

GROWTH OF SUNDAY SCHOOLS, 1809–19[74]

1809	12
1810	22
1811	39
1812	67
1813	62
1814	82
1815	92
1816	88
1817	107
1818	178
1819	279

NUMBER OF SUNDAY SCHOOLS IN PROPORTION TO POPULATION, 1821[75]

	Population	Schools	Scholars	Teachers
Ulster	2,001,966	1117	120,680	8833
Leinster	1,785,702	262	19,527	1950
Connaught	1,053,918	77	5122	425
Munster	2,005,363	63	4453	420

	Ratio
Ulster	1:17
Leinster	1:92
Connaught	1:206
Munster	1:450

This pattern reinforces other evidence showing that most of the schools were located in Ulster. The two areas in the south (outside of Dublin) where they were said to flourish were Powerscourt, County Wicklow, where the resident clergy were in the front ranks of the evangelical movement, and Youghal, County Cork, a traditional Protestant stronghold.[76]

Like the LHS, the Sunday School Society reported a decline in enrolment for the year 1824/5. This it attributed to the establishment of Sunday schools at

Catholic chapels, where religious education was now being provided for children who had formerly attended the Protestant schools. This development, however, does not appear to have seriously affected the system, which had a total of 202,000 pupils in attendance in 1831, as compared with 157,000 in 1824.[77] The commission of 1825 praised the work being done in the Sunday schools, which were run on a completely voluntary basis. Teachers gave their services gratuitously, and bibles and tracts were made available by the various evangelical agencies on both sides of the Irish Sea.

Much of the success of the Sunday School Society during its formative years was attributed to the commitment and energy of James Digges La Touche, who acted as secretary until his untimely death in 1827. La Touche was a conduit through which the radical and innovative ideas pioneered by Methodists and Independent evangelicals made their way into the Established Church. Around the time he undertook to make the Sunday school movement his personal crusade, his colleague Henry Monck Mason began to heed the appeals on behalf of the Bible in Irish that were issuing from the Independent evangelicals. Monck Mason had arrived at his vocation through a literary route. He had been a friend of the poet Thomas Moore at Trinity in the 1790s and a founding member of the Iberno-Celtic Society, a short-lived organization founded in Dublin in 1809 to promote the literature of Gaelic Ireland. More than any of his contemporaries, he was responsible for the Church of Ireland's espousal of the policy of using the Irish language for missionary purposes. The results of this were twofold.

First, it placed before the clergy of the Church of Ireland the challenge of acquiring the knowledge to speak and teach Irish, a necessity that forced them to employ the services of native scholars educated to the degree that they could produce dictionaries, grammar books and primers for use in schools. In terms of establishing links between the cultures of colonist and colonized, this was of far greater significance than the earlier attempts of the scholars of the first Celtic revival in the 1780s or the less well-known efforts of the United Irishmen in the 1790s. Its importance became evident when, via German Romanticism, the concept of the national language as the soul of a nation's identity became dominant around the middle decades of the century.[78]

This process was anticipated and even predicted by some of the individuals who promoted the Irish language for the purposes of furthering the cause of reformation. Certainly, there was no mistaking the tone of Christopher Anderson's address to Monck Mason and his friends when they solicited his advice on the question of whether the Gaelic or Roman character should be used for publications in Irish. Anderson was strongly in favour of the Gaelic character because native speakers preferred it, but he added:

> The question ... with respect to the letter is of small account, when compared with that of the necessity of teaching the language itself. And knowing that I am now addressing a committee with reference to their own countrymen, I would earnestly entreat their continued zealous attention to that object—teaching the native Irish to read their own language. Well assured as I am that whatever may be advanced at present against this,—the day will come when those who have taken up this object and prosecuted it will be regarded as the best benefactors of their country.[79]

Monck Mason's chief supporter in his crusade on behalf of the native language was the Rev. Robert Daly, rector of Powerscourt. Others included Thomas Lefroy, Joseph D'Arcy Sirr, Isaac D'Olier and Charles Edward Orpen. Together, this group represented the radical wing of episcopal evangelicalism that desired a much more open and active commitment of the Church of Ireland to the cause of a national reformation. They also represented a remarkably diverse range of opinions, which serves to illustrate the complex relationship between the legacy of Enlightenment idealism as expressed through religious revivalism and the polarities of the contemporary political world.

Initially, Monck Mason and the Rev. Daly attempted to work through the ADV by suggesting that it support the work of the LHS among the Irish-speaking population. But this proposal met with such opposition from the committee that they withdrew and began to lay plans for a separate organization, one that would be in more strict accordance with the religious principles of the Church of Ireland. These plans came to fruition with the founding of the Irish Society for Promoting the Education of the Native Irish through the Medium of Their Own Language in 1818. In the two years prior to its creation some of the chief supporters of the project had been engaged in the preparation of a historical defence of their objectives. Their findings were published by William Sankey in 1818 in *A Brief Sketch of the Various Attempts Which Have Been Made to Diffuse a Knowledge of the Holy Scriptures through the Medium of the Irish Language*. Except for its insistence that the work be undertaken and supported by the Established Church, this publication actually added little to the arguments of Anderson and Dewar, and in many instances merely repeated their proposals. According to one authority, however, the *Brief Sketch* 'had the immediate effect of removing much prejudice and of attracting many friends to a cause which it now appeared had the direct sanction of regal authority and of the convocation of the Church of Ireland held under Primate Ussher, A.D. 1664'.[80]

It certainly prompted the KPS to consider whether the native language should be incorporated into their educational policies. A subcommittee appointed in 1819 produced a lengthy report on the subject and concluded that the Society should become directly involved, particularly in the production of teaching materials:

> We conceive that the institution of an Irish school should not be compelled to languish for want of fundamental materials to set to work with. We have read several petitions concerning the establishment of schools in the south-west which state that nothing is wanting but elementary books in the Irish language to undertake forthwith the instruction of hundreds, and we have also seen several schools that were once established [that] have died away for want of such assistance ... Our society is the proper one for people to look to for providing such materials and we ought perhaps long ago to have turned our attention to the subject.[81]

The Sunday School Society also began to look favourably at the prospect of teaching through Irish wherever it was necessary, and reported applications for schools in remote Irish-speaking areas in 1818–19.[82] The Irish Society also reported substantial support, both financial and through donations of tracts and bibles, from several organizations in England and Scotland. A Scottish organization that called itself the Edinburgh Society for Promoting the Education of the Poor in Ireland sent documents of the work being done by Gaelic-speaking missionaries in the Highlands, and inevitably decided to transfer its support from the KPS, in the belief that

> there are advantages in the formation of separate and individual and, if you will, exclusive societies which may meet the various principles and even prejudices of those who wish well to the general cause, as a number of smaller streams flowing in many channels may do more to fertilize an extensive country than a torrent formed by a confluence of all their waters.[83]

In London a sister society was established in 1821 following a substantial gift from Sir Thomas Baring; William Wilberforce agreed to accept the office of vice-president and the patronage of Lord Teignmouth, president of the BFBS, was successfully solicited.[84]

Despite the ample discussion that had proceeded the founding of the Irish Society and the considerable publicity that attended the launching of its work, progress was initially quite modest. By 1825 the Society had in its employment seven schoolteachers who circulated among the 140 or so schools conducted by the Society, the majority of which were located in Connaught and Munster.[85] Payment from the Society was tied to the number of pupils who could prove their ability to read the scriptures to an inspector, who made a quarterly visit. The figures of those who could read proficiently were duly relayed to the Dublin headquarters of the Society for publication in the annual reports. The schools catered for adults as well as children, and in 1822 their work began to be supplemented by itinerant readers paid by the Scripture Readers' Society, founded in that year with a donation of £1000 from Thomas Lefroy, which was doubled by his friend Lord Powerscourt.[86]

The founding of the Irish Society heralded, if not the full commitment of the Church of Ireland to the cause of reformation among the Catholic population, then certainly the inability of its bishops to prevent the evangelical wing from having its own way. The trend terrified the Rev. Charles Forster (another of John Jebb's correspondents), who had always been sceptical of the involvement of laymen in religious affairs, and particularly of the influence of Bible societies. 'Have I not often been saying what penny-a-week Bible societies would lead to,' he lamented during the crisis precipitated by the papal directive of Cardinal Fontana warning Catholics against the reading of the Protestant Bible in the autumn of 1818.[87] Two years later, the attempts of the bishop of Killaloe, Dr Mant, to employ 'misdirected zeal' in promoting the Protestant religion among Catholic pupils in attendance at schools run by the ADV was more than enough to arouse the consternation of John Jebb. 'Such activities as those of the good bishop are precisely those which the hierarchy and priesthood on the popish side would wish to contend with,' he warned, 'and unless I am altogether in error, they will gain a temporary victory.'[88] Jebb's predictions were only too accurate. While it may have been politically judicious for Catholic authorities to ignore the efforts of Methodists and Independent evangelicals to influence the predilections of their flocks, it was an entirely different matter once high-ranking ecclesiastics and prominent laymen of the Church of Ireland started to involve themselves in the education and moral improvement of the Catholic population. This element could call upon the power of landlords and tithe-collectors and also, through the influence of supportive politicians, control the distribution of public funds allocated for educational needs.

None of the evangelical societies penetrated the upper echelons of the Church of Ireland quite as thoroughly as the Irish Society. Already by 1818 it could boast of the archbishop of Tuam, Dr Power le Poer Trench, as its president, and such prominent landowners as 1st Viscount Lorton and Viscount Jocelyn (the future Lord Roden) as vice-presidents. Among the committee were to be found the names of Robert Daly, Thomas Lefroy, William Smyth Guinness, Joseph D'Arcy Sirr and Charles Edward Orpen.[89] All of these men were committed evangelicals, but their opinions on the objective of the Irish Society, or indeed on the larger question of the social and economic condition of the Catholic Irish, were by no means unanimous. Robert Daly and Thomas Lefroy were known as two of the most bitter anti-Catholics in the country, whereas Archbishop Trench had already won a reputation as a sympathizer and a defender of the rights of the Catholic poor. Charles Edward Orpen's pronouncements on social and economic issues and defence of the language and culture of the native Irish, meanwhile, were directly in the tradition of the Christian humanism of Whitley Stokes and dangerously close to the radical republicanism of the 1790s.

Orpen's opinions are particularly revealing of the complexities of the evangelical mindset. His indignation at the political and economic degradation of the native Irish was matched by his anger over the low esteem accorded to their language and culture. The particular object of his anger was William Shaw Mason, who had suggested that the poverty of the Irish was a direct consequence of the 'barbarous' character of their native language: 'The common Irish are naturally shrewd but very ignorant and deficient in mental culture, from the barbarous tongue in which they converse, which operates as an effectual bar to any kind of literary attainment ...'. 'Whose fault is this', replied Orpen, 'but theirs who have hitherto refused to give them education in this language' and he went on to claim the number of Irish writers listed by the Iberno-Celtic Society and the manuscripts in Oxford and other great European universities as evidence of Irish literary and cultural achievement.[90]

There is some reason to believe that, like his predecessor Charlotte Brooke, Orpen was spurred into action by the movement gathering momentum in Scotland whereby the Gaelic culture of the Highlands was being pressed into service to provide a national identity as the country began to recover from the divisive trauma of the Jacobite rebellion. Since Gaelic Scotland had never been other than an 'overflow' or 'cultural colony' of Ireland, this 'invention of tradition' demanded some radical rearrangements, including, in the words of Hugh Trevor-Roper, 'the usurpation of Irish culture and the rewriting of early Scottish history, culminating in the insolent claim that Scotland—Celtic Scotland—was the mother nation and Ireland the cultural dependency'.[91] This attitude inevitably found its way across the Irish Sea and made its appearance in a statistical survey of County Kildare, where an account was given of the discovery by the Glengarry Regiment of Scotch Fencibles that they could communicate in Irish with the local peasantry. The incident itself was of no great consequence. It was the attitude of the author T.J. Rawson that was pounced upon by Orpen, who unflinchingly charged him with either ignorance or prejudice:

> The Scotch are mentioned as, speaking with correctness, the 'ancient Celtic' while the language of the Irish is called 'the corrupt Irish spoken by the natives'. How came the Gaelic, notoriously a minor dialect, to be more correct Celtic than the Irish, which all scholars allow to be the most pure?[92]

Orpen was a fellow traveller of Christopher Anderson and Whitley Stokes and a clear partisan of preserving Irish as the national language. To the smug conclusion of Shaw Mason that the spread of English was an indication of the acceptance of English law and civilization, he drew a distinction between language and religion: 'Thank God, say I, British policy is a distinct thing from the extension of the English language, and best advanced by diffusing Christian knowledge among all the tongues of this vast empire …'[93] In Orpen's ideal world Ireland's route to progress and a place among the nations would best be secured through the maintenance of the native language and the adoption of the Protestant faith.

Such views, in the short term at any rate, were drowned out by the sloganeering of polemicists like Robert Daly who dominated the public debate throughout the 1820s. But this is not to dismiss the influence of Orpen, or of Whitley Stokes. The ease with which the convictions inspired by religious feeling could be invested with equal passion in the worship of the nation was to become a common phenomenon in Victorian Ireland. Disillusioned or frustrated by the attempts to effect a religious reformation among the Catholic population, or simply with the rigidity and philistinism that had come to characterize the movement generally, many evangelicals transferred their passions to the study of language, antiquities and music. This movement would break into an open political expression at the end of the century when, shorn of its religious dimension, evangelical passion would find expression in Celtic revivalism.[94]

If the stated objectives of the Irish Society are any indication, however, the sympathies of Orpen were not shared by his colleagues. On the contrary, the committee repeatedly expressed its commitment to accommodate the prejudices of those who wanted to make the language an instrument of anglicization and Protestantization. At a meeting in October 1818 it was resolved to adopt as a standing rule:

> that the exclusive object of this society is to instruct the native Irish, who still use their vernacular language, how to employ it as a means for obtaining an accurate knowledge of English, and for this end, as also for their moral amelioration, to distribute among them the Irish version of the Scriptures ... and such other works as may be necessary for schoolbooks, disclaiming at the same time all intention of making the Irish language a vehicle for the communication of general knowledge.[95]

The use of this double standard notwithstanding, the fact remains that those who would promote the use of Irish for the purposes of evangelization were still obliged (to some degree) to enter into the linguistic and cultural world of the native Irish. The consequences of this could hardly be predicted. Consider the case of Henry Monck Mason, whose hatred of Catholicism was visceral but who nevertheless strove for much of his life to establish a chair of Irish in Trinity College and finally succeeded in 1844. Or take that of Canon James Goodman, the evangelical clergyman and Irish-speaking native of West Kerry, whose collection of traditional airs and dance tunes ranks as one of the four most important repositories of such material for the entire nineteenth century.[96]

The link between the worlds of Monck Mason, Canon Goodman, and the nationalist revival was a direct one. When the young John Millington Synge (in his own words) 'relinquished the kingdom of God' and 'discovered the kingdom of Ireland', his interest in the Irish language took him to the aged Canon Goodman, who had won the first Bedell scholarship to study Irish at Trinity in 1844 and who now occupied the chair established by Monck Mason.[97] Terence Brown has pointed out the need for an appraisal of the contribution of the evangelical movement to the cultural history of Ireland in the nineteenth century. Such an appraisal will undoubtedly foster a new understanding of the intersecting links between religion, culture and politics, and establish the place of the evangelical movement in the tangled genealogy of Irish nationalism. Of more immediate concern to our understanding of its impact on contemporary social and political affairs, however, is the reception of its promoters and agents among the Catholic poor, who were now confronted with an entirely new and unfamiliar invasion of the traditional sphere of their morality and religion.

THE POPULAR RESPONSE TO THE EVANGELICAL MISSION

That the aim of the evangelical crusade was to effect a moral reformation in the minds and hearts of the Irish peasantry was never in dispute. In the words of Thomas Lefroy, the idea was to educate them 'not by letters alone, but *really* to educate them by influencing their minds, moulding their habits, forming their principles, and training their faculties'.[98] Any attempt to assess objectively the degree of success enjoyed by the early phase of the evangelical mission is a potential minefield, particularly because the evangelical mission in later decades was tarnished by the accusation of wholesale bribery and coercion in the drive to make converts. The record of the first two decades of the century, however, at least up to the early 1820s when Catholic leaders launched a full-scale offensive against the movement at every level, suggests that ground was being won, particularly in the area of education.

Much of the evidence from the early years of the evangelical mission suggests that the common people simply did not know in what context or category they should place the itinerant Methodists, Baptist schoolteachers, Gaelic-speaking Scottish ministers and others who were loosed on the Irish countryside to distribute tracts and bibles and urge Catholic children to attend their schools. Their purpose was not at all clear to unlettered country people whose knowledge of the Protestant world did not extend much beyond what to them was the haughtily superior and tithe-exacting Church of Ireland. One of the most popular suspicions to circulate in connection with the schools of the Independent evangelicals was that Catholic children were to be taken for the army of the king of England, and that they would end up as 'sure soldiers'—no doubt a popular twist on the commonly invoked term employed by biblical enthusiasts to make people 'soldiers of Christ'.[99] On the other hand, the appearance of kindly Baptist missionaries in County Mayo, willing to establish schools and to educate children without charge, caused people to question whether the opposition of the priest was justified: they turned up to check it out for themselves, and when they found that they were not agents of the devil, they went against the wishes of the priest. Other instances surfaced where the situation was reversed: when the people of a County Sligo village refused to send their children to a school recently opened by the Baptists, 'fearing that the government would claim them', the local priest recommended from the altar that they attend and learn to read the scriptures.[100]

The characteristic evangelical method of infiltrating popular culture through subversive channels like popular reading material and substituting the reading of the scriptures for the *seanchaí* tradition of telling heroic tales around the fireside were apparently quite successful. Travelling evangelists frequently commented on the joy with which illiterate peasants heard passages from the Bible in their native language. Christopher Anderson recorded:

> Last summer the writer, in passing through a part of Connaught, found a schoolmaster teaching a school on his own account, who for several months had been in the habit of reading the Irish New Testament to his neighbours, and as a proof that his labour was not lost on those poor people, one of them brought a candle alternately, or at least they furnished light, while he read to them the Irish scriptures. On reading the affecting parable of the rich man and Lazarus, he said, they called out to him 'Read it again—read it again,' and they also had their favourite passages in consequence of this exercise.[101]

The testimony of his colleague Daniel Dewar was even more striking:

> Whenever it was announced that the scriptures would be read in the Irish language, crowds of Catholics came to hear, who never till then heard a Protestant read the bible; and I shall ever recollect the manifest pleasure with which they seemed to receive instruction.[102]

The great stumbling block, however, was the traditional association between the Protestant religion and the foreign oppressor, and this was always below the surface even when the overtures of the missionaries were made through the pleasing medium of Irish. When Gideon Ouseley visited the famous penitential shrine at Lough Derg (a bastion of what evangelicals considered the worst forms of Catholic superstition), a highly revealing exchange took place when he began to criticize the practice of purchasing penances:

> I expressed my unbelief [*sic*] with regard to a system so preposterous and unchristian: and to add to the absurdity, where the principal actor [the guide], himself a profane wretch, could perform works of merit and supererogation for the good of the souls of others. 'Ah!' he exclaimed, 'you are not Irish'. 'Indeed I am', was the reply: 'I have never been in England'.

'If you are not English', he retorted, 'you belong to them, so you do'. I then administered some suitable admonition and retired from the scene of moral degradation with sorrow and disgust.[103]

Once the education and school societies began to operate, however, such prejudice might be suppressed in favour of the educational and often the material benefits that stood to be gained. Writing from a remote part of Ulster in 1810, a teacher in the pay of the LHS complained of having lost pupils because of the opposition of the priest, and also of the dreadful poverty of the area where children barely had clothing and no shoes or stockings in the depth of winter:

> To see them come a mile or two in this condition, at this season of the year, is truly distressing. This is a country where one has an opportunity of clothing the naked and feeding the hungry, if he had but the ability. I wonder how many poor, naked creatures here will be able to get through the winter; and had I but a very few pounds to spare, I could lay them out in a very useful way; and a very few pounds laid out in this manner would procure me plenty both of hearers and scholars.[104]

The use of material incentives was not as yet associated with the opprobrium that was to accrue in later years when charges of wholesale bribery and outright coercion were levelled at evangelical missionaries. In one of his many epistolary discussions about moral reform with his archbishop, John Jebb described how a Sunday school run by the Church of Ireland had prospered in a part of Ulster where it was flanked by two opposing creeds:

> About seventeen years since, the bishop of Dromore established Sunday schools in his neighbourhood, which have since continued in a flourishing condition. The numbers at present are about 200, who, without distinction of religious tenets, are all taught the church catechism, and all attend the church service. Opposition was at one time experienced, *both from popish bigotry and Presbyterian pride*, but all opposition was rendered fruitless by the simple measure of giving each child a halfpenny for every Sunday's diligent attendance. Ever since the adoption of that plan the numbers have been progressively increasing and the good effects are fully ascertained by the civility and honesty of the children. [my emphasis][105]

The people most likely to take advantage of the material benefits offered by educational societies were schoolteachers, for whom the salaries of £25 and £30 a year and a decent schoolhouse were quite an improvement on the hedge schools. Hedge-school masters were quickly co-opted by the KPS, and also by the London Hibernian and Irish societies. Shortly after it began operations in Sligo, the LHS set up an academy to train young men as schoolteachers. Another institution, which professed itself a nondenominational body but appears to have had some connection with the ADV, was set up at Kildimo in County Limerick to train teachers for schools in which the scriptures were the basis of instruction.[106] It was the opinion of John Jebb that teachers who could make their way by their own abilities were far preferable to those paid by endowments 'because people think that there is a plot afoot to proselytize them. When the teacher is allowed to make his own way by the weight of his own attainments ... the people pride themselves on their good judgement'.[107] In spite of Jebb's expectations, however, the Kildimo Seminary was a constant source of controversy in the area, so much so that the Rev. William Maunsell of Limerick was obliged to advise the Commissioners of Education who were about to set up an investigative inquiry in 1817 to select superintendents 'free from local prejudice ... as it would be difficult to find anyone in this neighbourhood who had not formed a very unfavourable opinion of the seminary'.[108]

The attempts of the evangelical missionaries to make common cause with the native Irish led to some curious partnerships, but none was more remarkable than that of Thaddeus (or Thady) Connellan with the LHS, and later with the Irish Society. Born a Catholic in about 1780, Connellan was a native of Skreen in County Sligo and became one of the outstanding Irish scholars of his day. His career as a 'poor scholar' in the hedge schools of Connaught and Munster was recounted to Lady Morgan, who published an account of it in her *Patriotic Sketches* (1807). It bears a striking resemblance to that of the young William Carleton, especially because of the services rendered by both men to the cause of the evangelical moral crusade. Around 1807 Connellan came into contact with Albert Blest and the LHS, and either chose or was persuaded to link his cause with theirs. It is not clear at what point he converted to Protestantism, but the shift had certainly occurred by the time he took up employment to train Irish-speaking schoolmasters for the LHS in 1810. His conversion appears to have been a sincere one, and he remained a Protestant until his death in 1854.[109] His interest in education was nonetheless deeply and consciously motivated by a genuine desire to improve the condition of his countrymen:

> My own mind has long been most forcibly impressed, from a thorough knowledge of the character of my countrymen, their feelings, and their prejudices ... especially that large body of them who reside in the more distant part of the kingdom and among whom the Irish language universally

prevails ... that the only effective way to soften their passions was to cause their very prejudices to become an engine of good, and through their enthusiastic and natural love of their own language ... to lead them to a train of right thinking; and by opening to their minds the excellence of religion, to subdue their frightful disposition to anarchy, disloyalty, and confusion, and to render them loyal, industrious and happy.[110]

Connellan's faith in the reverence for learning to be found among the native Irish was such that he assured Lady Morgan that 'the labourer who earned but sixpence a day would sooner live upon potatoes and salt than refuse a little learning to his child'.[111] His estimation of their native language was hardly less restrained: 'The Irish is the first and loftiest tongue in the world: the English can never come near it, and the Greek alone is worthy of being compared to it.'[112] The possessor of such passionate convictions was unlikely to turn down any scheme designed to promote education through Irish. Predictably, one of the major tasks assigned to him by the LHS was the compilation of Irish textbooks and spelling books and the translation of the scriptures into Irish. Shortly after the founding of the Irish Society, Connellan was approached to work on an English–Irish dictionary and to help with the production of Irish grammars for use in the Society's schools. He was well informed about the progress that was being made in literacy in the native languages of Wales and Scotland:

> I believe the Highland Gaelic Society may help me in this object of printing useful works on husbandry such as they have in their Gaelic. They are long before us in very useful publications, and even the Welsh have many hundreds of new books in the vernacular language of the country and all the Scriptures these many years besides ...[113]

Useful works on husbandry, however, were precisely what Monck Mason and his colleagues wished to keep out of the hands of the Irish-speaking peasantry. The reformation they desired was to be confined to the realm of the spiritual, and Connellan's emphasis on the material was altogether at odds with the attitudes of those in control of the Irish Society.

Despite the consensus that existed between the various denominations on the desirability of effecting a change in the religious allegiance of the Catholic Irish, during the first twenty years of the evangelical crusade open conversion was considered less important than setting up an educational foundation on which a genuine reformation based on literacy and a knowledge of the scriptures might be advanced. Even under the best of circumstances it is doubtful whether this could have been accomplished, and the period that followed the ending of the Napoleonic Wars was far from providing the best of circumstances. Between 1815 and 1823 a deepening economic depression produced explosive developments in the political arena. It was against this background that evangelicals, driven by their faith in the Protestant Bible as the supreme source of moral authority, became identified in the popular mind with an unbending resistance to any measure that threatened Protestant hegemony. And the measure to which resistance was most fierce was precisely that in which the Catholics had come to invest all their hopes of salvation and deliverance, namely, Catholic Emancipation.

–FOUR–
The Politics of Catholic Emancipation

I see that our pretended friends, but real enemies, the Grattans, the Greys etc. are all bent on ensnaring us: and I am convinced that the Veto is the least part of the Protestant reformation they mean to enforce upon us.

JOHN MILNER[1]

You and I, sir, live at different sides of the channel, and as it is probable that you have never crossed it, allow me to tell you (and I fear my assertion will prove true) the Romanists want the tithes—the forfeited lands—the highest offices of the state—and power of every kind, not even excepting the kingly—and all as a right not as a favour. They ask like a sturdy beggar, armed with a bludgeon, and their language is—if you don't give quickly, we will make you.

PETER ROE[2]

Surely an all wise and over-ruling providence is our only refuge from the gloomy swell that threatens us with (sooner or later, how late or soon is not in us to know) no common storm. How mysterious a thing it is, that this tempest *whatever or whenever it be, is to be the result of so many good men.* [my emphasis]

CHARLES FORSTER[3]

AMBITIONS AND FRUSTRATIONS

From the Act of Union onwards, the 'Irish problem' and the 'Catholic question' were virtually synonymous terms at Westminster. The essence of the problem was how to appease Catholic expectations generated by the Union settlement in the face of opposition from the Irish Protestant ascendancy and its supporters in parliament. And the crux of the problem was that opponents of Catholic political equality could now point to the 1798 Rebellion to bolster their arguments. During the first decade of the new century, the spectre of Catholic vengefulness unleashed during the 1790s provided material for a virtual cottage industry implicating the Catholic Church in the Rebellion and recasting the 1790s in the sectarian tradition of 1641 and 1690.[4]

The ink on the parliamentary act that secured the Union was barely dry when conservative Protestant opinion united to revive Bishop Woodward's argument and to convince parliament and the public that the concession of what was called 'Emancipation' would spell the death of the Protestant interest in Ireland and the possible separation of the two islands. Once again the spectre of collusion between Catholic religious leaders and the fomenters of rebellion was raised in connection with the short-lived rising led by Robert Emmett in Dublin in 1803. The person who did the most to publicize this view was Lord Redesdale, who had been appointed to the office of lord chancellor in 1801. An acrimonious epistolary debate with a Catholic peer, Lord Fingal, appeared in published form in 1804 and provided a tremendous boost to the conservative cause.[5] It was all the more powerful because Redesdale was an Englishman (a scion of the Mitford family) with powerful connections among the English nobility.

The intransigent opposition to Emancipation personified by Redesdale was substantial enough to cause the resignation of Pitt in 1801 and the downfall of the 'Talents' ministry in 1807, when the cabinet was about to consider partial relief measures for Catholics.[6] The government's failure to fulfil its verbal pledge of 1800 had the effect of hardening the opinion of Catholic leaders into the conviction that Emancipation would not be won without a protracted struggle. Catholic opinion in Ireland as to what constituted 'Emancipation' was itself marked by sharp division. The veto controversy delineated this cleavage and, within the space of a few years, exposed where the real source of Catholic power lay. The veto was regarded, particularly by liberal Protestants, as a means whereby a compromise settlement agreeable to all parties might be achieved. Specifically, the government would command a veto over the nomination of candidates to the Catholic episcopal bench, in return for the removal of the remaining disabilities suffered by Catholics. This provision, it was hoped, would curb the independence of the bishops, and consequently the lower clergy, and keep them loyal both to the crown and to the Protestant position of privilege in Ireland.[7]

Catholic clerics were at first almost unanimous in accepting this condition. On the eve of the Union, under the conservative leadership of Archbishop Troy, the Catholic bishops had consented to the notion of state payment for the clergy and the possibility of the government having a say in the appointment of Catholic bishops.[8] It was, after all, the accepted practice in most countries in Europe (particularly in the lands of the Hapsburg Empire, the bastion of European Catholicism) for the monarch to claim an equal stake with the Pope in the nomination of episcopal candidates. The veto did not become a controversial political question in the immediate aftermath of the Union because Emancipation was shelved after Pitt resigned in 1801.[9] But by the time a petition on Catholic reform was presented to parliament in 1807, the climate of opinion in Ireland had clearly undergone a marked change. Protestant intransigence and the defence of the cause by Lord Redesdale not only united people like Denis Scully and Theobald McKenna, but also drew Daniel O'Connell into the political fray. It was now clear that it was not clerical but lay opinion that would have to be taken into account. Under O'Connell's guidance an anti-veto campaign was launched, which resulted in a majority of the bishops agreeing to reject any attempt by the government to interfere in episcopal appointments or indeed in any other matter having to do with Church authority.[10]

The decision of the hierarchy to follow the lead of O'Connell on this occasion was a telling revelation of the true nature of the Emancipation question. The issue of who should have the final say in the filling of vacant sees was directly related to the amount of autonomy that Catholics could exercise in the regulation of their own affairs, particularly those having to do with education, which, it was understood, would mould the political sympathies of the common people. The problem for Protestant opponents, of course, was the degree to which the political was linked to the religious. According to Oliver MacDonagh, the involvement of the Catholic clergy in politics during the first half of the nineteenth century was a step-by-step process in which 'the main body of the church had been harnessed to a nationalist agitation'.[11] If so, then the first of these steps was taken in 1807, and with almost every passing year the advance would become more pronounced.

The rejection of the Catholic relief bill of 1814 was the first real display of Catholic power and the imposing leadership of O'Connell. The bill, introduced by Henry Grattan in 1813 and promoted by Canning in the following year, contained the safeguards that the government deemed necessary for internal security if Emancipation was to take effect, namely, a veto on episcopal appointments and the provision of state support for the clergy. Although the bill won the approval of the English Catholic Board and the aristocratic elite of the Catholic Committee in Ireland, it was rejected outright by O'Connell and his followers. In an attempt to thwart their influence, the English Catholic Board submitted the matter to Rome. The proposed law was returned by the secretary of propaganda, Dr Quarantotti, with a definitive recommendation that it be adopted. This rescript produced turmoil in Ireland, where the more conservative members of the hierarchy and the Catholic Committee favoured acceptance while the radicals led by O'Connell attacked it with undisguised vehemence.[12] When it was rumoured that the Pope was prepared to yield to a British demand for a veto, O'Connell took his campaign to the people. To offset any backsliding by the bishops because of pressure from Rome, he threatened that if they agreed to papal advice on the veto, they would soon find themselves without a congregation:

> If the present clergy shall descend from the high station they hold to become the vile slaves of the Castle—a thing I believe impossible—but should it occur, I warn them in time to look to their master for support, for the people will despise them too much to contribute (great applause). The people would imitate their forefathers. They would communicate only with some holy priest who never bowed to the Dagon of power, and the Castle clergy would preach to still thinner numbers than attend in Munster or Connaught the reverend gentlemen of the present established Church.[13]

As a result of O'Connell's agitation the controversial rescript was withdrawn for reconsideration by the Pope. Its successor, which appeared in May 1815, was still in agreement with the original demand for a veto and state support for the clergy and was equally unacceptable to the O'Connellites, and to the hierarchy, who had by now come out publicly in support of the popular position. As one of their pamphlets explained,

> Because however anxiously the temporal aggrandizement of a

comparatively small number of Roman Catholics may solicit its revival and enactment, we know that it is abhorred by the great bulk of our community with so universal a ferment of detestation and with such convulsive alarm as we never before witnessesed.[14]

The negative response to the second rescript was the death knell of Canning's 1814 relief bill. If nothing else was achieved by the agitation and the exchanges with Rome, it was at least made clear that the Catholic bishops could not, without great risk to their Church, commit themselves to a policy abhorrent to their lay followers. This was the real source of the Church's power. Far from being the imperialistic arm of Rome, the Catholic Church in Ireland bowed more than a little in the direction of French democracy in its willingness to take popular feeling into account. The leadership role of the Catholic clergy in Ireland was described with stunning accuracy by a Presbyterian minister and long-time supporter of Catholic Emancipation Rev. James Carlisle as 'somewhat like a power vested in the leaders of a combination of workmen', which was almost absolute only so long as it led the people in the way in which they were determined to go.[15] It was evidently not a case of the clergy leading their flocks into the political arena, but rather a response to a popular demand that they fulfil the role that history had thrust upon them: that of representatives of the downtrodden Catholic population and guardians of the faith.

Nobody understood or exploited this better than Daniel O'Connell. At a public meeting of Catholics in County Clare in March 1814, he spelled out clearly his concept of the Church and its relation to the people:

> [The Church] has survived persecution; built upon a Rock, it has defied the storms of force and violence. But this emancipation bill would have undermined the church and the rock on which it is founded; and in the fall of both, the credulous people would be crushed to death and destruction ... there would be placed in every diocese, and then in every parish in Ireland, a ministerial dependent obliged to support the minister by the tenure of the ecclesiastical office; and then the expectants of the office would as usual be under the necessity of using double diligence in the ministry. Thus Canning's bill ... would have brought more numerous, better disciplined, and more effective recruits into the ranks of corruption than any one political measure ever yet invented or even imagined.[16]

O'Connell and his supporters saw the Catholic Church and the independence of its clergy as a bulwark between the designs of a hostile establishment and the vulnerability of the Catholic population. On this account they were even prepared to fly in the face of papal authority when it ran counter to their interests. Nevertheless, in response to Protestant insistence on the Bible as the supreme source of moral authority, they were compelled to support an equally dogmatic assertion on behalf of the claims of the Catholic Church and apostolic succession.

It was the nightmare of Protestant conservatives to see Emancipation only as a means to an end, that naturally being the destruction of the Protestant presence in Ireland. For many Protestants the prospect of a popular mass movement, well regulated and well led by O'Connell and the priests, held more terror than a recurrence of the *jacquerie* of 1798. As Archbishop William Magee was to express it so lucidly at the height of the Emancipation campaign:

> I do not believe that the Roman Catholic population attach to that specific object which is now looked upon as 'Catholic emancipation' any value of any moment. I consider that they look to it as a means, and that they have a greater object behind it; it is *their* country, *their* property, *their* religion. All this is incessantly forced upon them by persons who have a commanding influence over them.[17]

The growing strength of the Catholic movement had the effect of bringing Protestants closer together. It also added weight to one of the central elements of the evangelical world view: a deep-seated anti-Catholicism based on antagonism to the institutional forms and doctrinal beliefs of the Church of Rome. Evidence from a variety of sources indicates that evangelical influence in the Church of Ireland increased strikingly in the years 1812–16. Besides the domestic fear over the Emancipation question and the growing influence of O'Connell, it is clear that there was also an international dimension to be considered, and that events in Ireland were moving in tandem with others in Britain as a whole. Napoleon's defeat in Russia in 1812 and his subsequent capitulation and exile to St Helena were interpreted as the ultimate signs of providential deliverance and a vindication of all who had clung steadfastly to 'true religion' and the Bible in the face of the infidelity and anarchy unleashed in the previous twenty years.

The surest sign that the evangelicals had the wind in their sails with regard to public opinion was their triumphant success in the campaign to open India to the missionary efforts of the Church of England. During this campaign they invoked their own version of popular democracy, flooding parliament with petitions to illustrate the depth of popular sympathy for the missionary cause. It was an innovative and brilliant use of public opinion to effect political change and its lesson was not lost on others like O'Connell. The CMS's campaign of 1812–13 led by Wilberforce and others greatly exceeded the scope and extent of the abolition campaign and was considered by many in the evangelical camp to be a more important victory.

In the aftermath of that campaign three of the leading figures in the CMS organized a preaching tour in Ireland. Their first object was to promote the cause of the foreign missions and to organize an Irish branch of the Society, but they also had the effect of adding ballast to the revival currently gathering force in the Church of Ireland. The most obvious indication of this trend was the increase in the number of branches or auxiliaries of the HBS. From a total of eight such institutions founded between 1806 and 1812, the number had risen to fifty-three by the end of 1814.[18] This was a clear illustration that the Established religion was in the process of answering the challenge of the Methodists and Independent evangelicals, not only in the area of foreign missions but equally with developments on the domestic front.

Besides the increase in affiliated bodies, the HBS in this period received the support of several Church of Ireland bishops. The bishops of Cashel and Kildare openly gave their blessings to the aims of the Society, and Thomas Elrington, the bishop of Ferns and Leighlin, declared at a visitation in 1812 his wish that 'at no distant period we may expect to witness different auxiliary Bible societies established throughout the two dioceses'.[19] In the same year Elrington applied to the lord lieutenant on behalf of the ADV to import bibles and prayer books duty free.[20]

Even those who declined to support the HBS on grounds of churchmanship rejoiced at the launching of independent local organizations like the Cork Bible Society.[21] The younger evangelical clergy were also by this point beginning to make inroads in their drive for the cause of serious religion among the landed classes. The Rev. William Digby of Elphin, for example, was responsible for drawing into the movement two of the greatest names in the west of Ireland, Lord Lorton of Rockingham and the bishop of the diocese, Power le Poer Trench. In 1812 a branch of the HBS was founded in the Elphin diocese under the patronage of Lorton and Trench, and arrangements were made for depositories for the sale of bibles and testaments to be opened in the towns of Elphin, Boyle, Strokestown, Roscommon, Sligo and Ahascragh.[22] The combined influence of Lorton and Trench would form a nucleus from which the beams of the revival would radiate over all of Connaught in subsequent decades.

Increasingly landlords (and more particularly their wives) were coming forward to donate land for schools, to provide salaries for teachers, and to purchase quantities of bibles and testaments for free distribution. Nor were they exclusive in their support of the Church of Ireland. Lady O'Brien of Dromoland, for example, gave a hospitable reception to itinerant Baptists, was glad to subscribe to their society, and expressed her desire to open a female school on her estate.[23] Testimony to the popularity of the cause is also to be found in the voice of the opposition. Alarmed at the spread of Bible societies, a Protestant rector of County Kilkenny, Andrew O'Callaghan, warned that the distribution of bibles might produce 'less fruit than expected, [or] fruit in abundance but of a poisonous quality'. The liberal O'Callaghan questioned the value of circulating the Bible without note or comment. He also wondered why supporters of the scheme did not see fit instead to teach the peasantry the laws of their country and to circulate among them cheap editions of Blackstone or Littleton, which might help 'to humanize their minds, lessen their taste for nocturnal depredations, and quench their thirst for blood'.[24]

A more forceful argument was put forward by Rev. William Phelan, a convert from Catholicism and a rising star among those who defended the orthodoxy of the Established Church. Phelan argued essentially against the populist implications of the spread of Bible societies and compared the movement with the rise of democracy and 'mob rule' in the political world.[25] He objected, not to the distribution of the scriptures as such, but to this new mode of distribution that heralded interdenominationalism and lay involvement on a large scale.[26]

Still, the most obvious source of opposition to the evangelical missions was the Catholic clergy. On an individual level priests throughout the country had for years fulminated against itinerant preachers, Bible and tract distribution, and proselytizing schools. Among the bishops, however, there was for many years a tendency to minimize or ignore the implications of the evangelical crusade. As always, there were strong political motivations behind their long-held silence.

THE BIBLE SOCIETY CRISIS OF 1819–20

Between 1810 and 1818, when the evangelicals were assembling the institutional and ideological machinery necessary for a frontal assault on the sources of Catholic power in Ireland, the Catholic hierarchy remained judiciously silent about this challenge. The policy espoused by the bishops at this time was based on the twin pillars of political loyalty to the crown and religious toleration. To compensate for supporting O'Connell in his rejection of the relief bill, Catholic bishops made every effort to assuage fears of a Catholic ascendancy. Respect for the religious beliefs of non-Catholic denominations was encouraged, as were cordial relations between the different religious communities. This was the basis of the ecumenism of the pre-Emancipation period that has more than once been misinterpreted as a golden age of religious accommodation before the storms of the 1820s.[27]

On occasion, it appeared to some members of the Catholic episcopate, fealty to Rome took second place to the softening of religious differences within Ireland. At the height of the Bible War of 1824, Bishop Doyle of Kildare and Leighlin advocated a union between the Catholic Church and the Church of Ireland, somewhat reminiscent of the Gallican model in France.[28] He argued that doctrinal differences could be overcome by a conciliatory approach on the part of both churches, and that in any case it was 'pride and points of honour which keep us divided on many subjects, not a love of Christian humility, charity, and truth'. This opinion was shared by the archbishop of Tuam, Dr Oliver Kelly, who clearly thought Doyle's idea worthy of consideration but hoped that it might be preceded by a 'union in the bonds of Christian charity between the two religious groups'.[29]

These sentiments were undoubtedly a reflection of the bishops' concern over the chasm that sectarian controversy was creating between the religious communities. That a union might ever be brought to fruition was wishful thinking on the bishops' part. When Catholic bishops began to respond to the evangelical challenge, they defended their rights on civil and political as well as religious grounds. To withdraw while the debate was at its height in 1824–5 would be to concede defeat and to risk the loss of spiritual as well as temporal authority. As O'Connell had warned, without the strength of an independent Catholic Church in Ireland, the common people would be left, like so many sheep without a shepherd, 'to be crushed to death and destruction'. This was not idle rhetoric on O'Connnell's part, if one considers 'the elbowing aside of the resident population by powerful landowners' that was currently occurring in rural Wales and particularly in the Scottish Highlands where the poor were being cleared off the land in the name of economic efficiency and progress.[30] The economic and political dimension of the Catholic response to the evangelical challenge was therefore much more intense than the religious. While the evangelicals played against Catholics the trump cards of religious intolerance, the breaking of faith with heretics, and other forms of persecution believed to be sponsored by the Church of Rome, the Catholic defence was constructed upon a broad-based criticism of the establishment and its responsibility for the sufferings and miserable condition of the native population.[31]

The most significant feature of the Catholic defence was its origin in the lay-clerical alliance of O'Connell and the younger members of the episcopate. While older bishops like John Troy, archbishop of Dublin (1786–1823) deplored evangelical invective against Catholicism and prayed for peace between Catholic and Protestant, they were usually reluctant to go further. It was the younger members of the hierarchy, James Warren Doyle of Kildare and Leighlin (1819–34) and John MacHale of Maronia (1825–34) and later of Tuam (1834–81), who took the lead in defending their Church and its followers from attack. The alliance with O'Connell was mutually rewarding and highly effective. Throughout the 1820s, as the lines between the political and the religious became even more difficult to determine, this union developed into a behemoth of popular power that wrung Emancipation from a frightened government and legislature. Predictably, the successes of the alliance, instead of lessening evangelical anti-Catholicism, pushed it to greater heights of intensity.

The catalyst that set the wheels of Catholic reaction in motion was a letter in 1818 addressed to the Irish bishops by Cardinal Fontana, the prefect of Propaganda Fidei in Rome. Again, this was part of the larger canvas of religious affairs in England and Europe and not exclusively the product of particular conditions in Ireland. One of the consequences of the trammelling of papal power by Napoleon, and of the papacy's indebtedness to Britain for its major role in putting an end to his ambitions, was a tendency to ignore the challenge to papal power implicit in the launching of a Protestant missionary movement with global ambitions. This situation changed after the Congress of Vienna, when the Pope, as it were, woke up to discover the BFBS marching all over the globe, distributing its bibles in the vernacular and assisting modernizing rulers (such as Tsar Alexander I of Russia) with the organization of schools and the provision of educational material.[32] The first area in which the papacy locked horns with the BFBS was in Poland, where Catholic authorities opposed the starting up of Bible society activities in the Duchy of Warsaw, which was under Russian dominion at this time. Because the society had the official sanction of Tsar Alexander, it was able to proceed freely with its plans, which left the Catholic leader, Archbishop Raczynski, with no recourse but to appeal to Rome. Pius VII lost no time in informing Raczynski that 'these [Bible] societies are abhorrent to me, they tend to the subversion of the Christian religion, even to its very foundation; it is a plague which must be arrested by all possible means'.[33]

It was only a matter of time—given the dimensions and objectives of the evangelical mission in Ireland, and the diplomatic connections between Irish Catholic leaders and the Vatican over the vexed question of the veto—before news of what was afoot in Ireland reached the ear of Pius VII.[34] Indeed, for some time before the appearance of the Fontana letter, word was spreading through the evangelical grapevine that the Catholic bishops were about to issue an ordinance against the dissemination and reading of the Bible without note or comment.[35] Had Fontana's address never appeared, it is debatable how long the Catholic bishops in Ireland would have remained silent while their traditional territory was invaded by Protestant missionaries. What is certain, however, is that John MacHale took the Fontana letter as a clarion call to the Catholic clergy. In the famous *Hierophilus* letters of 1820–23, MacHale assumed the lead in responding to the evangelical challenge and raised the curtain on an era of bitter sectarian conflict that was to plague social, political, and religious life in Ireland for over half a century.

The primary purpose of MacHale's *Hierophilus* letters was to expose the proselytizing nature of evangelical societies involved in education and Bible distribution. The most damaging of the many charges issued by the author was aimed at the KPS, an organization hitherto free from the taint of proselytism and openly supported by many leading champions of the Catholic cause, notably Daniel O'Connell and Lord Cloncurry, both of whom sat on the board of directors.[36] From the time the Society was set up Catholics had willingly participated in the development of the system, and two places on the board of directors were reserved for Catholic laymen. By 1819–20, however, a number of trends that had been developing over the previous decade combined to heighten Catholic fears about the true nature of the Society's objectives. One was the ascendancy of evangelical opinion on the board of directors, in particular the influence of Thomas Lefroy, who was widely known as an intransigent foe of Catholic political demands and a staunch supporter of the evangelical crusade. Another was the growing suspicion that all educational and philanthropic enterprises directed by Protestants were working in unison towards the evangelization and ultimately the conversion of Catholics. The government's decision in 1816 to award an annual grant to the KPS, which would be deployed as the directors saw fit and would increase the scope of their activities enormously, lent further weight to the fear and indignation of Catholics.

The point on which O'Connell, no doubt taking his cue from the recent papal dictate, joined battle with his fellow directors of the KPS was the rule concerning the reading of the Bible without note or comment. This had not always been such a bone of contention for Catholics. In the early days many priests had even welcomed the idea. For those who were opposed to the reading of the Bible in the classroom a number of 'artful compromises' had been devised that enabled Catholics to meet the Society's demands without forsaking their religious principles. One of these involved the reading of the weekly scripture lesson from the altar on Sunday and the catechetical instruction of the pupils during school hours but outside the classroom. Another entailed what opponents labelled 'pious fraud', that is, the daily reading of the Bible in the classroom in the absence of the pupils.[37] By 1818, however, the 'Bible without note or comment' had entered political culture as a symbol of the triumph of Protestant Christianity over secularism and infidelity, and it was elevated as the standard under which British Protestantism would conquer the globe.[38] It is hardly surprising that Irish evangelicals would not tolerate the expenditure of government money on a school system that denied pupils access to this one fundamental source of Christianity. Neither is it difficult to see why Catholics interpreted this condition as a manifestation of Protestant cultural and political supremacy and saw it as part of a scheme to undermine the authority of their Church.

Moderate Catholics and their supporters in parliament went to great lengths to make a case for the damage that would ensue if the Kildare Place system were to fall apart over this issue. Catholic bishops were the first to agree that a want of education was responsible for so many of the country's problems, and that the Catholic body by itself could not meet the need as effectively as the KPS could. Archbishop Troy and Lord Fingal urged Charles Grant to recommend that the Catholic archbishop of Dublin be appointed to the board of directors and that an evangelical *Life of Christ* be made available as a religious text for use by Catholic children.[39] The great liberal champion of Emancipation, William Conyngham Plunket, turned to the wisdom of Montesquieu to make the point that 'nations have ever been tenacious of their customs, and the only mode of effecting change would be to engage the people themselves to change them'.[40] Lord Cloncurry (the well-known liberal peer who had been imprisoned in the aftermath of 1798 for his suspected sympathies with the republicans), claimed that the achievement of the Kildare Place schools was incalculable, and that children were not now being educated to display ingratitude and contempt for their parents, as had been the case in the Charter Schools.[41] Within a short time there was no room for moderates like Cloncurry, who struck a plaintive note years later in recounting the clash:

> As soon as the nature of the difficulty became fully known to me, I did all that in me lay to induce the society to remove it, and so, at all events, to secure for the children of the poor a free opportunity of moral and intellectual education. The committee, however, was in the hands of a few professional fanatics who in that day were in the habit of seeking, through Protestantism and piety, a ready road to the bench; and so my warnings were disregarded, and a barrier of bibles built up between the people and civilization. *Here was a new grievance brought above ground and within reach of professional agitators upon the other side; and as they did not at all lack the disposition to use it, a new war of opinion forthwith sprang up.* [my emphasis][42]

The most prominent of those 'not lacking the disposition' to attack the KPS was Daniel O'Connell. As a member of the board of directors, O'Connell had first voiced his opposition to the rule concerning the reading of the Bible at the annual general meeting in April 1819. He also convinced the other Catholics on the board, the duke of Leinster and Lord Cloncurry, that the system would never be acceptable to Catholics because of this condition. During the following year the controversy was heightened by the emergence of MacHale as an outspoken critic of every aspect of the evangelical mission. Both O'Connell and MacHale based their argument on the belief that the KPS could never win the approval of Catholics if its present constitution remained unchanged. In O'Connell's opinion government funds were not only being wasted but also abused. At the annual general meeting in February 1820 O'Connell proposed that the Society elect a subcommittee to examine the possibility of an alternative to the current reading of the Bible without note or comment. His proposal was answered by the assertion that this particular rule could be changed only with the assent of the directors—an unlikely event. At this point O'Connell resigned his seat on the board of directors. Shortly afterwards he publicly announced in the *Dublin Evening Post* how he had been 'rudely and violently hissed at merely for a necessary and unpresuming assertion of Catholic principles' on this occasion, and that this treatment was the result of the influence of a small number of partisans whom he described as 'the bitterest enemies of Catholic rights and religious liberty'.[43]

O'Connell's departure precipitated a crisis among Catholic and liberal Protestant supporters of the society. The duke of Leinster, an eminent Catholic peer and patron of the Society, assured the secretary, Joseph Devonshire Jackson, that he would not resign as patron but that he agreed with O'Connell that the Catholic poor were being deprived of education because of the regulation about the Bible.[44] Two years later, under the conviction that the Society had become more, not less, intransigent on this issue, he resigned his office as president of the Society.[45] The organ of liberal Protestant opinion, the *Dublin Evening Post*, likewise agreed that the Society had accomplished a great deal (particularly in its influence on popular reading matter), but that its work would be of no consequence if the priests chose to oppose it.

O'Connell's attack on the KPS and the consequent withdrawal of the leading Catholic patrons was a turning point in the history of Protestant–Catholic relations in Ireland. In the short term it meant that O'Connell and the hierarchy would participate in a government-sponsored educational system only on terms that recognized their right to an equal say in the moral and cultural agenda of the revolution in education. In the long run it secured the almost total exclusion of Protestant influence from Catholic educational concerns. The events of 1819–20 exposed a deep rift between the country's two main religious groups, a rift that widened over the following decade. O'Connell had taken the lead in confronting the evangelical mission, which he viewed as designed to prevent the emergence of the Catholic Irish as an independent and autonomous force. He interpreted the crusade as political rather than religious in nature, as yet another attempt to frustrate Catholic aspirations for full political freedom:

> In this country the bigots at last are compelled to confess among themselves the impossibility of long withholding emancipation; and so they would fain discount it. They would fritter away its value as much as they could; force failing them, they are resorting to every expedient of miserable and odious fraud. Look to the Kildare Place Society, established for the education of Irish children—necessarily of Catholic children. Watch their efforts and manouevres. See how insidiously they go to work—how active and persevering in their efforts to pervert the youthful mind of Ireland. Look to the tract distributors and the proselytizing societies of every name and shape, and say, do I allude to things of the imagination? Are not these facts, realities most necessary to be duly appreciated, attended to, and counteracted? How necessary, then, that we would show an equal vigilance with our enemies.[46]

The controversy over the use of the Bible without note or comment in the schools conducted by the KPS precipitated a furore at every level of religious life in Ireland. Sectarian conflict became more marked at the popular level, and clerical leaders of all denominations found it necessary to establish and defend their position with regard to the dissemination of the Bible. Even among the Catholic clergy, opinion on this subject was by no means unanimous. The greatest consternation, however, was experienced by some of the Church of Ireland bishops, who looked upon the rise of evangelical influence as the most serious threat to the security of their Church. When the policy of distributing the Bible without note or comment, 'thus encouraging the notion that men might draw their own religion from it',[47] was condemned by leading theologians of the Church of England, the bishops acting as vice-presidents of the BFBS (the majority of whom were Irish) were obliged to resign. The HBS suffered a similar exodus.

This did not mean, however, that the Irish bishops were about to abandon their sympathies for the evangelical movement. On the contrary, it appears that their support was strengthened as a result. What the resignations did encourage was the freedom of those members of the episcopate who disapproved of the evangelical crusade to voice their opinions in public. At his annual visitation in the cathedral city of Armagh in October 1821, the Protestant primate of Ireland, the Rev. Dr John George Beresford, issued a clear condemnation of the HBS. He urged that strict attention to the duties of clerical office was necessary if the Established Church was to be protected from 'the machinations so busily in operation to injure, if not destroy, the established religion [and] emanating, not from Dissenters who openly and candidly avowed their dissent, but from concealed enemies who were nourished and upheld by it, and were insidiously striving with all their energies to effect its destruction'.[48]

In the same year the outspoken bishop of Meath, Dr Thomas Lewis O'Beirne, penned a well-publicized letter to the rural deans of his diocese, warning them of the spread of Bible societies and the profusion of 'false teachers who are leading people astray' and 'who profess to teach articles of faith but actually pervert them by deducing doctrines which have been universally condemned as unknown in the Bible'.[49] Like most churchmen, O'Beirne did not object to the dissemination of the scriptures as such, but insisted that due regard be paid to the educational level of the recipients and to the need for careful instruction and interpretation of material that could easily be misconstrued by the uneducated. He also supported the idea that Bible reading form part of the education of Catholic children, but he believed that it should not be supervised by fanatics.[50]

While Catholic opponents of the Bible crusade were inclined to interpret the advocacy of the Bible without note or comment and the concerted efforts to proselytize among the Catholic population as one and the same thing, this was not true of the Protestant clergy. The thinking of Protestant clerics and laymen who opposed the evangelicals on grounds of churchmanship but who upheld the objectives of the Reformation movement is not as inconsistent as it appears. Legitimacy was the first concern of the Church of Ireland in the early nineteenth century, and no group defended it more strongly than the episcopal evangelicals. The cornerstone of the Church's legitimacy was its role as supreme arbiter in moral and spiritual matters. That it fulfilled this role only for a minority of the population was an unpleasant reality, one forcefully underscored by able Catholic polemicists, particularly Bishop Doyle of Kildare and Leighlin, who was goaded into action by the anti-Catholic polemics issuing from the ultra-Protestant press in the early 1820s.[51] The insecurity of the Church establishment was such that any offensive from the Catholic quarter was likely to guarantee a general outcry of 'the Church in danger'.

This is in fact what occurred after 1820. If the Church of Ireland could not justify its existence on grounds of representing the majority population, it could claim legitimacy on the basis of apostolic succession from the ancient Celtic Church founded by Saint Patrick. This was also a favourite theme of evangelicals, who liked to point out that the early Christian Church in Ireland had broken with Rome and had followed its own version of Christianity according to what it found in the scriptures.[52] This doctrine had a long-established pedigree, going all the way back to Wales in the sixteenth century when supporters of the Reformation had insisted that the independence of the ancient Celtic Church had set a precedent for separation from Rome and the founding of the Church of England.

The fact remained, nevertheless, that the allegiance of the majority population of Ireland still had not been won by the ecclesiastical body that claimed the mantle of Patrick: hence the demand for a 'reformation' both within the establishment and among the Catholic population. The evangelicals, both episcopal and Dissenting, had unquestionably laid the foundation of the new Reformation movement, and at the time when it was given official expression in 1822 by Archbishop Magee, they held control of all the agencies through which its expansion was to be attempted. Yet the movement was supported by many who were not evangelical in the sense of basing all spiritual authority on a personal interpretation of the Bible. Gradually, the finer points of distinction between the two groups became blurred, and evangelicals came to be defined, especially by their Catholic opponents, as all those who espoused converting Irish Catholics to the Protestant faith, regardless of the source to which they looked for spiritual authority, and regardless of whether they supported the distribution of the Bible without note or comment.

The evangelical attack on the Catholic religion in Ireland focused especially on the rule of the Catholic Church regarding the reading of the Bible. Once the lower orders were exposed to this true source of Christianity, the argument went, they would see for themselves the bondage of ignorance imposed on them by the servants of Rome. Once released from their state of spiritual darkness, they would proceed to moral and civil righteousness by casting off the rebellious spirit that inspired acts of outrage and murder. The alleged disavowal of the Bible by the Catholic priesthood was denounced as the most oppressive of the elements by which the peasantry were kept ignorant and poor.

To criticism of this kind the first response of Catholic leaders was to defend their Church's policy on the use of the Bible. In December 1819, obviously embarrassed at the recent uproar over the Fontana letter, Bishop Walsh of Waterford issued a pastoral letter urging his parishioners to study the scriptures.[53] Shortly afterwards, the Douay Bible, the version universally approved by the Catholic Church, was reprinted in a new translation, and a society was founded in Dublin for its distribution.[54] This was the beginning of a vast outpouring of literature, religious and otherwise, that was to issue from the Catholic press in the following decades in direct response to the taunts and threats of the evangelicals.

In contrast to Walsh, Archbishop Oliver Kelly of Tuam took his cue from the Fontana letter to warn about the dangers of distributing bibles among an illiterate people, and condemned the forces that 'under the semblance of a Christian education' were resorting to every art and insinuation 'in order to make proselytes among the innocent and unsuspecting youth of our communion'. Kelly used strong language to condemn the subversive workings of evangelical agencies, which, he claimed, were 'embellished with a thousand specious names but at the bottom of which evil lies concealed …. The enemies of our faith … like the serpent, creep and give death under flowers'.[55] The Catholic position on scripture reading and distribution was ably defended by Bishop Doyle, who accused the evangelicals of attempting to 'substitute the reading of the scriptures with the office of the ministry itself'.[56]

Although Doyle and his fellow ecclesiastics never departed from the principle that the dissemination of biblical material must be supervised by the priesthood, evangelical charges that they were consciously denying their followers access to the scriptures obliged the Catholic clergy to pay more attention to religious education. Catholic Sunday schools became very popular during the 1820s as a result, and enterprises like the breakfast institute set up by the Patrician Brothers in Galway 'for the purposes of opposing the inroads of proselytism' also had their origin in this period.[57] The revival underway in the Catholic Church was most obviously manifested in the increased construction of new churches, convents, monasteries and schools.

The evangelical challenge not only underlined the necessity for an educational system designed exclusively for the needs of Catholics, but it also ensured that control of such a system would be so jealously guarded that Protestant influence of any kind would be construed as an attempt to subvert the Catholic faith. It was some years, however, before this trend became starkly apparent. In the immediate context of the sectarian controversy of 1819–24 the preoccupation of the Catholic clergy was to prevent an explosive situation from developing among a peasantry beset by worsening economic conditions and driven by a millenarian belief that the downfall of the Protestant interest in Ireland was at hand.

MILLENARIANISM AND POPULAR SECTARIANISM

There was little cause for optimism about the general state of Ireland at the time of the outbreak of sectarian controversy in 1819–20. The conclusion of the Napoleonic Wars had ended a long period of prosperity in Britain and Europe generally, and the depression that followed had serious implications for the Irish economy, whose difficulties had to some extent been concealed during the boom years. The decline in grain and cattle prices, coupled with potato failure and increased population pressure, spelled disaster for many of the poorer peasants of the south and west.[58] Bad harvests in 1816 were the cause of widespread privation in many parts of Europe during the following winter and spring, but Ireland was unique for the degree of suffering and social unrest that accompanied the dearth. The effects of the scarcity began to be felt in the autumn of 1816 and increased alarmingly in the spring and summer of the following year. Reports of food riots began to arrive from several different parts of the country in the early months of 1817, with descriptions of hundreds of people breaking open grain and potato warehouses and preventing the transit of provisions.[59]

Deprivation during the spring months brought with it the spread of contagious fever, and the summer was marked by a raging typhus epidemic.

The impact of the crisis on a population that was already deeply alienated from the political system was a source of concern to all who were familiar with conditions in Ireland. It was the opinion of the bishop of Elphin, the Rev. Dr Power le Poer Trench, 'that there has hardly been a period in which a scarcity of food for the lower orders was more to be apprehended and the consequence of such scarcity from the difficulties and pressures of the times more to be dreaded'.[60] One estimate of the mortality for 1817 put the number of deaths at 40,000 out of an approximate population of four million, mainly the consequence of the fever epidemic.[61] As the quantifier, William Harty, claimed,

> Without fear of exaggeration, a more general epidemic never existed in any country of equal dimensions and population ... According to every account, whether public or private, not only every city, town, and village were visited by the disease but very few of the isolated cabins of the poor escaped.[62]

The recovery of the harvest and the waning of the typhus epidemic after the terrible summer of 1817 did little to mitigate the economic difficulties of spiralling unemployment and falling wages. The years 1821–3 were especially marked by economic hardship and warranted the organization of relief on a considerable scale. Public and private charity, however, did little to stem the tendency of country people to redress their grievances through the traditional means of the secret society. From 1821 to 1824 the Rockite movement (so called because its adherents styled themselves the followers of 'Captain Rock') spread throughout the south and south-west and visited upon landlords, large farmers, and the forces of the law an almost daily tally of murder and outrage. The Rockite movement in many respects contained elements common to such earlier agrarian rebellions as those of the Whiteboys (1761–5) and the Rightboys (1785–8). The recruitment of followers through the ritual binding of oaths, the raiding of houses for arms and ammunition, the use of various methods of intimidation and torture, and often the execution of hapless victims were all employed by the Rockites in their efforts to make the dominant classes bend to their notion of social justice. One of the singular characteristics of the movement, however, was a strain of millenarianism propelled by an anti-Protestant bias more vehement than in any of the earlier outbreaks of agrarian unrest.[63]

More than one commentator on the social history of Ireland in the nineteenth century has remarked on the absence or diminished influence of the millenarian vein in Irish culture.[64] This viewpoint is open to question. The spread of millenarian beliefs based on the prophecies of Pastorini, which coincided with the ascendancy of Captain Rock, contained many of the ingredients recognized as characteristic of a well-developed millenarian tradition. The theme common to all millenarian movements—that the current order would be overturned and the oppressed delivered from their state of bondage—was the central focus of the phenomenon. The governing impulse of Pastorini's disciples was the belief that the Protestants of Ireland would be swept away by a specific date, in this case 1825, after which the long-suffering Catholics would restore the golden age that they had enjoyed before the invasion of the heretical interlopers spawned by Henry VIII.

The ultimate source of this prophecy was an obscure treatise on the book of Revelation by an English Catholic bishop, Charles Walmesley, whose work entitled *A General History of the Christian Church* was published in Dublin in 1790 under the pen name of Signor Pastorini. Basing his predictions on a reading of the Apocalypse, he prophesied that a general punishment of heretics would occur about fifty years after 1771. In Ireland the date for retribution and deliverance was generally set at 1825, though the reasons for this are not clear. Neither is it evident at what point or on what account the widespread dissemination and acceptance of the prophecies began, though undoubtedly the phenomenon was connected with the impact of the famine and typhus epidemic in 1816–17. Apparently unknown at the popular level before 1817, Pastorini became a household name in Munster by 1822 and, according to contemporary evidence, kept the authorities and the Protestant population in a state of constant anxiety.[65]

The popular appeal of Pastorini was an embarrassment to the Catholic clergy, all the more so because the evangelicals were willing to seize upon it as further evidence of the covert anti-Protestant workings of the priests. There is nothing to suggest that there was any truth to this suspicion. The Catholic clergy as well as the Catholic middle classes were loath to ascribe any significance to the Pastorini phenomenon, and with good reason. As firm supporters of Emancipation, their first concern was to persuade the government and the Protestant establishment in Ireland of the loyalty and tolerance of the Catholic body. Nevertheless, the clergy often found it necessary to admit the influence and to condemn the prophecies from the pulpit and through pastoral addresses. Despite such opposition the prophecies enjoyed continued, though diminished, currency even after the year 1825 had passed without any remarkable happenings.

The mysterious appearance and rapid spread of the millenarian beliefs associated with Pastorini, and the way the challenge was met by both the Catholic Church and the Protestant establishment, provide important insights into the cultural conflicts at work in Irish society at this time. Some of the concepts used by social historians and anthropologists to explain the appearance of millenarian movements in different countries at various times can be usefully applied to Ireland in the early nineteenth century. The most obvious is the colonial hypothesis, which stresses the general conflict arising out of the pressures of a technologically advanced society on a backward or traditional one.[66] Forced acculturation and a sense of relative deprivation are particular aspects of the colonial experience emphasized in connection with millenarianism. With respect to forced acculturation, two trends may be noted as indicative of a society under threat. The first is the widespread demand for education, or the 'thirst for knowledge' that made its appearance in the late eighteenth century and was in full flower during the first two or three decades of the nineteenth. The second, a direct offspring of the first, was the general adoption of the English language during the same period.[67] It is not difficult to see in these complementary developments attempts at what A.F.C. Wallace called revitalization, 'the essence of [which] lies in the need of a society under excessive stress to either reinforce itself or die'.[68] This is yet another ingredient conducive to the growth of millenarianism.

Among the theories employed to explain the phenomenon, the two that bear most immediately on the Pastorini episode are those of relative deprivation and the disaster syndrome. In both the general and the particular senses, the causes of a deeply felt deprivation were abundant in Ireland, especially after 1815. Not only were deteriorating social and economic conditions working towards this end, but they were exacerbated by the perception of cultural loss exemplified in the reverence (so readily admitted to travellers, and so well documented by evangelical missionaries) that the country people bestowed upon their native language at precisely the same time that they were sloughing it off in favour of English. The fortunes of the campaign for Catholic Emancipation (seen by the common people as a general panacea for their many grievances), which reached its nadir between 1815 and 1822, would have added to the general sense of devastation. The events that drew these various forces together and filled the consciousness of the popular classes with hopes of their coming deliverance were probably the failure of the potato crop in 1816 and the famine and typhus epidemic of 1817. Disaster or the anticipation of disaster is one of the elements most common to millenarian outbreaks, according to Michael Barkun, because 'men cleave to the hopes of imminent worldly salvation only when the hammer blows of disaster destroy the world they have known and render them susceptible to ideas which they would have earlier cast aside'.[69]

The famine of 1821–2 witnessed the high-water mark of Pastorini's popularity in the counties most affected by agrarian violence, particularly Cork and Limerick. So widespread were the prophecies in County Limerick in the early 1820s that a government official who had specifically set out to collect information on what was currently influencing the minds of the peasantry in this disturbed region was obliged to admit: 'I do not think [that] in a single instance has one of these papers been produced to me that there was not a distinct allusion to the prophecies of Pastorini and the year 1825.'[70] The most alarming aspect of the prophecies for the authorities and for Protestants in general was the unbounded faith they appeared to inspire among the country people that, though Catholics were currently enveloped by a dark night of oppression, it had been ordained by God that the glorious morning of their deliverance was soon to dawn.

In 1822 an old woman on the earl of Rosse's estate in King's County told a Protestant neighbour to look to his life and property, for the Catholics 'were coming on like the waves of the Shannon, wave after wave, until they would overturn everything'. In the same area the belief was reportedly widespread that 'the Protestants will be green and flourishing in the evening, but that before midday they will be cut down and withered like thistles in the sun'. The words of a song that the earl of Rosse forwarded to his Tory colleague Lord Redesdale, designed to illustrate the fanaticism that had taken possession of the minds of the lower orders of Catholics, reveal similar metaphorical links between oppression and deliverance and night and morning:

> On yonder bower there grows a flower
> And some do call it Orange
> And over that there grows a branch
> That's called the blooming laurel
>
> It spreads so wide all in the night
> And in the morning early
> When the Orange rood it is cut down
> The laurel will flourish cheerly
>
> Our Church is built upon a Rock

Founded by our Saviour
And the gates of Hell that's roaring wide
Shall ne'er prevail against her

There is a spark *from France to Rome*
Call'd the glimmering light of Erin
There is a spark from France to Rome
Shall ne'er cease constant blazing

May it ne'er flinch, nor quench an inch
But still keep constant blazing
Till it destroy the race of Troy
King Henry's generation. [my emphasis][71]

Regardless of whether this kind of imagery originated in Catholic expectations or Protestant fears, what clearly emerges from these verses is the popular faith in the Catholic Church and religion as the source of strength and hope for the Irish, paralleled by the anticipated destruction of their enemies, less because they were English than because they were Protestant. The latter sentiment appeared repeatedly when Catholics who fraternized with Protestant neighbours were warned to have nothing further to do with them because their days were numbered.[72] The belief that the downfall of Protestantism in Ireland was imminent was not confined exclusively to the teachings ascribed to Pastorini. Anti-Protestant sentiments were also displayed in the Irish poetry of this period, along with appeals to the children of the Gael to stand firmly behind their Church. The verses of Anthony Raftery, for example, contain numerous references to the 'breed of Luther' as the cause of the country's afflictions.[73]

Sectarian animosity was not limited to popular ballads and poetry. Several of the outrages connected with the Rockite movement, such as the burning of Protestant churches, carried distinctly sectarian overtones. Open hostility was also shown by parents who withdrew their children from evangelical schools, and by crowds who threatened and harangued Bible preachers foolhardy enough to ply their trade in the streets. By 1824 the Catholic populace had been roused to the point that it was necessary to have troops stationed nearby to preserve the peace while the anniversary meeting of provincial auxiliaries of the HBS were in progress in the larger towns of the south and west. Hostility was returned in like manner by Protestants, especially those connected with the Orange Order. With the power of the State and the forces of the law in their favour, extremist Protestants did not find it necessary to adopt an apologetic tone in defence of their interests. Many, like the earl of Rosse, were ready to believe that if the Catholics rose, 'this time will be as memorable for the massacre of Protestants as 1641'.[74]

Protestant fears were fuelled in part by rumours that the plotters of rebellion were purchasing arms abroad to be used 'for the annihilation of reputed heretics which they are led to believe would be rendering a service to their God'.[75] When Sir Harcourt Lees, an ordained minister of the Church of Ireland with a penchant for incendiary polemics, warned the Catholic clergy that if they did not exhort the peasantry to surrender the 'immense store' of arms in their possession, he would consider it his duty 'to summon the Orangemen of Ireland to prepare themselves for the field, in defence of the king, the church, and the constitution', he gave expression both to the triumphalist attitude of Irish Protestants and to the fear inspired by rumours that the annihilation of Protestants was nigh.[76]

The atmosphere of fear and distrust generated by macabre prophecies at the popular level and verbal sabre-rattling among the upper classes inevitably found its way into the journalism and political discourse of the day. Eventually, it gave rise to new forms of expression in the controversial oratory of religious 'champions' and monster debates. What appeared to be at issue was cultural hegemony, in the struggle for which religion was to be the deciding factor. At one level the evangelical crusade may be seen as an attempt by the most intransigent and conservative of Irish Protestants to effect, through a process of cultural domination, the final stage of colonization. In the wider context of the global expansion of British power in the nineteenth century, however, it was a harbinger of the 'new imperialism' of the Victorian period in which the colonizing power would seek, through education and the legal system, to infiltrate and control the culture of the colonized, the better to improve their happiness and thus justify their subjection. India is the most familiar example of this model at work. As the colonizers of the seventeenth century had learned their trade in Ireland before they moved across the Atlantic, however, so too in the nineteenth would the model of cultural imperialism be attempted there before it was moved further afield.

At the heart of what Paul Johnson calls 'liberal imperialism' was a moral superiority manifested in the guise of a tolerant and benevolent attitude which demanded that 'the ruling power must respect the religion, customs, and susceptibilities of the ruled'.[77] This was precisely the line of approach followed by

English evangelicals when they considered the condition of Ireland. The tone was perfectly expressed by William Wilberforce at a meeting of the London Auxiliary of the Irish Society at the Freemasons' Tavern in 1822. Ireland had once been great and had known the experience of liberty and a national character, he argued. She had also known Christianity and Enlightenment before England had and, as many circumstances continued to remind her of her former superiority, she could not easily be brought to acknowledge her subjection. He also conceded that the Irish differed from the English in customs and manners, and that the term 'English' in their country evoked nothing but antipathy and alienation.[78]

Implicit in his address (and in the general line of English evangelical thought on the Irish question) was the idea that the time had come for this to change: through the benevolent impact of true Christianity, Ireland would be gently reinstated to a position of honour and respect in the 'moral empire' (the phrase is Paul Johnson's) governed by the blessings of British constitutional politics and the Protestant religion. Implicit also in this approach was an unspoken demand for the elimination of all obstacles that stood in the way of this necessary rehabilitation, not only the Catholic religion and its priests, who kept the population spiritually enslaved, but equally the attitudes and practices accumulated over centuries of neglect, which had given rise to the profligate economic habits of both rich and poor and which were seen as responsible for the alarming growth of a redundant surplus population. For the new moral order to succeed it was necessary that it be accompanied by a new economic order, one based on the interests of the market system in which sound fiscal management and the dictates of property-owners and the profit motive prevailed.

It was hardly a coincidence that the landlords who were most emphatic in their support of the evangelical crusade were also those committed to 'improvement' in the form of better estate management and stricter control over the lives of their tenants. This could be translated into the provision of schoolhouses, dispensaries and clothes depots and the supply of food in times of dearth. But it could also involve population clearance, for which an excuse, if such were deemed necessary, was provided in the refusal of parents to comply with the demand to send their children to schools in which the reading of the Bible was mandatory. The standard description applied to such landlords was that they were 'exterminators'—a term with roots in the eighteenth century but with particularly dangerous implications in the inflamed sectarian atmosphere of the nineteenth. The most hardline among them, such as Lord Lorton of Rockingham, were known to favour the introduction of Protestant tenants to lands from which Catholics had been evicted.

The obvious question that must be addressed in relation to the connection between evangelical religion and the new economic order is whether the trend that the marriage between the two had produced would have succeeded if its promoters had been allowed a free hand.[79] With manpower and financial resources—both public and private—available in abundance from Britain, and with colonies like Canada and Australia available for the transfer of displaced tenants, was it not realistic to think in terms of making Ireland a wholly Protestant country?[80] What stood in the way of such a projection, of course, was the Catholic Church with its claims to spiritual and pastoral leadership and its own revival underway after a century of the Penal Laws. By the early 1820s, the Catholic leadership was strong enough to provide effective resistance to the evangelical mission by laying claim to and finally taking control over the chief agency of modernization, namely, education. More than any other event it was the battle over education that brought the bishops and priests openly into the world of popular politics where they acted as a unifying force behind the campaign for Emancipation.

In reacting to the challenge of the evangelical moral crusade, the native population of Ireland rallied to the Catholic Church. The sense of identity, solidarity, and leadership it provided united the various manifestations of Catholic discontent, the rural followers of Pastorini as well as the politically sophisticated supporters of O'Connell, into an entirely new force in Irish life. In certain respects it is possible to see in this coalition the process of 'defensive structuring' to which Michael Barkun points, along with millenarianism and apathy or decay, as one of the three possible responses of the disaster-prone society.[81] Defensive structuring most frequently appears in the aftermath of a millenarian phase, but it requires certain conditions if it is to develop successfully: 'It can only work when it is possible to institute control of communications with other cultures, strong self-discipline, and authoritarian control.'[82] No student of Irish religious history would dispute the existence of 'strong self-discipline' and 'authoritarian control' as among the essential characteristics of Irish Catholicism as it took shape in the nineteenth century. Some would even see in these features the assumption, if not the imposition, of an entirely new culture in comparison with that of the eighteenth and early nineteenth centuries.[83]

The Great Famine of 1845–51, which is usually taken as a watershed in modern Irish history, has also been regarded as the dividing line between the traditional peasant religion of the pre-Famine years and the more severe and exacting 'Roman' Catholicism associated with Paul Cardinal Cullen in the post-Famine period. As Emmet Larkin has pointed out, however, all the ingredients of the 'devotional revolution' were in place before the Famine.[84] Recent research on the diocese of Kildare and Leighlin by Thomas McGrath has shown the extent of pastoral reform in the Catholic Church in the decades before the Famine, which suggests that the 'devotional revolution' was already well established by the 1820s in a part of the country fortunate enough to be endowed with a relatively wealthy population and a conscientious, energetic bishop.[85]

Unquestionably, the social consequences of the Famine contributed greatly to the ease with which the Catholic Church consolidated its position of moral and religious hegemony in Ireland. Nevertheless, the origins of its strength in this regard cannot be properly explained by pointing either to the devastating impact of the Famine or to the political designs of Rome. The integral role of Catholicism in Irish society can only be understood in the broadest sense against the background of economic and cultural transition that occurred throughout the British Isles during the period of modernization between 1750 and 1850. Although the historical roots of the phenomenon extend back to the seventeenth century, it was not until the early nineteenth century, particularly the decade of the 1820s, that the Catholic Church really assumed its role as the protector and defender of the interests of Irish poor. Its leaders understood the danger implicit in the combination of economic crisis and cultural destabilization threatened by the evangelical moral crusade. Colonial history is strewn with examples of indigenous peoples who fell prey to the destructive power of millennial visions, often informed by religious beliefs introduced from outside, during periods of destabilization brought on by imperial incursion. The Tai Ping rebellion in China (1851–64) falls into this category, as does the Cattle-Killing movement among the Xhosa of Natal in the 1850s and the Ghost Dance phenomenon of the Native Americans in the 1890s.[86]

In the crisis situation of the early 1820s Catholic leaders showed themselves able and willing to step into the breach and take control of the Emancipation movement, at once protecting the most vulnerable from self-destructive behaviour likely to draw the wrath of the authorities, and offering a sophisticated model of political action to the wealthier and more educated. In the final analysis what was at stake in the great cultural collision of the 1820s was what would define the terms on which the Catholic Irish would be integrated into the Union—whether they would join as free and equal subjects of a dominantly

Protestant Union in spite of their denominational allegiance to Rome, or whether they would submit to the dictates of a 'new moral order' that demanded a radical realignment of their cultural and religious traditions alongside a restructuring of the economy with its implications of population transfer.

The stakes involved were high, and resistance to the conservative Protestant vision for the future of Ireland was not for the faint-hearted, as witnessed by the belligerence that characterized the tactics and rhetoric of the Emancipation campaign. It was not for nothing that the evangelicals, the vanguard of triumphalist Protestantism, focused upon the priests as their greatest enemies. No calumny was too great to heap on the heads of those they considered artful, wicked and designing, who kept their flocks in a perpetual state of ignorance. Confronted with such a formidable Catholic bastion in the early 1820s, the evangelicals had no choice but to close ranks and abandon the subtleties and blandishments that had characterized their previous efforts. The time for open warfare had arrived.

–FIVE–
The 'Second Reformation' 1822–7

Had this charge, expressed as it was, in no very courteous or measured language, come from an individual less elevated in character and station than Archbishop Magee, it would have passed without any comment from us ... That he will be answered by disciples of Calvin and Knox, we believe ... That he will awaken the slumbering polemics of the Roman Catholic Church in Ireland we apprehend ... To us the charge presents itself as a political document of great importance.

Dublin Evening Post, 29 October 1822[1]

Another system was deemed more suitable to the objects of the establishment. Vituperation, virulence, fury—these were the weapons which they employed. Archbishop Magee had given the view hollow, and all the little dogs of the village—Tray, Sweetheart, and the rest, joined in the cry. War *ad internacionem* was declared. The Papists and their religion were to be crushed, not by brute force, for this, happily, is not yet in their power, but by slander, taunts, and insults, which the Catholics of Ireland would be less or more than men if they did not resent.

Dublin Evening Post, 24 January 1824[2]

There is seven times more Scripture reading in this parish and the adjacencies thereof than there was in the year prior to 1817; nay, if I would say fifteen times as much among certain classes; I believe few there would think me wrong.

JAMES EDWARD JACKSON[3]

ARCHBISHOP MAGEE AND THE CHURCH MILITANT

By 1822 it was abundantly clear that Protestantism in Ireland, encompassing both the religion and the class who professed it, was under serious attack. Between the ominous prophecies ascribed to Pastorini, the blatant outrages of Captain Rock, and the verbal thunderings of O'Connell and MacHale, Irish Protestants had good reason to be terrified.[4] The extent to which the abrasive anti-Catholicism of the evangelicals was responsible for arousing this hornet's nest of sectarianism was considerable. Undoubtedly, the struggle for Catholic Emancipation and the suffering associated with the economic crisis generated much anti-Protestant and anti-landlord sentiment. Nevertheless, the pervasive absorption with religious issues that characterized so much of the journalism and polemical literature of this period points to the overweening ambitions and divisive strategies of evangelical activists as a major source of the troubles.

The most obvious source of sectarian awareness at the popular level was the sheer amount of material in print. The mountain of bibles and tracts, controversial and otherwise, with which the country was now being deluged, along with the preaching of itinerant missionaries who travelled the country repeating the invective of their superiors in a more vulgar fashion, made the peasantry more familiar than ever with the age-old dispute between Protestantism and Rome. Knowledge thus obtained was put to the very opposite use from that intended by its distributors, and was often employed as evidence for the righteousness of the Catholic cause. As an employee of the Baptist Society lamented in 1819, after a period of scripture-reading in a Catholic district, 'the chief object of their conversation was controversy, wresting the Scriptures to support their superstitions'.[5] Even the Rockite movement had biblical overtones. In anonymous notices and particularly in the oaths binding members of the conspiracy together, the word 'rock' was used in association with the church of St Peter, 'founded upon a rock'.[6] The bibles, which the evangelicals hoped would teach the peasantry to live according to the word of God, were instead combed for any indication that the same word might sanction the extermination of heretics.[7]

In addition to the material disseminated by the various evangelical societies, the triumphalist tone of popular Protestantism became especially marked in a spate of new journals and newspapers that began to capitalize on the heady patriotism generated by the British victory over Napoleon. The standard fare of newspapers like *The Courier*, *The Patriot* and *The Watchman* was the moral supremacy of the Protestant faith, the cornerstone of British identity and patriotism, coupled with virulent attacks on Catholicism as the enemy within the gates, subversive and persecuting in intent, and committed to the triumph of slavery and superstition. The ugly tone adopted by the ultra-Protestant press was soon emulated in the streets, where assaults on Catholics were especially popular with supporters of the Orange Order, who appeared to be displaying a new sense of buoyancy and self-confidence. Certainly, in 1819, the *Dublin Evening Post* assessed the Orange authors of the 'Mountrath Declaration' as a set of men who 'in a period of comparatively profound peace, exhibit the banner of religious discord, rake up the embers of history, and make a declaration of interminable war against the Catholics of Ireland'.[8] Throughout the 1820s the *Dublin Evening Post* never ceased to lay the blame for the growing sectarian polarization on the ultra-Protestant propaganda that was disseminated with impunity under the nose of the government.[9]

By the early 1820s the effects of this propaganda were to be seen in abundance in the outbreaks of sectarian violence that frequently accompanied the commemoration of the Battle of the Boyne (12 July), the birthday of William III (4 November), and the Popish Plot (5 November). The mobilization of the forces that were used to preserve law and order during the Rockite disturbances—regular troops, yeomanry, and the new police force introduced by Robert Peel in 1822—was an additional provocation. In the consciousness of the Catholic population these forces were identified with Protestant supremacy, and their recruitment and deployment often served as avenues whereby Orange attitudes and tactics were introduced into areas that had never known sectarian discord.[10] Consider the incident reported in the *Dublin Evening Post* on 1 August 1822 that occurred in the village of Moylough in east Galway. There a convert by the name of Mannion, who had engaged in particularly riotous and inflammatory behaviour during the 12 July celebrations, had been allowed to go free because the chief of police, 'instead of trying to prevent insult and outrage, actually encouraged it'. According to the indignant *Post* reporter, Galway had always been renowned for good relations between Protestant and Catholic, 'until this year', when the chief of the police, a man 'paid for the preservation of the peace … encourages his men to violate it by his own example and provokes unoffending subjects to acts of a desperate nature by wantonly insulting them at their very doors'.[11]

The inflammatory tone of ultra-Protestant propaganda and the corresponding displays of vulgar supremacism in the streets was certainly fuelled and sustained by manifestations of Catholic defiance. But an even more potent source of fear and paranoia among the defenders of Protestant supremacy was the popularity of support for Emancipation among the educated elite in Britain and among liberal Protestants in Ireland. Ironically, the demise of Catholic leadership over the Quarantotti fiasco had left the field open for liberal Protestants to assert themselves. By 1820 the movement had united the various strands of liberalism that had survived the catastrophe of the 1790s—William Drennan of the United Irishmen, for example, as well as Henry Grattan of the 'Patriot Parliament'—into a powerful bloc of opinion that enjoyed widespread support among Britain's educated elite, and particularly among those who considered themselves the guardians of public morality such as William Wilberforce and Charles Grant. With the death of George III and the accession of George IV in 1820 there was hope that Emancipation would be carried by an enlightened legislature. The emergence of the youthful and dynamic William Conyngham Plunket as the leading spokesman for the liberal Protestant Emancipationists, following the death of Henry Grattan in 1820, put fresh enthusiasm into the movement. The decision of George IV to visit Ireland in the summer of 1821 gave optimists the impression that Emancipation would be carried.

This combination of Protestant leadership and royal sympathy had entirely the opposite effect on ultra-Protestant sympathizers, however, and inflammatory sectarianism in word as well as deed became the order of the day throughout the spring and summer of 1822. The celebration of the Orange festivals during the summer of that year was of such a character that the *Dublin Evening Post*, always in the forefront of the liberal cause, warned that they would 'steep Ireland into deeper horrors than any with which she has been hitherto scourged'. They interpreted the barefaced triumphalism of anniversaries in Enniscorthy and Bandon, where Orange incendiaries were often joined by troops of the militia who gloried in playing sectarian tunes and other provocative behaviour, as evidence that the Orangemen 'were about to enter into some new confederation'.[12] As the events of the latter part of 1822 were to reveal, they were not entirely mistaken in their assessment of the situation.

Into the cauldron of heightened sectarian tension dredged up by sectarian rivalry and inflammatory propaganda, an incendiary device of an entirely different kind was dropped from an unexpected quarter. On the occasion of his inauguration as archbishop of Dublin at St Patrick's Cathedral on 22 October, the Rev. Dr William Magee asserted openly that the Church of Ireland was the only legitimate ecclesiastical body in Ireland, and that its members should embrace a new mission to assert this orthodoxy and bring the general population into the fold. Because of his stature as the head of the country's most important diocese, it appeared to contemporaries that he had not only invited open conflict with the Catholic bishops but also placed himself and his Church at the forefront of the crude anti-Catholic crusade of the Orange Order. As the *Dublin Evening Post* observed, up until this time the fulminations of extremist Protestants had been ignored by upper-class Catholics, who 'provided a non-conducting medium between the fury of frantic polemics at one extremity of the chain and the irritable and volcanic passions of the multitude at the other'.[13] But Magee's sermon was seen as a turning point after which the highest echelons of the Church of Ireland came to be infected with the confrontational style of Orange supremacism. As George Ensor remarked of the sermon:

> This, observe, was not uttered at a subscription meeting to convert Dissenters and Catholics; nor after a charitable dinner to raise contributions for the sons of the clergy; they were not rash words, improvidently wrung from a petulant, presumptuous man; no, they were the *aura dicta* pronounced ... in a charge to the clergy of two dioceses—subjected to revision, after much popular animadversion and published at the unanimous request of the *influential* clergy (the Doctor's favourite epithet) of Dublin and Glendalough.[14]

Some years later, Magee himself asserted that there had been nothing extraordinary in his charge, certainly nothing that he had not said many times before. In light of similar opinions expressed on other occasions by his episcopal contemporaries, this rings true. What set the incident apart was the decision of Bishop Doyle and other Catholic prelates, including Dr Patrick Curtis, archbishop of Armagh and primate of Ireland, and Dr John MacHale, to respond publicly to Archbishop Magee's claims concerning the rights and duties of the Established Church. This was a radical departure on the part of the Catholic clergy and marked the beginning of officially sanctioned Catholic resistance to Protestant ambitions to extend the principles of the Reformation in Ireland.

Why did Archbishop Magee choose this particular time to give official sanction to the Reformation movement? The answer must be sought in the nature of the campaign for Catholic rights, which increasingly emphasized legal and constitutional issues. All supporters of Catholic claims based their charges against the establishment on legal grounds, and it was surely no coincidence that the leading spokesmen for the movement were themselves lawyers.

Selina Hastings, countess of Huntingdon (1707–91).

Gideon Ouseley (1762–1839).

Methodist Meeting House, The Mall, Castlebar, County Mayo. Built by the earl of Lucan. The foundation stone was laid by John Wesley in 1785.

Robert Jocelyn (1788–1870), 1st Viscount Jocelyn (later Lord Roden). Artist: George Harlow, 1817.

James Warren Doyle (1786–1834), bishop of Kildare and Leighlin (1819–34).

Tollymore House, Castlewellan, County Down.

Robert Edward King (1773–1881), 1st Viscount Lorton.

View of Rockingham House and Lough Key, Boyle, County Roscommon, from John D'Alton's *Annals of Boyle* (Dublin 1845).

Dr William Magee
(1766–1831), archbishop
of Dublin (1822–31).

Dr John MacHale (1791–1881),
archbishop of Tuam (1834–81).

№ 1

A CHARGE

DELIVERED

At His Primary Visitation,

IN

ST. PATRICK'S CATHEDRAL, DUBLIN,

ON THURSDAY THE 24TH OF OCTOBER,

1822.

BY

WILLIAM MAGEE, D.D. F.R.S. M.R.I.A., &c.
ARCHBISHOP OF DUBLIN.

Dublin:
GEORGE & JOHN GRIERSON AND MARTIN KEENE,
HIS MAJESTY'S PRINTERS.
1822.

Frontispiece of Archbishop Magee's sermon in St Patrick's Cathedral, Dublin, 24 October 1822.

A VINDICATION

OF THE

RELIGIOUS AND CIVIL PRINCIPLES

OF THE

IRISH CATHOLICS;

IN A LETTER, ADDRESSED TO

HIS EXCELLENCY

THE MARQUIS WELLESLEY, K. G.

LORD LIEUTENANT GENERAL, AND GENERAL
GOVERNOR OF IRELAND, &c. &c.

SECOND EDITION.

BY

J. K. L.

[James (Doyle) R.C. Bishop of Kildare & Loughlin]

AUTHOR OF "LETTERS TO HIS GRACE THE PROTESTANT ARCHBISHOP
OF DUBLIN;" OF "ESSAYS ON DOMESTIC NOMINATION," &c. &c.

"*Rerum ego vitia collegi non hominum, sublato enim tyranno tyrannida manere video.*" CIC. EP. LIB. 14, AD ATTICUM.

DUBLIN: PRINTED
BY RICHARD COYNE,
4, CAPEL-ST.
BOOKSELLER, PRINTER, AND PUBLISHER TO THE ROYAL
COLLEGE OF ST. PATRICK, MAYNOOTH.
1823.

Frontispiece of Bishop Doyle's *Vindication of the Rights and Civil Principles of the Irish Catholics* (Dublin 1823).

Memorial to Bishop Doyle by John Hogan in Carlow Cathedral. George Petrie wrote in 1840 that 'the subject is the last appeal of a Christian prelate to heaven for the regeneration of his country'.

Memorial to John Jebb (1775–1833), bishop of Limerick (1822–33), in St Mary's Cathedral, Limerick.

View of the Church of Ireland, Ardcarne, County Roscommon, from John D'Alton's *Annals of Boyle* (Dublin 1845).

Postcard of the Achill Mission from the early twentieth century.

Since the passage of the Act of Union in 1800 a clear-cut body of liberal thought had been developed to the effect that Catholicism was compatible with constitutional freedom, and indeed that if this freedom counted for anything, Catholics could no longer be denied political equality. Increasingly the position of lay theorists like Denys Scully and Theobald McKenna was reinforced by clerical opinion, particularly that of James Warren Doyle, the youthful bishop of Kildare and Leighlin, whose acronym of 'JKL' (James of Kildare and Leighlin) would shortly become a household word.

In addition to the legal weapons that were being sharpened by able Catholic defenders, during the early 1820s the subject of tithes was again brought into the public sphere by the spread of the Rockite disturbances, and resolutions for tithe commutation began to issue from the highest reaches of the political world.[15] Once again the cry of 'the Church in danger' began to be invoked, and once again another scion of the Woodward family spoke for his community, only this time the complaint included the fear that the Established Church

> had as much to fear from parliament as from the whiteboys ... The landlords have allowed the results of absenteeism and rackrenting to fall on the backs of the poor clergy and the 'saints' are open to any charge that might be made against us. The Irish Church is in great danger and government ministers have given up entirely, saying that changes in the Irish Church need not involve the Church of England ... I consider this as letting slip the dogs of war against us.[16]

In light of such fears Magee's sermon may be seen as an attempt to regain the high moral ground for the Church of Ireland and its followers, from the legal and constitutional reformers on the one hand, but equally from the criticism and challenge of evangelical purifiers on the other. In assuming the mantle of the Reformation movement, Archbishop Magee was not so much pushing aside the claims of the evangelical crusade as jumping on board and taking over the reins in the name of the Church of Ireland.[17]

While Magee's strident declaration that the Church of Ireland should assert its supremacy as the 'national' church may have been impolitic in the charged political climate of the early 1820s, it was an opinion that was not without support among many of his colleagues. Magee was one of a group of energetic and reforming churchmen who were elevated to the episcopal bench in the first quarter of the century, and who had come to recognize that the new circumstances afforded by the Union afforded an unprecedented opportunity for the established religion to extend its claims in Ireland. Those circumstances included the union of the churches of Ireland and England and the commitment of the government to support a program of church-building and an increase in the ministry. The trend was underpinned by the growing religiosity generated by the reaction to events in France. This, and the competition and example of Independent evangelicals, fuelled the movement towards episcopal orthodoxy in the period in question. There is also abundant evidence that the Church of Ireland was becoming increasingly defensive both of its right to be a national church and to work towards orthodoxy in religious life, which was becoming increasingly common in England and Scotland.[18]

Until the 1820s, however, reformers in the Church of Ireland were content to proceed quietly in the manner exemplified by John Jebb. But the politics of the early part of that decade did a great deal to change this and to compel the most committed of the new bishops into a more open and confident assertion of their aims and objectives. The inaugural sermon of Bishop Jebb in 1823, for example, echoed the same theme of increased attention to pastoral duties and included the implication that the Church of Ireland clergy should seek to include the Catholic population in its mission.[19] In a similar vein, at his triennial sermon in Tuam Cathedral in 1822, Archbishop Power le Poer Trench addressed Catholics present in a polite but strong rhetorical tone as to why they should consider the doctrines of the reformed faith superior to those of Rome.[20] Magee's sermon was unusual only in its intemperate attack on the Catholic body as being 'a Church without a Religion'—a comment that was immediately recognized by the *Dublin Evening Post* as not only insulting but dangerous in the highly combustible sectarian atmosphere of the time.

In assessing the impact of the famous 'antithetical' sermon, Magee's personality should also be taken into account. Prior to his appointment as archbishop of Dublin, he had enjoyed an outstanding scholarly reputation as a fellow of Trinity College, famed for his rhetorical flourishes and for his good opinion of his own abilities. Through his outspoken support for the political ambitions of his friend William Conyngham Plunket, he had earned a reputation as a liberal in politics. It was to this reputation—if W.J. Fitzpatrick is to be believed—that he owed his appointment as archbishop.[21] But if the subject of his visitation sermon was any indication of his political leanings, he had apparently fallen into line very quickly with the evangelical ideal of religious duty and its accompanying spirit of Protestant partisanship.[22] Indulging in the love of antithesis that had characterized his oratory since his student days, Magee preached at length on the two great obstacles confronting the Church of Ireland:

> We, my Rev Brethren, are placed in a station in which we are hemmed in by two opposite descriptions of Christians: the one possessing a Church without what *we* can call a Religion and the other possessing a Religion without what *we* can call a Church: the one so blindly enslaved as to suppose infallible Ecclesiastical authority, as not to seek in the Word of God a reason for the faith they possess; the other so confident in the infallibility of their individual judgment as to the reasons of their faith that they deem it their duty to resist all authority in matters of religion. We, my Brethren, are to keep free of both extremes, and holding the Scriptures as our great charge, whilst we maintain the liberty with which Christ has made us free, we are to submit ourselves to the authority to which he had made us subject. From this spirit of tempered freedom and qualified submission sprung the glorious work of the Reformation, by which the Church of these countries, having thrown off the slough of slavish superstition, burst into the purified form of Christian renovation.[23]

These adverse references were unmistakably directed at the Catholics and the Presbyterians. As had been predicted by the *Dublin Evening Post*, neither group was prepared to tolerate such an obvious insult without striking back. The Presbyterian response, however, was overshadowed by Bishop Doyle's reply on behalf of the Catholics, which appeared two weeks later in the *Dublin Evening Post*. Doyle's decision to enter into public controversy with such a distinguished prelate of the Church of Ireland was an unprecedented move for a Catholic bishop. Magee had argued that the Established Church possessed the sole legitimate claim to apostolic succession in Ireland. In the opinion of the historian W.D. Killen, this was a fatal mistake on the archbishop's part. By taking his stand on what Killen called 'the essentially popish ground of so-called apostolical succession' instead of 'the impregnable foundations of Protestantism', Magee had placed himself at the mercy of the young prelate of Kildare, who 'had long been furbishing his weapons of theological warfare'.[24]

Doyle's reply to Magee's charge was equal to its author's reputation as the rising star of the Catholic episcopate and had the immediate effect of infusing an extraordinary sense of confidence into the Catholic body as a whole. In a formidable display of legal, historical and theological learning, Doyle took Magee to task on the apostolic-succession question. Not content with having demolished his adversary's reasoning in this matter, he went on to declare that the property of the Church of Ireland was held not by dint of any divine sanction, but 'only by virtue of the civil law, and that law is penal—*highly* penal'.[25]

Like O'Connell, Doyle was capable of grasping and highlighting the contradictions between the privileges enjoyed by the Church of Ireland and the moral framework of the legal system. This was especially true with regard to tithes. 'But what', enquired Doyle, 'does the establishment give the peasant in return for his tithe?' Confident that the only truthful reply was 'nothing', he advised his opponent not to accuse of injustice anyone who might think differently

> as you will never succeed in convincing your countrymen that they are conscientiously bound to pay for what they don't receive ... There is not a peasant in Ireland who does not know, as well as Ulpian, that commutative justice requires an equivalent to be given for what is received.[26]

This last criticism had implications that went far beyond the purely spiritual realm, since it vindicated the right of Catholics to withhold tithes and consequently threatened the very foundations of the Established Church. To stalwart defenders of the Protestant interest like Magee and Sir Harcourt Lees, it meant that the sword of Catholic tyranny, which had been glittering in the scabbard for so many years, was now drawn and ready to strike.

The contest between Doyle and Magee let loose a flood of polemical treatises from the pens of less renowned, though hardly less vigourous, apologists for the respective denominational interests. Local and national newspapers became forums for religious controversy, and Bible society meetings were turned into occasions for whipping up the enthusiasm of militant Protestants. While the controversy between the bishops was in full swing, sectarian hostilities at the popular level became more open and aggressive. One notorious incident associated with the controversy was the clandestine desecration of a Catholic altar in Ardee, County Louth, with a calf's head, understood to be a symbol of gross insult and ridicule.[27]

A more disturbing prospect for the Catholic clergy, however, was the strength of the Protestant response to Magee's proclamation of a reformation crusade. Before 1822, evangelical overtures to the Catholic population had not gone further than Bible and tract distribution and the enticement of children to schools run by one or another of the various societies. Between 1822 and 1827 this system was supplemented by more direct efforts to increase the number of converts from Catholicism. In line with Magee's proclamation that the Established Church was under a severe and immediate obligation to unfurl the banner of the Reformation, the making of converts assumed pre-eminent importance and became the source of particularly bitter hostility between the two major religious groups.

MORAL ASCENDANCY AND THE LANDED ELITE

The 'Second Reformation' of 1822–7 revealed the degree to which the evangelical message had fallen on fertile soil among the landed aristocrats of the Church of Ireland. The intensification of the Reformation movement after 1822 was strongly linked to its popularity among the great landowning families, and support from this quarter was largely responsible for its institutionalization at the local level. Although the patronage of the nobility was also an essential element in the growth and popularity of the evangelical movement in Britain, most visitors from Britain were amazed at the extent to which it prevailed in Ireland. The great Cambridge revivalist, the Rev. Charles Simeon, confided to a colleague following an extended visit in 1822:

> You, who know the precise line in which I walk at Cambridge, would be astonished, as I myself was, to find earls and viscounts, deans and dignitaries, judges, etc. calling upon me ... I dined at the Countess of Westmeath's and met Judge Daly and many other characters of the highest respectability.[28]

Evidence from a variety of sources, not least the critical and satirical, suggests that the 'spiritual flooding' that Elizabeth Bowen spoke of as having occurred sometime around 1817 was by no means an isolated incident. Indeed, the amount of attention that the phenomenon was attracting prompts the question whether what was taking place was not in fact the equivalent of an 'awakening' among certain sections of the Church of Ireland community. What kind of evidence should we use for this? Clearly, the enthusiasm of itinerant preachers about the progress that was being made among the landed classes might be explained as congratulatory self-indulgence; but there is simply such an abundance of it for the years in question (roughly 1816–21) that it cannot all be coincidental. James Edward Jackson's annoyance at the 'bustling activity' and 'proselytizing spirit carried even to obtrusiveness' of the HBS is clearly suggestive of revivalist excitement:

> In point of fact the Bible Society everywhere presents itself to your eye, in the Anniversary and the Committee Meeting, in the city and the village, in advertisements in the newspapers and in placards on the walls. It crosses you in your walks, with troops of female associates; it is the theme

of your social parties, and of your domestic circles. It ascends your pulpits, and 'canvasses' for charity at your doors. You repel it, and it returns; you make objections, and it shifts its ground, until at length wearied out with importunity and perhaps unconsciously moved by insinuations against your zeal, you give the sanction of your name to measures which you secretly dislike, that you may not be singular, or that you may be quiet.[29]

Several of the major figures who were to dominate the Church of Ireland's evangelical wing over the next several decades in one degree or another underwent a conversion experience during this period, and memories recorded later in the century invest these years with a special significance. More significantly, millenarian beliefs associated with perfecting the world in anticipation of the Second Coming began to gain serious followers among prominent aristocratic families like the Rodens of County Down and the Powerscourts of County Wicklow.

In Dublin the celebration of the 'April meetings', as the week-long series of annual meetings of the various evangelical societies came to be known, provided remarkable evidence of the popularity of evangelicalism among the upper classes. A correspondent of the Baptist Society commented in 1821 that:

> not less than 2,000 people attended, and these of the first respectability ... Many of the speeches of the bishops, clergy, and laymen were excellent, and I believe not exceeded by any meeting in London.[30]

In the provinces the sense of drama and expectation was equally pronounced. Following a visit to Lord Lorton's demesne at Rockingham in 1821, where he preached to a crowd of two or three hundred, the Baptist missionary Isaac MacCarthy wrote:

> I cannot describe the interest which seems to be excited in the minds of the people to hear the word of God all through this neighbourhood, particularly in the town of Boyle. The crowd was so great that we deemed it expedient to prop the left of the Sessions House, as some were apprehensive of danger if it were left without it.[31]

The Lorton estate was already well known as the centre of a local revival in north Roscommon, but the Lortons were by no means alone as prominent local sponsors of the evangelical crusade. By 1822 there was a growing network of great landed families who subscribed to the objectives of the Reformation movement and who exerted enormous influence, locally and nationally, because of their social and political prominence. Who were these families, and what distinguished them from their peers who chose not to answer the evangelical challenge?

In one of his attacks on the clergy of the Established Church, Bishop Doyle had pointed to 'the saints' (i.e. the evangelical clergy) as having disseminated the hostile anti-popery spirit among 'the little gentry with whom they associate'.[32] This was undoubtedly true, but such practices were by no means confined to the smaller gentry, as the names of Farnham, Roden, Powerscourt, Lorton, Manchester, Mountcashel and Gosford in the front ranks of the evangelical family roster testify. Many of these great evangelical families were related through marriage, and in some cases their prominence in the movement could be attributed to the influence of a younger son, nephew, or son-in-law trained for clerical orders at Trinity College.

That the cultivation of habits of personal piety, duty and responsibility was the rising fashion among the youthful aristocracy is powerfully evident in one of the few personal accounts to have survived from this period, the diary of Lady Anne Jocelyn of the Roden family. It is strewn with references to the great evangelical families of Dublin and Wicklow who made up the young girl's social circle—the Parnells, Synges, Le Despencers, Dalys, La Touches, Howards and Wingfields, but her private musings reflected her absorption with religious issues after the death of her beloved sister, Fanny, who had married into the Powerscourt family. Her preoccupation with death and fear of the day of judgment was never far from her thoughts, not only on occasions when she has been exposed to death but often quite spontaneously, as, for example, with the entry for 22 May 1812:

> I was standing on a dangerous rock today, and it occurred to me, suppose I tumbled in and was drowned, was I fit to die suddenly in that kind of way. Oh I fear not, what an awful idea death is; I trust my heavenly father will support me at that dread hour. How guarded all my thoughts and actions should be.[33]

It was this mentality that pushed her to engage in good works on her father's estate at Tollymore in County Down. She persisted in ministering to the needs of the poor even as the shadow of death hung over her and finally claimed her in 1822, at the age of twenty-one.[34]

Contemporary critics frequently pointed to the relationship between women and clergymen as the basis of much of the fanaticism that appeared to take hold of otherwise reasonable men. In a thinly disguised account of the Reformation movement on the Roden estate in County Down, Eyre Crowe Evans drew a revealing and humorous picture of this feminine–clerical alliance in his novella *Old and New Light* in 1825. Of the local evangelical curate, Mr O'Syng, he observed:

> His proselytes in and about Ardenmore were numerous, especially among the weaker sex, whom his pathos, and cambric handkerchief moistened with pulpit tears, never failed to move. Even the good squires, who slumbered or snored through the young apostle's preaching, heard his doctrines subsequently repreached to them by domestic missionaries with whom for peace-sake it was always best to coincide.[35]

The role of women in the movement was of unquestionable importance, even if it did provide critics with an excuse for treating the subject flippantly.[36]

The most essential reason for the commitment of Irish Protestants to evangelicalism, however, was an unbounded confidence that adherence to duty and responsibility as directed by the teachings of the Bible would secure their position as property owners and the natural leaders of society. This attitude was in keeping with that of their British counterparts, who had survived the upheaval created by the democratic threat of the late eighteenth century and the Napoleonic Wars and were currently in a position of greater strength than ever. The confidence generated by political victory and an exceptionally strong economic foundation (guaranteed by the demand for agricultural produce stemming from the war effort and the rising population of the industrial cities) allowed the landed aristocracy to believe that providence had indeed favoured their way of life and that hierarchy and tradition had won out over democracy and infidelity.[37] The duty of this class in Ireland, as expressed in 1822 in the *Christian Observer* was:

> To encourage the agriculture, commerce, and manufacturers of Ireland, to give her an able and upright magistracy, a resident gentry, and a resident and pious clergy; to raise the degraded condition of the peasantry and enable them to enjoy a fair portion of the produce of their labours, to allay the religious dissensions which pervade every part of the country and embitter the quiet of every hamlet within it; and to devise a substitute for the tithe system, that everlasting source of discontent and disorder, are a few, and but a few, of the obligations imposed upon them [the rulers of the country].[38]

To this litany of desirable objectives, Irish evangelicals would have added, as a prerequisite, the eradication of Catholicism and priestly influence, which they held responsible for the wretched state of the country in the first place.

Evangelical myopia about the cause of Ireland's lamentable condition and the cure necessary to relieve it gave rise to a whole new series of derisive appellations. As William Urwick complained, 'all workers for the gospel were contemptuously and sneeringly called in common "Methodists", "New Lights", "Swaddlers", etc., as best suited the taste, or slang, or convenience of their opponents'.[39] In 1837 the diarist Humphrey O'Sullivan referred to the 'wretched swaddlers [*suadleirige beaga*] who are trying to see whether they can wheedle away the children of the Gael to their accursed new religion'.[40] The contemptuous use of the word 'saint' had a long history, extending back to the Puritan revolution of the mid-seventeenth century and currently enjoying a new lease on life in association with William Wilberforce and his followers in the Clapham Sect. It was used with equal vigour in Ireland.[41] The most popular epithet for Irish evangelicals during the 1820s, however, was 'New Light', a term that had come into general vogue in America in connection with the anti-establishment revivalist movement that had originated in New England.[42]

In *Old and New Light*, Crowe Evans evidently did not feel the need for a subtitle to inform his readers that the work was a study of the conflict between the easy-going traditional followers of the Church of Ireland and the ill-founded and socially disruptive enthusiasm of the evangelicals. His protagonist, the amiable Charles St George, cuts an implausible figure (considering the book was published in 1825) as a naïve, well-meaning young clergyman, fresh from Trinity College, who arrives in County Louth completely unfamiliar with the New Light phenomenon. His innocence provides an opportunity for the writer to present us with the opinions of the high-spirited younger members of a local gentry family, the Penningtons, as well as with those of the tormented Harry Lowrie, heir to the Laylands estate, where the newly acquired sanctity of his sisters and parents has literally driven him out of the place. Upon enquiring what the New Light marvel was all about, St George is greeted with the following reproachful comments:

> 'When Mr. St. George has spent an evening at Laylands', said Miss Mary Pennington, 'he will know perfectly well what New Light means. Why, they would not allow dancing there on any account!'
>
> 'Of reading a novel they would abhor the thought', cried Miss Pennington, equally horrified at such rigidity, 'and their pianos would not stoop to music less grave than "Let the bright Seraphim", or "Angels ever bright and fair".'
>
> 'For heaven's sake, Louisa, don't mention that Seraphim', cried Harry.

'I have heard that tune so frequently of late that Shaun caught me whistling it to the hounds last week and asked me from what witch I had learned that confounded *cronon* [wail] that was setting the dogs off their sport'. 'My father, Sir', continued the young man to St George, 'has sold his hunter the other day and gave away his pack, not to me or to any honest sportsman who would use them—he should distribute them in separate couples to every poacher about the country, spoiling the sport that he now thinks it a sin to partake of—now that's what I call New Light'.[43]

One of the phenomena strongly underlined in Crowe Evans' novella is the popularity of the evangelical movement in the counties of north Leinster.[44] While the geographical expansion of the movement did not conform to any clear pattern, some areas of the country were definitely more susceptible than others to the spread of religious revivalism. This was particularly true of areas that had experienced heavy Protestant settlement and where a substantial Protestant middle class helped to bolster the confidence of the landed elite. The influence of evangelical landlords was heaviest in an arc that stretched from the Atlantic to the Irish Sea across Sligo, north Roscommon, Cavan, Monaghan, Armagh, Louth and south Down. This was the southern flank of the Ulster plantation, a border country where sectarian passions were never far below the surface, and where the triumphalism of the resident gentry reflected a frontier mentality. This was also the territory where the Orange Order had taken root most firmly in the 1790s, and many of the leading gentry who had been associated with the Society since the 1790s would emerge as leaders of the 'Second Reformation' movement in the 1820s. To a certain extent this was also true of Wicklow, Carlow and Wexford, where Protestant settlement was much more extensive than in any other part of the country outside the north-east.[45]

Marriages between the great evangelical families in these areas were very common. The most powerful champions of evangelicalism in Leinster—the Powerscourt family of Wicklow—maintained strong connections with the Roden family of Down, traditional stalwarts of the Protestant cause. Intermarriage between various branches of these two families extended over three generations. Lady Louisa Jocelyn, a sister of Robert Jocelyn (1756–1820), 2nd earl of Roden, was married to Rev. Edward Wingfield, brother of Richard Wingfield (1762–1802), 4th Viscount Powerscourt. The latter's son, Richard Wingfield (1790–1823), 5th Viscount Powerscourt, married Lady Frances Jocelyn, eldest daughter of the 2nd earl of Roden. One of the offspring of this union, the eldest son and heir, Richard Wingfield (1815–?) married Lady Elizabeth Jocelyn, his first cousin once removed. Although this is undoubtedly the most striking example of marital linkages between evangelical families, many similar instances can be found among the aristocrats whose names repeatedly appeared on the lists of patrons and vice-presidents of the HBS and kindred organizations, and whose estates provided havens for evangelical clergymen, scripture-readers and Bible schools. The Kingston and Mountcashel families, for example, two of the most prominent aristocratic names in Cork and Tipperary, were connected through marriage and were both closely associated with the evangelical movement. Viscount Lorton, whose estate at Rockingham, County Roscommon, was well known for its evangelizing activities, was a brother of the earl of Kingston and a son-in-law of the earl of Rosse, another fervent advocate of the cause. The practice of intermarriage extended down the ranks to include the professional classes. The eldest daughter of Viscount Lorton, for example, was married to a son of Thomas Lefroy, and the offspring of the Lefroy and La Touche clans could be found in the highest reaches of the evangelical aristocracy. These marriage alliances undoubtedly reflected mutual recognition by kindred spirits travelling the same road.

With the notable exception of Theodosia Howard, Viscountess Powerscourt, no woman gained national recognition for involvement in the evangelical movement. Yet much evidence points to the role of women as central figures in such practical operations as distributing bibles, visiting the sick and the imprisoned, and supervising Bible schools. Besides giving women opportunities to escape the domestic environment, evangelical philanthropy also made it possible for the wives and daughters of landlords and clergymen to cooperate with men in a way that did not threaten Victorian ideals of womanhood.[46]

In a sardonic description of what he calls 'that appalling smugness' that overtook the Irish gentry during this period, Hubert Butler includes an interesting note on the involvement of women in philanthropic activity:

> At first it had quite a genial aspect, there was less abuse, less violence, less drink, less extravagance. I think it was merely that the Rakes of Mallow had taken their money and their merriment to Bath and Brighton. A great crop of charitable institutions and alms houses grew up, there were bible classes and farming classes. In the drawing rooms, where chair covers had been embroidered to the sound of the harpsichord, acres upon acres of warm cross-over shawls were knitted, in the kitchens where rum punch had been brewed, gallons of soup and mountains of nourishing

jellies were prepared for the deserving poor. It is said that Lady Elizabeth Fownes literally killed herself with woolwork; and at Piltown the four daughters of Lord Duncannon regularly taught in the village school.[47]

This is an imaginative portrait of serious religion at work in the domestic environment. But some of the more important features to be found on the larger canvas of Irish evangelicalism are absent, and they are not to be found when Butler attempts to answer the question he sets himself—'How was it that these improved manners did not lead to friendlier feelings but instead the old bitterness intensified, the old divisions deepened?'[48]

The effects of misplaced philanthropy are more vividly documented in *Old and New Light*, and go a long way towards explaining the bitterness and ill-feeling generated by the now-fashionable philanthropy of evangelical aristocrats. Crowe Evans' work is set in the early 1820s, when the country was suffering the full effects of the post-Napoleonic depression. Jemima Lowrie has recently opened a Bible school on her father's estate at Laylands and has succeeded in enrolling the children of a tenant, Tim Byrne, a once-prosperous farmer now fallen on hard times. All goes well for a while, and the youngsters are regularly sent to Miss Jemima to receive instructions, 'which, whenever they were accompanied by a wedge of bread or a trencher of stirabout, were exceedingly welcome to young scholars'.[49] The trouble starts when Jemima rewards the eldest child with a gift of a new Bible, which is introduced to the Byrne household at a most unfortunate moment, when the local Catholic curate, Fr McDowd, happens to have stopped by for a social visit. The ensuing conflict over who should have control over the minds of the hopeless Byrne children is related to the sympathetic Charles St George by Tim Byrne:

> 'But as I was goin to 'quaint your reverence, when Miss axed for the childer, sure Judy couldn't but send em. And sure as she did, it war'nt to spell at all, at all, that Miss Jemima taught 'em, but tip-top larnin to—to puzzle the priest; and if you war but to see Father McDowd, how mad he was at the hathen knowledge that had been put into the craturs. For all that, I got round the priest, and talked to him oncet or twicet, for he is a good sort of a body, and likes a drop, and isn't malevolent the laste taste in the world. Ontil las Saturday night it was come five weeks, who should be with us but Father McDowd, when the childer cam home. And what should little Judy have in her fist but a bran-new Bible, given her, she said, by Miss, all as one as if it was a story book. Och, by my sowl! Ye might as well ha' been tying Dundalk Bay in a big storm down wid a rope

of suggawns (i.e. straw ropes) as thought of quieting him. Puillialoo! your reverence knows what the clargy are like when they're vexed; troth, they're as bad as the women, every bit; and that's saying enough for 'em. And the long and the short of it was, that Father McDowd wouldn't hear of me sending the childer any more, at all, at all.

'Well?'

'And sure that angered Miss, and Miss angered Master; and it's all fallen upon poor Tim's head. Judy and Martha were first forbidden the big house; Martha went up the day after the bible row to the big house, and all the young ladies flew at and abused her; and the poor girl would ha' cried, if she could, but the tears din't come to the broken-hearted cratur. And then the cow was pounded every hour in the day, and the childer frighted and threatened; and at lasht, down comes the agent and asks Tim for what he hasn't. And he driv off our heifer, your reverence, and we're to be turned out to the ditch; and all our bits o' things, the remains of our ould days o' comfort are to be canted immadiately ...

'There's more like me in the country persecuted, and all for some trifle o' the kind! And I know what they'll do is to unite and ruin the country, by burning and slaying and massacreeing every new tenant that dares to step into their shoes. But I'm a pacable man, and the women dependent on me, and what to do in the wide world this blessed day, I don't know.'[50]

This is one of the few realistic (if fictional) accounts of the 'priestly intimidation' highlighted in the evangelical press, and of corresponding charges from outraged Catholics that landowners and employers were using economic pressure to force parents into sending children to the Bible schools. If it accurately represents the end product of the 'improved manners' of the gentry, it is not difficult to see why the bitterness between landlord and tenant intensified. To the evangelical mind, the source of the problem was the interference of the Catholic clergy, and little sympathy was wasted on the ill-fated peasant caught between the economic power of the landlord and the social and cultural demands of his religion.

Evidence that landlords were in fact pressuring Catholic tenants to attend schools in which the reading of the Protestant Bible was obligatory surfaced on several occasions. In June 1824 Fr James Mulcahy of Castletownroche in County Cork reported that twenty-three labourers and servants had been dismissed by Lord Ennismore because they would not send their children to a school run by the KPS on his estate. Some months later, the *Dublin Evening Post* alleged that Lord Ennismore, along with Lords Carbery, Lorton and Roden, were known to be involved in proselytism of this kind.[51] In October 1827 another priest in Bray,

County Wicklow, reported to Archbishop Murray that some thirty or forty families on the estate of the earl of Rathdrum were threatened with eviction the following spring if they did not send their children to the local Protestant school.[52]

A recurring theme in the evangelical propaganda of the 1820s was the spirit of enquiry allegedly developing among the peasantry as a result of exposure to itinerant preachers and Bible schools. After centuries of bondage to Rome, Irish Catholics were depicted as having finally awakened to the source of their misery; they were said to be ready and eager to dismiss the authority of the priests and to absorb the true word of God as contained in the Bible. It is a measure of the popularity of the movement and of the effectiveness of its propaganda that this belief was widely accepted. Occasionally, a sober voice commented on the true state of the Catholic Church in Ireland, but even a candid acknowledgment of its strength was unlikely to curtail the evangelicals' enthusiasm and served, if anything, to strengthen their sense of purpose and commitment. In 1817 an itinerant Baptist preacher working in the southern counties made the following admission:

> Some people say popery is on the decline in this nation, but if I must give you my candid opinion on that subject, I think to the contrary. Let anyone travel as much as I have done, and see the preparations they are making to establish their interest—the number of priests and friars they are educating, the monasteries and superb chapels they are building in cities, towns, and villages all through this country—you would not imagine popery was losing power here; but especially if you knew the dreadful and despotic influence the priests have over the bodies and souls of the poor people, you would be more convinced of the reality of my idea.[53]

Contrary to what the propagandists liked to claim, the intensification of the evangelical crusade in the early 1820s had the effect of strengthening the authority of the priests. A further dimension of sectarian awareness was forced upon Catholics who were exposed both verbally and in print to the arguments between the reformed faith and Rome. The exclamation of the peasant child who led the Rev. Caesar Otway to the summit of Croagh Patrick—'God help the poor heretics, they have no religion at all, at all!'[54]—provides one glimpse of the sectarian division embedded in the popular consciousness. It would be fatuous to suggest that the Irish peasantry were at any previous time oblivious to the religious differences that set them apart from their Protestant neighbours. Yet there is much contemporary evidence in literature and journalism to suggest that the 1820s and 1830s were years in which Irish Catholicism at the popular level assumed the jealous, exclusive and self-righteous tone that was to characterize it for the remainder of the century and beyond. Undoubtedly, the vigilance of the priests and the repeated denunciations of many aspects of the reformed faith, especially the Protestant Bible, accounted for this tightening of Catholic ranks. The fictitious conflict between Fr McDowd and Miss Jemima may again be employed to illustrate what took place in communities where the evangelical spirit was abroad:

> Father McDowd was not a shepherd that could rest ignorant or patient at these inroads upon his flock. He paid daily visits to the Byrnes and to all the cottiers who dwelt around; and he zealously instilled antidotes stronger than the poison that he sought to counteract. Except for the purpose of opposing Miss Lowrie's endeavours at proselytism, the good father would not have thought it necessary to instruct his young flock as to the diabolical condition of all who went to church [i.e. the Church of Ireland]. But he was now under the necessity of depicting them in the most fearful and abominable light to his little flock, and his teaching was all the more powerful, independent of parental example, for the lessons of Father McDowd were imaginative, full of impressive horrors, miracles, and divine interpositions; to which Miss Lowrie had nothing to oppose but very naked common sense, stupid morality, the pragmatic maxims of religion, which the young and the ignorant are incapable of comprehending or reverencing. The consequence was not only that Miss Jemima failed utterly in spreading of natural religion through the rising generation around her, but that her ill-imagined endeavours had the effect of causing the blackest bigotry to be instilled into the youthful poor, joined necessarily with a detestation of herself, her family, and all her persuasion.[55]

This account stands in sharp contrast to the euphoric reports of Catholics deserting their traditional allegiance to the priests for the blessings of true religion, which became a standard feature of evangelical propaganda. Within the wider context of denominational relations, it is also closer in spirit to the actual consequences of the evangelical mission. In a letter to Lord Lansdowne complaining of the treatment of tenants on the estate of the earl of Rathdrum, Archbishop Murray accurately acknowledged the effects of proselytism when backed up by the economic clout of the landlord class:

> Can peace or happiness be expected to continue when such occurrences take place? We too look to the present government with the most confident hope that it will not identify with the authors of these proceedings and by the grant of funds which can be turned into such vexatious pur-

poses. We want much the means of education. We would receive them from the government with great gratitude, but we cannot accept them if accompanied by any inroad on our religious principles, which we hold dearer than education or than life itself.[56]

CONVERSIONS AND CONTROVERSY: KINGSCOURT AND ASKEATON

Between 1822 and 1827 the two areas of the country that experienced the most successful attempts at Reformation were Kingscourt, County Cavan, and Askeaton, County Limerick. For many years Kingscourt was the prototypical example of the Reformation movement in operation at the local level. With its moral-agency system (a new departure in estate management in which a 'moral agent' supervised the lives of the tenantry in accordance with the landlord's demands) and its network of teachers supplied by the Irish Society, it rapidly became a missionary centre for the whole of south-east Ulster, until what was known as the Kingscourt District embraced the counties of Cavan, Louth, Meath, Monaghan and Tyrone.[57] The term 'Second Reformation' was at first used almost exclusively in connection with the Kingscourt District, but it shortly came to be used in connection with the general evangelical mission to the Catholic population.

The work begun on the estate of Lord Farnham at Kingscourt in 1821–2 was part of the general drive to intensify the mission to the Catholic population that had gathered force with the founding of the Irish Society and the Scripture Readers' Society in 1818 and 1822 respectively. The 2nd Baron Farnham, John James Maxwell (1760–1823), who occupied the seat when the experiment was begun, had been among those who had supported the ultra-Protestant cause since the 1790s. His only surviving child, a daughter, Lady Harriet, was married to Denis Daly of Galway, who had died in 1791. Although Daly had been known as a liberal, his son, the Rev. Robert Daly, was an ultra-conservative supporter of the Union and a committed advocate of the new spirit of reform generated by the evangelical movement.[58] Following his appointment as rector of Powerscourt in 1814, Robert Daly became an intimate member of the Roden–Powerscourt evangelical circle, and his missionary inclinations were given full freedom in this hospitable environment. Along with Henry Monck Mason he had become a firm supporter of the Bible-in-Irish movement and was a founding member of the Irish Society. The 5th Baron Farnham, John Maxwell (1767–1838), under whose stewardship Kingscourt became the mecca of the Reformation movement, was married to the former Lady Lucy Annesley of the Gosford family of Armagh, who was also a fervent supporter of the cause. There was no offspring from this union but the evangelical link was sustained by a nephew, Henry Maxwell, who succeeded to the title in 1838 and was married to Lord Roden's sister-in-law.

The movement to convert the Catholic tenants on the Kingscourt estate began in 1822, when the Rev. Winning, a Presbyterian minister connected with the Farnham household, invited the Irish Society to provide teachers for the schools that were to be established with Lord Farnham's financial support.[59] The committee furnished nine teachers at the outset, but this number was greatly increased as the district became the main base for the Society's activities. Winning had apparently begun this work of his own volition and had set up three or four schools with the assistance of an inspector, Thomas Russell, and two circulating masters. Once the Irish Society became involved, the number of schools and scholars rose dramatically. Between 1822 and 1825, 83 schools were opened and 3090 students, including 2110 adults, were enrolled. The most spectacular increase occurred in the latter part of 1825, as the following table indicates:

SCHOOLS ON THE KINGSCOURT ESTATE, 1822–5[60]

	Schools	Scholars
May 1823	3	75
June 1824	41	278
May 1825	86	652
Nov. 1825	115	1719

Precisely why such a big increase took place between May and November 1825 is not clear. Given the bias of evangelical propaganda, which was constantly under fire from the Catholic and liberal Protestant press for fraudulence, it seems reasonable to treat these figures with caution. It must also be remembered that a certain percentage of those attending the schools would have been Protestant. The only safe conclusion is that after the onslaught of the Catholic clergy against the Reformation movement in 1824, the evangelicals greatly increased their campaign, and the Kingscourt area was the focus of their strongest efforts in this regard.

The prominence of the Kingscourt District as a centre of the new Reformation was further heightened in 1826 with the appointment of a moral agent, William Krause. This office, in contrast to that of the regular agent who oversaw the granting of leases and the collection of rent, had no equivalent in Britain. It entailed the supervision of the moral welfare of the tenantry, with particular emphasis on school attendance, and to a lesser extent on the provision of medical services and the general improvement of living conditions. The moral-agency system spread across the great estates of south Ulster in the 1820s and nothing better reflected the ideological ambitions of these landlords.[61]

The man appointed as Lord Farnham's moral agent, William Krause, was the very model of a self-conscious British patriot who took up the cause of Protestantism and the Union when other outlets for his nationalistic aggression closed off.[62] A native of the West Indies, Krause had seen active service in the Napoleonic Wars. Following a visit to Ireland in 1822 he had a near-fatal illness, as a result of which, in the words of his biographer, 'his heart was turned from sin and the world to the Lord'. The change was also consonant with his political sympathies. By his own admission he had been born a 'lover of aristocracy', with a 'sovereign contempt for the mob, misnamed the people'.[63] The political claims of the people he described as 'low-born Irish papists' were the particular object of this contempt:

> There are no people that could be more quickly tamed than the Irish papists. The fact is, a real and thorough papist is trained up a slave; his system of religion inculcates this, and the effects of their moral bondage are seen in the character of their crimes.[64]

His enthusiasm for his new vocation as the moral agent of Lord Farnham may be inferred from his stated preference for cholera over 'popery' as the lesser of the two evils. He was eventually ordained a minister of the Church of Ireland and ended his days, in what had by then become a tradition, as an incumbent of the Bethesda Chapel between 1840 and 1852.

The fruits of the combined industry of Krause, Winning, the Farnham household and the Irish Society began to appear around Kingscourt in the latter part of 1826, when reports of converts were broadcast in the ultra-Protestant evangelical press. In a two-month period alone, 300 Catholics were said to have made public recantations of their faith in Cavan town. The evangelicals claimed that this remarkable occurrence was the result of the curiosity aroused by the Bible War of 1824, but it was really the impact of the general election of 1826 that provided the context for the extraordinary upsurge in conversions that caught the imagination of the country. The decision of the Catholic Association to back liberal Protestant supporters of Emancipation in this election resulted in the so called 'revolt of the forty-shilling freeholders', which convincingly illustrated that the landlords' hold on electoral politics could be broken by discipline and organization in the Catholic ranks. In four constituencies a candidate backed by the Catholic Association had succeeded in defeating an anti-Emancipationist contender, and in a fifth the conservative incumbent held on to his seat by a mere five votes. The only county in which the ultra-Protestant camp managed to hold its ground was Cavan, where the Farnham interest was strong enough to withstand the challenge launched by Robert Southwell, the candidate backed by the Catholic Association.[65] To promoters of the Reformation movement, the defeat of Southwell appeared as providential approval for the work in which they were engaged. As adherents of a millenarian interpretation of worldly events, Lord Farnham, along with Robert Winning and William Krause, was now ready to believe that Cavan was indeed favoured by divine providence to take the lead in a movement that would deliver the country from the advancing forces of the Antichrist.

From Cavan the movement spread to other parts of the country where evangelical missionaries had been active and before long it began to be broadcast that the entire country was about to be embraced by the spirit of a wildfire revival. Krause in particular was emphatic on this point and spoke in glowing terms of the thirst for knowledge currently sweeping the country and of the hundreds of Catholics in County Cavan 'who want only protection and the countenance of the gentry to induce them to come forward'.[66]

In January 1827 Lord Farnham launched the Cavan Association for Promoting the 'Second Reformation' in Ireland. His inaugural address contained a resounding account of the successes in his own district and a lengthy analysis of how the peace and security of the country were dependent on the Reformation movement. Underpinning his attachment to this belief was the old argument of Bishop Woodward, by now an article of faith among conservative aristocrats, that the political Emancipation of Catholics would lead to the collapse of the Established Church, the destruction of the Protestant interest in Ireland and the eventual separation of the two islands. Like Archbishop Magee's famous sermon of 1822, Lord Farnham's address prompted Bishop Doyle once again to take up his pen to defend the rights of the Catholic population. Declining to indulge in religious controversy, Doyle defended Emancipation on the grounds of its sheer inevitability and discounted Farnham's assertion that the political integrity of the United Kingdom would be greatly endangered as a result of its passage. He questioned the peer as to why, if he was so fearful about Emancipation, he entertained no anxiety whatever of the consequences, should it be indefinitely withheld. Agreeing with Lord Farnham's belief that the Church establishment must fall sooner or later, Doyle warned that the evangelical campaign against the Catholic religion would be fruitless: 'Fruitless, I mean, of such conversions as you contemplate, but probably fruitful in results far and widely different from those which you would have the public to believe you to expect.'[67] Doyle was eventually obliged to enquire into the truth of reports that hundreds of people were being converted in the Cavan area. In so doing, he was at least acknowledging that the existence of converts was not wholly a figment of the imagination of evangelical propagandists.

Lord Farnham's proclamation of the successes of the evangelicals in his native county drew an extraordinary amount of attention to the Reformation movement not only in Cavan but throughout the country generally and also in Britain. This was due in large measure to the effectiveness of the evangelical propaganda machine, which deluged regional and national newspapers with accounts of the self-sacrificing work of dedicated missionaries and the harvest of souls they were reaping. In Cavan town weekly bulletins of the latest number of converts were posted in public places and carried through the streets on placards by hired persons.

Three months after Lord Farnham's famous inauguration speech, Bishop Jebb of Limerick, whose opinions on the ascendancy of evangelical influence had always fluctuated between admiration for their commitment and dedication and fear of what their enthusiasm implied for denominational relations, candidly admitted to a correspondent in England that the news from Cavan had changed his mind:

> Within these few weeks my opinion has undergone a considerable change. I have learned from various trustworthy quarters that in almost every part of Ireland inquiry and thirst for knowledge, and even in some instances a degree of religious anxiety, are gaining ground among the Roman Catholics. Numbers, I am well informed, in neighbourhoods predominantly popish, are thinking and inquiring and reading the scriptures, who have not as yet proposed to conform: and what is especially remarkable, in the county of Tipperary several of the priests wish to place the scriptures in the hands of their people and are still withheld from doing so only by the injunctions of their superiors. From the papers you

can learn what is going on in Dublin as well as in Cavan; you see also weekly notices of conversions in all parts of the country. So far as I can learn, the clergy of the diocese of Ferns are acting very systematically to produce this effect; several of the parochial clergy, with the sanction and under the guidance of the bishop, preach controversial sermons; they have divided among themselves the prominent subjects in debate and preach rotationally in each other's pulpits, thus giving each congregation a view of the whole controversy.[68]

Bishop Jebb was not alone in his belief that 1827 was the *annus mirabilis* of the Protestant Reformation in Ireland. Like Lord Farnham, his fears had been fuelled by recent political events. The victory of the Emancipationist candidates in the 1826 election had shown what discipline and organization in the Catholic ranks might achieve, and it pointed ominously to the political sophistication of O'Connell and his supporters. Catholic hopes were further heightened, and the Emancipation debate given more scope than ever, when Canning succeeded Lord Liverpool as prime minister in 1827. The hubbub in press and parliament over the pros and cons of Emancipation ensured a hospitable reception among ultra-Protestants for the harbingers of Reformation. Robert Daly, writing as 'Senex' in *Blackwood's Magazine*, kept readers informed of the horrors that lay in store for the kingdom, and for the Protestants of Ireland in particular, if Catholics were granted full political freedom.[69]

In May 1827 the writer of a long article on the Catholic question strongly defended the benefits, temporal as well as spiritual, that a Reformation would generate among the benighted inhabitants of Ireland:

> If its people were Protestants, it would be free from its present divisions and distractions; the Catholic question, which is now used as an instrument for filling it with almost every kind of evil and for placing its eternal peace and the peace between it and Britain in peril, would be unknown. If its people were Protestants, they would be free from spiritual tyranny; they would be accessible to instruction and civilization; the subject would not be arrayed against the ruler, and the tenant against the landlord; neighbour would not be seeking the ruin of neighbour; society would be placed under these bonds, feelings, and regulations without which it can never know prosperity.[70]

This essay provides a succinct and telling revelation of the overlap between religion and politics that characterized the evangelical mentality. To this way of thinking there was only one solution to the country's problems, this being the elimination of the Catholic question through the elimination of the Catholic religion. The main purpose of the article was to respond to a speech recently made in parliament in which the attorney general for Ireland, William Conyngham Plunket, had attacked the evangelical crusade, referring to it as 'the merest chimera that ever bewildered the mind of man'.[71]

Neither the warnings of Doyle nor the criticism of Plunket, however, were likely to deflect anti-Emancipationists on both sides of the Irish Sea from believing what they wished about the prospects of the 'Second Reformation' in Ireland. What this belief, or delusion, as some would have it, amounted to was the inevitability of the triumph of the Protestant religion now that the priests had been openly challenged on the dogmas and despotic tendencies of the Catholic Church, and scriptural education made universally available. Given the successes of the evangelicals in education and controversial preaching, it seemed entirely logical that substantial numbers would renounce the errors of popery, and that the process, once begun, would accelerate rapidly. When Lord Farnham announced the conversion of seven or eight hundred Catholics in his own district, it was interpreted as a sign of divine intervention. The evangelicals went through 1826 on a wave of popularity, with approval for their work coming from many different quarters. This was sufficient to propel Bishop Doyle into organizing defensive action on behalf of the Catholics. Predictably, his first concern was to investigate the truth behind the Cavan conversions.

The man to whom he entrusted the task of reporting on events in Cavan was George Ensor, a Protestant lawyer of impeccable liberal views and a strong supporter of Catholic Emancipation. Ensor published a total of seven letters on the Cavan conversions and the Reformation movement generally. The first of these appeared in February 1827, and the remaining six were published in rapid succession between November 1827 and February 1828. Later in 1828 they were published in collected form by Richard Coyne of Capel Street, Dublin, under the title *Letters Showing the Inutility and Exhibiting the Absurdity of What Is Rather Fantastically Termed 'The New Reformation'*. Ensor's approach to his subject may be inferred from the title. Like his English contemporaries William Cobbett and the Rev. Sydney Smith, his support for the Catholic cause had more to do with his detestation for all that evangelicalism represented rather than an attachment to or appreciation of the doctrines of the Catholic faith. As a Protestant, he could afford to indulge in biting sarcasm without fear of being labelled a bigot, and as a liberal, he was entirely dismissive of the commitment to evangelizing the heathens abroad and the Jews and Catholics at home while society in Britain was rife with inequality and crime. Of the foreign missionary agencies, he wrote, 'I wonder that they do not send out a mission with Franklin to the Pole, for the *Quarterly Review*, No. 68, felicitates its readers on Parry's sailors learning their catechism at the Arctic Circle.'[72] But his wrath was reserved for the Irish evangelicals, 'who hate them [the Catholics] and their kindred, and Ireland's self, except what they can wring from its misery'.[73] Doyle had chosen his rapporteur well, it would appear.

In the most damaging of the charges levelled in the *New Reformation* letters, Ensor accused the Cavan evangelists of exploiting the economic destitution of the peasantry to attract converts. That conversions occurred was not denied. What was strongly implied, however, was that a combination of economic hardship and political disappointment in 1826–7 had left the Catholic peasantry of Cavan in a state of extreme vulnerability. Although he asserted that 'a season of great distress, want of food, and want of employment prepared the Cavan conversions', Ensor did not dwell on the precise causes of the economic crisis.[74] Since the country did not experience famine, even on a regional or local basis, during this period, the economic distress to which Ensor alluded can most likely be attributed to the decline of handloom weaving associated with the cotton and linen industries. The prominence of weaving in Cavan had made it one of the most prosperous and densely populated of Irish counties by the end of the eighteenth century. All this was to change, however, when mechanization turned handloom weaving into an obsolete trade. The earnings of the once-prosperous weavers went into an irreversible decline, bringing widespread immiseration in its wake. Between 1820 and 1835, the income of cotton weavers declined by more than 50 per cent, while the cost of food and housing remained steady.[75]

Relief was afforded to displaced artisans only through emigration and eventually through absorption into the factory system. Until the transition was made, suffering and deprivation were inevitable. A visitor to Kingscourt in 1836 gave the following account of the conditions of the inhabitants:

> In several hovels we found widows in extreme want. Naked mud holes, rather than rooms, with half a rood of ground attached, pay 24*s*., 28*s*. and even 30*s*. per annum rent. One man, with an asthma, and several women told us they lived 'by begging in the name of God'. The houses of labourers were scarcely better. In one cabin a youth, almost grown up, said that his father was gone to seek work but had been long without it and that he himself could only get work at harvest for 4*d*. a day. In this wretched place, blackened with smoke, dark, damp, and dirty, without

even the corner for the pig, the spade resting idly against the wall, and a little heap of very bad turf, with a broken loom, the only property besides, did the father and his five children sleep on one bedstead (if the rude collection of stakes nailed to each other deserve that name) without mattrass [*sic*], without clothing, nay, even without straw. In another cabin we found a woman spinning, who said she could earn by her wheel about $1\frac{1}{2}d$. in the day, which was confirmed by a lady of Kingscourt with whom we were walking, who further said that she could get a number of women to work for her at that rate.[76]

Along with economic deprivation, Ensor had listed 'the Malthusian doctrines of clearing estates of redundant population in order to increase surplus produce' as having contributed to the poverty of Cavan Catholics. It is certainly not difficult to appreciate how tenants faced with eviction on top of all their other miseries might agree to attend Bible schools or even to change their religion so as to preserve their slender subsistence. The final blow to Catholic solidarity in Cavan, in Ensor's opinion, was the failure of the forty-shilling freeholders to unite in support of an Emancipationist candidate in the 1826 election: 'When the people of Cavan failed as electors, they were prepared to take another step downwards.'[77] Whatever number of them converted to Protestantism in 1826–7—'this famishing, land-clearing, expatriating, vindictive Protestant year', as Ensor called it—they allegedly returned to their traditional faith once the threat to their subsistence was removed. Ensor compared their experience to that of birds 'which visit milder climates at intervals, but their coming is proof of a great severity in their native country, and who return when the iron days are passed and the sun cheers them home'.[78]

Despite Ensor's repeated assertions that the Cavan converts were driven by hunger and deprivation to become Protestants, and that they had returned to the Catholic fold when the crisis receded, at no point did he refer to the number of people involved. In the metropolitan parish of Armagh he learned of six Catholics who had converted, and in a Tyrone parish he did not name, a further two.[79] But the fate of the 'hundreds of converts' in the Kingscourt area was left unspecified, except for a general comment on their eventual return to the Catholic faith. In January 1828 the *British Critic*, in a leading article entitled 'The Irish Reformation', claimed that by September of the previous year the total number of converts for the country as a whole had reached 2357, and that more than half of these resided in the Kingscourt District.[80] In view of the social ostracism that usually accompanied a change of faith, it would have been unusual if that many people enjoyed the direct protection of the landlord and the authorities. In the 1830s such protection was frequently afforded in 'colonies' in which the converts lived, together with clergymen and teachers, but there is no evidence that such a settlement was ever planned in Kingscourt. What we do know is that, whatever the number of converts, the entire area was in the throes of sectarian conflict throughout the 1830s.[81] Popular animosity was repeatedly vented against converts and especially against the Bible readers and teachers employed by the Irish Society. According to the Society's annual report for 1833, the hatred aroused by its schoolmasters and students was a consequence of their being the only Catholics locally who were not involved in illegal associations: 'of the thirty or forty families connected with the enterprise, none are ribbonmen, and several have had a narrow escape from being murdered'.[82] Baptist Wriothesley Noel encountered several people who had renounced Catholicism and who were forced as a result to move to distant parishes. One woman told how she had been recognized at a fair by her former neighbours, 'who damned her soul, declared her a disgrace to her church, and called out in the crowded street, "turn coat, turn coat"'.[83]

Teachers and readers were continually beaten and persecuted, and on occasion murdered. In July 1830, when a man named Moore was arraigned for having fired shots at some of the Irish Society's masters, the Rev. Winning impressed upon Lord Farnham the importance of his attendance at the trial:

> The Committee think—and think justly—that the interests of their schools in that district are intimately concerned with the issues of this trial. The hostility of the priesthood is incessant against these schools— the characters of the teachers are vilified—threats, intimidation, and every hostility are resorted to. Three of our men have already been murdered— and if Moore now evades justice, their lives will be greatly exposed.[84]

Despite the terrible risks connected with working for the Irish Society, the Rev. Noel was proud to note in 1836 that men persisted in offering themselves for training. The Rev. Winning had informed him that if the Irish Society were to give permission, 500 new teachers could immediately be trained and put to work. Noel drew no connection between this remarkable assertion and the dire poverty that he had witnessed in the area. At a time when the wages of occasional workers averaged 10*d.* a day in summer and 6*d.* in winter, when many labourers could hardly obtain two days' work in the week, and when by the author's own admission many of the inhabitants were on the verge of starvation, the average wage of 6s. a week paid to the teachers of the Irish Society must have seemed handsome indeed.[85]

The most thorough account of the Cavan conversions appeared in the *British Critic* in January 1828, in a seminal article whose author was wholly familiar with the impulses and objectives of the movement. The article shows what the reading public in England was learning about the current state of religious affairs in Ireland. Rather than being the work of dedicated clergymen labouring to spread the light among the enslaved masses, the Irish 'Second Reformation' was represented as a reaction by lay Catholics against the excesses and abuses of their own Church. Bible and school societies and evangelical landlords and clergymen were portrayed as merely responding to rather than initiating the development. Such an interpretation drew the Irish experience into line with that of northern Europe in the sixteenth century, and this was precisely the intention.[86]

Cavan, needless to say, was presented as the fountainhead of the revival, though this was attributed not to the zeal of the Farnham family, but to its proximity to County Fermanagh, 'the very gangway of Irish superstition'.[87] This was of course a reference to the road leading to Lough Derg, the famous penitential shrine in the southern part of County Donegal. The Catholic clergy of Cavan, allegedly envious of the profits pouring into Lough Derg, had set up a place of pilgrimage in their own county at Coronea. Popular opposition to this venture was said to have been the beginning of the Reformation in Ireland. Within a short period entire communities went over to the reformed faith and the light was beginning to spread even further afield: 'The whole country seemed to have waited only to receive a signal from some peculiarly favoured district, that it might be encouraged to express its general impatience.'[88]

Just as evangelicals had once seen the hand of God at work in the country's deliverance from the horrors of the French Revolution and Napoleon, so they now perceived the same influence operating to save them from the threat implicit in the passage of Catholic Emancipation. That zealous clergymen and landlords were on hand to assist the Reformation was taken as further evidence of divine sanction. To stop the Reformation at this point, said Lord Farnham's cousin Leslie Foster in the House of Commons, would be like stopping the falls of Niagara.[89] Thus was the English public made aware of what they might expect in Ireland.

Outside of the Kingscourt District the greatest number of conversions during the heyday of the 'Second Reformation' in 1825–7 was recorded in

Askeaton, County Limerick. They were investigated by Bishop Jebb, then head of the diocese in which they took place, in response to an enquiry from a colleague in England, the Tory MP Sir Robert H. Inglis. The evidence forwarded by Jebb, in addition to that contained in his private correspondence, suggests that the Askeaton conversions were a much more complex affair than those at Kingscourt, involving genuine popular anti-clericalism on the part of those who converted, in addition to the usual presence of evangelical activity by a local Protestant clergyman.

The person mainly responsible for planting the evangelical standard in Askeaton was one Rev. Daniel Murray, a Church of Ireland clergyman who had been appointed vicar of Askeaton in the summer of 1824. We know little about his background or education, but his dedication to parochial work, especially to education, marked him as one of the body of 'superior young divines' whom Bishop Jebb rejoiced to see replacing the apathetic older generation of clergymen, not only in Limerick but throughout the country.[90] Having been entrusted with a sum of £200 a year for charitable purposes, the vicar and his wife established schools in the area. Three were set up altogether, one under the patronage of the KPS and the other two under their own direction but with Catholic masters so as 'to meet the prejudices of the people'. The scheme was violently opposed by the local priest, Fr Fitzgerald, who ordered parents to withdraw their children from the schools. This they refused to do, and gradually they began to register their opposition to the priest's directive by adopting the Protestant faith. According to Jebb, two families withdrew in June 1825, and they were followed during the next eighteen months by about 170 adults and 300 adolescents and children.[91]

The most remarkable feature of the Askeaton conversions was the apparent absence of the type of coordinated activity between landlords and evangelical agencies that characterized other areas of the country where the Reformation movement took root. Although the Rev. Murray was a member of the HBS and the CMS, he received no assistance from external sources. According to Jebb, he preferred it that way. When help was offered by the Methodists and by representatives of other evangelical organizations it was politely declined. Murray was said to be on the best of terms with his Catholic parishioners, a fact that his diocesan superior attributed to his unwillingness to engage in sectarian controversy and his disavowal of itinerant preaching and other forms of evangelical activity likely to arouse the hatred of Catholics. Bishop Jebb was of the opinion that it was this attitude that endeared him to the local people and had led to their departure from the Catholic Church.[92]

The motives of the Askeaton converts are difficult to determine. In view of the denominational rivalry and religious controversy that had been openly raging since 1822, and considering that Catholic popular opinion held that Protestants were not only usurpers but heretics to boot, the question arises as to why a relatively large group of people should have decided to join the enemy camp at this time. Bishop Jebb's assertion that they were moved by the benign influence of the Rev. Murray, behind whose work lay the hand of God, seems less than convincing. But his allusions to the dispute between the local parish priest and Catholic parents who wished to avail of education for their children points to a more realistic explanation.

Although the relationship between priests and people was frequently misrepresented by the propagandists of the 'Second Reformation' in the 1820s and '30s, tension between the two was not entirely illusory. Since the middle of the eighteenth century popular hostility to the demands of the Catholic clergy had surfaced on numerous occasions, though it had noticeably diminished by the 1820s. There were two areas in particular in which priests were likely to fall afoul of their parishioners: the exaction of fees for services such as weddings and baptisms, and the opposition to agrarian secret societies.[93] Since agrarian combination was generally a response to economic deprivation, a condition that might be traced in part to the exactions of the clergy, it was not uncommon to find these two grievances voiced at the same time. During the Rockite disturbances of 1821–4, the western part of County Limerick, including Askeaton, was one of the most disturbed areas in the whole country. Agrarian outrages were repeatedly denounced from the altars of Catholic chapels, and the clergy from the bishop downwards did their utmost to dissuade the popular classes from violence.

The interest of the Limerick clergy in the preservation of public order was evidently stronger than that of their colleagues in most areas affected by disturbances. Why this should have been so is not clear, but contemporary opinion suggests that the authorities and the clergy, Protestant and Catholic alike, suspected that there was a more sophisticated revolutionary process at work behind the disturbances, which usually tended to spread like wildfire from county to county and to abate just as quickly on the passage of reform or the improvement in the economy. As early as 1816, John Jebb confided to the archbishop of Cashel that the most disturbed parts of County Limerick were also the most prosperous ones, and that tithes formed no part whatever of the popular grievances in these areas: 'In many instances, indeed, tithes were but too fatally put forward

… as a stalking horse; and the people were industriously drilled on that subject by persons who kept themselves out of view, and who had other, and infinitely more desperate objects to carry.'[94] This tone was still current in 1822. A correspondent of the *Dublin Evening Post* noted that the anti-tithe movement in Limerick was burning less brightly than in the neighbouring counties of Cork and Tipperary, but interpreted the quietude in ominous terms: 'there is a silent fermentation in that county, an apparent quietness of purpose maturing, which threatens this devoted district with the most direful calamities'. As further evidence, he pointed to the singular change that had occurred in the manners and habits of the common people, who appeared to have departed from their usual indulgence in drinking and fighting at fairs.[95]

One measure of the popular hostility encountered by the Catholic clergy in their strivings to preserve the peace in County Limerick was the physical violence they had to endure. On two occasions priests were attacked for preaching against outrages; in one of these cases the priest was actually killed on the altar of his chapel. Another priest, Fr John Mulqueen, was shot to death in 1819, though his assailants were said to have been unaware of his identity.[96] Such incidents were almost unique to County Limerick at this time, a fact that suggests that the clergy of this county were intensely committed to the maintenance of law and order, and that anti-clericalism was still running strong there when it appears to have abated elsewhere. Conversely, the Church of Ireland clergy were considered to be well regarded in County Limerick, though the grounds for this claim are somewhat dubious. Certainly, the renown of Bishop Jebb as the most fair-minded and conciliatory prelate of the Church of Ireland did much to enhance denominational relations.

The most famous expression of such goodwill occurred in the parish of Murroe on 16 December 1821, when Jebb was still archdeacon of Emly. During a particularly severe outbreak of disturbances the parish had been kept peaceful 'by the good disposition of the people and the indefatigable exertions of the parish priest', but the great fear was the incursion of 'emissaries from disturbed parts'. According to Jebb's account, the farmers and the lower classes were well pleased with the protection afforded them by the police and the military, and promised to turn in any emissaries who appeared among them. When they asked Jebb how they might be of further service in keeping the peace, he replied that he would like to be granted leave to preach to the congregation after Mass on Sunday. This he did with the support of his Catholic counterpart, Fr O'Brien Costelloe. The response of the congregation was overwhelming.

> Nothing could exceed their attention and the expression on their countenances was actually delightful … some shed tears. When called upon, if they approved the resolutions to hold up their right hands, they held them up to a man. Even the children imitated the gesture.[97]

In political terms, and especially on the subject of Catholic Emancipation, Jebb was no liberal. Yet his sympathy for the Catholic poor and his willingness to treat their clerical superiors respectfully and diplomatically won him the abiding respect of middle-class Catholics, who regarded him with some justification as the Protestant equivalent of Bishop Doyle. The comparison is reasonably valid when his mildness and charity are compared with the fury of Archbishop Magee. But whether his appointment as bishop of Limerick in 1823 did anything to lessen popular sectarianism in the county is impossible to determine. The most that can safely be said is that the Catholics of Limerick had some reason for thinking well of the Protestant clergy and bishop at the same time that they were at odds with some of their own priests.

The district around Askeaton was a traditional Protestant stronghold, though it is most unlikely that this lent itself to good denominational relations. The Palatine settlers whose villages dotted the area had never been integrated into the local community and were a constant source of sectarian friction because of their ultra-Protestant sympathies and their eagerness to join the yeomanry and the militia, forces frequently used to put down rebellious Catholics.[98] According to the reporter from the *British Critic*, however, the Palatines had no influence, either positive or negative, on the Catholics who opted to join the Church of Ireland in 1825–6. The Oliver family, whose clerical offspring had introduced evangelical ideals to the district around the turn of the century, was not mentioned in any contemporary account as having been involved with the conversions. The social composition of the converts is unknown, but an interesting piece of evidence was provided by Bishop Jebb, who recalled that one of the most upright among them had formerly been a leader of a faction known as the 'Four Year Olds'. This may indicate that the man in question had been involved in a conflict between labourers and cottiers on the one hand and graziers and strong farmers on the other. The latter group was closely aligned with and supported by the Catholic clergy, a fact that may have helped to push the landless element in the direction of Protestantism.

Askeaton was not the only area where a Catholic exodus occurred following a dispute of a social or religious nature within the Catholic body itself. The

Crotty cousins of Parsonstown in King's County, for example, were accompanied by over a thousand of their parishioners when they took leave of the Catholic Church in 1829.[99] Despite the large number of people involved, very little noise was made either by the Catholic clergy or the press on this occasion. The same was true of Askeaton. According to Bishop Jebb, the Askeaton converts were quietly received into the Church of Ireland after a lengthy period of instruction, during which the Rev. Murray assessed their motives and weeded out all whom he considered unsuitable.[100] Jebb's letters contain no evidence that the converts were persecuted by their Catholic neighbours, a response that became almost axiomatic in other parts of the country where similar events took place. What eventually became of the converts is not known. After 1826 the Askeaton area remained relatively calm and did not develop into a missionary centre like Kingscourt or the colonies established on Achill Island and the Dingle peninsula in the early 1830s. When Baptist Wriothesley Noel toured the country in 1826 specifically to chart the progress of the Reformation, Askeaton was not on his itinerary, and it received no mention in the accounts of subsequent evangelical travellers. A remnant of the popular response to the conversions, however, was recorded in a popular ballad collected by Douglas Hyde in County Galway at the end of the nineteenth century:

> Ye muses now come aid me in admonishing the pagans
> The New Lights of Askeaton whose fate I do deplore
> From innocence and reason they are led to condemnation
> Their faith they have violated, the occasion of their woe
> The mass they have forsaken, their source and renovation
> To free them from damnation and Satan's violent yoke
> The means of their salvation at the great accounting table
> When mountains shall be shaken and nations overthrown.[101]

CONVERSIONS AND SOCIAL CONFLICT

From 1825 onwards, the evangelical drive to win converts for the 'Second Reformation' added yet a further dimension of violence to life in Ireland. During the late 1820s and throughout the 1830s the Kingscourt District was rife with sectarian disturbances, as were parts of County Sligo, the diocese of Tuam, and the diocese of Kildare and Leighlin, where the evangelicals were also beginning to make inroads into Catholic ranks. Converts were denounced from Catholic altars and excommunicated if they persisted in their apostasy. More seriously, they were frequently attacked by their neighbours, refused goods when they went to purchase them, and often driven out of their homes altogether. Several cases were reported of Catholics who were murdered because of their involvement with the evangelical crusade, either as converts or schoolteachers. The protection of the local gentry was not sufficient to guard against such excesses.

Protection was nowhere more in evidence than on Lord Farnham's Cavan estate, and yet this area was the scene of some of the greatest atrocities. Of the 900 or so teachers whom the Rev. Noel claimed had been employed in the Kingscourt area since the inception of the Reformation, many had allegedly been beaten and persecuted and a few had been killed. In one case the victim was a relative and tenant of the parish priest, who eventually evicted him because he had refused to quit his work as a reader of the scriptures in Irish; he was waylaid and murdered one evening while returning from Kingscourt with a parcel of books. Reports were also made to Noel about teachers who had their faces bloodied and their jaws broken. The Rev. Winning gave his own account of how schoolmasters employed by the Irish Society were driven out of rural areas and forced to live in the towns after their houses had been broken open and their property destroyed. He claimed to have seen schoolmasters 'covered with wounds and bruises, their faces disfigured, their eyes closed, and one with his teeth knocked out'.[102]

By far the most serious incident took place in 1829, when a body of armed Catholics descended on a Protestant village near Kingscourt in search of some individuals on whom they wished to exact vengeance. They were dispersed by gunfire, but when it was observed that the police and militia were assembling in the area, frightened local Catholics sought support from elsewhere and a body of 20,000 men reportedly surrounded Kingscourt. The town, which was predominantly Protestant, was kept in a virtual state of siege and the inhabitants were badly frightened. The besiegers were eventually repelled by the military, and several of the ringleaders were later hanged or transported.[103] This incident was probably the work of the Ribbon organization, which was said to be very strong in the area at this time. Sectarian motives were certainly to the forefront.

One of the instigators of the attack was said to have been the local Catholic curate, a Fr Nolan, who was obliged to leave the area as a result. By immersing himself in scriptural studies, the better to improve his talents as a controversialist, Nolan apparently saw the light and decided to convert to Protestantism and carry the banner of the 'Second Reformation'. In so doing, he joined a small band of convert priests who drew on themselves the everlasting venom of their erstwhile clerical colleagues. Shortly after Nolan conformed, he was appointed a minister of the Church of Ireland in Athboy, County Meath, which was considered part of the Kingscourt District. He quickly made a name for himself as a controversial speaker and conducted preaching tours around the country. Two pamphlets explaining his change of religious allegiance—*Nolan's Reasons for Leaving the Church of Rome* and *A Second Pamphlet*—each went through five editions in the 1830s.[104]

Nolan's case was exceptional, however. Most of the Catholic priests in the area joined forces in condemning the Reformation movement. From the altars on Sunday they preached against the use of the Bible, branding it (so their critics claimed) 'the black book' or the work of the devil. Efforts were mounted to keep Catholic children away from the Bible schools and to persuade adults to turn in bibles, tracts and controversial literature that had been distributed gratuitously. In 1839 a supporter of the Irish Society named Richard Benson of Fatham, near Kingscourt, informed the Dublin headquarters of the Irish Society that its teachers were being denounced from Catholic altars and were in constant fear of their lives. The priests of the area were said to be circulating pamphlets calculated to mobilize their followers against the designs of the Irish Society. Benson described the contents of one of these pamphlets:

> The system of Irish teaching is represented as having been introduced into this county by three heretic lords—Roden, Wicklow, and Farnham—that it first took root in Kingscourt, sprang up, and brought forth many branches there, and that within the last few years, some of its seeds had been blown over and had taken root in the Fatham woods, from whence it was the author's determination to cast it out, and ... he invites his fellow countrymen to collect all the bibles, testaments, and elementary books issued by the society into one pile on the top of Thangullian and there in the face of heaven to make one glorious bonfire of the whole.[105]

This is a fair representation of the opposition encountered by the Reformation evangelists wherever they sought to ply their trade. And hostility was not always confined to denunciation from the altar. Many converts and preachers paid dearly in person for their zeal.[106]

Outside of Cavan and the adjoining counties that made up the Kingscourt

District, the most active evangelical missionaries and their equally energetic opponents were to be found in County Sligo. The main reason for this was that Sligo served as the centre of operations for the LHS. Besides the schools run by this organization, the Scripture Readers' Society had about thirty workers employed in the area. By 1828 Sligo was not far behind Kingscourt in converts and controversy. In one seven-month period about 160 adults were received into the Established Church, and their dependents, who numbered about 200, were also expected to be raised as Protestants.[107] Some of the most blatant aggression against evangelical missionaries and their proselytes took place in the Sligo area.[108] In the parish of Ardagh, in an effort to prevent Catholic children from attending Bible schools, the local priest reputedly offered up a special prayer during Sunday Mass to the effect that if 'any parent should not withdraw his child from the free schools, his horse and his cow, his foal and his calf, and any other living stock, with himself and his child, might be dead within the year'.[109]

The investigator for the *British Critic* noted a marked difference in the attitudes of the Catholic clergy towards schools conducted under the sanction of the gentry and those under the direct management of one or another evangelical agency. What the priests were said to fear was the development of an attachment between the gentry and the peasantry that would interfere with their own authority.[110] On these grounds, it was said, they were not nearly so condemnatory of schools run by the Irish Society, where classes were conducted in Irish, thereby preventing any involvement by the gentry, who were ignorant of the language. In the parish of Killenummery in County Sligo, where the resident landlord was closely identified with the evangelical cause, the Catholic bishop made a special visit to warn his flock about the dangers of proselytism. Shortly afterwards, a schoolmaster was murdered in broad daylight while on his way to a Protestant church to recant his former faith. A local priest, finding religious tracts on his body, informed the crowd that had gathered at the scene that the murder was the work of the devil to punish the schoolmaster for reading such material. It was reported from a neighbouring parish that a man who had made known his intention to conform had had his cow killed.[111]

It is clear from the pattern of Catholic clerical opposition to the evangelical movement that the struggle was concerned not only with ecclesiastical legitimacy but also with the issue of which party, the priests or the Protestant landed classes, would emerge as the natural leaders of the Catholic peasantry.[112] Irish Protestants were correct in identifying the priests as their greatest adversaries. No force in Irish life at the local level did more than the priesthood to undermine the influence of the landlords, and it is not surprising that by the end of the nineteenth century the Catholic presbytery had replaced the 'big house' as the focus of local authority. The jealousy and bitterness that characterized relations between the priests and the landed classes, who warily eyed each other from a distance, each convinced that the other was the scourge of the country, can best be understood in this light. Historical and contemporary conditions dictated that evangelical Protestants stood little chance against the priests when it came to promoting themselves as representatives and protectors of the people. Yet this is not to deny the evangelicals' sincerity. In 1840 the diarist Elizabeth Smith, who worked tirelessly to improve her County Wicklow estate and the living standards of the tenants, captured the dilemma of the conscientious evangelical:

> I think, nay I feel sure, that if we Protestants did our duty, if we acted up to our principles, if the landlord visited and assisted them and became acquainted with their tenantry, and our clergy laboured with zeal in their vocation, there would be few papists in this country in twenty years.[113]

Like most of her contemporaries, Mrs Smith persisted in the belief that the peasantry were browbeaten by the clergy, and 'would be happy and prosperous if those priests would let them alone', by which she meant, in this instance, that if the priests had not interfered with the political allegiance of the tenants, the tenants would not have been faced with the hostility of the landlords.[114] It was a conflict in which there was little room for compromise. The stakes were assessed in 1827 by a writer in *Blackwood's Magazine*, in an ominous portent of the tone that Catholic–Protestant relations in Ireland were to assume over the remainder of the century:

> The reformation is a measure of defence as well as of aggression; it is one of self-preservation as well as of conquest. The war between the two churches is a war of extermination; and if the established one lay down its arms or act merely on the defensive, it must inevitably perish. The dissenting body of Protestants exist through it; it is their shield; and if it fall, Presbyterianism and every other form of Protestantism will soon be banished from Ireland.[115]

—SIX—
The Catholic Counter-Attack

Let all our proceedings be in strict conformity with the law, that those who are on the opposite side may have no evil to say of us, and that our conscience or our posterity may not reproach us with having swerved from the patience and long suffering which our religion and our interest enjoin ... For all the implacable enemies of our just claims ... will seek new pretexts for continuing their injustice in the slightest indiscretion into which any portion or individuals of our body might be betrayed.

JAMES WARREN DOYLE[1]

Yet the Irish, because a few here and there believe and fear, shall be reputed as all gaping and swallowing every extravagance. If they were, they have their excuse. They might expect miracles where politically and morally all things are extraordinary in their object and progress. Nor should they be reproached for believing abrupt interpositions of Providence; for in great misery the afflicted naturally ejaculate—those abandoned by man invoke God's aid, and surely none should be more disposed to expect supernatural relief than the Irish, and none more likely to receive it, for who have endured such protracted and complicated affliction.

GEORGE ENSOR[2]

The Catholic Association has its emissaries in every part of the country ... It pursues the same course of exciting the passions of the people by manifestoes and seditious harangues and above all by the active, insidious influence of the Roman Catholic clergy. Like the Catholic Committee, it levies taxes upon the people and assumes to itself all the prerogatives of government. What is to be done under such circumstances? Why, put it down. Let ministers appeal to parliament to suppress this monstrous evil, and the appeal will not be made in vain. If not soon extinguished, a rebellion more dreadful, more sanguinary, and more dangerous than any on record will be the consequence.

The Courier, 1824[3]

THE VINDICATION OF CATHOLIC IRELAND: BISHOP DOYLE AND PRINCE HOHENLOHE

Over a period of about eighteen months after Archbishop Magee's famous 'antithetical' sermon in St Patrick's cathedral in October 1822, Catholic leaders came together in a unified and sustained counter-offensive against every manifestation of Protestant supremacy and particularly against the aims and ambitions of those who claimed moral hegemony in religious and educational affairs. What 'took off' among the Catholic population at this time was not the type of wildfire revival or awakening that the evangelicals had been predicting, but a popular democratic movement on a scale unprecedented in European politics. In 1823–4 the Catholic Irish were welded into a single force united behind the grand objective of winning Emancipation through constitutional means. Bishop Jebb, with his usual clear-sighted view of public events, described the achievement as something 'we of this generation have never before witnessed … In truth, an Irish revolution has in great measure been effected'.[4] In the early years of the century, Peter Burrowes had predicted such an eventuality as soon as some force—what he called 'cement'—would rally the Catholic body into a unified whole. It remains to be seen to what degree this cement was provided by the defenders of Protestant supremacy and particularly by the proponents of the new Reformation.

The emergence of the priest-in-politics is continually cited as one of the major reasons behind the cohesive structure and eventual success of the Catholic Association. This is undoubtedly true. Less well known, however, is the manner in which priests and bishops were drawn into the political fray through a need to defend their faith and their office from the repeated denunciations of their detractors. In the aftermath of the controversy over Magee's famous sermon, the tempers of educated Catholics in general and Bishop Doyle in particular were not readily appeased. Indeed, Doyle's defiant gesture of picking up the gauntlet thrown down by Magee set the tone for his political pronouncements of the following year, which had an enormous impact, particularly on the key figures who dominated public opinion, such as W.F. Conway and Michael Staunton, editors of the *Dublin Evening Post* and the *Freeman's Journal* respectively.

During the spring of 1823, dismayed by the stagnancy of the Emancipation question and the beaten state of the country, O'Connell and Sheil, who had long been at loggerheads over strategy and tactics (Sheil supported the veto while O'Connell opposed it), finally joined forces with the formation of the Catholic Association. Like the old Catholic Committee, the Catholic Association was organized to petition parliament for Catholic rights. O'Connell's plan was to fashion it into a broader, more popular organization to publicize Catholic grievances, to collect money to help defend Catholic rights in a legal system dominated by Orange sympathizers, and to provide resources for the education of Catholic children.[5]

The modest nature of the initial collaborative effort that gave birth to the Catholic Association has since passed into historical legend.[6] Equally inauspicious was the event that was to raise Doyle to the ranks of a political propagandist of the first order in the same year. During the early months of 1823, when O'Connell and Sheil were laying the foundations for their new campaign in a meeting room on the upper floor of Coyne's bookshop in Capel Street, Dublin, Doyle was apparently watching for an opportunity to reinforce the authority of his Church and the morale of his followers. He discovered a worthy means of fulfilling his ambitions in the person of a German priest, Alexander Emmerich, dean of Bamberg and prince of Hohenlohe, whose reputation for effecting miraculous cures had recently gained wide currency in France and Germany.[7]

Doyle sent a letter to Prince Hohenlohe asking him to intercede on behalf of Maria Lalor, a young woman who had lost her speech as a child. The case afforded a perfect opportunity to test the particular method employed by the prince, who specialized in what can only be called 'long-distance' cures. Hohenlohe agreed to pray for the deaf woman's recovery at a special Mass scheduled for 9 a.m. on 10 June; the deaf woman and her confessors were to join in prayer and Holy Communion at exactly the same time. The arrangement went ahead as planned. According to Fr O'Connor, the priest who administered the sacrament on the appointed day, the young woman, just as she was about to receive the host, heard a voice in the distance asking, 'Mary, are you well?' to which she replied, 'Oh Lord, am I,' and fell prostrate. Upon regaining consciousness, she was found to have recovered her powers of speech.[8]

When Doyle received word that Hohenlohe's intercession had proved successful, he proceeded in haste to the scene of the miracle in order to verify it and to make a public pronouncement. Having established the authenticity of the miracle to his own satisfaction, he decided to publicize the case through a pastoral letter, which was circulated throughout Ireland and Britain as well as in some European countries. The letter itself was less a proclamation of gratitude for divine favour and more an intensely political statement designed to bolster the confidence of Irish Catholics by declaring that God was on their side. It was aimed directly at their detractors, especially the evangelicals:

> At this time and in this place it was worthy of His providence that the light of His countenance should be shed upon His faithful people. We have long experienced the truth of His prediction to those who were to walk in His footsteps and carry after them their cross—namely 'that the world would rejoice but that they would be sad'; and the present period has added sorrow to our sorrow, and pressure to our distress. Our religion is traduced, our rights are withheld, our good name is maligned, our best actions are misrepresented, crimes are imputed to us against which our very nature revolts, our friends are silenced, and our enemies insult us and glory in our humiliation. It is meet, therefore, and just that He for whose name and faith we suffer, should cast upon us a look of compassion, lest we faint in the way or be overcome by temptation—that He should comfort His people and renew to them by visible signs an assurance that He watches over them—that a hair of their heads will not perish—and that, possessing their soul in patience, they may expect His return 'to wipe away every tear from their cheek and fill them with that joy which no one can take away'.[9]

In a plea worthy of a masterful diplomat, Doyle went on to explain the nature of the current anti-Catholic agitation and why it should be borne with Christian tolerance. He countenanced charity and understanding as the most effective antidotes against the bigotry and prejudice the enemies of the Catholic cause had imbibed with their mothers' milk and that 'nothing but education, of which many of them are destitute, and a free intercourse with Catholics could remove'. When every source of influence from the nursery to the law courts informed Protestants that Catholics were enemies of God and the State, how could things be different?

> But, you will ask me, are we then to suffer in silence and not vindicate our good name: Far from it, brethren; you should uphold by every lawful means your own character and promote your own interests. These interests are the interests of truth and justice, and they must advance. The ways of their progress are obvious, and nothing can retard them but your own imprudence.[10]

In Doyle's opinion the righteousness of the Catholic cause would triumph, not only because it was just in the eyes of God, but because His church on earth was coming forward as the instrument of deliverance:

> You have increased in property, in numbers, and in strength; these give you a moral weight which carries you forward with an accelerated motion. Education has arrived to a state of excellence amongst those of you who are blessed with the means of obtaining it, and is united with a pure and sound morality. These will illuminate and enliven and direct the movements of our body that we may act in concert, dissipate prejudice, make our merits manifest, and attach to our cause the virtuous and intelligent of every creed and class. The progress of our religion, which is such as to excite even our own surprise, will of itself make known our principles and refute every calumny; the piety and zeal of your priesthood, the appearance of your places of worship, the multitudes who frequent them, their pious demeanour, their strict integrity, their faithful attachment to the ever faithful creed of the saints, will have—as they daily have—an insensible but powerful effect ... These are the lawful and efficient means of mitigating the evils you now endure, and a few of the grounds of your future hope. These will plead for you in a language which will speak to the understanding of the wise, to the interests of legislators, and to the hearts of men. Supported on these pillars, let your cause rest.[11]

This proclamation was nothing less than the theoretical foundation for the Emancipation campaign, for which O'Connell and Sheil were shortly to improvise a practical strategy. The timing of its publication was very significant. Throughout the summer of 1823 the activities of the Orange Order reached new heights of provocation. The government's refusal to ban these demonstrations, especially those scheduled for the Twelfth of July, appeared as further evidence of Protestant triumphalism, and the Catholic Association, still in its infancy, was in no position to offer any meaningful resistance. In this context Doyle's epistle had a galvanizing effect on Catholic public opinion; it was all the more effective because it was the dictate of a bishop who was universally acclaimed for integrity and moderation.[12]

The cure of Maria Lalor was held up as tangible proof that the Catholic faith enjoyed divine sanction, and Doyle's letter publicly proclaimed the Church's role as the instrument that would deliver its people from bondage and degradation. The impact of the Lalor case was further strengthened by another miraculous cure attributed to Prince Hohenlohe, this time involving a Carmelite nun, Maria Stewart, whose recovery was verified by the Catholic archbishop of Dublin, Dr Daniel Murray. Murray's decision to follow Doyle's example indicated that the Catholic resurgence initiated almost singlehandedly by Doyle was beginning to gain momentum.[13]

During the summer of 1823 Hohenlohe had become a household name in Ireland, synonymous with the legitimacy of the Catholic faith. In the decade leading up to Emancipation, perhaps no individual episode did more to unite the religious and the political aspects of the Catholic question than these 'cures' attributed to a German priest who had never set foot on Irish soil.[14] Much of the publicity for the Hohenlohe cures derived from the taunts and jeers of the ultra-Protestant press at this affirmation of one of the most hallowed traditions of the Catholic faith. In the face of the sworn evidence of medical authorities and the relatives of the women who had been cured, as well as the testimony of leading members of the Catholic episcopate, however, such denunciations carried a hollow ring. What mattered in the long term was the amount of publicity that the events had received, and how this publicity acted as a conduit to bring Doyle's ideas before the public.

In October 1823, with the publication of the famous *Vindication of the Rights and Civil Principles of Irish Catholics*, Doyle secured his reputation as the theorist of Catholic resurgence. The *Vindication*, which appeared in the form of a letter to the lord lieutenant, the marquess of Wellesley, has been described by Fergus O'Ferrall as having had the same effect on the consciousness of Irish Catholics as Tom Paine's *Common Sense* on the Americans in 1776.[15] A more appropriate parallel, perhaps, would be the impact of the Abbé Joseph Sieyès' celebrated pamphlet *What Is the Third Estate?* during the debates leading up to the convocation of the Estates General in May 1789.[16] This is true more especially if the *Vindication* is taken together with Doyle's other political writings of the 1820s, in particular the famous *Letters on the State of Ireland* ... (1825).

Invoking the principles of utility and the 'career open to talent' so evocative of the rhetoric common to both the French and American revolutions, Doyle attacked the colonial gentry as having enslaved the native Catholic population, and described them as a useless and parasitical entity on the health and well-being of the whole:

> Their *esprit de corps*—the prejudices which encompass them—their family circumstances—the insolence, often, and immorality of their sons—the pomp and vanity of their wives and daughters—their ephemeral and transitory rank unfit them for the office of gentry. Lighten the pressure of them on the country, give good and equal laws, and talents and industry will produce a gentry.[17]

Describing the Church of Ireland as an establishment 'as should not be suffered to exist in any civilized country'[18] he questioned its legal and ecclesiastical legitimacy, and claimed it enjoyed its illegal patrimony at the expense of the suffering and degradation of the majority Catholic population. As Sieyès did when he attacked the feudal privileges of the French aristocracy, Doyle went far beyond mere criticism when he attacked the tithe system, the economic foundation of the Church of Ireland and the ultimate guarantor of its legitimacy and permanence. His rhetoric embodied all the indignation and anger of an unacknowledged and despised class suddenly awakening to a realization of its own power and importance in the nation. In a pattern that was remarkably evocative of the impact of Sieyès' famous pamphlet, Doyle combined moral righteousness with rational analysis to provide a script for the revolution in consciousness that was about to unfold. The Catholic cause had unquestionably found its theorist and propagandist, who hammered the moral and legal justification for Catholic equality into place as O'Connell assumed the mantle of tactical strategist and political spokesman.[19] That the theorist was the most respected member of the Catholic hierarchy was perhaps the most consequential event in the entire Emancipation campaign.

With Doyle's response to the problems of the time, the spiritual and the political were never far apart. A native of County Carlow, he had been educated in the Augustinian seminary at Coimbra in Portugal, where he witnessed the Peninsular Campaign and came to know the duke of Wellington. A professed admirer of John Locke and the British constitutional tradition (which he considered far superior to the governing systems of the old regime he had been exposed to in Spain and Portugal), he returned to Ireland and was appointed bishop of Kildare and Leighlin in 1819 at the age of thirty-three. His youth, his European education, his political liberalism, and not least his courage and eloquence immediately set him apart from his episcopal colleagues. He could not be branded an ingratiating 'Castle bishop' by the radicals, nor an uncouth peasant raised by the influence of Maynooth and the power of the Roman collar to arrogance and demagoguery, as the evangelical press continually represented his vociferous colleague, Rev. John MacHale. Doyle commanded universal respect, even from his enemies, who liked to point to the Protestant element in his family background (his mother's family, the Warrens, had originally been Quakers) and allegedly circulated the rumour that he converted to the reformed faith on his deathbed in 1833.[20]

Doyle's thinking on the Catholic question had a long pedigree, extending back to Charles O'Conor and Edmund Burke in the eighteenth century, but more thoroughly developed as a political ideology by Denys Scully, Theobald McKenna, William and Henry Parnell, and the poet Thomas Moore, among others, in the early nineteenth century. The essence of this ideology, which has been variously described as 'liberal unionist' or 'Catholic liberal', was that loyalty to the constitution (as opposed to French republicanism) was the most effective way to secure the political rights still denied to Catholics; that legal and constitutional justice demanded the restoration of such rights; and that once restored to their rights the Catholics of Ireland would be proud to see their country rehabilitated and admitted as a full and equal partner in the British union of nations and would prove the equal of any of the other nations when it came to loyalty.[21]

Doyle seldom appeared on a public platform, preferring to spread his influence through pastoral letters, pamphlets, and his favourite journalistic mouthpiece, the liberal-Protestant *Dublin Evening Post*. His endorsement of political action was remarkable for a churchman, and his attitude may be gauged from a statement in his private correspondence:

> Much is granted to prayer, much to importunity, much even to clamour, but the silent slave will be converted into a beast of burden. 'Arise,' says the apostle, 'and Christ will enlighten thee'. And another, 'he that is in filth, let him lie in filth still'.[22]

Through his writings and sermons in 1823 he demonstrated to fellow clerics how the spiritual office might be employed in the temporal service of alleviating the conditions under which the Catholic population was forced to live. The events of 1823 brought about a remarkable change in the consciousness of Irish Catholics. From this point onward, there can be discerned a sense of confidence and unity in the pursuit of a common goal, more obvious at first among prominent figures in political and religious life, but soon reaching the urban middle classes and the peasantry.

Doyle articulated two major objectives to which O'Connell and the Catholic Association wholly subscribed. The first was to wean the popular classes away from their reliance on secret societies and addiction to millennial prophecies by advocating obedience to the leadership of the clergy and hierarchy, and by substituting a program of constitutional action in which Catholics of every social class could participate. The second was to undermine the criticism of ultra-

Protestants by demonstrating Catholic loyalty to the constitution, and to uphold the prestige of the Catholic Church against evangelical charges that it was a subversive and tyrannical force in Irish affairs. No force in Irish society at this time provided a stronger incentive towards the accomplishment of these ends than the provocative and triumphalist tactics of the ultra-Protestant party.

It had long been the practice of ultra-Protestant polemicists and supporters of the Orange Order to engage in provocative anti-Catholic agitation through commemorations of anniversaries and public festivals as well as inflammatory rhetoric in the popular press. After the impact of Archbishop Magee's 1822 sermon, however, it became clear that a strategy that focused more specifically on the Catholic hierarchy and priesthood was beginning to take shape. In March 1823, for example, the famous controversialist, the Rev. Robert McGhee, urged Lord Farnham to introduce a motion in the House of Lords requiring that Catholic bishops and priests be made to answer openly to the government for their beliefs, particularly on the question of whether they considered all Protestants 'accursed heretics'.[23]

In August of the same year at St Kevin's churchyard in Dublin, a Catholic burial service was interrupted and the priest, the Rev. Michael Blake, prevented from officiating at the grave. This situation had arisen because graveyards were usually sited alongside churches that had been Catholic in medieval times but had been expropriated by the Church of Ireland during the Reformation. Catholics were thus obliged to use burial facilities in Protestant property, a situation that was permitted so long as priests did not attend with the usual accoutrements of their office such as vestments, prayer books, and holy water on open display. As a result, the custom had developed whereby priests attended the funeral without any mark of distinction and stepped forward at the appropriate moment to offer, from memory, prayers for the deceased.[24] By his own account, this is what the Rev. Blake had been doing when 'the order of Dr Magee was rung in my ear', as he put it, and he was obliged to retire from the scene.[25] Dr Magee, it would appear, had insisted that the practice of accommodation in use for centuries was yet another example of the Catholic priesthood's flagrant disregard for the law and the rights of the Established Church, and had ordered his chaplains to discountenance it. Amid the uproar and indignation that ensued, the Catholic Association organized a petition to persuade parliament to introduce a burial bill that would allow Catholics to purchase land for their own graveyards and also to collect funds to provide for the costs of purchase.[26]

The controversy over burials extended into the new year and also into other parts of the country. An incident similar to that at St Kevin's reportedly occurred in January at a Presbyterian funeral in Holywood, County Down, where the pastor was interrupted on the instructions of the bishop of Down, Dr Mant, who ordered that he not only be prevented from officiating but be put out of the churchyard.[27] In Limerick, Bishop Jebb lamented the 'incalculable mischief' done by a Church of Ireland minister named Fitzgibbon, who antagonized the crowd by putting in a personal appearance at one funeral, then proceeded to call out the military, and followed it up by engaging in a newspaper war. Jebb's evaluation of Fitzgibbon's influence speaks to the amount of damage such an individual could do:

> Had Mr. F.[itzgibbon] (for he is the only established clergyman of Limerick who continued to get into these scrapes) conducted himself from the beginning with common prudence, all might now be well. But the sword is drawn perhaps beyond my power of getting it replaced in the scabbard. I do not mean to say that there is not a systematic plan, adopted on the instigation of O'Connell, for usurping authority in the Church of England burial ground and exhibiting to a heated populace the triumphant insignia of popish superstition; but I will say that but for the intemperance of ultra-protestants who know little, and feel less, of that faith for which they think themselves particularly zealous, Limerick would at this day exhibit a fair specimen of mutual toleration and goodwill.[28]

The burial controversy was temporarily shelved when parliament passed a bill that granted Catholics the right to hold funeral services according to the rites of their own Church once they had secured permission from the sexton. The matter did not end there, however, and eventually Catholics bought land for their own graveyards, usually quite near to the lavish new churches that were springing up all over the country at this time.[29]

As one of the grievances the Catholic Association used to increase its political capital with the Catholic clergy, the burials controversy was of great importance. But it was minor compared to the uproar that took place in March 1824 when English MP John Henry North, in his maiden speech in the House of Commons, charged the Catholic priesthood with neglecting the education of Irish children because of their opposition to the use of the scriptures. He managed to add insult to injury by alleging that *Moll Flanders* was commonly used as a schoolbook in Ireland. North was Irish by birth and a member of the KPS. While his speech might have been foolhardy and ill-conceived, it was hardly unique at the time; similar charges had been the common currency of evangelical critics from the very beginning of the moral crusade. What touched the sensitive nerve of national pride was his open assertion before the assembled parliament of the kingdom that Irish Catholic children were being educated through the medium of immoral and licentious literature while the word of God was being purposefully denied them.[30]

First to reply to North's allegations, predictably, was Bishop Doyle in the *Dublin Evening Post*. The particular source of Doyle's outrage was the fact that the Catholic clergy were denied money for educational purposes from public funds while their critics and detractors were in open receipt of such resources. Doyle's letter was taken by his great supporter, W.F. Conway of the *Dublin Evening Post*, to a meeting of the Catholic Association on 6 April. Conway astutely suggested that the Association solicit accounts from priests all over the country about the state of education in their parishes. The ostensible reason was to get some measure of the educational picture at the national level, the better to counter North's allegations, and also to see to what degree the suspicion of proselytism on the part of the KPS was warranted. But the real motive was the linking of the impassioned debate over education to the political movement.[31]

Despite the crescendo of criticism that had been growing ever since John MacHale's *Hierophilus* letters had revealed that public money was being made available to proselytizing agencies, nothing had changed with regard to the allocation of government funds. Until the Catholic Association stepped into the breach, priests could counteract the designs of the societies only on an individual level by warning their congregations, writing letters to the papers, or other gestures of this kind. The emergence of the Catholic Association as a vehicle to gather and publicize information at the national level rapidly changed this situation. Not only did it provide a forum for the airing of grievances about proselytism, but it also gave priests experience in participatory democracy that would reap enormous dividends in the future. In addition it bolstered confidence by revealing how successful were the voluntary efforts of the Catholic community to provide an acceptable education for their children in the face of poverty and the well-financed competition afforded by the Protestant societies.

The response of the Catholic clergy and hierarchy to the appeal for information on education and proselytism was so overwhelming that the Catholic Association threatened to sink under its weight. Members began to complain about the amount of time spent at public meetings listening to Conway reading aloud from the thousands of letters that began to pour in from all over the country. The letters contained information about the organization and financing of schools, the curriculum used, and often the denominational interests involved. They revealed a mixed picture of voluntary effort at every level, from the most humble hedge schools to those run by religious orders.[32] It was a matter of great pride with many of the priests to point out, as did Fr James Roche of Donard to Archbishop Murray, that 'there is not, even in England, a peasantry better informed with respect to religion than in Ireland, notwithstanding all the persecution of ages'.[33] Although many instances were given where the Kildare Place schools were run on principles perfectly acceptable to Catholics, the overall consensus suggested that the suspicion of proselytism could never be overcome, and that the Catholic community would never be satisfied with the Kildare Place system. The testimony of the Rev. James O'Shaughnessy, bishop of Killaloe, reflected the general opinion of Catholics on the subject:

> So convinced are the Catholic clergy and laity that proselytism is the avowed aim of the Kildare Place Society that they have zealously set their face against them ... These bible schools are in general a source of acrimony ... and are the cause of diminishing considerably that mutual harmony and friendship between Catholics and Protestants that had subsisted until the unfortunate period of their existence.[34]

O'Shaughnessy's evidence, like much of its kind, was reprinted in the *Dublin Evening Post*. By the end of May, after six weeks of debate in the national newspapers, it was clear that education had superseded every other item on the Catholic list of grievances. The opinion was virtually unanimous that the KPS schools should be rejected and the government called upon to establish a commission of inquiry to investigate charges of proselytism and to establish how its money was being spent.[35] This laid the issue to rest momentarily, but as far as the clergy's attachment to the Catholic Association was concerned, the link was established. As a result of their politicizing of the education question, the Association had shown the priests what could be accomplished by political influence backed by public opinion. It was a lesson they would make good use of.

The public debate over the burials controversy and the education question resulted in the Catholic hierarchy and clergy becoming deeply politicized by the summer of 1824. Their mood of open defiance became evident in the autumn and winter of that year when they opted to respond to public challenges to defend their faith and their office at a series of meetings organized by evangelical societies throughout the country. It was this affair above all others that spread the militancy of the Catholic Association down the social ranks and into every part of the country. By the year's end the authorities and the sources they depended upon for their information were speaking in terms that suggested their fear of a national rebellion or revolution.

THE BIBLE WAR OF 1824

The celebrated confrontation between representatives of the Catholic Church and the evangelical mission was occasioned by a preaching tour that involved two well-known speakers who were scheduled to attend anniversary meetings of various evangelical societies in the autumn of 1824.[36] The event was unquestionably designed to precipitate a confrontation with the priests. Subsequent accounts of the proceedings in the evangelical press portrayed the meetings as having been forcibly interrupted and broken up by garrulous priests, supported by Catholic mobs, despite clear evidence that the priests had in most cases been invited to participate. The strategy was apparently to 'cordially invite' priests to attend the meetings on the assumption that if they stayed away, as the evangelicals apparently believed they would, the Catholic cause would appear to have lost face. If, on the other hand, the priests did accept, it was assumed that the moral strength of the Protestant position would easily win the day.

As it happened, the Catholic clergy not only accepted the invitations but were accompanied in some cases by the most prominent political figures of the day. Besides featuring debates on spiritual questions, the Bible society meetings of 1824 became forums for the discussion of major political issues, including the tithe system, the disturbed state of the country, and especially Catholic Emancipation. The whole affair lasted three months and received extraordinary coverage in the newspapers. The *Freeman's Journal* printed the complete speeches of all the leading orators, including Daniel O'Connell, who made full use of the opportunity to assert himself as the champion of Catholic rights.

The two preachers who arrived in the country in September 1824 were the Rev. Baptist Wriothesley Noel, an evangelical minister prominently associated with the Clapham Sect, and Captain James Edward Gordon of the Royal Navy, who was closely connected with the Independent evangelical community in Sligo. Both Noel and Gordon had Scottish connections, and Gordon already had an established reputation as stalwart of the evangelical moral crusade and a particular foe of Catholic ambitions.[37] The *Freeman's Journal* portrayed them as a pair of misguided enthusiasts completely out of their depth in the stormy waters of Irish religious controversy. This opinion seems to have been widespread, and shortly after their arrival in the country the two became known as 'the Scotch captain' and 'the schoolboy', and their tour through the provinces provided a great deal of amusement to the wags of the time. In their progress from town to town Noel and Gordon left a trail of controversy and sectarian strife in their wake, to the extent that the police and even the military had to intervene frequently.

The first major incident occurred in Cork early in September at a meeting of the Cork Ladies' Auxiliary of the HBS. The meeting was well publicized, for among those present were O'Connell and Sheil to defend the Catholic position, and the Rev. Richard Pope, a Church of Ireland minister whose stock in trade was religious controversy.[38] The speeches of Noel and Gordon cited the usual evangelical explanation for the cause of the country's woes: the lack of knowledge of the scriptures. Sheil countered that the Irish poor were less in need of bibles than of bread, and that the visiting speakers would be better employed if they exerted their energies among the higher orders, to whom they might teach a little humanity. When the discussion turned to the state of morality in Ireland, O'Connell took the floor and left nothing unsaid on the same subject in England. Using the evidence of a recent parliamentary report on the poor laws, he asserted that nineteen out of twenty women in England were already mothers a month before they were married. For the representatives of religion and morality in that country to attempt to educate poor Irish women was in his view a ludicrous state of affairs; they had more than enough to do in looking after their own. Sheil and O'Connell were successful in preventing the passage of a motion on the value of scriptural education in Ireland, and the meeting was adjourned.

When the company reassembled on the following day to complete the proceedings, a repeat performance took place. Eventually, both parties reached a gentleman's agreement to end the discussion, with neither conceding defeat.[39] The marathon debate was not accompanied by physical violence, but the Catholics of Cork were roused to the point of organizing a defence committee to counter the activities of the HBS. When the bishop of Cork, Dr Murphy, was urged to support such an organization, he issued a public statement to the effect that he wished the people themselves to express their opinions freely, because the supporters of the Bible society had asserted that the Irish people would be favourable to the evangelical preachers were it not for the work of the priests.[40]

The meetings in the smaller towns of the south and south-west took place without disturbance, presumably because Catholic spokesmen were not in attendance. At the Waterford meeting in early October the priests played no part in the discussions, but a large group of Catholics gathered outside the hall where Gordon and Noel were speaking; troops were stationed nearby to prevent violence. The crowd was addressed by a local priest, who ordered them to keep the peace and disperse quietly, which they apparently did.[41] Catholic clerics and laymen accepted the invitation to attend the Kilkenny meeting on 14 October. Only a select few were admitted, however; the mayor's bailiffs and the city police stood guard at the door to prevent undesirables from entering and to keep order in the hall. At this particular meeting, which was chaired by Lord Ormond, the evangelical cause was well represented by the ubiquitous Richard Pope and the local stalwarts, Peter Roe and Robert Shaw.[42] Great indignation was expressed in the *Freeman's Journal* because a reporter sent to cover the event was roughly prevented from doing so. Having waited three days to obtain an account, the editor finally exposed what had happened, adding that the anti-Catholic press in both islands, particularly the *Dublin Evening Mail*, had published false accounts of the proceedings.[43]

The most notorious event of the whole campaign occurred on 19 October at Loughrea, County Galway. The meeting was to be held at the Quarter Sessions House, with the archbishop of Tuam, Dr Power le Poer Trench, in the chair. When the bishop and his colleagues went to enter the courthouse, they found it packed with Catholic clergy and their supporters; the priests had apparently been invited by a letter circulated among them during the previous week. Inside the building the clamour was so great that the bishop and the guest speakers could make their way to the platform only with the help of the police. When the leading Catholic spokesman, Fr Peter Daly, attempted to speak, the archbishop refused to allow him to proceed on the grounds that he was not a subscribing member of the Bible society. At this point John Guthrie, a liberal Protestant barrister, interposed on behalf of the Catholics and was also refused a hearing. In the tumult that followed (according to the Catholic account), the Catholics attempted to leave the meeting in indignation at the way they had been treated, but found their way barred by a unit of the 10th Hussars with drawn sabres.[44] According to the Protestant account, the Catholics raised such a racket and so interrupted the proceedings that the archbishop and his colleagues were forced to leave.[45] The large and hostile crowd in the street outside the courthouse made the presence of the military a necessity for the safe exit of the Protestant group.

After Trench and his followers had taken their leave, the company who remained behind elected John Guthrie as chairman and proceeded to pass several resolutions condemning the activities and objectives of the Bible society. Most of the proposals were put forward by Protestants sympathetic to Catholic claims, including Matthew St George of Kilcolgan, and Robert D'Arcy of Woodville, the agent of Lord Clanricarde.[46] The event was celebrated by Anthony Raftery, a contemporary poet well known in the Loughrea area:

> Gannon and Daly were reading the commission
> Long life to Dan Egan and Councillor Guthrie
> True flower of the Powers country, and no doubt Bob D'Arcy
> The people who eat meat on Good Friday were stealing away and departing
> And they could not see the door for shame.[47]

Outrage over the events at Loughrea was expressed in several newspapers and periodicals. The loudest voice in defence of the Catholics was as usual Daniel O'Connell's in the *Freeman's Journal*. A week after the Loughrea debacle, he made a point of attending a public dinner there that grateful Catholics held in honour of John Guthrie 'for his constant advocacy of Catholic freedom and especially for his conduct among the Saints last week'. In the course of the evening O'Connell expressed the wish to form a committee to prepare an address to the people of England, explaining why Bible societies were opposed in Ireland. In his opinion the various evangelical bodies were raising a torrent of fanaticism among the Protestant gentry, which was completely destructive to all the decencies and normal intercourse of social life. Reinforcing this proposal was a motion, introduced by a priest and seconded by a Protestant gentleman, that no more public Bible meetings be held, 'as they appear to create disunion and widen the breach that exists between the two religions'.[48]

The Loughrea experience did not deter Noel and Gordon from proceeding to Ballina in the following week. Once again, the meeting turned into a melee when local priests were refused permission to address the crowds, and one priest was assaulted by a policeman.[49] The next venue on the west coast was Easky, a small town near Sligo, where by all reports an exemplary meeting was held. Three priests of the locality were matched against the Rev. William Urwick and two scripture-readers. The discussion was confined to doctrinal issues, and both sides came away satisfied that their cases had been well represented.[50] At Carrick-on-Shannon in early November three Catholic priests—Fathers Browne, McKeown and O'Beirne—were appointed to speak against Oldfield, Percy, and Bushe, ministers of the Established Church. No ugly incidents were reported in the press, but as the *Freeman's Journal* sarcastically commented, 'admirable arrangements were made to preserve the peace'.[51]

An air of intense expectation surrounded the Carlow meeting, which began on 18 November. The debating teams included some of the best orators in the country, including Robert Daly and Richard Pope on the Protestant side and Fr Edward Nolan on the Catholic. But the centre of attention was Bishop Doyle, who had recently published a pamphlet attacking the work of Bible societies.[52] Contrary to expectations, however, Doyle did not participate in the discussions, much to the disappointment of the editor of the *Freeman's Journal*, who had stopped the press at three o'clock on 24 November to inform readers that the meeting had been resumed for the third day, and that the bishop was expected to take up the cudgels at any moment.[53]

Doyle preferred to leave the task to his coadjutor, Fr Nolan, who was to succeed him as head of the diocese ten years later.[54] Nolan presented a sane and reasonable account of why the Catholic Church opposed the ambitions of the various Bible and education societies, and made no attempt to disguise the fact that such opposition was based on self-protection:

> When they [i.e. the societies] take the field against the Catholic Church and unfurl the banner of evangelical licentiousness, we need no prophet to warn us of the danger. Many of the individuals who support it, I am sure, are activated by good motives, but the principles and objectives of the society are essentially hostile to the Catholic Church.[55]

The Carlow gathering was the last event of the tour to appear in the national headlines, although Gordon and Noel remained in the country until December. The controversy surrounding the public meetings had a catalytic effect on public opinion. The Catholic clergy emerged from the contest secure in the knowledge that they had established the authority of their Church on the use of the scriptures, and they were therefore even more firmly determined to keep evangelical missionaries from influencing their flocks. Henceforth, their opposition to the evangelicals became more organized, involving sophisticated methods of defence and attack, especially in their collaboration with the Catholic Association and in their use of propaganda. They also lived up to the reputation that the evangelicals had been ascribing to them for years, namely, as the strongest opponents of free distribution of the Bible and the chief obstacle in the way of the new Reformation. After 1824 hostility between the evangelical vanguard and the priests subsided in proportion to the degree that the Protestant landed classes lost their social and political power, except in the province of Ulster, where religious division continued to defy all political solutions.

PROPAGANDA AND COUNTER-PROPAGANDA

One of the more significant facts highlighted by the Bible controversy of 1824 was the importance of propaganda. The forces arrayed against each other had always had their slogans, pamphleteers, and partisan journals and newspapers. Nevertheless, a new dimension was introduced with the extensive coverage given to the debates on education, proselytism, and the Bible controversy in the pages of national daily newspapers like the *Freeman's Journal* and the *Dublin Evening Post*. After 1824 it appeared that sectarian controversy had become a staple diet of the reading public, and no contemporary political issue gave rise to such a deluge of pamphlets, newsletters, journals and other polemical literature.

In the area of printed matter generally, the evangelical press for years had had the upper hand. Once the Catholics embarked on a counter-offensive, many of the methods they employed to publicize their cause were borrowed directly from their opponents. No Protestant Bible society was without its handbook of general rules and its series of monthly reports, often supplemented by extracts of correspondence. In general, these carried accounts of regular business matters, lists of patrons and subscribers, and statements on the intake and outlay of funds. Special attention was always given to the correspondence of workers in the mission stations or of clergymen on the preaching circuits. Very often, the reports carried news about other agencies engaged in similar activities, and the societies also enjoyed access to journals such as the *Christian Observer* (the official mouthpiece of the Church of England), *The Quarterly Review*, *The British Critic*, *Blackwood's Magazine* and the *Edinburgh Review*. By the 1820s the evangelical press in Britain was one vast publicity machine that was certainly doing more to inform the reading public about foreign countries and their inhabitants than any journalistic enterprise up to that time. After 1824 the Irish organizations became especially adept at getting their material into British journals, where they had a particularly powerful influence on the debate over Catholic Emancipation.

The furore over the notorious Bible meetings in 1824 had almost as much effect on public opinion in England as it did in Ireland. The *Christian Observer*, which had always adhered to a moderate position on the Emancipation question, now assumed a distinctly hostile tone, especially towards the Catholic Church. The Bible society meetings were reported as having been tumultuously interrupted by Catholic clergy and laymen, who in some cases, as at Loughrea, allegedly proceeded to gross outrages.[56] Attention was drawn to recent meetings at which Catholics had not only proposed to start a fund-raising campaign to halt the progress of scriptural education in Ireland but had even appointed an agent to manage their affairs in London. The City of London Bible Auxiliary denounced the 'conspiracy' against the Bible in Ireland and claimed that the society had sent 'arms' to support it, and would send more in the future, 'for the people of Ireland were beginning ardently to desire the bible and it would be unjust to withhold it from them'.[57] This attitude reflected the view generally propagated in the British evangelical press that the Catholic Irish were themselves conscious of their spiritual enslavement and anxious to be liberated from the controls of Rome. It was deftly exploited by anti-Catholic propagandists, increasingly in receipt of fresh material to support their claim that Catholicism was indeed subversive of the constitution. Such material flowed mainly from two sources: the writings of talented propagandists like the Rev. Caesar Otway and Bishop Robert Daly; and second, the eyewitness accounts disseminated by preachers like the Rev. Mortimer O'Sullivan and the Rev. Robert McGhee, who began the practice of preaching tours in England on behalf of the evangelical cause at home.[58]

Of the many polemicists who involved themselves on behalf of the Bible in Ireland, no single individual contributed more to the substance and success of evangelical propaganda than the Rev. Caesar Otway. A younger son of a Tipperary landed family, Otway was yet another minister of the Church of Ireland who had attended Trinity at the close of the eighteenth century. He began to make a name for himself as a controversialist in the early 1820s, and in 1825, along with Rev. Joseph Singer, he founded the *Christian Examiner and Church of Ireland Magazine*. This was the first periodical of its kind to represent the Established Church in Ireland, and in some ways it was modelled on the *Christian Observer*. Its main purpose was to promote and defend Protestant opinion in the face of the current 'Roman controversy'.

Otway's personal speciality lay in exposing the superstitions believed by Catholics, especially those connected with pilgrimages and the miraculous powers attributed to the priesthood. Besides editing the *Christian Examiner* he was personally responsible for much of its content. An intrepid traveller with a keen appreciation for popular culture, he was also the author of several travel books on Ireland, especially the far-western fastnesses of Connemara and Donegal that were currently in the process of being 'discovered' as fashionable tourist venues by the wealthy and sophisticated. Invariably composed with a view towards exposing Romish superstition, these works contain valuable material on folk life in the immediate pre-Famine period and betray a sympathy, if not a love, for the customs of the country people that is seldom matched in contemporary accounts of other foreign visitors.[59] Ironically, Otway was never more entertaining than when he was describing the petty sectarian tensions that gave spice and hilarity to everyday affairs, and that he personally appreciated more than most people. His travel books abound with stories of suspicious Protestants and inscrutable Catholics managing to live side by side, seldom escaping the influences of each other's religion, and frequently showing remarkable tolerance and good humour in their dealings with one another.

As one seeks to place the Irish evangelical movement in cultural perspective, the seemingly contradictory aspect of Otway's regard for the 'hidden Ireland' of the Catholic peasantry is of the greatest importance. Along with a small group of fellow travellers, he bridged the gap between the earlier phase of the evangelical movement and the emergence of a literary and intellectual trend among Protestant conservatives who looked to culture as well as religion as a possible foundation for uniting the interests of native and colonial. This ethos was propagated through the *Dublin University Magazine* and inaugurated a new phase in the study of Irish antiquities and literature. Otway was a regular contributor to the magazine, as were Samuel Ferguson and Isaac Butt.[60] Of equal importance in securing Otway's place in Irish literary history was his sponsorship of the young William Carleton.

The career of William Carleton offers a unique portrait of an ambitious Catholic caught up in the cultural and religious tensions of the times. A native of the Clogher Valley in County Tyrone, Carleton arrived in Dublin in 1817 as a penniless youth hoping to earn a living by teaching or writing. Within a few years he married and took up employment as a clerk with the Sunday School Society. His entry to the world of letters began when he read Otway's first travel volume, *Sketches in Ireland*, published in 1827. Among the aspects of Catholic superstition discussed in this book, considerable attention was paid to the penitential station on an island in Lough Derg in County Donegal. When Carleton met with Otway and told him how he had made the pilgrimage as a boy and why he agreed with the way it had been described in the *Sketches*, Otway invited him to submit his own recollections for possible publication in the *Christian Examiner*. The result was 'The Lough Derg pilgrim', the first of Carleton's masterly sketches of peasant life before the Famine.[61]

Otway recognized talent when he saw it. For the next four years Carleton became a regular contributor to the *Christian Examiner*, combining his marvellous and intimate knowledge of peasant life with 'a sectarian bias laid on with a trowel' as Benedict Kiely has described it. By the time of his first meeting with Otway, Carleton had already become a Protestant, which he remained until his death. Religious controversy was never his forte, however, and many critics insist that the bigotry with which his earlier literary efforts abound was the result of Otway's skilful editing. In the 1830s, especially after the publication of *Tales of Ireland* (1834), he began to move away from the influences of Otway and evangelicalism, and towards the cultural and political outlook of the literary intellectuals later known as Young Ireland. In the 1840s, in what amounted almost to a public recantation, he expressed regret for having previously misrepresented the Irish people, their religion and their clergy. Whether to redress the balance, or simply to depict the true nature of the evangelical mission as he saw it, he drew one of the most damning fictional accounts ever penned of the new Reformation in *Valentine McClutchy* (1848). This contribution notwithstanding, Catholic writers of later generations never forgave his betrayal of their religion and his decision to live and die a Protestant. It was mainly through the efforts of another Protestant, William Butler Yeats, that his place in Irish literary history was established.[62]

By the 1830s Otway was himself beginning to widen his literary horizons, though it is clear that while his writing may have become more 'national' in character, it lost little of the old animosity towards the doctrines and practices of the Catholic Church. In 1831 he resigned as editor of the *Christian Examiner* and thereafter gave of his literary talents to the *Dublin University Magazine*, which he had helped to found in 1833. Hardly less unionist in spirit than the *Christian Examiner*, this publication did not concern itself directly with sectarian matters and gave an elevated tone to literary and intellectual subjects in general. Under the editorial supervision of Isaac Butt and later Charles Lever, it promoted the country's most talented writers, including William Carleton, Sheridan Le Fanu and James Clarence Mangan.

Otway's resignation as editor of the *Christian Examiner* did not dampen that magazine's taste for religious controversy, and it continued to enjoy reasonable success until the Church of Ireland was disestablished in 1869. To the end it retained its official status as the voice of the Irish evangelical movement, but as Barbara Hayley has observed, 'without the literary and fictional content that [Otway] had commissioned or supplied himself, it degenerated into a run-of-the-press pious bickering'.[63] Neither did Otway's literary ambitions serve to lessen his personal antagonism to Catholicism. In books published in the mid- and late 1830s, which made his name as a travel writer, he seldom lost an opportunity to comment on the moral and intellectual slavery imposed on the peasantry by the Church of Rome and its agents. The following is characteristic:

> The truth is that it is not only the bible but the accompaniments of the bible that the priest dreads; he fears the spirit of inquiry, the illumination that succeeds the liberality of feeling, the disenthralling of intellect; above all he fears the contact with Protestantism. Let but the serene and manly front of that creed be presented to popery, which, prostrate before its clergy is only erect in subordination, and that clergy will fear lest the attitude belonging to man will be assumed by their vassals too.[64]

Up to 1824 the anti-Protestant sentiment in Catholic literature was to be found mostly in the popular ballads and poetry that were the preserve of the peasantry and the urban working classes. Pastorini, of course, was a prime source of inspiration for compositions of this kind, which were filled with dire predictions of the downfall of Protestants and the resurgence of the Catholics. Because of their openly seditious character, they were a matter of great irritation to the Protestant authorities. As Bishop Jebb, who always kept a watchful eye on public opinion at the lower end of the social scale, remarked:

> These ballads are listened to and bought up with great avidity. The itinerant minstrels, by way of interlude, haranguing the people after each stanza with much vehemence and gesticulation and inciting them to nothing short of rebellion. Several have been taken up both in Cork and in this city [Limerick] in the very act.[65]

The tone of many clerical pronouncements in the early 1820s indicates that the Catholic clergy and hierarchy were willing almost to bend over backwards to suppress sentiments that the more vulgar among their flocks were circulating in broadsides or cheerfully bellowing from street corners.[66] Bishop Murray, intensely conscious of the power of words and how they might be used against his Church, informed a parliamentary commission in 1825: 'we at present use the word "heretic" very sparingly; we chose, rather, as it is an offensive word, to say "our dissenting brethren", or "our separated brethren" or something of that kind'.[67] Bishop Doyle was prepared to advocate remarkable compromises, such as mixed education and even a union of the Catholic Church and the Church of Ireland.[68]

This last gesture, which was one of the most radical ever put forward as a solution to the Irish problem, was an effort to forestall the polarization that Doyle saw as inevitable in the spring of 1824 if events should continue on their present course.[69] After the Bible War of the following autumn and winter, however, Doyle's ambitions in this direction were increasingly fruitless. Once the priests had taken to the public platform, there was no stemming of either their political involvement or their anti-evangelical belligerence. When the forceful (and often highly entertaining) polemics of the folk hero Fr Tom Maguire came in the door, as it were, the soothing words of Doyle and Murray went out the window.

The events of the latter part of 1824 are critical to understanding the fusion of religion and politics that endowed the Emancipation campaign with such extraordinary strength and unity. During the controversy generated by the Bible War in the autumn and winter of 1824, the priests began to combine their role as public defenders of the faith with that of local organizers of the Catholic Association. Since their involvement with the education survey in the previous spring and summer, most were familiar with the aims and objectives of the Association. It was hardly a coincidence that the controversial meetings organized by the evangelical societies gave rise to the formation of defensive alliances of Catholics. In Waterford, for example, the campaign that succeeded in electing a pro-Emancipation candidate in the general election of 1826 was launched at a meeting to counteract the work of the Bible societies.[70] Side by side with lengthy accounts of the Bible meetings in the national press, there appeared news of recently organized branches of the Catholic Association and membership lists that grew longer by the day. The Bible debates probably did at least as much to mobilize priests and people behind the Catholic Association as the exhortations of O'Connell. A forthright commentary in the *Dublin Evening Post* accurately predicted the popular response to the inflammatory attacks on the Catholic religion:

> We admit that these things are constantly done in pamphlets and newspapers, charges and in sermons; but this is the first time in Ireland or in any country that two sets of orators have been found discussing knotty points of scripture in an aggregate assembly. The Catholics of Ireland, the

priests of Ireland, have long been accustomed to outrage and insult; but this is the first time that the experiment has been tried of rousing a whole population into madness.[71]

But it was not only Catholics who were successfully welded to the side of O'Connell and Emancipation by the events of 1824. Liberal Protestants, angered and disgusted by the blatant inflammatory attacks on their Catholic countrymen, were also driven into the O'Connellite camp. Immediately after the famous Bible meeting at Loughrea, John Guthrie came forward and declared that the whole purpose of the meeting had been the assembly of Catholics 'for the predetermined purpose of insulting them', and that while

> Biblicals of all sects, whether Established Church or Dissenters, were heard, [there was] not a word from a Roman Catholic. The Catholic pastors were to look on, and with indifference to behold their flocks seduced from them. The Catholic clergy were to stand by in silence, like convicted criminals, to hear sentence passed on themselves and their religion. He felt the injustice done to his Catholic brethren and entreated as a Protestant to be heard but Bishop Trench would not hear anyone who was not a member of the Bible Society.[72]

Similarly, in 1828, William Smith O'Brien (the son of Lady O'Brien of Dromoland, County Clare) declared his support for O'Connell and Emancipation because he wished to express his 'concurrence in any act which would put an end to the ascendancy of a faction which already revelled in the anticipated triumph of a civil war'.[73] Without the support of those liberal Protestants who threw the weight of their influence behind the Emancipation campaign, O'Connell would never have broken the hold of conservative landlords on electoral politics in 1826.

The genius of O'Connell's scheme to make the Catholic Association the representative organization of the entire Catholic community was the so-called 'Catholic rent': the penny-a-month that every Catholic in the country would pay to subscribe. O'Connell's strategy had been developed earlier in 1824 in connection with his ambition to broaden the base of the Catholic Association; it was not a new idea, and indeed it owed not a little to the example of the penny-a-week subscriptions collected by the Methodists and Bible society supporters. What O'Connell lacked was a network of organizers to implement his strategy at the local level. The priests were the ideal candidates for this task, and once their services were engaged in organization and rent collection, the scheme took off with phenomenal success.[74] It marks, as J.A. Reynolds has stated, the transition of the Catholic Association from a small club into a mass movement. With the rent scheme the organization in Dublin shot out roots into the soil of Ireland to provide countrymen everywhere with a diet of political food as universal and staple as the national potato.[75]

Both priests and people were politicized in the process, to the great consternation of the authorities. A correspondent of Francis Blackburne of Rathkeale described the situation as 1824 drew to a close:

> The influence of the clergy over the people is now greatly increased; this system of the Catholic rent has brought the people and their clergy closer than ever to one another; *their connection before was religious, now it is political.* The priests tell the people that it is for their good to pay the rent; they tell them this and significantly withhold any further explanation. This undefined and mysterious mode of acting leaves the people to their own construction; therefore, a rumour or a feeling prevails among them universally that we are to have a rebellion. I find that Pastorini's prophecies about the extinction of heretics in 1825 are again revived. [my emphasis][76]

The evidence coming in from government informers suggested something even more alarming: that the Catholic forces were engaged in preparations for a general rebellion. One of Chief Secretary Henry Goulburn's informants described the situation in Imaal in County Wicklow, where priests, middle classes, and peasantry were all united in a plot to stage an armed uprising and 'had received instructions to behave civilly to Protestants until the time arrives to throw off the mask'. The informant did not know who was at the head of the planned rebellion, but 'the people say that Counsellor O'Connell is an instrument appointed by God almighty to effect their wishes'. The local priest Fr Kavanagh, when exhorting his congregation in the chapel to pay the rent, reportedly stated 'it will be one side or the other this year 1825'. The informer went on to add that

> the opinion of the people on leaving the chapel was that they would certainly succeed. Everything that passes convinces them more and more that the prophecies of Pastorini will be fulfilled in 1825. All are sure of an explosion but do not know when it will take place.[77]

The most immediate and powerful evidence of a revolution in consciousness was the pride attached to the word 'Catholic'. If revolutions are brought about by words (as the critic La Harpe had claimed of the French Revolution), then it was fitting that that master of the rhetorical device, Archbishop Magee, should be among the first to recognize what had occurred. In a letter to John Jebb in the spring of 1824 he referred to the petition currently before the House of Lords:

> Instead of petitioning on behalf of Roman Catholics, they decided on deliberation to use the word 'Catholic' ... you may therefore see the determination of defiance. In truth, in the very term 'Catholic' the papists in Ireland have a strength that even now is difficult to resist.[78]

Clearly, Bishop Doyle's ambition had been realized. The symbolism and expectation previously attached to Captain Rock and Pastorini was now being transferred to O'Connell and the Catholic Association.[79]

The linkage between these two phases of the popular politicization that occurred during the 1820s is clearly reflected in the work of the poet Anthony Raftery. Born in Mayo, Raftery spent most of his life in east Galway and built up a reputation as one of the last of the wandering bards.[80] Blind from youth onwards, he was evidently well acquainted with history and contemporary politics. He wrote in Irish and his work constitutes one of the few and certainly one of the most valuable channels through which to observe the mentality of pre-Famine Gaelic Ireland. Raftery's poems dealing with political or religious themes reveal how the peasantry identified and blended the forces of political, religious and social oppression. As a resident of the part of County Galway dominated by the Trench family and affected by the sectarian conflict of the early 1820s, Raftery would have found it difficult to avoid commenting on the close alignment between the evangelical movement and Protestant supremacism. Time and again, he warned his readers to have no truck with the evangelicals and their Bible. Unlike anti-clerical poets of an earlier generation such as Eoin Ruadh Ó Suilleabháin, Raftery strongly approved of the priests' right to speak unconditionally on behalf of the people and gave his readers the following advice:

> But trust ye the clergy and the discourse of the church
> And the holy sermon that the saints and apostles have written for us
> Do not seek the bible or it shall come across you.[81]

His condemnation of the unauthorized use of the scriptures was taken straight from Catholic dogma:

> Many is the humpbacked lying discourse
> That was drawn out of the Irish bible
> Every man out of his own head, picking learning from it
> Asserting the right on top of the perjury.[82]

The following passage on the dangers of proselytizing schools shows how effectively the message of O'Connell and Doyle about the symbiotic relationship between church and people, and the Church as the instrument of deliverance, was making its way into the popular consciousness:

> I heard, if it be true, a rumour strange and new
> That they mean to plant schools in each corner
> The plan is, for scaith, to steal away our faith
> And to train up the spy and informer
> Our clergy's word is good, then seek no other food
> God's church has his own arm around her
> But if ye will embark on this vessel in the dark
> It will turn in the sea and founder[83]

Raftery's most famous exposition of popular Catholic feeling is to be found in a long poem called 'The Catholic rent', evidently written shortly after the famous Bible meeting at Loughrea in October 1824. It is at once an attack on tithes and Bible preachers and an invocation of O'Connell and Catholic rights. The underlying theme is the usurpation of the Irish Catholics' rights and religion by a Church founded on false doctrines. According to his interpretation of Pastorini, this ecclesiastical edifice and its fanatical representatives would be the first to fall:

> On observing the signs, I see fear for the fanatics
> Who fast not on Fridays and jeer at the Catholics
> Success is denied them, defeat shall be absolute
> As Peter and Jesus have spoken.
> Wrote Pastorini, you'll see it made manifest
> A rascally meeting each month in each hamlet
> But Clonmel shall make pieces of New Lights and Orangemen
> And Loughrea shall defeat them and beat their rascality;
> We have lost our good Clayton, but Daly's as bad for them
> Their bible's mendacious, we'll shame them and sadden them
> We'll give them ('twill please us) a token.[84]

Although Catholic deliverance had been prophesied by Pastorini and the book of Revelation, it would be secured, according to Raftery, only if the people co-operated with the methods of O'Connell:

I call ye, ye people, and be not under reproach
I shall praise ye forever if ye pay the Catholic rent
It is very little in the month is a farthing a week
And do not earn for yourselves scandal and shame
It is a little thing in the rent and it will free the land
Tithes shall not be called for, as used to be done to ye before
There shall be right and law for ye in respect to country and land
There is no danger of us forever, so long as O'Connell lives
Believe ye with truth the saints and the apostles who say the foreigners shall be scattered.[85]

Popular poetry and street ballads were not the only literature that condemned the Reformation movement, nor were they perhaps the most effective vehicles of opposition. During the period 1824–7 the foundations were laid for the vast outpouring of popular theological pamphlets that became a feature of Irish Catholicism in the nineteenth century.[86] The importance of such literature in regularizing religious observance and in enshrining Catholic doctrine as the supreme moral authority in the country stands as yet another example of how the Protestant evangelical movement served to entrench Catholicism in the lives of ordinary people.

The demand for what might be called 'serious' theological literature first became evident in the aftermath of Magee's sermon and gathered momentum in 1823–4.[87] The debates themselves contributed to the demand. Not only were they carried in national newspapers, but additional accounts, always highly partisan in tone, were later published by rival printing houses in Dublin. Shortly after the campaign began, the priests of Dublin, 'not hesitating to accept as an ally the importer of Tom Paine's bones', as J.A. Reynolds sardonically notes, were circulating copies of William Cobbett's *History of the Protestant Reformation* among the Catholic population. This particular history was remarkably popular in Dublin in early 1825. A correspondent of Robert Peel described the scene outside a bookshop where the work was on sale as resembling 'a mob pressing to the galleries of a theatre'. The bookseller, a man named Scully, who was considered Cobbett's agent in Dublin, was overheard telling a friend that 'he was at that moment writing to London for ten thousand copies by return of the mail, and that he had no doubt of requiring ten thousand more'.[88]

Whether the priests were actually responsible for the popularity of Cobbett's work is open to question. Cobbett was one of O'Connell's strongest supporters in London, and his *Reformation* was written with the very specific end of supporting the Catholic cause. He argued that the Reformation had its origins in an insatiable greed and materialism that had devoured the medieval Church and victimized in perpetuity the unfortunate inhabitants of Ireland.[89] The appeal of this argument (like that of the other contemporary bestseller that defended the Catholic cause, Thomas Moore's *Memoir of Captain Rock*), was its insistence on a secular cause (and by implication, a secular solution) for the country's problems, in contrast to the ultra-Protestants' insistence that Rome was the source of every evil.[90] The popularity of Cobbett and Moore notwithstanding, the Catholic clergy still felt pressed by the need to establish the teachings of their Church on the proper use of the scriptures and to proclaim the precise basis of their opposition to the evangelical moral crusade.

Bishop Doyle's most influential writings on education and the use of the scriptures appeared in 1825 in his *Letters on the State of Ireland*.[91] As much as he disavowed religious controversy, his sweeping condemnation of the methods and objectives of the Bible and education societies could only have encouraged the militancy of priests at the local level. Besides furnishing a lengthy and learned defence of Catholic teaching on the use of the scriptures, he attempted to place the evangelical mission in historical perspective. Striking a chord that went much deeper than the purely spiritual or theological, he unhesitatingly underlined the connections between political and religious persecution, with an explicit recognition of the ideology behind the 'Second Reformation':

> Behold ... the conditions implied on which alone these societies and their dupes and abettors will educate the poor of Ireland. Behold also and at the same time the force with which these societies press on an impoverished and broken-hearted people. Funds to the amount of, or exceeding £200,000 a year are at their disposal; the influence of the landlord—an influence paramount to every other; the zeal of the inspector, the power of the press and of the tongue—calumnies incessantly repeated against the hallowed name of the Word of God; the thirst of the people for education, all these form a moral phalanx more formidable than that of Macedon, and if God and the spirit of the people did not assist us, we could not resist it. We have borne many things, but we have never borne a persecution more bitter than what now assails us ... What we suffer from these societies, and the power and prejudice they have embodied against us, is more tormenting than what we endured under Anne or the second George.[92]

Doyle and his episcopal colleagues were clearly aware of the need for something more than a display of theological acumen to counter evangelical successes and the enormous publicity that accompanied them. The appointing of Eneas McDonnell to represent the opinion of the Catholic Association in London was part of this strategy. An unashamed defender of ultramontane Catholicism, McDonnell was the individual who, more than any of his contemporaries, gave journalistic vent to the idea that the evangelicals were out to destroy Catholicism. But McDonnell's attempts at counter-propaganda were not on their own sufficient.

As early as 1824 discussion was begun on the need for some kind of organization that would provide reading material sanctioned by the Catholic Church: in other words, a Catholic equivalent to the HBS. The leading light behind this scheme was a Dublin publisher named William Joseph Battersby. From the beginning Bishop Doyle gave his full support to the enterprise and was responsible for drawing up the plans on which it would be organized.[93] These bore a remarkable similarity to the system in use by the HBS. The headquarters were to be located in Dublin and the chief officers to be residents of the city. The Society was to spread through the provinces by means of cooperative societies, which would oversee the development of distribution centres, such as book depositories and lending libraries. On the regional and local levels these activities were to be under the direct sanction of the bishops and the clergy. Close ties were to be maintained between the local chapters and the headquarters in Dublin. As Doyle himself proclaimed when the Society was inaugurated in 1827:

> Every parish clergyman, nay, every society and confraternity concerned in the education of youth, are at liberty and would do well to place themselves in communication with the secretary or agent of the society. By that means they could forward their contributions without difficulty; they could have their orders for books executed without delay; they could obtain in the easiest manner the most useful information respecting the selection of books, the formation of parish libraries, as well as the improvement and management of schools, and the supplying of them with lessons and books of elementary instruction.[94]

The formal title of the organization launched by Doyle and Battersby and sanctioned by the Catholic episcopate was the Irish Catholic Society for the Diffusion of Useful Knowledge. It shortly came to be known as the Catholic Book Society. With the exception of an ancillary body—the Catholic Society of Ireland, founded in 1834 to promote the free distribution of religious material—the

Catholic Book Society appears to have been the only organization of its kind in nineteenth-century Ireland. One of the resolutions put forward by Doyle when the initial plans were under discussion in 1824 was that 'such books as are calculated to excite dissensions amongst Irishmen be carefully excluded'. In 1836, however, the *Catholic Directory* (another of Battersby's projects) asserted that the objectives of the Book Society were: 'to furnish people in the most cheap and convenient manner with useful information on the truths and duties of the Christian religion; to supply all classes of persons with satisfactory refutations of the prevailing errors and heresies of the present age; and to assist in supplying schools with the most approved books of elementary instruction'.[95] These objectives, especially the second, breathed hostility to the evangelical mission.

By 1836 it was claimed that the Catholic Book Society had already published 5 million books and circulated them in cheap editions, not only in Ireland but also throughout Britain and the overseas possessions of the empire.[96] It seems likely that much of the material distributed in Ireland consisted of prayer books, tracts and bibles in the vernacular, which came into widespread use for the first time in the 1830s. This was partly in keeping with the Church's strategy of enlightening its flock on the doctrinal foundations of the Catholic religion, and partly a response to the evangelicals' repeated taunts that the priests were withholding the scriptures from the people in order to keep them in ignorance.

In 1834 Dr William Crolly, bishop of Down and Connor, arranged with the Catholic publisher Richard Coyne of Capel Street to publish an entire version of the Catholic Bible; Crolly even applied to the excise office to have the paper tax removed so that it might be sold more cheaply. Coyne's edition of 1224 octavo pages was sold by the Catholic Book Society for eight shillings, an extremely low price considering the amount of print. The first edition of 'Crolly's Bible' was sold out within a few weeks, with the bishop himself spending £600 on copies, which presumably were distributed for free.[97]

In 1836 the Rev. Noel met a Catholic tradesman in Drogheda who informed him that Crolly's Bible, then selling for six shillings and threepence, was enjoying great popularity among Catholics. Noel was also shown two smaller works—*The Abridgement of Christian Doctrine, Permissum Superiorum* and *The Christian's Guide to Heaven* (both published in Dublin in 1835)—that he painstakingly combed for evidence of the Catholic Church's opposition to the free interpretation of the scriptures. Like most evangelicals, Noel preferred to see some version of the scriptures in use by Catholics rather than none at all. What he abhorred, however, was that the teaching contained in the tracts and catechism further instilled Catholic orthodoxy in the minds of ordinary people, thus rendering them more inimical than ever to the evangelicals and to the Bible without note or comment.[98]

While the literature distributed by the Catholic Book Society was definitely designed to undercut that of the evangelical agencies, the tone and indeed the very nature of the material—prayer books, catechisms, and the like—were aimed more at building up Catholicism than at pulling down Protestantism. This could not be said of the many Catholic journals that sprang up to challenge the *Christian Examiner* and others of its kind. Up to 1829 the market for periodicals in Ireland was occupied, according to Barbara Hayley, by magazines that were 'almost exclusively polemical, disseminating violently Protestant or Catholic, unionist or anti-unionist propaganda, and very little else'.[99] With the exception of the *Christian Examiner*, most of these, especially the Catholic ones, enjoyed only a brief existence, the reasons for which will be considered presently.

The first of the blatantly pro-Catholic journals (that is, in the religious as opposed to the political sense) was the *Irish Catholic Magazine*, which began publication in Cork in 1829 and 'struck the *Christian Examiner* from the Catholic side'.[100] Little is known about its popularity or lifespan. A somewhat better-known publication was *The Catholic Penny Magazine*, launched by W.J. Battersby in 1834 and envisaged as the mouthpiece of the Catholic Book Society. It was a weekly booklet, similar in form to those published by the British missionary societies, containing articles on the lives of the saints, Catholic religious observance, new churches and religious houses, foreign intelligence, and contemporary social and political events of particular importance to the Catholic Church.[101] The refutation of the anti-Catholic propaganda emanating from the evangelical press became one of the magazine's standard features. Readers were urged to ignore rather than to take personal action against proselytizers. News of converted priests and laypeople was often exposed as fraudulent. One evangelical author who called himself the 'Rev. E.B. Delany, formerly a Catholic priest' was said to be only a poor, deluded schoolmaster.[102] Another report that appeared in several evangelical periodicals concerning the content of controversial sermons delivered by a leading Catholic polemicist in 1835 was attacked as grossly untrue.[103]

Two years after it was founded, *The Catholic Penny Magazine* encountered serious financial difficulties and was forced to cease publication. It was superseded by the *Irish Catholic Magazine of Entertaining Knowledge*, another project of Battersby's. Even more than its predecessor, this journal became embroiled in sectarian controversy. As Thomas Wall remarks:

Gone is the elation over the building of new churches, and the reader is given instead page after page of religious polemic. And how dreary, inglorious, and even shabby was the religious controversy of the eighteen-thirties. There was then no thought of dialogue, no quest of a common ground of agreement, no scruple over offending charity. There was a small group of renegade priests who made Maynooth the particular target of their scurrilous attacks, and the *Irish Catholic Magazine* gave too many pages to exposing their iniquities.[104]

Both of these magazines, like the *Christian Examiner*, contained some cultural and intellectual content, publishing articles on travel, literature, history, and antiquities. Neither enjoyed much success, however, and it was the repeated complaint of Battersby that although there were seven million Catholics in Ireland, he could sell only 3000 copies of his weekly magazine. Wall has described Battersby's magazines as 'rather mean and shabby in appearance ... with something of the catchpenny in all of them'.[105] This, and the often vulgar tone of their polemics, was probably responsible for alienating many of the more respectable Catholics, including the clergy. The poorer classes provided no market for literature of this kind, a fact for which poverty and illiteracy have been held accountable.[106]

CONTROVERSIAL SERMONS AND MONSTER DEBATES

Great public meetings associated with voluntary philanthropy, particularly the home and foreign missionary endeavours, had become a standard feature of religious life in Britain by the 1820s. Usually associated with the anniversaries of organizations like the CMS and the BFBS, they attracted people from all over the country and from various walks of life. For an entire week they would attend lectures and sermons by preachers and workers in the field, fraternize with like-minded colleagues and renew their commitment to the evangelical way of life. The 'April meetings', as they were called, were soon as popular in Dublin as they were in London and they brought something like a festive spirit to the capital each spring.

Just as the Orange activities of July and August did for the lower classes, they provided an opportunity for 'respectable' Protestants to display solidarity with one another and also to partake in the excitement generated by the feeling that they were part of a great national movement. Fifty years later the well-known Nonconformist minister, the Rev. James Godkin, gave a nostalgic account of the annual event as he knew it in his youth:

> for a young man who attends the April meetings now, it would be very difficult to conceive the excitement they produced and the attraction they put forth forty or fifty years ago. The spirit of revival seemed to pervade the very atmosphere; every eloquent speaker was a champion, a hero, who was looked upon with admiration as he passed along the streets. For hours, day after day, as society after society came upon the stage to tell the story of the year and record its triumphs, a select audience from all parts of the kingdom, of which a majority were ladies, sat listening with rapt attention or were thrilled into wild excitement by the impassioned appeals of their favourite orators. Some of these were certainly the most eloquent men that ever appeared upon a religious or political platform. Their speeches were fully reported in the Protestant newspapers, which were circulated by thousands throughout the country.[107]

This account captures the excitement of a community who felt that the wind was at its back. There was little to compare with such displays on the Catholic side. In the Bible debates of 1824 the priests defended themselves ably, but they stayed within their own districts, and no clerical figure emerged to compare with the well-known (but unfortunately named) Rev. Richard Pope, who travelled and debated tirelessly on behalf of Protestant cause, winning national recognition as a result. Not until 1826 did the Catholics discover an orator capable of rivalling Pope in public debate. This was the celebrated Fr Tom Maguire—'from the bogs of Leitrim'—one of the most colourful figures of the pre-Famine period and the bane of evangelical controversialists. Maguire's oratory raised the art of polemic to a new and altogether more entertaining level.

Fr Maguire first drew attention to his oratorical skills when he visited Dublin in 1826 to deliver a series of Lenten sermons at the Franciscan church.[108] The supporters of religious controversy on the Catholic side, especially the publishers, evidently saw in the big country priest an opponent likely to raise the hackles of the Protestant controversialists. Shortly thereafter, Maguire moved to the capital, where his natural talent for polemic was nurtured. A unique and mutually rewarding relationship sprang up between him and the publisher Richard Coyne. As the largest distributor of Catholic literature in the country, Coyne had a vested interest in religious controversy. He was well versed in obscure theological detail, and he put his knowledge at Maguire's disposal. He also acted as Maguire's agent in scheduling public appearances and debates, and he held the copyright to all material that went into print. The cooperation and friendship between the two was described by Bishop Ullathorne and repeated by Thomas Wall in Dickensian terms:

> Father Maguire was a 'tall man with a high tapering forehead, broad jaws, florid features, and a small mouth, with tall teeth, and for his proportions, narrow shoulders'. Coyne was a small man, dapper and dainty, with a precise mind well-stored with references, especially in controversial literature. The priest addressed the printer familiarly as 'Dicky, my father', and the printer spoke to the priest as 'Tom, my son'.[109]

The event that made a national hero of Maguire was a marathon debate with Pope held in the Sackville Institute in Dublin in April 1827. Lasting all of six days, it proved to be the most publicized event connected with the Reformation crusade since the Loughrea affair of 1824. It ended in a resounding victory for Maguire, and Pope was said to have lost his health as a result.[110] In October 1827 it was reported in the *Dublin Evening Post* that Fr Maguire had made a statement during a meeting of the Catholic Association in Roscommon town to the effect that an unnamed Protestant parson, acting on behalf of a Protestant archbishop, had offered him £1000 at once and £800 a year for life if he would join the Protestant side.[111] This item of news produced a storm of denials and counter-denials by the parties concerned and inevitably ended up in the law courts. Maguire claimed that the account of his speech given to the newspaper was false to begin with. While advances were certainly made to him by a Protestant clergyman, it looked in retrospect like a case of entrapment. He strongly denied that he had ever mentioned the name of Dr Trench in connection with the affair.[112] The *Morning Herald* of 8 November had announced that Trench was indeed the archbishop alluded to, and moreover that this information had been volunteered to the *Herald* by Maguire.[113] Trench promptly sued the editor of this newspaper for libel, but Maguire was able to clear his name once again by showing that his statement had been misrepresented.[114]

Hot on the heels of this flap came another, more serious case against Maguire: a paternity suit in which he was charged with having seduced the daughter of Bernard McGarahan, an innkeeper of Drumkerrin, County Leitrim. Daniel O'Connell acted as his counsel and managed to prove that the slander had been concocted by members of an Orange faction who wished to punish Maguire for having trounced Pope earlier in the year. The Catholics of Dublin illuminated their houses when the court ruled against the prosecution.[115]

Throughout the 1830s Maguire maintained his reputation as the leading Catholic orator and was always in great demand in the Dublin area. The busiest time of year for controversial sermons and debates was the Lenten season just before Easter. Catholic observance of Lent gave Protestant critics an opportunity to pour obloquy on the practices of fasting and abstaining from meat on Fridays, as well as on the use of images, rosary beads, scapulars, etc. The drama was naturally heightened by the April meetings that took place around the same time. In March 1835 *The Catholic Penny Magazine* noted that Fr Maguire was preaching controversial sermons to overwhelming congregations in St Teresa's Church in Clarendon Street on Sundays, Wednesdays and Fridays. In the same issue it was reported that Protestant fanatics were engaged in putting up scurrilous anti-Catholic posters all over the city.[116] Maguire certainly contributed his share to stoking the fires of discord. It was the strength of his oratory rather than his grasp of theology that served to overwhelm his opponents. When he could not prompt an opponent to come forward and engage in a platform debate, he struck out at his written work. As the following passage illustrates, theology was not always the object of his attack; in this case it was the writing style of the Rev. Robert McGhee, one of the most famous of the Protestant orators:

> From such English as this, O Lord deliver us! I defy any man to make either grammar or sense out of such language. I have always hated pettifogging and all supercilious criticism ... I know a man may be a very good Christian without knowing the rules of Etymology, Syntax, or Prosody, but I would leave it to this respectable assembly, if a man is not bound to make restitution when he makes money for teaching what he knows nothing of? ... I have discovered not less than seventeen violations of the rules of grammar in one of his columns alone.[117]

It is not surprising that Maguire was almost as much of an embarrassment to later generations of Catholics as he was to Protestants during his own lifetime. He died in 1847, poisoned by one of his own relatives in a dispute over land.[118]

Theological debates occurred less often in the provinces, but they did become a familiar feature of local life in the period between 1825 and 1830. Often lasting several days at a time, they provided an open forum for debates about Church structure and Church–State relations, as well as doctrine, and could involve some peculiar alliances. At one such debate that took place in Downpatrick in April 1828, for example, the subjects for discussion were 'The right of Luther to Dissent from the General Church', and 'The alleged dependence of the Established Church of England and Ireland on the State'. The second topic, according to the *Christian Examiner*,

> was one which afforded them [the Catholic priests] full scope for declamatory addresses to their own people; and it was one which they probably calculated that the Presbyterian part of the audience would be at least neutral, if not inclined to take their part. In fact, it was from the Presbyterian armoury that they took the greater part of their weapons, with which they carried on this part of the combat. Towgood's *Dissent Justified* and Palmer's *Catechism* which have been circulated pretty extensively through the north of Ireland were carefully studied and what appeared to be their strongest points were adopted in many cases verbatim.[119]

Besides the marathon debates lasting days at a time between clerical (and sometimes lay) representatives of the rival denominations, the regular scheduling of controversial sermons in Protestant churches appears to have become widespread during the late 1820s. One such series was begun at Ballymahon, County Longford, in the spring of 1827, which was said to have been 'well attended by Roman Catholics' and another at Newtownmountkennedy, County Wicklow, in December of the same year.[120] Even small-scale local venues were made use of to air the controversy. The diarist Humphrey O'Sullivan, for example, recorded an event that took place in County Kilkenny in a 'poor school' between a local priest, Fr Doran, and a Protestant minister, the Rev. Dobbin. According to O'Sullivan, 'Fr. Doran gave enough to Mr. Dobbin.'[121]

The era of controversial sermons and debates was marked by increasing unity among different Protestant denominations. This was not especially remarkable among the Baptists and Congregationalists of the southern counties, who had a similar stake as the Church of Ireland in the Reformation crusade. But a new note was sounded, to the alarm of local Catholics, when the Presbyterian clergy of the northern counties began to take up the practice during the course of 1827.[122]

The level of controversy in any given district was almost always a measure of the involvement of the local clergy—whether the Protestant minister was sympathetic to the evangelical cause, and whether his Catholic counterpart was willing to respond to the challenge. In some dioceses, such as Kildare and Leighlin, the priests were actually forbidden to attend controversial meetings.[123] In others they simply kept quiet, sometimes to the disappointment of the local Protestants. Writing from Cork in 1827, a correspondent of the dowager Countess Massereene regretted that there had not been any sectarian debate for several years 'the R.C. clergy having declined it long since'. She occasionally attended the Bible society meetings in Kinsale, 'which go on without any disputings, as our two quiet priests do not attend them'.[124]

Indeed, the entertainment value was no small factor in the popularity of the theological disputes, and the rivalry inevitably tended to spill over into many other areas of popular culture. During the 1830s it began to appear that competition and controversy had become the preferred mode of discourse between the denominations, and this fashion embedded itself in Protestant–Catholic as well as Anglo–Irish relations. Theological differences were naturally at the centre of the division, and it followed as a matter of course that there was always a good market for controversial material, whether written or oral. If the public could not attend controversial sermons, the mass circulation of pamphlets and debates would sustain their interest. The mixture of religion, politics, popular entertainment and profit was marvellously captured in a squib published by Richard Lalor Sheil (originally a playwright of some talent) about the attempts to perform an exorcism on Archbishop Magee at Clongowes Wood College, to rid him of the 'devil of polemics'—a task even the Jesuits were unable to accomplish (see appendix B).

The output of propaganda from the Catholic side seems generally to have been lower than that of the evangelicals. The main reason for this was that the hierarchy, through the priests, had direct access to the mass of the Catholic population. Episcopal guidelines on any matter of controversy could be read from the altar on Sunday. Such dictates, of course, could always be supplemented by the priests' own advice on the most effective deterrents to be used against Bible preachers. The example to which evangelical apologists loved to refer in this regard was the advice that homeowners should always keep on hand a pot of boiling water with which to douse the missionaries before they could cross the threshold.

Since it was the evangelicals who were engaged in a missionary endeavour, it might be expected that they would tout statistics of converts, school enrolments, and other indictors of their progress. Catholics, however, were not slow in responding with their own figures on the number of converts from Protestantism.[125] No other aspect of the religious conflict gave rise to such distortions of reality or indeed, in many instances, to severe personal psychosis.

Nineteenth-century Irish history is strewn with cases of people 'jumping' from one religion to the other and often back again. Consider the case of Margaret Anna Cusack (a niece of the rabidly anti-Catholic Rev. William Stoney of Newport, County Mayo), who converted to Catholicism, took religious vows, gained prominence in the latter part of the century as the eccentric Nun of Kenmare and ended her days back in the Protestant fold.[126] A milder but more significant case was that of Catherine McCauley, a young woman from a mixed background who was raised in a Protestant household. Her anger at the prejudice against Catholicism she saw exhibited by her Protestant relatives inspired her to found the Sisters of Mercy, a religious order dedicated to the education of the poor in direct imitation of a Protestant ladies' organization with an emphasis on 'lack of ceremony' and dedication to the 'useful' works of nursing and teaching.[127]

The distortion of reality went much wider than the individual cases mentioned above. If Catholic opinion on the subject were to be accepted at face value, the evangelical mission, aside from its negative impact on sectarian relations, amounted to nothing more than what William Conyngham Plunket had called it in 1827 in the House of Commons: 'the merest chimera that ever bewildered the mind of man'. Meanwhile the evangelicals were predicting a rout of popery in the outlying and impoverished regions of Connaught and Munster. Neither side, as it turned out, was correct in its assessment of the situation. So deep-seated was the division between them, however, that neither could appreciate that the other had some grounds for adhering to its beliefs.

—SEVEN—
New Directions, 1828–40

Though Britain be safe from the incursions of foreign foes, and though peace and prosperity encompass our sea-girt isle, yet is she in imminent danger as long as she nourishes in her bosom men who under the garbled form of liberality, with 'Emancipation' in their mouths, but contemplated 'ascendency' [*sic*] in their hearts, aim at no less than the utter subversion of the British constitution.

The Watchman, 3 February 1827[1]

We found some caution at first, but on a further acquaintance we were well received, especially by the clergy, who opened their pulpits to us and came in numbers to our meetings. No religious society ever attracted such crowds in that country. We left the best of the clergy preparing to study the controversy. From what I saw, I am convinced there is a splendid and unfathomed mine of good Protestant feeling in England which only requires to be well worked. When I spoke of the persecution suffered by Protestant clergy and people, I excited a feeling that must be seen to be understood.

M.G. BERESFORD[2]

In the story of the Church, the landed aristocracy may see their own perils predicted. Because the clergy of Ireland had not opportunity or power to defend themselves, their rights have been violated and injuries unredressed ... Aristocracy should take counsel. They are a colony in a hostile country, and if not closely and effectively united, they are lost!

Dublin University Magazine, October 1833[3]

RETRENCHMENT AND REDEFINITION

The ideological and political showdown of the 1820s had consequences for denominational relations that can hardly be overestimated. The Catholic Association's strategy of popular mobilization, particularly the collection of the 'Catholic rent', proved remarkably successful despite all attempts of the government to outlaw its activities. When the Association was suppressed by an act of parliament in March 1825, it was reconstituted by O'Connell as the New Catholic Association and succeeded in having four pro-Emancipation candidates elected to parliament in the general election of 1826. When O'Connell himself was elected as a member of parliament for County Clare in the famous by-election of 1828, the implication was clear: as a Catholic he would have to be allowed to take his seat, or his success could be multiplied all over the country in the next general election. The prospect in that event was a withdrawal of Catholic members from Westminster and possible civil war in Ireland. Against this situation, Wellington yielded, and the Catholic Relief Act was passed and came into operation in April 1829.[4]

The sustained momentum of the Emancipation campaign had the predictable effect of reinforcing ultra-Protestant sentiments. The natural alliance between the defenders of the Protestant interest in politics and the evangelical organizations became even more sharply defined. In 1828 it was cemented by the foundation of the Brunswick Clubs, a voluntary organization militantly dedicated to preventing the passage of an Emancipation bill. The men behind the formation of the clubs were those whose names were synonymous with the Reformation cause, including Lord Farnham, Lord Roden and Thomas Lefroy. Their tactics included the popular mobilization of Protestants in the border counties and a propaganda blitz to inform public opinion in Britain about the dangers facing the Protestant community in Ireland.

The depth of popular Protestant hostility to the Emancipation campaign was revealed during the famous 'march on Ulster' in 1828. On this occasion O'Connell unwisely commissioned a Belfast journalist, John Lawless, to lead a non-violent pilgrimage of thousands of Catholics from the southern counties for the purpose of holding political meetings to mobilize the Catholics of Ulster behind the Emancipation banner. As the marchers approached the border counties, armed bands of Orange supporters massed to prevent their passage.

Only O'Connell's sensible decision to call off the march prevented bloodshed on a large scale, as there were not enough troops in the area to keep the peace.[5] Given the overwhelming numerical superiority of the Catholics and the avowed militancy of armed Protestants, it seemed to Peel and Wellington that civil war in Ireland would be inevitable if Emancipation were not granted. They struck a deal with O'Connell that if the forty-shilling freehold voters on whose power the entire Emancipation movement had been carried forward were disenfranchised, an Emancipation bill would be passed.[6]

The passage of the Catholic Relief Act brought one phase of the Catholic question to a close, but it did not inaugurate religious peace in Ireland. On the contrary, Catholics became more militant in asserting their numerical superiority in civil and religious affairs, and Protestants ever more embattled and disposed to close denominational ranks against the threat of Catholic ascendancy. The first salvo of Catholic resurgence, predictably, was manifested in the anti-tithe movement, which began to assume serious momentum in the autumn of 1830. The movement began in Graiguenamanagh, County Carlow, with the refusal of a Catholic priest and relative of Bishop Doyle to pay tithe to the local Protestant clergyman, who was known to be a passionate supporter of the Reformation movement. His gesture was widely supported among the local community and the movement soon spread to the surrounding counties. The movement was not supported by the Catholic Church nor by Daniel O'Connell, but it was vehemently defended by Bishop Doyle, whose fulminations against tithe had been a central feature of his writings throughout the 1820s and whose hallmark rhetorical flourish 'may your hatred of tithe be as lasting as your love of justice' had provided the campaign with its most popular slogan.[7] When military force proved ineffectual against popular resistance, a consensus emerged on the reform of the system to make both the collection and payment of tithe the responsibility of the landlord class. This was preceded by the Church Temporalities Act of 1833, which restructured the diocesan system and reduced the number of archbishoprics. That the government was willing to back such legislation was at one and the same time a recognition that the Church of Ireland was an institution separate from the Church of England, and an ultimate admission that it would never become the church of the majority population, in other words a recognition of the failure of the Reformation crusade. It was the first nail in the coffin of the Church of Ireland that would culminate in its disestablishment in 1869.

The launching of the anti-tithe campaign so soon after the Emancipation victory deepened fears about Catholic resurgence and its ultimate objective. Strident defenders of Protestant supremacy such as Henry Maxwell, heir to the Farnham Estate, and the Rev. Hans Hamilton of Knocktopher, County Kilkenny, were convinced that the political activism of the priests was part of a Jesuitical scheme that had been plotted years in advance to bring down not only the Protestant presence in Ireland but the entire British empire.[8] The dividends that accrued to the evangelical movement on this account were enormous. Preachers and polemicists were afforded a platform from which to voice their fears of Catholic ascendancy and unquestionably attracted a great deal of moral and financial support that they might not otherwise have received, particularly from Britain.

Insofar as the ultimate success of the Emancipation movement and the progress of the anti-tithe campaign affected the progress of the Reformation movement, however, it was confined mainly to the area of public opinion. The granting of Emancipation and the Church Temporalities Act did not in themselves affect the programs that were already underway to convert Catholics, or if they did, it was on the credit side of attracting further support for the work of the evangelicals. The reform of the education system, however, which followed on the heels of the Emancipation act, dealt a death blow to what had become the central foundation of the evangelical mission. With the advent of a national system of primary schools funded by public money, the evangelicals were deprived of their most important bridgehead to the primary source through which they sought to effect their ends—the vast majority of children of school age.

Long before the setting up of the National Board of Education in 1831, it was understood that the Catholic hierarchy would never agree to the attendance of Catholic children at government-sponsored schools in which the reading of the Bible without note or comment was obligatory. The formidable lay and clerical opposition launched by O'Connell and MacHale in the early 1820s, and subsequently upheld by Bishop Doyle and the Catholic Association, succeeded in demolishing the KPS's system over this issue. In 1824 the government had established a commission of inquiry to investigate the entire range of educational agencies currently operating in Ireland.[9] Between 1824 and 1827 this commission produced a total of nine reports based on the evidence of witnesses who represented the various educational interests. The first and most substantive of the reports, released in 1825, clearly revealed the Catholic hierarchy's fear that 'a combined and systematic attempt' was underway to wean schoolchildren away from the Catholic faith, not only by the more aggressive of the evangelical agencies, such as LHS, but also by the KPS, and that in reality there was little difference between them. The commissioners noted that

> this confusion has in some degree arisen from the circumstances that the same persons in several instances take a prominent and active part in the management of more than one of these societies, and the Roman Catholics have concluded that their objects are alike in all.[10]

The bishops' allegations were borne out by the unapologetic admission of certain agencies, particularly the LHS, that they were indeed educating Catholic children with a view to their ultimate conversion to the Protestant faith. It was the opinion of the commissioners after surveying the evidence that neither threats nor rewards could induce Catholic parents to send their children to schools of which their clergy disapproved.[11]

The debate over state-sponsored education continued for another six years, by which time the government agreed to support a system in which religious education would be provided by the pastors of the respective denominations. This system was originally envisaged as nondenominational in character, but since the management of the schools at the local level was effectively placed in the hands of that clergyman whose denomination was overwhelmingly represented in the school, it did not take long for sectarian interests to assert themselves. 'The main result of the introduction of the National System', as S.J. Connolly has neatly concluded, 'was to bring about a dramatic increase in the educational resources of the Irish Catholic Church.'[12]

The government's decision to develop the National System destroyed the prospects of the evangelical educational agencies in one blow. In the first place, they were deprived of their most important and reliable source of income. They were also, needless to say, deprived of pupils. The LHS and the KPS rapidly fell into decline. Many of their schools simply applied for funding to the National Board and refashioned their objectives under the aegis of the new system. Others aligned themselves with projects such as the one currently underway in the Kingscourt District. The Irish Society and the Scripture Readers' Society appear to have followed a similar route and became heavily involved in the experiment with colonies in the west, which, from the 1830s onwards, began to absorb the energies of the evangelical movement generally.

The demise of the educational societies, however, does not appear to have affected the popularity of the evangelical movement among the Protestant population. The figures available for the growth of the HBS provide one measure of this popularity. From a total of 147 contributory institutions in 1822, the number increased to over 600 by the early 1830s.

DISTRIBUTION OF HBS AUXILIARIES, 1831[13]

Province	Auxiliaries	Branches	Associations	Total
Connaught	5	3	27	35
Leinster	22	76	80	178
Munster	11	263	32	306
Ulster	34	44	54	132
Total	72	386	193	651

Comparative surveys of the distribution of these societies on a county basis give some indication of how the system had set down roots in the provinces. The areas in question, Westmeath and east Galway, occupy a fertile stretch of the midlands on each side of the River Shannon, and the towns represented are either county towns or substantial market centres, with a sprinkling of smaller villages in each case.

SAMPLE DISTRIBUTION OF HBS AUXILIARIES, 1832[14]

Westmeath	East Galway
Athlone Ladies' Association	Ahascragh
Castletowndelvin	Ballinasloe Ladies' Association
Killucan	Galway city
Mayne	Loughrea (county society)
Mullingar (county society)	Monivea
Moate	Tuam

In addition, the founding of the Established Church Home Mission Society in 1828 heralded the formal commitment of the Church of Ireland to the ideals of the evangelical wing. Its main function appears to have been the organizing of preaching tours and itinerancies for ministers supportive of the cause. Noel's account of the Home Mission in 1836 gives the impression that the Protestant community throughout the country was alive with activity:

Besides a diocesan mission in the diocese of Meath and another in the diocese of Tuam, there are now ten missionary circuits, travelled by above 100 zealous ministers of the Church of Ireland, the majority being incumbents. These circuits extend through Donegal, Londonderry, and Down; they occupy Fermanagh, Monaghan, and Cavan; they come into Westmeath and Meath; they fill Kildare; they run from Sligo across Ireland, through Athlone and Carlow to Wexford; they extend along the southwestern coast from Wexford to Youghal; and lastly, from Youghal they pass through Killarney to the remotest parts of Kerry and through Charleville to the mouth of the Shannon. Each circuit has about 24 stations and almost all the stations are visited once a fortnight; so that now the mission sends a pious clergyman every fortnight to about 240 stations, scattered across the four provinces. Each missionary is on the circuit for a fortnight; he has usually 24 places to visit, preaches two sermons daily, and is conducted to the different stations in a car or gig at the expense of the mission. The missionaries do not at present reach the Roman Catholics or the great landowners, their work lying chiefly among the smaller gentry and the middle class of Protestants. Most of all are they useful to the clergyman in whose parishes they labour. If a clergyman is devoted to his work, they confirm his doctrine, silence his opponents, who find how many able men think with him, teach even ungodly persons to respect his ministry, and carry conviction to the minds of some he could not previously impress. If he is a good man but indolent, he is usually roused into activity. If he be ignorant of the gospel and careless in his life, he stands rebuked by their zeal, and through it, may both himself and those who hear him be saved from eternal death. In this manner the talent and piety of a minister of the Irish church, instead of being monopolised by the 60 or 100 Protestants in his own parish, become subservient to the welfare of many congregations in many towns.[15]

During the late 1820s and the early 1830s the Kingscourt District remained the most successful example of the combined influence of landlord and clergy to evangelize at the grassroots level, and it was in Kingscourt that new initiatives were undertaken to expand the movement to other parts of the country and to consolidate gains already made. The most significant of these initiatives was the design to introduce Protestant colonists, often to lands from which Catholics had been evicted, in order to maintain numerical superiority. Part of the idea behind the desire to establish colonies was the fear that Protestants were going to emigrate en masse because of the threat of Catholic ascendancy. It was not in Ulster, however, but in some of the most remote districts of the west that the colony movement took root most firmly. This was the result of a combination of factors, not least the presence in the archbishopric of Tuam of the most evangelical-minded prelate of the Church of Ireland, the Rev. Power le Poer Trench.

ARCHBISHOP TRENCH AND THE EVANGELICAL MOVEMENT
IN THE WEST

Like many of his evangelical contemporaries, the Rev. Power le Poer Trench was of Huguenot descent. The family had originated in the Seigneurie of La Tranche in the traditionally Protestant territory of Poitou, but had fled the religious persecutions of the late sixteenth century and settled in the north of England. One branch of the family acquired estates in Ireland during the confiscations of the seventeenth century, first in Cavan and later in east Galway, where the family seat was located, at Garbally near Ballinasloe.[16] The history of the Trench family in the late eighteenth and early nineteenth centuries reveals an extraordinary record of success obtained largely through clerical preferment and support for the Union and the ultra-Protestant cause. The main protagonist in this spiral of progress was William Power Keating. He had married Anne Gardiner, the sister of Viscount Mountjoy, in 1762. He served as an MP for County Galway from 1769 to 1797, and in 1798 he was elevated to the peerage with the title of Baron Kilconnell. According to Michael Davitt, this was a reward for his services to Earl Camden in connection with the 1798 Rebellion. In 1801 he was made 1st earl of Clancarty, allegedly for his role in suppressing the Rebellion, but more likely for his support of the Union.[17] One of his daughters married into the Gregory family and another into the La Touches. William Power Keating's eldest son, Richard, succeeded to the earldom, while his second son, Power, became archbishop of Tuam and another son, Charles, was made archdeacon of Ardagh.[18]

Depending on which source is used to assess contemporary opinion, the Trench family was looked upon in east Galway either as patriotic benefactors or reactionary tyrants. Several of the younger members of the family, including the future archbishop (who was a captain in the yeomanry) and his brother the archdeacon, were involved in the bloody purge of suspected rebels in the aftermath of 1798, the ferocity of which shocked even hardened campaigners like Lord Cornwallis. One of the most notorious incidents to have survived in the popular memory regarding the family's record for cruelty was associated with

Charles Trench, future archdeacon of Ardagh, who, as captain of the Galway militia stationed in Cork, had a woman named Winifred Hynes flogged in public for the crime of stealing a candlestick. When the soldier appointed to the task balked at the order, the archdeacon is said to have torn the clothes from the victim's back and administered the lash himself in the full view of her husband.[19] Even if the more gory details of this story are apocryphal there is abundant evidence in the poetry of Raftery of the odium attached to the Trench family by the Catholics of east Galway. On the other hand, the archbishop's biographer, Joseph D'Arcy Sirr, recounts the statements of several Catholics who testified that he was the most fair-minded and charitable of men.[20]

At the outset of his career as a clergyman, Dr Power le Poer Trench was not kindly disposed to the evangelical cause, though he apparently established a reputation for attention to duty that would have rivaled that of the most conscientious evangelical. In 1802 he was appointed to the bishopric of Waterford and Lismore, and immediately set about introducing reforms in what had previously been a much neglected diocese. Chief among these reforms was the maintenance and improvement of church buildings, the regularizing of church services and the foundation of a widows' fund for the wives of poor clergymen.[21] In 1810 he was transferred to the diocese of Elphin, where he upheld his reputation as a conscientious administrator and a friend of the poor. He personally sponsored industrial schemes in spinning and weaving, and also the establishment of a dispensary and a school, efforts that were generally appreciated by local Catholics, especially during the famine and typhus epidemic of 1816–17.[22] The dispensary physician, a Catholic named Michael Dillon, gave the following account of Dr Trench's benevolence during this period:

> The years of 1816–17 were years of great distress. Famine and pestilence stalked over the land. Elphin felt severely their effects, having a wretched population, without a market, without business of any kind, and very remote from turbary [i.e. peat bogs, or a fuel supply]. The poor of the town and its precincts were supplied with fuel, blankets, clothing, plenty of milk, etc. by his Lordship. The wandering beggars, who were attracted to the place by the report of this beneficence, had food such as soup, rice, plentifully dispensed to them; at the distribution of which he and some members of his family frequently attended. He also provided a place for the sick poor labouring under typhus, had them attended to by the dispensary physician, and supplied with every requisite.[23]

Interestingly, Dillon went on to note the change in religious feelings that overtook Trench while he was bishop of Elphin, and added a comment on his motivations:

> When his lordship first came to Elphin, that weak and mistaken zeal for proselytism, which has obtained the approval of some otherwise good men, was not much encouraged by him; but at the close of his sojourn here he seemed to partake a little of that religious feeling, which appears to me not so well calculated to secure the happiness of mankind, as its advocates on either side seem to think. He thought and acted, I believe, from the dictates and impulse of a good conscience. What he said and felt arose not from any selfish or mean principle, but were, I believe, intended to promote the religious and moral good of his neighbours.[24]

Two incidents occurred in 1816 that helped to push Trench into a closer identification with the ideals of the evangelical movement. The first was the death of his beloved sister, Lady Emily, the fervently religious wife of Robert La Touche. Her death in childbirth at the age of twenty-seven deeply affected the entire Trench household, especially her brother the bishop, who had attended her deathbed. As an acquaintance later revealed, 'in watering her soul as God's minister, his own soul was indeed blessedly watered. This, I know, was a season he never forgot. He frequently spoke of it to me.'[25] Shortly after this, he engaged in an exchange of opinion with Archdeacon William Digby of Elphin, as a result of which he wholeheartedly embraced evangelicalism as his guiding inspiration in civil and religious affairs.

The Rev. William Digby was one of those energetic clergymen whose work at the parochial level by the second decade of the century was turning the area around Boyle in County Roscommon into a powerful local expression of a spiritual 'awakening' among the Protestant community. Born into a long-established clerical family in the area (his grandfather had been bishop of Elphin) he assumed his duties as archdeacon of Elphin in 1809. According to Maiben Motherwell, the biographer of Albert Blest, Digby was 'instrumental in introducing real religion into the upper classes of society to an extent hitherto unknown' in the region.[26] Certainly, the Lorton family of Rockingham lent the whole weight of their social and economic eminence to the campaign. Since many of the Lorton family's marriage connections in other parts of the country were active evangelicals, their collective involvement appears to have been a family affair, as indeed was true of virtually all the nobility and gentry associated with the movement. Digby's energy and enthusiasm, backed by the social and economic clout of the Lorton family, made the area around Boyle into a centre that radiated with the excitement of religious revivalism.

Shortly after Dr Trench was transferred to Elphin, the diocese was alive with the evangelistic zeal of energetic young curates, including the Rev. Robert McGhee, who went on to become famous as a controversial orator, and the Rev. Charles Seymour, the apostle of evangelicalism in Connemara. These men owed their promotion to the influence of Archdeacon Digby and Viscount Lorton. During the winter of 1816–17, at the instigation of a clergyman who was a tutor in the Lorton household, clerical meetings for ministers of the diocese were begun on a regular basis. They were fully sanctioned by Bishop Trench and proved an enormous success with clergy and laity alike. Digby's description of the involvement of local Protestants in these monthly meetings is one of the most valuable accounts of the momentum that accompanied the spread of the evangelical movement in the provinces:

> For now clergymen from all parts of the diocese began to attend, and the few that did not were the exceptions. The word of God increased remarkably in the neighbourhood, and the number of disciples (especially among the gentry) multiplied, so that there was scarce a great company of the parochial clergy which had not one or more of its members with us; and a great number of the parochial clergy became obedient to the faith. At our clerical meetings there was nothing done through strife or vainglory, nor were there any vain janglings about unprofitable questions; but each came prepared to receive or to impart what good they could. The happy result of this was that our pulpits generally uttered the same sound, and that no uncertain sound ... And those meetings, having led to a closer examination of scripture or the articles, liturgy, and formularies of our church, and by the solemn promises made by our clergy at their ordination, proved a blessing unto many—a revival of religion took place, and vital piety gradually spread among clergy and people.[27]

Archdeacon Digby's greatest contribution to these developments lay in the personal influence he wielded over the proclivities of his diocesan superior. Shortly before he was transferred to Tuam, Trench acknowledged his indebtedness to the archdeacon in this regard:

> He is full of zeal in God's service, and I confess that if it pleases God ever to make me a Christian, he has been much the means of my hitherto weak and feeble conversion. If ever I shall be a child of God, I shall, humbly speaking, in a great measure be his son in the gospel.[28]

Trench's experience of evangelicalism while he was bishop of Elphin is crucial to our understanding of his record as archbishop of Tuam. There he had direct exposure to the revival in the Church of Ireland. He endeavoured to make clergy and laity alike aware of their duty to improve the moral and spiritual welfare of all Christian subjects in Ireland, Catholic as well as Protestant. He had also sanctioned cooperation between the Church of Ireland community and the Dissenting evangelicals associated with the LHS in Sligo.[29] His accession to the see of Tuam opened enormous and exciting possibilities for the expansion of evangelicalism throughout a diocese that was undoubtedly the most backward in the country, in terms of both the material welfare of its Catholic population and the manpower of the Catholic Church.[30] His coming brought with it dramatic change. The procurement of livings for zealous curates, the enlistment of landlords and other lay Protestants (especially magistrates, doctors, coastguards and military officers), and naturally the introduction of Bible schools and scripture readers were now pursued on a grander scale in Connaught than they had ever been in any other part of the country.

Immediately upon succeeding to the archbishopric of Tuam in 1819 Trench turned his attention to the advancement of those interests that had occupied so much of his energy at Elphin. Clerical meetings, or 'diocesan synods' as one commentator called them, were scheduled for the third Thursday of every month. Attendance at these meetings by ministers from all over the archdiocese was often so heavy that accommodation began to be a problem. The education of the poor, especially the promotion of Sunday schools, the repair of church buildings and the organization of a widows' fund, were likewise the objects of his concern. But the crisis that above all absorbed his attention and energy very shortly after his transfer was the famine that struck the western counties in the summer of 1822.

The failure of the potato harvest in 1821 had left the peasantry of the west facing starvation in the following spring, without either crops for consumption or seed for planting. The response of Archbishop Trench to this calamitous situation was both swift and effective, and probably without equal in the records of episcopal charity anywhere in the British Isles. Indeed, the personage with whom he was most frequently and eulogistically compared was Bishop Belzunce of Marseilles (immortalized by Alexander Pope), who had 'walked through the valley of the shadow of death' ministering to his parishioners during the plague that struck that city in 1720. Trench personally assumed the responsibility of travelling to the most afflicted areas and reporting on conditions to the newspapers and the government. Besides contributing to relief efforts out of his own pocket, he supervised the distribution of aid from outside sources, especially that of the London Tavern Committee, an organization specifically committed to the relief of famine in the west. In May and June 1822 he visited the western parts of County Mayo around Castlebar, Newport and Westport, and made the following report to the London organization:

> Here, much fever, dysentery, and cholera prevail. I have, everywhere I went, and I presided at all their committees, advised their more extended relief, and to endeavour to keep as many alive as they can for one fortnight to three weeks, when I was assured large further supplies would be sent, from the strong representation I made to the government. I wrote on Tuesday last to Mr. Goulburn such a statement as could only be equalled by the scenes I have since seen. In short, sir, if thousands are not immediately sent into these counties, particularly to Mayo and the West of Galway, without the fear of contradiction, I say large proportions must die! It is now become so bad, that it would be folly to talk about immediate employment. The people in general are too weak to work, and must be fed and strengthened gradually before employment could be available. If our government has not sufficient funds to relieve this most *extraordinary* demand, I hope they will again apply to parliament for a liberal supply. There is no time to discuss the matter; our case cannot be met by *ordinary* rules or reasonings. If we are not supplied, we must die. If we are promptly supplied, many may yet be saved. I SHALL LIVE AMONG THESE FAMISHING PEOPLE TILL THE SUMMER IS OVER, when I pray that the Lord may bless us with a plentiful harvest; FOR ALTHOUGH I CAN DO THEM NO GOOD, I THINK IT CHEERS THEM TO SEE ONE ANXIOUSLY INQUIRING ABOUT THEM, and it encourages the gentlemen (who indeed in most parts are doing their job well) to go on in their work of mercy.[31]

Throughout July and August the archbishop laboured unceasingly on behalf of famine victims in the Tuam area and in Galway city, which was being swept by a fever epidemic. The dispersal of aid in outlying regions he entrusted to local relief committees, in most cases supervised by Protestant clergymen, among whom the evangelical Archdeacon Thomas Grace of Westport was distinguished by his dedication.[32] But the cooperation of the Catholic clergy was likewise not in short supply, and their gratitude to Trench was expressed on several occasions. On 3 August 1822 a Catholic priest in Galway informed the local newspaper that Archbishop Trench had entered every wretched cabin in that part of his parish known as Bohermore, a suburb on the main Dublin road outside Galway city. Trench comforted the inmates and promised that 'their days of bitterness and trial would shortly pass away, and plenty and comfort be their future lot'. This was no idle promise on the archbishop's part. When the crisis of the famine finally passed its peak (relief provisions had kept it from assuming catastrophic proportions), the first project to occupy his attention was the development of cottage industries based on spinning and weaving throughout Galway and Mayo.[33]

Exposure to the actual conditions of everyday life among the peasantry of the west had a profound effect on Archbishop Trench. His heroic labours on their behalf during the terrible summer of 1822 created for him a bond of attachment that embraced the social as well as the spiritual aspects of their well-being. At one point he came dangerously close to identifying the true source of their misery, but his intellectual and spiritual disposition and his role as a leading representative of the Church of Ireland precluded any radical demands that the existing social and political system should be overhauled in favour of a more equitable distribution of the sources of wealth. Thus the most that he could achieve was to intercede with the government on behalf of the unfortunate peasantry and to exert his own energies to the full in contributing to their relief. His awareness of these limitations is clearly revealed in correspondence addressed to the London Tavern Committee in August 1822:

> At all times a large proportion of our peasantry have no beds, little or no covering at night, a few miserable articles of furniture, and clothing scarcely fit for decency; wretched hovels—some without any gardens and some with a few perches, for which of course they must be under some rent. I am now speaking from my own knowledge. There is not regular employment for one-quarter of our labouring poor, and the wages are six pence, eight pence, or ten pence per day, with which they are to pay their rent, subsist, and clothe their families, provide fuel, etc … Those whose cases were a little improved by possessing something are most extensively reduced from the pressure of the present famine; they have sold their clothes, their blankets, their furniture, their pigs, horses, cows, sheep—in short—every article upon the earth, to procure food in the early part of the current distress and to avoid their seeking relief by public or private alms … In relieving much of the want I have stated as arising from the state of this particular year, one great difficulty occurs to me. Most of these unhappy people are in considerable arrears to their landlords. Much danger is to be apprehended that, were you now to replace such articles as they may have sold in order to procure for themselves and their families' food,

they would be seized for the payment of the rent, and thus your funds would not mend their condition, but go into the landlords' pockets, a class of people who no doubt have a right to the rent for their land, and who are very great sufferers from the present distressed state of the times.[34]

The archbishop's efforts did not go unappreciated by local Catholics. In his own locality the country people bestowed on him the traditional gesture of gratitude by collectively harvesting his crops. When he got word of what was taking place and hastened to provide beer for their refreshment, they refused to partake of it 'in order to avoid even the appearance of receiving any recompense for their unsolicited and gratuitous services'.[35] On a more formal level the Catholic archbishop of Tuam, Dr Oliver Kelly, at the last meeting of the local relief committee on 19 August 1822, on behalf of himself, his clergy, and their parishioners, offered Dr Trench 'the humble tribute of our sincere gratitude, hoping that his benignity of character and his active and well-directed beneficence (qualities worthy of our emulation) may long continue to shed their light over us'.[36]

With the possible exception of Bishop Jebb of Limerick, no prelate of the Established Church stood higher in the esteem of his countrymen at this time. Even the *Dublin Evening Post* at the height of the Bible War of 1824 would not allow his good name to be tarnished, despite his fervent commitment to the evangelical cause. The editor reminded his readers of the archbishop's Herculean labours in the west in 1822; while many of his compatriots, who,

> with a species of bitter irony, are called the natural protectors of the poor, were uttering fine sentiments on the banks of the Thames or the Seine, he was visiting every part of his extensive and starving see, distributing food and raiment, comforting the afflicted, and saving hundreds from the jaws of death.[37]

The question that must be addressed at this point is why a man of such integrity did not appreciate the risk involved in throwing the whole weight of his influence behind the 'Second Reformation' movement. It seems reasonable to presume that the generous bestowal of his energy and personal resources on the starving poor of the west in 1822 might have awakened his conscience to the benefits to be gained if Protestants and Catholics joined forces in a meaningful effort to improve the condition of the peasantry. But such a presumption would of necessity omit a consideration of the evangelical conscience, which was at all times the guiding spirit of his actions, spiritual as well as temporal. His work among the famine victims of the west only strengthened his belief that they were flocks within his keeping, for whose salvation he stood accountable in the eyes of God. Because of his good standing with the Catholic community, he thought it fitting to devote to this subject a large portion of the sermon delivered at his triennial visitation in 1823.

The visitation was held at the Protestant cathedral in Tuam, and a sizeable proportion of the congregation was Catholic. That part of the sermon directed at the Catholics was wholly concerned with the right of the individual to base his religious convictions on the diligent and serious examination of the scriptures, as opposed to 'the intentions and traditions of men [which have been] made the fundamental basis of your creed'.[38] The tone of his address had none of the militancy of Archbishop Magee's visitation sermon at St Patrick's Cathedral in Dublin in the previous year. Yet it was, for all its sincerity, a ringing declaration of the spiritual dimensions of the evangelical mission to the Catholic population:

> My friends, you are kept in ignorance, and darkness, and delusion, and prohibited the use of God's holy word, which can *alone* enlighten your understandings and open your eyes to behold the wondrous things of God. Let the most wicked and abominable books, books of sedition, of treason, of rebellion, of blasphemy, of impurity, be disseminated among you, not one word is said from your altars to caution you against their evil tendency or to guard the people against reading or listening to them. But if one of your communion dares to look into the precious Gospel of Christ—if he there looks for the true way of deliverance from the curse of the law and for the truth which can make him free—if he ventures to seek in that sacred volume the means of saving his immortal soul—the heaviest denunciations and curses of his church are immediately pronounced against him. And what, my friends, is all this for; is it for an hearty desire for your salvation—is it that you may become good Christians—is it that you may pass from earth to heaven and ever rest in the bosom of your heavenly Father? No; but it is from fear that you should discover your error and protest against it.[39]

Trench was criticized in many quarters for his resolute adherence to evangelical principles, but critics were largely without influence on this single-minded prelate, who proceeded to put into practice what he had long been preaching. He shortly had a vanguard of evangelical curates operating in strategic locations throughout the diocese: the Rev. Charles Seymour in

Clifden, the Rev. William Stoney in Newport, the Rev. Thomas Burgh in Ballinrobe, the Rev. Giles Eyre in Galway and the Rev. Thomas Walker in Westport. Most of these men were recent products of Trinity College. In the dissemination of vital religion they cooperated with each other, with the gentry of the districts in which they held their livings, with the agents dispatched by the educational societies in Dublin, and above all with their diocesan superior in Tuam. The results of their combined activities became immediately apparent in the years after 1824, when the 'Second Reformation' was in full flower. The amount of sectarian controversy prevailing in a given district was usually a reliable measure of the influence of the local evangelical clergyman. A case in point was the area around Newport, County Mayo, where the Rev. William Stoney kept up a continual battle with the local priests over his right to minister to the Catholic population.[40]

Connemara, to which Trench dispatched Rev. Charles Seymour in the early 1820s, was notorious as one of the few remaining spots in Ireland where the writ of English law often did not apply.[41] The first two decades of the nineteenth century brought about great changes, however, as speculators newly enriched by the booming economy of the war years began to purchase land and to build splendid new houses.[42] The most prominent of those who established themselves in Connemara in this fashion were men whose names suggest their association with the 'tribes' of Galway—Hiberno–Norman merchant families that had dominated that city's economic and political life since the heyday of the Spanish trade in the fifteenth and sixteenth centuries. By the early nineteenth century many of these families, such as the Blakes, Burkes, Martins and D'Arcy's, were classic examples of members of the Catholic upper classes who had converted to the Protestant religion in the eighteenth century, and who had capitalized on the commercial revolution, particularly the West Indian trade. Henry Blake, whose modern residence at Renvyle was said to have been built on the proceeds of his family's plantation in Montserrat, began his career as an improving landlord when he settled in the area with a fashionable English wife and an equally fashionable commitment to promoting 'the Irish Highlands' of Connemara for wealthy tourists in search of romantic scenery and antique remains.[43]

The Martins of Ballinahinch had a somewhat longer history in the area, but they more than equalled the Blakes in their penchant for modernization and development. The flamboyant Richard Martin, the popular 'Humanity Dick', founder of the Royal Society for the Prevention of Cruelty to Animals and lord of the sprawling Ballinahinch estate, could hold his own with the most fashionable of Westminster's aristocratic philanthropists.[44] Henry Blake and Richard Martin were both outmatched by John D'Arcy, who in 1815 founded the town of Clifden, which he planned to develop as the commercial hub of the surrounding area, and built a magnificent neo-Gothic castellated mansion on his model estate west of the town.[45]

While Martin and D'Arcy were ardent supporters of O'Connell and Emancipation, they (or, perhaps more accurately, their wives) were enthusiastic promoters of the trend for improving the lives of the peasantry. The schools of the KPS were thus introduced to Clifden, and land was provided by the Martins for a school run by the LHS in Ballinahinch. The Blakes of Renvyle were by far the most enthusiastic 'improvers' in Connemara, engaging in famine relief as well as attempts to introduce industry and education to the area. In April 1824, on the publication of a letter from Martha Louisa Blake complaining of the opposition of the local priest to the children attending her school, the *Dublin Evening Post* saw fit to describe Connemara as an area 'where all the proprietors are extremely litigious and are infected with the most virulent description of the biblical mania'.[46]

The source of the 'infection' undoubtedly was the man chosen as the instrument of evangelization by Archbishop Trench: the Rev. Charles Seymour, formerly curate of Ardcarne, and Archdeacon Digby's most diligent footsoldier in the Elphin diocese. In 1820 Seymour was appointed to the union of Ballinakill, which embraced almost the whole of Connemara and Joyce's Country, including the town of Clifden and the extensive estates of the Martin family at Ballinahinch. Seymour's proficiency in Irish was particularly suited to his mission, and he aspired to carry out a 'holy war' with what he called his two-edged sword—the Irish and English testaments. In a letter to Joseph D'Arcy Sirr, who was working for the Irish Society in Dublin at this time, he described the prospects for the Irish Bible in Connemara:

> It is a truth learned better by experience than by reasoning that the Irish language in some parts of Ireland (particularly Connemara) is a better introduction to the English than the English to the Irish. I have found my Irish sword (Irish testament) of singular service in clearing away the obstacles that opposed my English weapon (the English testament). I am every day polishing, sharpening, and, I thank God, in some degree successfully brandishing my Irish sword, and I long for some powerful ally to be sent down by the society to help me.[47]

Seymour's mission predictably met with strong opposition from the local Catholic clergy. The Kildare Place school in Clifden was put under severe prohibition on these grounds; even the use of a spelling book published by the Irish Society, which contained some parables from the Bible, was forbidden. Among the local gentry, however, Seymour's exertions were warmly supported. The Martins provided land for a London Hibernian school at Ballinahinch and supported the education of an Irish-speaking master. A Sunday school was established in Clifden and a weekly school for girls was patronized by Mrs Blake at Renvyle. The promising start made by Seymour in the Clifden area prompted his transfer to Louisburgh, County Mayo, in 1822. He was replaced by his nephew, the Rev. Anthony Thomas. Sirr suggests that Seymour's removal to Louisburgh was occasioned by the reputation of the surrounding area as a centre of Catholic pilgrimage. (In addition, the settlement of refugees who had fled the northern counties during the terror of the 1790s lent an ultra-Catholic character to the area.[48]) Between the activities of Seymour and those of Stoney in Newport and the Rev. Edward Nangle in Achill, the whole of western Mayo was characterized by bitter sectarian conflict throughout the middle decades of the nineteenth century.

In Connemara, meanwhile, largely because of the active involvement of the local gentry, the evangelical crusade was making distinct progress. Until the early 1830s the Rev. Thomas worked alone from his vicarage in Ballinakill. His dedication and energy may be illustrated by his Sabbath duties, which took him first to Ballinahinch, a distance of about twelve miles from his home; from there he travelled on horseback to Clifden, another six miles, and then proceeded to his base at Ballinakill to repeat the ceremony. Because of his wife's ill health he was obliged to leave Connemara in 1834, but his work was carried on by two curates whom Archbishop Trench had dispatched earlier to assist him. These were the Rev. Mark Anthony Forster, who ministered in the village of Tully from 1830 to 1832, before moving to Roundstone on the southern coastal flank of the district, and the Rev. Brabazon Ellis, who was appointed to the curacy of Moyrus near Carna in 1831.[49]

Between them these men were the guiding spirits of the Connemara mission and were responsible for founding the Connemara Christian Committee in 1836.[50] This organization, which included lay as well as clerical members, was dedicated to the holding of clerical meetings and the evangelization of local Catholics. An appeal for local support signed by Forster and Ellis, representing the 'Connemara Christian Committee, under the sanction and approval of his grace, the archbishop of Tuam', stated clearly that the mission to the Catholics was the organization's first concern. The strategy proposed to achieve this end was based in its entirety on the methods developed over long years of experience in other parts of the country:

> The MEANS by which they seek to effect this high and holy object are the apostolic means of *united deliberation, united prayer, and united exertion*. The plans which they propose adopting will embrace—First, Bible associations; second, Scriptural schools; third, Scripture readers; fourth, public lectures; fifth, public meetings for reading the Scriptures; sixth, tract shops; seventh, periodical publications; eight, protection of approved converts.[51]

In addition to the evangelical clergymen appointed by Archbishop Trench, the Connemara Christian Committee was actively supported by the younger generation of the local gentry. Of these the most significant was Hyacinth D'Arcy, the eldest son of John D'Arcy of Clifden Castle, who had returned from Trinity College in the early 1830s to inherit his father's estate and to devote himself to the evangelization of Connemara. From the very beginning he was active on the Connemara Christian Committee, having been elected treasurer at the Society's first meeting in Clifden on 11 February 1836.[52] Largely because of Hyacinth D'Arcy's influence, Clifden became the centre for the work of the Society for the Irish Church Missions, an organization infamous in the popular memory for what became known as 'souperism' during the years of the Famine between 1845 and 1850. This practice in brief was the alleged refusal of evangelical missionaries to deploy their substantial resources among any but those who either apostatized or, at the very least, allowed their children to attend evangelical schools. The record of Hyacinth D'Arcy and his fellow workers in this regard does not lie within the scope of the present work. What is of vital importance, however, is the degree to which the native soil had been prepared and the requisite connections set in place when Alexander Dallas, with substantial funds and manpower from England, opted for Connemara as a base from which to launch his proselytizing offensive on the eve of the Great Famine.[53]

One of the greatest challenges faced by the Connemara Christian Committee was the protection of converts faced with the ostracism and hostility of their Catholic neighbours. The Rev. Brabazon Ellis reported how the sixty or so converts under his care in the years 1835–6 were constantly persecuted. One family, several of whose members were teachers in the Clifden area, was subjected to the following treatment after converting: 'Persecution set in—their schools were denounced; their scholars withdrawn; they were left without the means of subsistence, and they had no *apparent* alternative but to perish from starvation or to return to Rome.'[54] Ellis and his wife were likewise subjected to denunciations from the altar, threatening letters, and even physical abuse. By his own admission they were virtual prisoners in their home in Clifden, though he claimed that he was always treated with kindness by the country people of the surrounding area.[55] In view of the overwhelming local opposition to the mission Ellis, D'Arcy and Forster, with the approval of Archbishop Trench, began to consider the prospects of developing a Protestant colony. This project was based on the evident success of the Rev. Edward Nangle's experiment on Achill Island. Land was purchased on a desolate and windswept stretch of moorland between Clifden and Letterfrack called Sionnanach, but this scheme never materialized during the archbishop's lifetime (he died in 1839). Instead, Protestant settlement in Connemara confined itself to small enclaves of dispersed settlements like those at Ballinakill, Kingstown, Moyrus, Errislannon and Castlekerke near Oughterard, which were usually centred on the residence of the local landlord or clergyman.

The development of Protestant colonies was responsible for much of the success, such as it was, that the evangelical movement enjoyed during the 1830s and 1840s. Perhaps no other aspect of the Reformation movement so clearly reflected its connections with the militant defenders of Protestant supremacy, or the degree to which the enterprise was an exercise in cultural imperialism.

THE IDEA OF PROTESTANT COLONIES: THE ACHILL AND DINGLE EXPERIMENTS

A combination of several trends in the late 1820s gave rise to discussion among the leaders of the evangelical movement about the utility of setting up Protestant settlements that would serve as a bulwark against the undermining of the ultra-Protestant cause. If the number of converts were to be increased, some form of protection would be necessary to enable them to be socially and economically independent of their local communities, which subjected them to ostracism and physical abuse. Fears were also expressed in certain quarters that the lower classes of Protestants were emigrating in vast numbers because of the threat of Catholic ascendancy implicit in the passage of the Emancipation act.[56]

In 1833 the *Dublin University Magazine* claimed that Protestants were leaving Ireland in such numbers that

> it was impossible to state fully, and if so stated would not be credited. It is not from this or that district alone. Panic and disgust have seized upon the Protestant yeomanry throughout Ireland. The country is not bleeding merely, it is sweating blood.

In all, it was claimed that 94,000 Protestants had left Ireland since 1829.[57]

It was this aspect of the debate that led to the establishment of the Protestant Colonisation Society. The Society took its inspiration from a work published in Edinburgh in 1828, *An Account of the Poor Colonies and Agricultural Workhouses of the Benevolent Society of Holland,* which described the success of Dutch settlements organized on the cooperative principle, devoted to land reclamation, agricultural innovation and the increase of capital.[58] In November 1829 plans for the launching of the Society were drawn up by a group of influential landlords, clergymen and laymen well known for their anti-Catholic sympathies. The committee of management included the earl of Enniskillen, Lord Mountcashel, Lord Lorton, Marcus Beresford, Colonel Blacker, N.D. Crommellin and Anthony Lefroy. Among the vice-presidents were Archbishop William Magee, the marquis of Donegal, Lord Bantry, Viscount Dungannon, Lord Farnham, Lord Longford and the earl of Muskerry. Dignitaries such as the bishops of Bath and Salisbury, the duke of Newcastle and the earl of Winchelsea lent their support.[59] It was agreed that settlements would prove an effective means of halting the emigration of poorer Protestants and of introducing industry, discipline and obedience to the law in those parts of the country where they were needed most. More fundamentally, it was hoped that the plan would prove to be an important stepping stone in the creation of political stability. One of the clergymen present claimed:

> Protestant colonies would be found most useful in preserving the connection between this country and England. The poorer class of Irish Protestants were in truth the chain that bound conquered Ireland to the conqueror England; and it was as much the interest of England as of Ireland to encourage those Protestants by whom this connection was preserved.[60]

But the aims of the Protestant Colonisation Society went far beyond the vision of self-sufficient cooperative enclaves that would provide protection and support for converts from Catholicism. According to the earliest pronouncements issued by the management committee, it was clear that they were envisaged as missionary centres from which influence would radiate to the surrounding areas through the work of preachers, Bible readers and schools, as well as through the example of what Protestant investment, industry and good management could achieve in backward areas.[61] The connection between the Protestant Colonisation Society and the various settlements started in the 1830s is unclear.[62] Although the Society was clearly involved in small-scale efforts undertaken at Aughkeely, County Donegal, and Kilmeague, County Kildare, it is not at all clear that it was connected with the more substantial colonies of Achill and Dingle.

What is certain, however, is that it was closely connected with the Brunswick Clubs. The *Dublin Evening Post* in 1830 reported that an attempt to set up an auxiliary in Sligo in that year was the work of two men, James Gore Jones and James Wood, who were well known locally as Brunswick sympathizers.[63] Even more revealing was the transfer of the Brunswick Society funds to the Colonisation Society when the former was disbanded in the early 1830s. The justification for the transfer was that the Colonisation Society offered, so it was claimed, 'the only immediate practical means for effectively countervailing the growing national calamity of Protestant emigration'.[64]

Among the earliest experiments of the Protestant Colonisation Society was that in Aughkeely, County Donegal, a townland between Letterkenny and Stranorlar, on the estate of Sir Edmund Hayes of Drumbo Castle.[65] Applicants were invited to apply for homesteads consisting of a comfortable house and five acres of ground (the allotment could be extended to twenty-five or thirty acres where desirable) at a rent of fifty shillings a year. Families from Scotland and England were welcomed, but the majority of the twelve households of the Aughkeely colony in 1832 were of Ulster origin, with a sprinkling of representatives from the southern counties.[66] It is not known to what degree the Aughkeely colony functioned as a refuge for converts, and no mention of it occurs in the subsequent historiography of the evangelical movement. Another experimental settlement of this kind was founded at Kilmeague, County Kildare, and up to a hundred families were said to have taken occupancy there in the decade before the Famine.[67] In 1835 Kilmeague was brought to the attention of Lord Farnham as an example of a project that had aroused great interest in England. According to Farnham's correspondent, funds were being raised by no less a personage than the Rev. Wood, tutor to Prince George, who had already collected almost £100 for the persecuted inhabitants of the colony.[68]

The colonies started at Achill and Dingle in the early 1830s were by far the most substantial of their kind and also the most famous. The Colonisation Society appears to have had little to do with the launching and development of these particular colonies. While talk of colonies was very much in the air at this time, and while the policies of Archbishop Trench in the Tuam archdiocese indicated favourable prospects for missionary expansion in that area, the specific event that turned the evangelical focus westward was a severe outbreak of famine and cholera that swept the coastal regions in the years 1830–1. In the case of both Achill and Dingle, it was famine relief that drew the attention of evangelicals to the possibilities for missionary work based on the colony system. The labours of individual clergymen were soon reinforced by agents supported by the Irish Society and the Scripture Readers' Society, and leading Dublin evangelicals, especially those connected with the Home Mission Society, were in frequent contact with the west. In the case of Dingle, this combination of influences was clearly behind the launching of an integrated system of missions on the peninsula in the 1830s.

The evangelical tradition in County Kerry went back to the days of Charles Graham and the Methodist mission to the Irish-speaking population in the late eighteenth century. The choice of Kerry as an area in which to begin this mission may have been influenced by an Anglican clergyman, the Rev. Nash, who lived near Dingle in the 1790s and was a close friend of Adam Averell, the head of the Methodist convocation in Ireland at that time.[69] It is unlikely that Graham's mission produced any remarkable results in converting the Catholics of Kerry. What is certain, nevertheless, is that there was a sustained interest in this idea during the first three decades of the century. When George Ensor published his famous attack on the 'Second Reformation' in 1828, he referred to an allegation that 'hundreds of families' had been converted in Kerry.[70] Similarly, during the winter of 1826, when reports of converts were coming in from Kingscourt and Askeaton, *The Watchman* commented that people in the Dingle area were 'all ablaze for the Irish scriptures'.[71] Despite the lack of solid evidence on this point, it does suggest that something was afoot, a view that finds support in the record of a tour by two representatives of the Home Mission Society, the Rev. Denis Browne of Santry and the Rev. John Gregg of the Bethesda Chapel, who were invited to Kerry by the Rev. Arthur B. Rowan, an evangelical minister who had been appointed to the curacy of Blennerville near Tralee in 1824.[72] They mentioned the Dingle peninsula as an area badly in need of further visits from the Society's agents. The reason given was the 'singularly enthusiastic overture' they had received from the enthusiastic curate of Dingle, the Rev. Thomas Chute Goodman.[73]

Thomas Goodman, or 'Parson Tom' as he was called locally, was the product of a remarkable blending of the older presence of the Church of Ireland with the local Catholic community and also with the administrative innovations of the modern state that were beginning to penetrate the remote fastnesses of the west by the 1820s. The Dingle peninsula was remarkably similar to Connemara in that it was largely Irish-speaking and relatively untouched by the modern world. Among the more significant modern intrusions in the 1820s was the building of four coastguard stations, staffed by officers and their families who were mostly Protestant. It was concern for the spiritual welfare of this community, which averaged between thirty and forty souls per station, that first brought the attention of Bishop Jebb to 'this westernmost parish in Europe, the wildest country he ever beheld'.[74] Jebb's estimation of the excellent conduct of the coastguard community, particularly the good relations the residents enjoyed with their Catholic neighbours and even the local priest, convinced him that it might function as a centre from which the influence of Protestantism would radiate in the quiet and unobtrusive fashion that had always appealed to him. His plan to provide a pastor to minister to the coastguards and their families, if carried into effect, he said, would

> not merely be a provision for the welfare of 120 or 130 souls (though that of itself is a most important consideration) but the nourishing and perhaps with God's blessing dispersing the seed of Protestantism in a remote and extensive district: a seed too, from all appearance, of the most promising quality. A nucleus might then be formed round which the scattered and lapsed Protestants (of which there are several in that part of the country) might rally. This has partially been the case hitherto. And what is remarkable, Roman Catholics have occasionally attended the sermons and have expressed themselves surprised to find so much religion among Protestants.[75]

Jebb's concern to provide a pastor for the coastguard community was occasioned by his disappointment with the rector of Dingle, Rev. John Goodman, who had held the living since 1787. The elder Goodman was English and also held a living in Kemerton, Gloucestershire, but in the opinion of Bishop Jebb, after his many years in Dingle he had practically gone native. A fluent Irish-speaker, he was on extremely good terms with his Catholic neighbours, and according to Jebb, 'did as little as he could with any decency'.[76] The son Thomas, however, was considered to be more promising material: 'though far more respectable than his father ... from his defective education and aboriginal habits, [he is] incompetent to act without assistance'. Jebb saw the needs of the coastguard community and the particular weaknesses of Thomas Chute Goodman—his lack of training coupled with his close affinity with the native Catholic community—as affording the perfect opportunity for the placement of a pastor devoted to the evangelical mission of the Church of Ireland.[77]

In 1831 a clergyman named George Gubbins took up residency in Dingle, reputedly to assist Goodman in relieving the distress caused by famine and cholera, which were once again scourging the seaboard counties of the west. Little is known about this man's background, and it is not clear to what degree Bishop Jebb was behind the appointment, but it is apparent that he came primarily to carry on missionary activity. An exemplary evangelical in every way, he was as remarkable for his humble lifestyle and dedicated relief work as for his desire to advance the missionary cause. He is generally credited with the initiation of proselytism in the area.

Significantly, it was during this outbreak of famine, when the evangelical mission in Kerry gained real momentum, that the baneful term 'souper' first came into popular usage. According to Mrs D.P. Thompson, the chronicler of the Dingle Mission, 'a benevolent lady in Dingle' opened a soup kitchen to provide sustenance for the starving inhabitants in 1831. The local priest forbade them to have anything to do with it, and anyone who did so was consequently labelled a 'souper'.[78] Eventually, the expression 'to take the soup' implied not only the acceptance of food or clothing but also the assumption of the Protestant religion, outlook and behaviour in return for material advancement, especially in the forms of housing, land or employment.

The most important figure behind the expansion of evangelical missions in Dingle was Lord Ventry, the proprietor of a vast estate on the peninsula. His name was not to be found along with those of Roden, Farnham, Lorton and de Vesci on the lists of patrons of evangelical societies, and the occasion of his conversion to the cause is unknown. But by the early 1830s he was prepared to place his enormous personal influence behind the enterprise. In 1833 he invited a young clergyman, the Rev. Charles Gayer, to become his personal chaplain.[79] Though of English birth, Gayer had been educated in Ireland and had held two previous livings at Slawin, County Fermanagh, and Kinnegad, County Westmeath. On assuming his position as chaplain to Lord Ventry, he set as his first objective the organization of a comprehensive mission that would be centred on the town of Dingle and extend to the five parishes of the peninsula, including the Small Blasket Island. With the sustained financial support of Lord Ventry behind him, he made rapid progress and succeeded in developing a full-scale missionary enterprise that covered the whole of the peninsula by the late 1830s.[80]

Along with a small number of assistants, including Goodman and Gubbins, Gayer first sought converts in the immediate vicinity of the town of Dingle. When a sufficient number of local Catholics responded to his overtures, a schoolhouse was built and formal instruction in the reformed faith begun. The next step was to procure the conversion of those in attendance at the school and to enlist their aid in spreading the Reformation to the adjoining parishes.[81] For the first two or three years the progress of the mission was gradual but steady. Several prominent members of the local Protestant community were active supporters of the mission. These included Lieutenant Clifford of the Coastguard, David Thompson, the local magistrate and agent of Lord Ventry, whose wife wrote a history of the mission in 1846, and Catherine Hartland Mahon.[82] Here the chief attraction was the use of Irish as the primary medium of instruction. As was often reported by agents of the Irish Society working in other parts of the west, the directors of the Dingle Mission perceived that hostility to the scriptures was reduced remarkably when the Irish version was used, and they made the oft-repeated claim that Irish country people truly believed that no evil could be transmitted through their native language.[83] Though Gayer himself could not speak Irish, its use as the primary means of communication between the missionaries and the Catholic Irish of Dingle was a virtual necessity, since the area was wholly Irish-speaking.

In 1836 the Irish Society became heavily involved with the mission when one of its inspectors visited the school and reported on its progress. An agreement was made to supply twenty instructors to augment the mission staff, with wages and other support drawn from the Society's funds. These teachers were not necessarily Protestants, but they were fluent Irish-speakers prepared to give lessons in the scriptures through Irish whenever opportunity offered, usually during domiciliary visits under cover of night. Before the end of 1836, upwards of 170 men were in regular attendance at the Dingle school, and reports of converts were arriving from several parishes on the peninsula.[84]

In the decade before the Famine the fortunes of the Dingle Mission continued their upward course, and several conversions of well-known Catholics took place. The most celebrated of these was a priest, Fr Brasbie of Kilmalkedar, who had originally been sent into the area to counter the work of the evangelicals but who had ended up joining their ranks. According to Mrs Thompson, he had been extremely popular prior to his conversion, but afterward he dared not appear in public without protection, and when he attempted to deliver sermons the military had to be called out to prevent violence.[85]

Another famous case of conversion, this time on a family scale, was that of the Moriartys, four of whom took up the evangelical banner. The most remarkable among them was Thomas Moriarty, who joined the Irish Society and worked for a time in the Kingscourt District. In 1838 Gayer requested that he return to Dingle, in all likelihood because his services were considered necessary; in the following year Gayer himself was appointed rector of Dunurlin on the departure of George Gubbins, who was transferred to Ballingarry, County Tipperary, to attempt a repetition of the Dingle experiment. The Irish Society not only consented to release Moriarty from his duties at Kingscourt but also undertook to support him, along with a number of Bible readers and a schoolmaster and mistress who were to work under his direction at the newly opened mission station at Ventry. Two of Thomas Moriarty's brothers followed his example in adopting the Protestant faith and serving the cause of Reformation; one was employed in the nearby town of Castleisland and the other went farther afield to County Tyrone.[86] Their sister, who remained a Catholic for seven years after the conversion of her brothers, was looked upon as a great example by local Catholic stalwarts. When she finally relented and apostatized, there was a tremendous local uproar, followed by great hostility to the converts.[87]

The evangelical mission in Dingle was a continual source of social and sectarian conflict, although there is some evidence that a degree of tolerance was accorded those of local origin, particularly the Rev. Thomas Chute Goodman. One piece of evidence in support of this view is to be found in the postscript to a threatening letter received by the Rev. Gayer. The letter warned Gayer to look out for his life, but it also added: 'Parson Goodman is a good man. He interfaries [*sic*] with no man's religion. I lave him to you.'[88] Even Gayer was not always the object of execration. However misguided his efforts were thought to have been, local Catholics appear to have appreciated that he was genuinely interested in their welfare. This was especially true during periods of dearth, when he did not hesitate to use the resources of the mission for temporal relief.

The Dingle Mission assumed a more permanent character and its resources were greatly advanced when Gayer's ambitions for a full-scale colony were realized in 1839. A number of cottages were built to house converts, along with a church, a glebe house and schools. Farmland was leased from Lord Ventry, and attempts were made to develop the fishing industry. The evangelization of the surrounding area continued unrelentingly. At one point Gayer sent a Bible reader to the Blasket Islands, but he was obliged to beat a hasty retreat when the islanders threatened to hurl him over the cliffs. Three years later, they reportedly sent a deputation to the headquarters at Dingle, asking that a teacher be sent among them.[89] This was typical of the ambivalence with which the Kerry people responded to the missionaries. Gayer succeeded in having a church built on the Blaskets only by invoking the protection of the law; the owner of the islands was a Catholic lady who would not allow her tenants to work on the project.[90] Yet in 1845, when a schoolmaster from the mission visited the islands, he was kindly received in a Catholic household, one of whose members informed him that it was only the relief sent by Gayer that had kept them from starving the previous summer.[91]

The record of the Dingle colony during the years of the Great Famine has never received detailed scrutiny. Gayer, along with his co-workers and the converts, was never free from local hostility, especially after the Catholic Church began a more organized defence of its interests in the 1840s. When the American philanthropist Asenath Nicholson visited the colony during her tour of Ireland in 1844–5, she was greeted with suspicion and resentment by the local priest and by Charles Gayer's wife, who admonished her for having deigned, as a Protestant, to have anything whatever to do with Catholics, especially a priest: 'And what did you call on him for? I will never go near any of them. They are a persecuting people.'[92] Outraged at the rude and arrogant manner in which she had been received, Mrs Nicholson lamented that 'so noble, so apostolic a work was in the hands of those whose hospitality, whose humility, whose courteousness to strangers, and whose self-denial were so far behind the principles they professed to inculcate'.

When she interviewed the converts, she found that they had only a faint understanding of the differences between the faith they had departed from and that into which they had been received. The only answer she repeatedly encountered when she enquired about the nature of their new-found enlightenment was, 'We do not worship images.' She was appalled at the educational methods in use, which seemed designed to teach the poor to know their place, and which were especially discriminatory against females. This latter aspect she compared very unfavourably with a school run by Catholic nuns 'whose lessons in grammar, geography, and history would do honour to any school, and [whose] needlework was of the highest order'. One of the teachers observed of the three hundred or so pupils in attendance: 'Though they are the children of the poor, we do not know what station God may call them to fill. We advance them as far as possible while they are with us.'[93]

The death of Charles Gayer in 1847 was a severe blow to the mission. The colony survived into the 1850s, but many of the converts emigrated during the Famine years, and the remainder gradually drifted back to the Catholic faith.[94] The visible remains of Gayer's mission is the row of houses of the 'Colony' in Dingle, which is still known by this name. A less tangible legacy may have been the introduction of literacy in Irish through the work of the Irish Society. It is impossible to determine what the relationship was, if any, between the introduction of literacy in Irish and the emergence of the famous school of writers associated with Tomás Ó Criomthain and others in the early twentieth century. It is believed locally that Ó Criomthain, the greatest of the Blasket writers, learned to read in Irish from the primers issued by the Irish Society.[95]

Whatever the record of the Dingle evangelical missionaries during the Famine years toward the local people who received their spiritual bounty, good care was taken of all who deserted the Catholic ranks. When Henry Wilberforce visited the area in 1852, he was informed that the inhabitants of the colony paid no rent and had plenty of work, in glaring contrast to their ragged and starving neighbours.[96] A Catholic labourer remarked of Gayer that 'he was a good warrant to help any poor man that would go his way'. Wilberforce, who had converted to Catholicism as a result of the Oxford Movement, was a leading opponent of the evangelical mission in Ireland and had taken up residence in Connemara, where he headed the Catholic Defence Association to counter the work of the Irish Church Missions.[97] In his view the enterprise was a 'demoralising system of wholesale bribery'. He probably reflected the viewpoint of most critics when, on observing the comfortable situation of the Dingle converts with their rent-free houses and land, he tartly commented 'it was worthwhile to be Protestant at that rate'.[98]

No project cast up by the campaign to evangelize the west of Ireland created more controversy and sectarian conflict than the Achill colony established by the Rev. Edward Nangle in 1834. Nangle's overpowering presence often made it appear that he was singlehandedly responsible for turning Achill into the 'Mecca of all true believers', as the *Freeman's Journal* sarcastically referred to it.[99] Certainly, it is not difficult to see why his personality and demeanour enabled those who interviewed him and observed his approach at first hand to arrive at this conclusion. In an interview with the Rev. Caesar Otway, he once compared his task on Achill with that of Martin Luther:

Their colony, he said, was established in direct hostility to popery; that it lost all claim to a religious and proselytising establishment if they treat gently which was like the nettle, a thing that, when only touched lightly, stung the hand severely, but when grasped lustily, might be plucked and eradicated without injury.[100]

Despite the furious controversy and polemics that could be traced to his door and his printing press, Edward Nangle was only the most visible aspect of the westward thrust of the evangelical movement, which was based largely on two organizations—the Irish Society, already a veteran in the field, and the recently formed Irish Islands and Coasts Society. In the case of both organizations the impulse to expand in the west came largely from the Kingscourt District.

By 1830 the evangelical mission in Kingscourt was the project on which the Irish Society was concentrating its resources.[101] More than any other area where missionary work was underway, Kingscourt was particularly remarkable for the virulence and blatancy with which its successes were publicized. Converts were paraded in church on Sunday, and teachers obliged to publish petitions to the effect that the policy of teaching the scriptures in Irish was both popular and acceptable to Catholics. Because the prospect in the northern counties appeared more promising in the years 1825–8, the Irish Society had virtually deserted the west, although Archbishop Trench of Tuam was clearly in close contact with the directors of the Society in Dublin, particularly Joseph D'Arcy Sirr and Henry Monck Mason. Between 1826 and 1829 he frequently discussed with Monck Mason the possibility of introducing the Kingscourt system on a broader scale in Connaught. The outcome of these deliberations was the foundation of the Connaught Auxiliary of the Irish Society on 22 January 1829. So enthusiastic was Dr Trench about the possibilities that now appeared before him that he committed himself to a policy under which he would not ordain clergymen for work in the Tuam archdiocese unless they were proficient in Irish. His concern for educating future clergymen in the native language was a motivating force behind the endowment of a professorship in Irish in Trinity College.[102]

Archbishop Trench's promotion of the evangelization of the Irish-speaking west gave renewed impetus to the Irish Society and its supporters in the Kingscourt District. Tactics and strategies were soon being discussed, and the Irish Islands and Coasts Society made its appearance, a corollary of the Irish Society designed to extend its operations to the 50,000 or so inhabitants of the islands along the west and south-west coasts.[103]

The founder and lifelong secretary was Mrs Henrietta Pendleton, a native of Fatham near Kingscourt. She was married to the Rev. E.C. Pendleton, who was employed by the Irish Society in the area.[104] Formerly, she had acted as secretary to the Ladies' Auxiliary of the Irish Society and had engaged herself with projects involving the islands. In 1833 it was decided to set up an independent agency for this branch of the work, since the Irish Society could not meet the demand, 'the field of its labours in the interior requiring all the resources it could command'.[105]

The Islands and Coasts Society appears to have been largely a female concern. Money was raised through letter-writing and private appeals, while individual ladies undertook the education of future scripture readers and preachers. Work was underway by 1834, and the Society began issuing its own reports in the same year. Little is known about the extent of the efforts involved. In 1836 the Rev. Noel drew attention to the needs of the islands and seemed unaware of Mrs Pendleton's organization. Likewise, there is no mention of the organization in the records of the Achill Mission, although Achill, while connected by a causeway to the mainland, was certainly considered an island.

The events that led to the foundation of the Achill colony in 1834 clearly illustrate the links between the various support centres of Irish evangelicalism in Kingscourt, Dublin and Tuam. The founder of the colony, Edward Nangle, was not a well-known figure in evangelical circles prior to 1830. A native of Athboy, County Meath, he had graduated from Trinity College in 1823 and was ordained a minister of the Church of Ireland in 1824. He spent a brief period as a curate in his native Athboy and another at Monkstown near Dublin. Sometime between 1825 and 1830 he was transferred to the curacy of Arva, County Cavan, where he probably had exposure to the progress of the evangelical mission centred at Kingscourt. After a year and a half of this work his health broke down, and he was obliged to convalesce for a period. During this time he chanced to read Christopher Anderson's *Historical Sketches of the Native Irish* (first published in 1828). This induced in him something like a conversion experience, from which he emerged committed to making the evangelization of the Irish-speaking west his life's work.[106]

Nangle's first opportunity to survey the scene of his future labours came when he accompanied an expedition on the *S.S. Nottingham*, which carried a cargo of relief provisions to Achill in the summer of 1831. Like the Dingle peninsula, western Mayo had been severely hit by famine and cholera in 1830–1, and relief efforts were similarly characterized by bitter rivalry between Catholic priests and evangelical missionaries resident in the area. In the vicinity of Ballina, for example, the local Baptist minister, the Rev. James Allen, became the object of particular hostility when he charged that the priests were monopolizing the relief funds in the town and refusing relief to country people who were in any way connected with the Baptists. Led by Archbishop MacHale, the Catholic majority on the local relief committee demanded Allen's expulsion on grounds that he was using relief funds to assist his proselytizing campaign. Local Protestants, however, representing 'all the wealth, independence, and influence of the town' came to his defence, determined not to be put down by the 'popish faction'. This situation confronted the beleaguered Rev. Allen with a set of equally undesirable alternatives:

> Should the supplies, at this stage of the proceeding, be handed over to the popish party, a complete triumph both over myself and the independence of the town would be effected. On the other hand, should the supplies be withdrawn, the most fatal consequences would ensue.[107]

It is not known if Nangle had any knowlege of the controversy over the handling of relief in the Ballina area. But it is clear that, in addition to its cargo of food and clothing, the expedition of the *S.S. Nottingham* was also designed to test the ground for missionary work on Achill.[108] It was sponsored by people of influence in Dublin, particularly Thomas Parnell of the Religious Tract and Book Society and Henry Monck Mason and the Rev. Robert Daly of the Irish Society.[109] Also in 1831 a committee was formed with the intention of leasing land for reclamation and development and laying the foundation of a settlement. When Nangle was appointed director in 1834, the mission already consisted of a house and farm occupied by two families, and a schoolmaster and scripture reader had begun work among the local population. The substantial support made available from Dublin and also from English sources guaranteed rapid progress for the Achill Mission. Land was leased from the absentee proprietor of the island, Sir Richard O'Donnell, and four schools were in operation by 1835.[110] A church was built around the same time, and a printing press was donated by supporters in London and York.

By 1836 it was clear that the Mission was not simply to function as a refuge for converts, as the Rev. Nangle so emphatically claimed, but as a missionary centre from which agents could be sent out to evangelize the whole of western Mayo. This was the main objective pursued during the Mission's heyday, which lasted from 1835 to about 1860.[111] It was also the source of bitter controversy and even physical violence. Few people—even Protestants—who might ordinarily have been sympathetic to the enterprise had anything good to say about the Rev. Nangle and his tactics. Yet, as one of his most outspoken critics, the travel writer Samuel Carter Hall, was obliged to admit, the colony unquestionably contributed a great deal to the development and modernization of the island.[112]

The first physician to take up residence in Achill, Dr Neason Adams, left a profitable practice in Dublin to supervise the dispensary at the colony; formerly, the nearest medical help available to the Achill people was at Newport, some twenty-five miles distant. Adams was universally lauded as 'the St Luke of Achill', and it was the opinion of an English visitor in 1844 that local opposition would have long since broken up the colony were it not for the good influence of Dr Adams among the Catholic population.[113] The colony schools were also said to be well run, but it is not clear whether the children in attendance were of local parentage or orphans brought from other parts of the country. The land-reclamation scheme likewise met with approval. But most visitors who published accounts of their visits to Achill implied that a great deal more might have been accomplished by the project if the proselytizing dimensions had been absent. The Rev. Caesar Otway had this to say of Nangle's experiment:

> Why not establish a settlement, where, by introducing better modes of rural economy, setting examples of cleanly, regular, and sober habits, showing the natives by well-tried experiments the advantage of attending the winter feeding of cattle, the cultivation of green crops; also by giving premiums for home industry and cleanliness amongst females, and establishing schools for the teaching of needlework ... Even suppose literary and religious instruction were quite left out of the question, why do not some of your patriots, your liberal well-wishers, for the good of Ireland, bestir themselves? Why in this way confine themselves to benevolence, while all the beneficence is left to Mr. Nangle and his supporters.[114]

The more outspoken Asenath Nicholson thought little of the Rev. Nangle's beneficence. The more that she saw of the Achill colony, the more willing she was to compare it with the slavery of the southern United States, where tyrannical slave-owners lectured their unfortunate chattels from the scriptures on the obedience owed to masters. The converts in her opinion had yielded more than spiritual allegiance when they crossed the religious divide:

> I had looked into the cabins of many of the converts of Dingle and Achill, and though their feet were washed cleaner, their stools scoured whiter, and their hearths swept better than in many of the mountain cabins, yet their eight pence a day will never put shoes upon their feet,

convert their stools into chairs, or give them any better broom than the mountain heath for sweeping their cabins. It will never give them the palatable, well-spread board around which their masters sit, and which they have earned for them by their scantily paid toil. Those converts turned from worshipping images to the living and true God, as they are told, holding a Protestant prayer book in their hands which they cannot read, can no more be sure that this religion, inculcated by proxy, emanates from the pure scriptures than did the prayer book which they held in their hands when standing before a popish altar.[115]

An intelligent and courageous woman, Mrs Nicholson perceived very clearly what the evangelical mission in Ireland was about: in her opinion, it had less to do with the social or spiritual welfare of those to whom it was directed than with the upholding of a social hierarchy built upon the subservience of the native population.

Undoubtedly there were many evangelical Protestants whose devotion was based upon their faith that they were liberating Catholics from spiritual slavery. But the alliance between evangelicalism and political conservatism that broke into open expression in the 1820s obliterated any possibility that the evangelicals would be considered in a neutral light. The events that followed Magee's famous sermon of 1822 united the issues of religious and political liberty for Catholics and opened the door that enabled the Catholic clergy to assume political as well as moral authority. The success with which they assumed this role placed an intractable barrier in the path of both the integration of the Catholic population into the Union and the prospects of future harmony between Protestants and Catholics in Ireland.

The unbounded evangelical belief in Providence reached particularly worrisome proportions when famine struck in the 1840s, and struck hardest in precisely those areas of the west where the evangelicals were entrenched. The willingness of the most extreme elements to look upon the Famine as providing an opportunity to expand the work already underway coloured the already disastrous history of evangelical missions in Ireland. Now their ambitions really would be seen in the cold light of an effort to exterminate Catholicism, and the Catholic Church for the remainder of the century and beyond would be provided with an ironclad claim to its position as defender of the people and the faith.

Conclusion

The role of religion in defining identity in private as well as public life has been the most dominant and enduring reality of modern Irish history. While the roots of the phenomenon date back to the Reformation and the conquests of the sixteenth and seventeenth centuries, it was during the period of political and economic modernization in the late eighteenth and early nineteenth centuries that religion become entrenched as the ultimate dividing line between native and colonial. This was an era in which national identity was formulated according to how people perceived the history and tradition of the community to which they belonged, a vision that would in large measure dictate the sense of national destiny and the trajectory of political life. The evolution in Ireland of two polarized and oppositional 'nations' illustrates the continuing importance of religion in the national psyche and the degree to which it answered people's basic needs in a period of upheaval and change.

By 1835 the evangelical movement had established itself as the most invigorating and energetic force within the Irish Protestant world. This was an indication of the extent to which it answered the needs of a community increasingly threatened by the growth of popular democracy and the accompanying demand for political equality among the Catholic population. Like its British counterpart, the character of Irish evangelicalism was determined by the particular environment in which it was nurtured, particularly the unfolding of the political struggle between Catholic and Protestant. In this sense it may be said to have had a unique and indigenous character, though undoubtedly it owed a great deal to the influence of both people and events often far removed from the world of denominational rivalries in Ireland.

The spread to Ireland of the religious enthusiasm associated with the 'Second Great Awakening' was a forceful reminder of the country's place in the wider British colonial world. Early evangelists like George Whitefield, John Wesley and John Cennick certainly saw their work in Ireland as an extension of their missionary efforts in Britain and the American colonies. Nevertheless, it was not until the early nineteenth century that evangelical leaders began to think in terms of an organized movement to convert the Catholic population. The overwhelming sense of urgency that characterized the mission to the Catholic Irish was a consequence of the political breakdown of the last two decades of the century. Following the Union the Irish problem essentially became one of assimilating a minority Catholic population into a dominantly Protestant union of nations. A 'common investment in Protestantism' in Linda Colley's words, was the adhesive that bound this union.[1] It is hardly surprising that the challenge of integrating the Catholic Irish was seen primarily in terms of the necessity of a 'moral transformation' in which the principles of the Protestant faith, along with respect for the constitution and the existing social and political order, would be made the basis of their belief and conduct. Initially, the idea that a common Christian culture could be made the basis of such a transformation gained currency in some quarters. Inevitably, however, the more extreme opinion prevailed that the influence of the Catholic religion was what lay at the root of the ignorance, poverty and rebellious disposition of the native Irish. The eradication of Catholicism in consequence became the driving force of the evangelical mission in Ireland.

Dynamic and committed adherents of the Independent groups, particularly the Methodists and Congregationalists, provided the leadership and inspiration for the first phase of the evangelical moral crusade. Revealingly, these men were not solely the products of the Irish evangelical world (though some, like Gideon Ouseley, certainly were) but partners in the great expansion of home and foreign missions that spawned the evangelization of the Celtic fringe areas of Scotland and Wales, as well as the overseas missions to Africa and India. The challenge mounted by these pioneers inspired a sense of denominational rivalry in the Church of Ireland, which proceeded to develop its own strategy to rescue the Catholic Irish from ignorance and superstition. By the second decade of the century Church of Ireland evangelicals had undoubtedly taken the lead in the moral crusade through the many voluntary agencies that made their appearance at this time, particularly the ADV, the Sunday School Society and the KPS.

The initial phase of the moral crusade was not especially productive of sectarian tension. Indeed, funds made available by voluntary agencies were often accepted and even welcomed by Catholic priests and schoolteachers eager to participate in the work of national regeneration through the spread of literacy and education. The problem arose when a series of events between 1816 and 1821 combined to produce a situation in which religion was made the centre of the political discourse on the admission of Catholics to full political equality. In the first instance, the rising tide of popular triumphalism following the victory over revolutionary France contributed to the belief that Providence had favoured the British social and political order grounded in tradition, social hierarchy, an economic system based on the principles of the free market, and the Protestant faith. Secondly, the economic crisis that followed the war produced a dangerously unstable situation in Ireland, a situation intensified by the almost total collapse of the Catholic-led Emancipation effort and the rise of an agrarian movement driven by a marked sectarian undercurrent. And thirdly, there was the readiness with which liberal Protestants stepped into the breach to take over the leadership of the Emancipation campaign. This development coincided with a growing trend among the leaders of political opinion in Britain—including prominent members of the evangelical movement such as William Wilberforce and Charles Grant—to consider that the Emancipation of Catholics, like the liberation of slaves in the West Indies, was an idea whose time had come.

The commitment of liberal Protestants to an Emancipation bill, together with the fear of popular revolution and the emergence of men like Daniel O'Connell, Rev. John MacHale and Bishop James Warren Doyle as outspoken and fearless leaders of Catholic public opinion, amounted to a grave threat to the continuation of Protestant supremacy in Ireland. This threat infused a renewed, indeed revolutionary, vigour into the traditional intransigence of conservative Protestants. Inspired by the belief that Britain had been saved because of its fidelity to the Christian faith, Protestant conservatives emphasized their traditional loyalty to Church and constitution, and rallied to the standards of the religion they now saw as enjoying undisputed ascendancy. With the strength of the United Kingdom and its immense commercial empire at their back, and the global imperative of awakened Christianity to provide wind for their sails, they were now emboldened to launch an ideological crusade to undermine the threat to their liberty from the forces of Catholic subversion.

This disposition found expression in a hardening of the attitudes on the use of the Protestant Bible in schools run by evangelical agencies, in the renewed activity of the Orange Order in provoking Catholics, and above all in the renewal of the debate on the safety of the Church of Ireland begun by Bishop Woodward in the 1780s. The combined effect of these developments was to inject religion, or rather religious division, solidly into the centre of the debate on Catholic Emancipation. This, of course, was nothing new. In the past, however, there had not been in existence either a developed ideology, which professed the necessity of converting Catholics, or a body of institutions with which to effect the transformation. Both elements were now in place, backed by a rising tide of conservative opinion in Britain as well as Ireland that public funds be used to advance the process.

It was the realization that public money was being utilized to undermine the doctrinal authority of Catholic teaching by insisting on 'the Bible without note or comment'—the ultimate symbol of Protestant superiority and righteousness—that caused Daniel O'Connell and Rev. John MacHale to come out in open opposition to the aims and methods of the evangelical educational agencies in 1819. The particular object of their attack was the KPS, an organization originally devoted to neutrality in religious affairs, but which had been overtaken by the ascendancy of evangelical opinion on its board of directors during the second decade of the century. This heralded an open confrontation between Catholic spokesmen and increasingly strident defenders of the Established Church, fearful of the implications of Emancipation and tithe reform. New heights were reached in the dispute when the newly appointed archbishop of Dublin, William Magee, in his inaugural sermon in St Patrick's cathedral in October 1822, claimed apostolic succession for the Church of Ireland and challenged its members to work towards making it a national church that would eventually absorb both the Catholic and Dissenting communities.

Archbishop Magee's famous sermon has rightly been interpreted as a turning point in denominational relations in Ireland. What made it so was the response it evoked from Catholic leaders, particularly Bishop Doyle, a rising star in the religious and political world. Doyle's response to Magee's charge began what would be a brief but extraordinary career as a theorist and propagandist of Catholic freedom. His defence and vindication of the Catholic Irish infused new vigour and confidence into the community as a whole, and his advocacy of peaceful, constitutional action provided a modus operandi for the newly formed Catholic Association. The coherence of Doyle's arguments, the force of his vision and the power of his rhetoric united people across class, geographical and even denominational lines, and made it appear that the cause of Catholic freedom was irresistible, if not providentially ordained. It drew to the Catholic Association leaders of extraordinary talent who exploited every opportunity and effected a political revolution based on peaceful mass mobilization that would be the first of its kind in Europe.

The perception that the evangelical mission underpinned the ideological assumptions of ultra-Protestantism, and was geared towards changing the attitudes and assumptions of the Catholic Irish, made the conflict into a war of cultural defence. It was this feature above all else that provided unity and cohesion among the disparate supporters of Emancipation. It also provided a clear opportunity for the clergy to become involved in political organization and policy making, particularly in the area of education, where they established an influence that would fundamentally control the direction in which the mindset of Catholic Ireland would develop.

The fact that the theorist of native resurgence was the work of a Catholic bishop, and that the popular democratic movement was driven forward by the unity of priests and people at the local level, was more than enough to cause conservative Protestants to see the hand of Rome behind the process. Where previously it had been perceived as the agency behind the violence of the agrarian rebels and the treason of the republicans, now the papacy would be seen as the arch manipulator of the forces of popular democracy unleashed by the revolutions of the late eighteenth century. This ennabled Protestant critics to insist that Catholic democracy was a sham because its followers were slaves to Rome. It was a worldview that became embedded in the very foundation of Protestant national identity and would for generations stand as a barrier against the acceptance of Catholics as equal citizens within a constitutional system.

Archbishop Magee's famous charge of 1822 baffled contemporary observers as well as later historians, including Desmond Bowen, who referred to it as a declaration of religious war, unprovoked and uncalled for in the circumstances of the early 1820s. But this opinion carries weight only if one chooses to ignore what had been taking place in the previous two decades with regard to evangelical ambitions for the native Irish, and the marriage between the overweening ambitions of the evangelicals and the hard-line political conservatism that began to take solid form in the years after 1816. Having established this claim, it is not altogether fair to lay the blame for the explosive events of the 1820s totally on the doorstep of the moral reformers and missionaries. It is entirely possible that agencies like the KPS and the LHS could have gone about their work of educating Catholics until a national system made its appearance, which it undoubtedly would as it did everywhere in Europe. Their work might even have come to be regarded as having contributed to a great deal of good. Bishop John Jebb of Limerick, for example, despite his lifelong adherence to the principle of the Church of Ireland taking the lead in the movement for moral reform and his rigid opposition to Emancipation, was enormously well regarded by Catholics. It was the politicization of the movement in the second decade of the century that opened the door for the Catholic Church to assert itself in the public sphere as the protector of the native Irish and the guardian of their traditions and way of life.

The manner in which the political modernization of the Catholic population took place must be regarded as one of the fundamental turning points in modern Irish history. The revolution in mass politics that occurred during the propaganda war of the mid-1820s meant that the bulk of the Catholic Irish were educated into citizenship in an atmosphere charged with the rhetoric of religious warfare. Victory in the Emancipation campaign was an unstinting reflection of the power of mass mobilization and the leadership role of the clergy. The defence of Catholic doctrine and the strident assertion of its righteousness, if not superiority, had an extraordinary influence on the role assumed by the Catholic Church in later decades in matters relating to education and morality. The net result was the growth of a political Catholicism in which religion and national identity would become synonymous.

Success in the Emancipation campaign and the securing of an educational system to suit the needs of the Catholic majority was not a prelude either to denominational peace or the decline of evangelical influence among the Protestant community. Indeed, the opposite was the case. For conservative Protestants, every passing year saw the links between Catholic democracy and the resurgence of papal power became more transparent. Anti-Catholicism as a result became more entrenched and also more widespread, and it is not an overstatement to say that by the 1830s it had become a political doctrine in its own right. Its impact on attitudes towards Ireland and the Irish, among the British population generally and in political circles in particular, can hardly be overestimated. It is impossible to understand the attitude of a government official like Charles Trevelyan during the Famine, for example, without taking it into account.

Religious prejudice born out of the great cultural collision of the 1820s was also exported in tandem with the dispersal of the Irish, both Catholic and Protestant, to Britain and the United States, Canada and Australia. It deeply influenced the way in which the Catholic Irish were treated by the host countries, and the way in which their culture evolved at an institutional as well as a social level. The creation of a 'fortress' structure to protect its flocks from assimilation into the dominant Protestant cultures of the English-speaking diaspora was the first prerogative of the emigrant Church. By creating wholly alternative structures to provide services in such critical areas as health, welfare and education, the Catholic Church secured the loyalty of Irish emigrants to a degree that no other institution could match. Since Irish Catholicism internationally took its culture as well as its personnel in large measure from home, it was deeply conscious of its role both as a defender of the faith and a protector of the poor and dispossessed.

The legacy of Bishop Doyle's vision of the Catholic Irish as an 'elect'—a people special in the eyes of God because of all they had suffered and endured for the faith—fed the creation of a self-image that would provide both identity and coherence as the Irish diaspora spread in the late nineteenth and early twentieth centuries. It was central to the creation of the concept of a 'spiritual empire': the special role of the Irish as the vanguard of international Catholicism in the English-speaking world. The 'spiritual empire' thesis was the ideological fuel behind the explosion of the Irish Catholic missionary movement worldwide, which was fed by the 'devotional revolution' at home, and particularly by the expansion of religious orders like the Sisters of Mercy and the Christian Brothers into secondary education. It gave the Catholic Church an entirely exclusive role in Irish society, nationally and internationally, and to those employed in its ranks a unique status underpinned by the belief that they were engaged in both serving their own people and in helping to spread the faith worldwide. The extraordinary power and status accrued by the Catholic Church was the ultimate measure of the success with which it had utilized the Protestant challenge as a lever to assert itself as the supreme arbiter of morality, both public and private, among the native population. It goes a long way towards understanding what promoted the growth of the moral totalitarianism that became the particular hallmark of Irish Catholic culture, both at home and abroad.

The fusion of religion and politics that has characterized so much of modern Irish history has long been recognized as a particularly poisonous brew. For all the recognition of this reality, however, and despite the mountain of scholarly literature that has attempted to make sense of the bitter religious and political differences that have plagued Irish society, there have been few attempts to chart the course of Protestant–Catholic relations within the framework of denominational rivalry, to examine how the character of the respective churches and their communities were formed in reaction or opposition to each other and how this influenced, or was influenced by, developments in the political world. But this failure is not unique to Ireland. As Gertrude Himmelfarb has noted, the political influence of religion is one of the great lacunae in the field of modern history.[2] Part of my purpose in undertaking this work was to seek an understanding of the relationship between religion and politics in a country where religious division became so entrenched as to have become virtually a national characteristic in its own right. At a time when fundamentalism is again a major influence in many of the world's leading religions, and millions across the globe are flocking to the standards of religious nationalism, the Irish experience affords a useful case history in which scholars of other divided societies may find valuable insights and comparisons.

—APPENDIX A—
Tracts on the Popish Controversy

Selection of reading matter forwarded by the Rev. John Jebb to Archbishop Charles Brodrick of Cashel for possible use among clergymen connected with the Association for Discountenancing Vice, 7 May 1804.[1]

1. *Sermons Against Popery* by Zachary Pearce
2. *Meagher's Popish Mass*. Limerick, 1771 (Welsh)
3. *O'Farrell's Comparative View of the Primitive and Romish Church*. Dublin, 1780 (Mills).
4. *A Short Account of the Doctrine and Practices of the Church of Rome*. Dublin, 1788 (Watsons) Written by old Dr Beaufort.
5. An Edition of Dr Butler's *Justification*, with notes by A.G., N.J.D. Dublin, 1787. Preview by Dean Erskine.
6. *A Recent Address to the Roman Catholic Nobility and Gentry*. By a Protestant, Dublin, 1804.
7. Crito's *Letter to Dr Troy*, Republished, London.
8. Schleusner's *Lexican*. Leipzig, 1801, 2nd ed., 4 vols, octavo.

—APPENDIX B—
Richard Lalor Sheil's Account of a Contest between Doyle and Magee[1]

Richard Lalor Sheil's satirical account of the contest between Doyle and Magee, situated at Clongowes Wood College where the Jesuits have taken Archbishop Magee in order to rid him of a variety of demons it was believed he was possessed by:

> Having thus expelled the devil of avarice, Father Kenny was proceeding to eject the devil of polemics, when it was suggested that Dr Doyle was the best qualified theologian to perform this operation. Accordingly Father Kenny yielded his place to the Bachelor of Coimbra, and the Bishop advanced to the offices of exorcism. He did not, however, adopt the ordinary ritual of diabolical ejection; but in order to allure this devil out, who he knew was always prompt and willing to appear, he challenged him to a controversial disputation respecting the comparative claims of the two rival religions, when instantly a direful hissing was heard and the devil of polemics sprang from the Doctor into the midst of the fraternity.
>
> The young Jesuits immediately assailed it, and the Rev. Mr. Esmonde laid his hand boldly upon the fiend; but the fierce adder turned upon him and giving him a formidable sting, he was compelled to let him loose. The fiend went hissing in triumph around the chapel, spitting its venom on the images of the saints and crucifixes, rearing itself aloft, and erecting itself upon its burnished spires. It must be owned that, however hateful its venomous qualities, it was not destitute of beauty, and its brilliant skin and glossy scales were appropriately emblematic of the Doctor's

intellectual qualifications. It was manifest that Dr Doyle was the only divine competent to contend with this devil, and he was loudly called upon to attack it. The fiend, who did not at first appear to entertain any dread of the Carlow theologian, turned round, and seemed to collect and concentrate all its power to make a single dreadful spring upon him; but Dr Doyle subdued it with a single word. He merely articulated 'Plagiarism'! and instantaneously the serpent shrunk back, and made an effort to escape; but Dr Doyle set his foot upon his head, and crushing it to the ground, commanded it to confess the misdeeds which it had caused the doctor to perpetuate. The fiend, after twisting and contorting itself in vain, assumed a human voice, and answered—

> That it was the devil of polemics
> And all religions have gone amiss
> Since he flung his fierce antithesis,
> If discord rages through the land,
> If controversy's furious band,
> From north to south and east to west,
> The country with their howls infest,
> The doctor has the fearful merit
> Of having raised this frantic spirit,
> That long has set, and will for years
> Still set the people by the ears.
> Now, holy father, I entreat you
> Since I could never yet defeat you
> And since 'tis by opposing me
> You owe your fame in theology,
> And if you lose an antagonist,
> Your name in the papers will be miss'd,
> I humbly pray you, J.K.L.,
> Don't trample me too soon to hell,
> But long in Kildare Street let me dwell.
> 'Twould never answer me or you,
> That neither should have nought to do

'No!' exclaimed Dr Doyle; 'I will drive thee from the face of the country.'

He was about to put his menace into execution, when there was a general remonstrance from the Jesuits, who felt the force of the devil's logic and the cogency of the last argument.

Notes

Introduction

1. Desmond Bowen, *The Protestant Crusade in Ireland, 1800–70: A Study of Protestant–Catholic Relations between the Act of Union and Disestablishment* (Dublin and Montreal 1978), p. xi.

One: Eighteenth-Century Antecedents

1. Quoted on the title page of *The Monstrosities of Methodism: Being an Impartial Examination into the Pretension of our Modern Sectaries, to Prophetic Inspiration, Providential Interferences, and Spiritual Impulse. With a preliminary notice of Dr Walker's New Sect, and the Disputing Society in Stafford Street. By a Curate of the Church of England* (Dublin 1808).
2. A.C.H. Seymour, *The Life and Times of Selina, Countess of Huntingdon, by a Member of the House of Shirley and Hastings*, vol. 1 (London 1839), p. 346.
3. Charlotte Brooke, *Reliques of Irish Poetry* (1789; Gainesville, Florida 1970), preface, pp. vii–viii.
4. Jacob Boehme (1575–1624)—more commonly known as Behman in England—a German theosophist and mystic, was considered the source of continental pietism in the British Isles. His writings on the nature of God and the problem of evil were translated into many languages. William Law (1686–1761) was a devotional writer and a great admirer of Boehme. Law's *Serious Call to a Devout and Holy Life* (1728) deeply influenced the early evangelicals, especially the Wesley brothers. Mrs Law is most likely a reference to Hester Gibbon, sister of the historian Edward Gibbon, to whom in fact Law was not married. Along with a wealthy widow, Mrs Hutchinson (or Hutcheson), she shared Law's household until his death in 1761. Nicholas Zinzendorf (1700–60), a German nobleman and native of Dresden, was inspired by Moravian refugees to devote himself to the religious life. He had a significant influence on the international evangelical movement, particularly through his conception of a 'Pilgrim Church', which was at the centre of the Protestant missionary enterprise. John Wesley (1703–91) and his

brother Charles (1708–88) owed a great deal, in both practical and spiritual terms, to the influence of Law and Zinzendorf. George Whitefield (1714–70), the most active and travelled preacher of his day, began his career in close cooperation with the Wesleys but later diverged from them on theological grounds. Gordon Rupp, *Religion in England, 1698–1791* (Oxford 1986), pp. 218–32 (Jacob Boehme and William Law); pp. 342–63 (John and Charles Wesley); pp. 339–42 (George Whitefield).

5. J.L. Kincheloe, Jr, 'European roots of evangelical revivalism: Methodist transmission of the pietistic socio-religious tradition', *Methodist History*, 18 (July 1980), 262–71; Susan O'Brien, 'A transatlantic community of saints: The Great Awakening and the first evangelical network, 1735–1755', *American Historical Review*, 91 (Oct. 1986), 811–32; W.R. Ward, 'Power and piety: The origins of religious revival in the early eighteenth century', *Bulletin of the John Rylands Library of Manchester*, 63, 1 (1980), 231–52; Andrew F. Walls, 'The eighteenth-century Protestant missionary awakening in its European context' in Brian Stanley (ed.), *Christian Missions and the Enlightenment* (Grand Rapids, Michigan and Cambridge 2001), pp. 22–44.
6. Ward, 'Power and piety', 236–8.
7. Edward Langton, *The History of the Moravian Church: The Story of the First International Protestant Church* (London 1956), p. 75.
8. Ward, 'Power and piety', 242–3; David Hempton, *Methodism and Politics in British Society, 1750–1850* (London 1984), p. 23.
9. Langton, *Moravian Church*, p. 67.
10. *Ibid.* pp. 72–5.
11. For the influence of the Moravian Church on the missionary movement in England in the late eighteenth century see J.C.S. Mason, *The Moravian Church and the Missionary Awakening in England, 1760–1800* (Woodbridge, Suffolk and Rochester, New York 2001).
12. Langton, *Moravian Church*, pp. 131–2; John Warburton, Rev. J. Whitelaw, and Rev. Robert Walsh, *History of the City of Dublin from the Earliest Accounts to the Present Time; containing its annals, antiquities, ecclesiastical history, and charters; its present extent, public buildings, schools, institutions, etc. to which are added, biographical notices of eminent men, and copious appendices of its population, revenue, commerce, and literature*, vol. II (London 1818), p. 827.
13. Warburton et al., *City of Dublin*, vol. II.
14. Langton, *Moravian Church*, pp. 131–2. A full account of the Moravian colony at Gracehill is contained in S.G. Hanna, 'The origin and nature of the Gracehill Moravian settlement, 1764–1855, with special reference to the work of John Cennick in Ireland, 1746–1755' (unpublished MA thesis, Queen's University, Belfast 1964).
15. David Hempton and Myrtle Hill, *Evangelical Protestantism in Ulster Society, 1740–1890* (London and New York 1992), p. 7.
16. The standard account of the early development of Irish Methodism and John Wesley's role is C.H. Crookshank, *History of Methodism in Ireland* (London 1885–8).
17. David Hempton, 'Methodism in Irish society, 1770–1830', *Transactions of the Royal Historical Society*, 5, 36 (1986), 117–42.
18. Robert Haire, *Wesley's One and Twenty Visits to Ireland* (London 1947), p. 23.
19. Rupp, *Religion in England*, pp. 372–7.

20. Quoted in Haire, *Wesley's One and Twenty Visits*, pp. 30–1.
21. Hempton, 'Methodism in Irish Society', 118.
22. The most comprehensive account of Ouseley's career is William Reilly, *Memorial of the Ministerial Life of Gideon Ouseley, Irish Missionary* (New York 1852). For a more recent evaluation of his contribution to the Irish evangelical movement see David Hempton, 'Gideon Ouseley: Rural revivalist, 1791–1839', *Studies in Church History*, 25 (1989), 203–14.
23. Myrtle Hill, 'Evangelicalism and the churches in Ulster society, 1750–1850', (unpublished PhD thesis, Queen's University, Belfast 1987), p. 31.
24. Selina Hastings, Countess of Huntington, played a pivotal role in spreading evangelical religion among the upper classes in eighteenth-century Britain. An early admirer of the Wesleys and Whitefield, she used the provisions of the Conventicle Act of 1687 to attach chapels to aristocratic houses where clergymen who were not ordained in the Church of England could preach without fear of the law. In order to train ministers for her Connexion she founded a college at Trevecca in North Wales. Her aristocratic associations did not always agree with the Wesleys, but her contribution to the growth of the evangelical movement in the Church of England is beyond question. Rupp, *Religion in England*, pp. 462–71. See also Boyd Stanley Schlenther, *Queen of the Methodists: The Countess of Huntingdon and the Eighteenth-Century Crisis of Faith* (Durham 1997).
25. Langton, *Moravian Church*, p. 41.
26. Walter Shirley to Lady Huntingdon, 20 Feb. 1760 (Westminster College, Cambridge, Cheshunt Foundation Papers, E41/1).
27. Henry Mead to Lady Huntingdon, 15 Nov. 1771 (*Ibid.* F1/139).
28. L.M. Cullen, *The Emergence of Modern Ireland, 1600–1900* (Dublin and New York 1981), pp. 57–8.
29. Rev. Maiben C. Motherwell, *A Memoir of the Late Albert Blest, for Many Years Agent and Secretary for Ireland of the London Hibernian Society* (Dublin 1843), pp. 13–24.
30. *Ibid.* p. 35.
31. According to his biographer, 'the motives which influenced Mr. Blest's conduct contributed much to the cordiality of religious feeling which then prevailed between members of the Established Church and evangelical Dissenters in Sligo. Education in doing good and not the advancement of the sectarian interest was the characteristic feature of every measure adopted for general usefulness. The revival and extension of religion was accompanied by a corresponding solicitude for the welfare of the leading religious societies. Their respective anniversaries were well-attended and liberal contributions made to their funds.' Motherwell, *Albert Blest*, p. 119.
32. Roger H. Martin, *Evangelicals United: Ecumenical Stirrings in Pre-Victorian Britain, 1795–1830* (London and Metuchen, New Jersey 1983), p. 3.
33. Edwin Welch, *Spiritual Pilgrim: A Reassessment of the Life of the Countess of Huntingdon* (Cardiff 1995), pp. 120–4.
34. Martin, *Evangelicals United*, pp. 5–14. See also Rupp, *Religion in England*, pp. 368–72.
35. Motherwell, *Albert Blest*, pp. 145–6.
36. To take hospital care as one example, with institutions like Dr Steevens's (1733), Mercer's (1734), St Patrick's (1757), and the Rotunda (1757), Dublin could compare with the best in the kingdom, if not in Europe. J.L. McCracken, 'The social structure and

social life, 1714–60' in T.W. Moody and W.E. Vaughan (eds), *A New History of Ireland, Vol. IV: Eighteenth-Century Ireland, 1691–1800* (Oxford 1986), p. 50.
37. Rupp, *Religion in England*, p. 309.
38. Warburton et al., *City of Dublin*, vol. II, p. 309.
39. Constantia Maxwell, *Country and Town in Ireland under the Georges* (Dundalk 1949), pp. 321–5. See also Toby Barnard, *A New Anatomy of Ireland: The Irish Protestants, 1649–1770* (New Haven, Connecticut and London 2003), p. 277.
40. Helen M. Jones, 'A spiritual aristocracy: Female patrons of religion in eighteenth-century England' in Deryck W. Lovegrove (ed.), *The Rise of the Laity in Evangelical Protestantism* (London and New York 2002), pp. 85–94.
41. R.B. McDowell, *Ireland in the Age of Imperialism and Revolution, 1760–1801* (Oxford 1979), p. 141.
42. Noel Annan et al., *Ideas and Beliefs of the Victorians: An Historic Revaluation of the Victorian Age* (New York 1966), p. 36.
43. V. Kiernan, 'Evangelicalism and the French Revolution', *Past and Present*, 1 (Feb. 1952), 44.
44. Harold Perkin, *The Origins of Modern English Society, 1780–1880* (London 1969), pp. 281.
45. Kiernan, 'Evangelicalism'; E.P. Thompson, *The Making of the English Working Class* (New York 1966), especially chapter 3, 'The transforming power of the cross', pp. 350–400.
46. Stuart Piggin, *Making Evangelical Missionaries, 1789–1858: The Social Background, Motives, and Training of British Protestant Missionaries to India* (Abingdon 1984), appendix 5, pp. 294–305; Paul Johnson, *A Shopkeeper's Millennium: Society and Revivals in Rochester, New York, 1815–1837* (New York 1985), pp. 138–41.
47. Gerald Newman, *The Rise of English Nationalism: A Cultural History, 1740–1830* (New York 1987), chapters 2–7.
48. *Ibid.* p. 234.
49. *Ibid.*
50. *Ibid.* p. 235.
51. Ian Bradley, *The Call to Seriousness: The Evangelical Impact on the Victorians* (London 1976), p. 156.
52. David Hempton, 'Evangelicalism in English and Irish society, 1790–1840' in Mark A. Noll, David W. Bebbington, George A. Rawlyk (eds), *Evangelicalism: Comparative Studies of Popular Protestantism in North America, the British Isles, and Beyond, 1700–1990* (Oxford 1994), pp. 156–76.
53. Alan R. Acheson, 'The Evangelicals in the Church of Ireland, 1784–1859' (unpublished PhD thesis, Queen's University, Belfast 1967), p. 30.
54. *Ibid.* p. 29.
55. *Ibid.* p. 77.
56. The most forceful argument to project Irish society of the eighteenth century as reflecting the general character and conditions of *ancien régime* Europe is S.J. Connolly, *Religion, Law and Power: The Making of Protestant Ireland, 1660–1760* (Oxford 1995).
57. Cullen, *Modern Ireland*, p. 13.
58. S.J. Connolly, 'Law, order, and popular protest in early eighteenth-century Ireland: The case of the Houghers' in P.J. Corish (ed.), *Radicals, Rebels, and Establishments: Historical Studies XV* (Belfast 1985), pp. 51–68.

59. Thomas P. Power, *Land, Politics and Society in Eighteenth-Century Tipperary* (Oxford 1997); Kevin Whelan, 'The Catholic Church in County Tipperary, 1700–1900' in William Nolan and Thomas McGrath (eds), *Tipperary: History and Society: Interdisciplinary Essays on the History of an Irish County* (Dublin 1985), pp. 215–55.
60. For an account of the debate about conversion in the eighteenth century, see Connolly, *Religion, Law and Power*, pp. 294–9.
61. Brian Ó Cuív, 'Irish language and literature, 1691–1845' in Moody and Vaughan (eds), *Eighteenth-Century Ireland*, p. 375. John Richardson, *A Proposal for the Conversion of the Popish Natives of Ireland to the Established Religion, with the Reasons upon Which It Is Grounded and an Answer to the Objections Made to It* (London 1712), p. 95.
62. The most complete account of the Charter Schools is Kenneth Milne, *The Irish Charter Schools, 1730–1830* (Dublin 1997).
63. Carl Becker, *The Heavenly City of the Eighteenth-Century Philosophers* (London 1932; New Haven, Connecticut 1966), especially chapter 3, 'The new history: Philosophy teaching by example', pp. 71–118.
64. Among the practitioners of this kind of scholarship Charles Vallancey was the most famous, but he was by no means an isolated figure. *An Essay on the Celtic Language: Showing the Importance of the Iberno-Celtic, or Irish Dialect, to Students in History, Antiquity, and the Greek and Roman Classics*, which was published by Vallancey in 1782, was preceded by Rev. David Malcolme's *Letters, Essays and Other Tracts Illustrating the Antiquities of Great Britain and Ireland* (London 1744), and by John Cleland's *The Way to Things by Words* (London 1766), which advance more or less a similar argument.
65. David Dickson, *New Foundations: Ireland, 1600–1800* (Dublin 1987), pp. 102–3.
66. Whelan, 'Catholic Church in County Tipperary', p. 216.
67. Power, *Eighteenth-Century Tipperary*, pp. 245–52.
68. *Ibid*, pp. 228–31.
69. James S. Donnelly, Jr, 'The Whiteboy movement, 1761–5', *Irish Historical Studies*, 21, 81 (March 1978), 20–54.
70. *Ibid.*; Power, *Eighteenth-Century Tipperary*, pp. 241–2.
71. Power, *Eighteenth-Century Tipperary*, pp. 263–5.
72. *Ibid.* p. 256; Dickson, *New Foundations*, pp. 134–5.
73. Cullen, *Modern Ireland*, p. 123.
74. J.C. Beckett, *The Making of Modern Ireland: 1603–1923* (London 1972), p. 212.
75. Marianne Elliott, *Partners in Revolution: The United Irishmen and France* (New Haven and London 1982), p. 14.
76. James S. Donnelly, Jr, 'The Rightboy movement, 1785–88', *Studia Hibernica*, 17/18 (1977–8), 126–7.
77. Maurice Bric, 'The Rightboy movement, 1785–1788', *Past and Present*, 100 (Aug. 1983), 102.
78. Edited and introduced by James S. Donnelly, Jr, 'A contemporary account of the Rightboy movement: The John Barter Bennett manuscript', *Journal of the Cork Historical and Archaeological Society*, LXXXVIII, 247 (1983), 1–50.
79. *Ibid.*
80. *Ibid.* 27–8.
81. *Ibid.* 12–13.

82. Dominic Trant, *Considerations on the Present Disturbances in the Province of Munster, Their Causes, Extent, Probable Consequences, and Remedies* (Dublin 1787), pp. 56–7.
83. Donnelly, 'Rightboy movement', 147.
84. S.J. Connolly, *Priests and People in Pre-Famine Ireland, 1780–1845* (Dublin 1982), pp. 243–52; John A. Murphy, 'The support of the Catholic clergy in Ireland, 1750–1850' in J.L. McCracken (ed.), *Historical Studies*, vol. v (London 1965), pp. 103–21.
85. Bric, 'Rightboy Movement', 115.
86. *Ibid.* 114–15.
87. Donnelly, 'John Barter Bennett manuscript', 18.
88. A more complete account of Arabella Jefferies' involvement with the Rightboy campaign may be found in Ann C. Kavanaugh, *John Fitzgibbon, Earl of Clare: Protestant Reaction and English Authority in Late Eighteenth-Century Ireland* (Dublin 1997), pp. 105–7; her difficult relationship with her brother is considered on pp. 205–8.
89. Donnelly, 'Rightboy movement', 175; Donnelly, 'John Barter Bennett manuscript', 22.
90. Donnelly, 'Rightboy movement', 175.
91. The origin of the term 'Protestant ascendancy' has provided fertile ground for debate among scholars of the late eighteenth century. See James Kelly, 'The genesis of "Protestant Ascendancy": the Rightboy disturbances of the 1780s and their impact upon Protestant opinion' in Gerard O'Brien (ed.), *Parliament, Politics, and People: Essays in Eighteenth-Century Irish History* (Dublin 1989), pp. 93–127.
92. Richard Woodward, *The Present State of the Church of Ireland, Containing a Description of Its Precarious Situation and the Consequent Danger to the Public, Recommended to the Serious Consideration of the Friends of the Protestant Interest, to which are Subjoined Some Reflections on the Impractability of a Proper Commutation for Tithes and a General Account of the Origin and Progress of the Insurrection in Munster* (Dublin 1787), preface, pp. iii–xv.
93. *Ibid.* pp. 75–6.
94. Patrick Duigenan [Theophilus], *An Address to the Nobility and Gentry of the Church of Ireland as by law established. Explaining the real causes of the commotions and insurrections in the southern parts of the Kingdom resprecting tithes* (Dublin 1787), p. 2–4.
95. Woodward, *Present State of the Church of Ireland*, pp. 87–92.
96. James Kelly, 'Interdenominational relations and religious toleration in late eighteenth-century Ireland: The "Paper War" of 1786–8', *Eighteenth-Century Ireland*, 3 (1988), 39–67.
97. James Kelly, 'Relations between the Protestant Church of Ireland and the Presbyterian Church in late eighteenth-century Ireland', *Éire–Ireland*, XXIII, 3 (Fall 1988), 38–56.
98. Donnelly, 'Rightboy movement', 147.
99. Donnelly, 'John Barter Bennett manuscript', 38.
100. The 'Protestant ascendancy' debate of the late 1780s is discussed in Jacqueline Hill, 'Popery and Protestantism, civil and religious liberty: The disputed lessons of Irish history, 1690–1812', *Past and Present*, 118 (Feb. 1988), 124–6; and W.J. McCormack, *Ascendancy and Tradition in Anglo–Irish Literary History from 1789 to 1939* (Oxford 1985), pp. 67–96.
101. Elliott, *Partners in Revolution*, p. 21.
102. McCormack, *Ascendancy and Tradition*, p. 66.
103. Norman Vance, 'Celts, Carthaginians, and constitutions: Anglo–Irish literary relations, 1780–1820', *Irish Historical Studies*, 22, 85 (1981), 218.

104. Ned Lebow, 'British historians and Irish history', *Éire–Ireland*, VIII (1973), 3–38.
105. Walter D. Love, 'Charles O'Conor of Belnagare and Thomas Leland's "Philosophical" history of Ireland', *Irish Historical Studies*, 13, 49 (March 1962), 2–3.
106. Hill, 'Popery and Protestantism', 106.
107. Patrick Duigenan, *A Fair Representation of the Present Political State of Ireland* (Dublin 1800), p. 80.
108. Love, 'O'Conor of Belnagare', 2–6.
109. David Berman, 'David Hume on the 1641 rebellion in Ireland', *Studies*, XV (1976), 101–12.
110. John Curry, *Historical Memoirs of the Irish Rebellion in the year 1641; Extracted from Parliamentary Journals, State-acts, and The Most Eminent Protestant Historians* (London 1758).
111. Robert and Catherine Coogan Ward, 'The Catholic pamphlets of Charles O'Conor', *Studies*, LXVIII (1979), 259–64.
112. Love, 'O'Conor of Belnagare', 17–22.
113. *Ibid.* 11–15.
114. *Ibid.*
115. Donal MacCartney, 'The writing of history in Ireland, 1800–1850,' *Irish Historical Studies*, 10 (Sept. 1957), 347–63.
116. Hill, 'Popery and Protestantism', 118.
117. Peter Burke, *Popular Culture in Early Modern Europe* (New York 1978), pp. 3–22.
118. Newman, *English Nationalism*, pp. 115–18. The most famous contemporary example of this model was, of course, that advanced by the Abbé Joseph Sieyès in his celebrated pamphlet *What Is the Third Estate?* in which he charged the French aristocracy with being descendants of the invading Franks who had enslaved the native Gauls. For an evaluation of the role of Sieyès rhetoric in the events leading up to the French Revolution see William H. Sewell, Jr, *A Rhetoric of Bourgeois Revolution: The Abbé Sieyès and What Is the Third Estate?* (Durham, North Carolina 1994).
119. Brooke, *Reliques of Irish Poetry*, preface, pp. VII–VIII.
120. Newman, *English Nationalism*, p. 159.
121. Oliver MacDonagh, *States of Mind: A Study of Anglo–Irish Conflict, 1780–1980* (London 1983), pp. 1–3.
122. Hill, 'Popery and Protestantism', 129.
123. James Kelly, 'The context and cause of Thomas Orde's Plan of Education of 1787', *Irish Journal of Education*, XX, 1 (1986), 3–26.
124. Quoted in *ibid.* 18.
125. *Ibid.* 20–1.
126. Ian McBride, 'The common name of Irishman: Protestantism and patriotism in eighteenth-century Ireland' in Tony Claydon and Ian McBride (eds), *Protestantism and National Identity: Britain and Ireland, c. 1650–1850* (Cambridge 1998), pp. 236–61.
127. Joseph Liechty, 'Irish evangelicalism, Trinity College Dublin and the mission of the Church of Ireland at the end of the eighteenth century' (unpublished PhD thesis, St Patrick's College, Maynooth 1987), especially chapter 3, 'Trinity College Dublin in the late eighteenth century: The Irish Establishment's custodian of faith and morals', pp. 121–82.
128. *Ibid.* p. 122.

129. *Ibid.* pp. 165–6.
130. Nancy Curtin, 'The transformation of the United Irishmen into a mass-based organization, 1794–6', *Irish Historical Studies*, 24 (Nov. 1985), 463–92.
131. Thomas Bartlett, *The Fall and Rise of the Irish Nation: The Catholic Question, 1690–1830* (Dublin 1992), p. 153.
132. Quoted in McDowell, *Ireland*, pp. 396–7.
133. Gearóid Ó Tuathaigh, *Ireland before the Famine, 1798–1848* (Dublin 1972), p. 45.
134. Quoted in McDowell, *Ireland*, p. 398.
135. Alexander Knox, *Essays on the Political Circumstances of Ireland Written during the Administration of Earl Camden, with an Appendix Containing Thoughts on the Will of the People and a Postscript Now First Published* (Dublin 1799), especially essay 2, 'Remarks on Lord Fitzwilliam's statement on the Roman Catholics', p. 19.
136. Kevin Whelan, *The Tree of Liberty: Radicalism, Catholicism and the Construction of Irish Identity, 1760–1830* (Notre Dame and Cork 1996), pp. 115–19.
137. Ian d'Alton, *Protestant Society and Politics in Cork, 1812–1844* (Cork 1980), p. 55.
138. Ó Tuathaigh, *Ireland*, p. 31.
139. Bowen's description of her ancestor Eliza Galwey provides a classic picture of the moral seriousness that overtook the Irish gentry in the early nineteenth century: 'Her reforms were moral as well as spiritual, she is said among things to have purged the library—the absence from among Henry III's family's representative stock of eighteenth-century books, of any novel, has been traced to her.' Elizabeth Bowen, *Bowen's Court* (1942; New York 1979), p. 247.

Two: The Age of Moral Reform

1. Warburton et al., *City of Dublin*, vol. II, p. 886.
2. *Fourth Report of the Sunday School Society for Ireland* (1814), p. 13.
3. John Jebb to Charles Brodrick, 22 Oct. 1815 (NLI, Brodrick Papers, MS 8866/4).
4. Mark A. Noll, 'Revolution and the rise of evangelical social influence in North Atlantic societies' in Noll et al. (eds), *Evangelicalism: Comparative Studies*, pp. 113–36.
5. Perkin, *Origins of Modern English Society*, p. 280.
6. Peter Burrowes to Sir Laurence Parsons, 23 Oct. 1800 (PRONI, Rosse Papers, D/2/11).
7. Whitley Stokes, *Projects for Establishing Internal Peace* (Dublin 1799), pp. 44–8.
8. The Rev. Joseph Stopford, scion of a long-established clerical family and famous for his piety and charity, was well known as the spiritual benefactor of many of the younger generation of Trinity evangelicals. His best-known protégé was the Rev. Peter Roe of Kilkenny. Another case is that of Thomas Lefroy who was taken into the family of Peter Burrowes during his student days. Liechty, 'Irish evangelicalism', p. 149.
9. *Ibid.* pp. 165–6.
10. Rev. Singleton Harpur, *A Sermon against the Excessive Use of Spiritous Liquors* (Dublin 1788). The same clergyman was also the probable author of an anonymous pamphlet *Observations on the Consequences of the Excessive Use of Spirituous Liquors and the Ruinous Policy of Permitting Distillation in this Country*, also published in 1788. In both pieces the

connection between improvements in manners and morals and the economic prosperity of the nation was strongly underlined.
11. Bradley, *Call to Seriousness*, pp. 95–7.
12. *Hints on the Means of Forming a Plan for Advancing Religious Education, Addressed to the Members of the Association for Discountenancing Vice and Promoting the Practice of Religion and Virtue* (Dublin 1788). Several sources, including Warburton et al.'s *City of Dublin*, cite 1792 as the year in which the Association was founded, although the above pamphlet makes it clear that it existed in some fashion four years earlier.
13. Warburton et al., *City of Dublin*, vol. II, pp. 887–91. For an account of Hannah More's popularity in the 1790s see Niall Ó Ciosáin, *Print and Popular Culture in Ireland, 1750–1850* (London and New York 1997), pp. 136–8.
14. Ford K. Brown, *Fathers of the Victorians: The Age of Wilberforce* (Cambridge 1961), p. 257.
15. Warburton et al., *City of Dublin*, vol. II, p. 87. Myrtle Hill, 'Evangelicalism and the churches in Ulster society', p. 112.
16. Acheson, 'Evangelicals', p. 70.
17. Samuel Madden, *Memoir of the Life of the Late Rev. Peter Roe* (Dublin 1842), p. 64.
18. Acheson, 'Evangelicals', p. 53.
19. *Ibid.* p. 72.
20. Madden, *Peter Roe*, p. 82.
21. Acheson, 'Evangelicals', p. 75.
22. *Ibid.* p. 68.
23. Madden, *Peter Roe*, p. 144. The Rev. Walter Blake Kirwan was the most famous preacher of the 'charity sermon' in Dublin during the early nineteenth century. He was a native of Galway and a convert from Catholicism who had been educated at Douay. There is no evidence that he sympathized with the evangelical doctrine, but he nevertheless put his preaching skills at the disposal of institutions with strong evangelical affiliations like the Magdalen Asylum. For an account of his background and career, see Desmond Bowen, *Souperism: Myth or Reality? A Study in Souperism* (Cork 1970), pp. 31–3.
24. Madden, *Peter Roe*, p. 152.
25. W.D. Killen, *The Ecclesiastical History of Ireland from the Earliest Period to the Present Times*, vol. II (London 1875), p. 382.
26. *Ibid.*
27. For an account of the background of the La Touche family and their extensive influence in banking and politics in the eighteenth and early nineteenth centuries, see David Dickson and Richard English, 'The La Touche dynasty' in David Dickson (ed.), *The Gorgeous Mask: Dublin 1700–1850* (Dublin 1987), pp. 17–29.
28. *Diary of John David La Touche, 1799–1800* (NLI, MS 3153), p. 11.
29. *Diary of John David La Touche, ibid.* p. 29; Mathias Joyce to Thomas Coke, 21 Aug. 1804 (SOAS/MMSA [Ireland] 1802–25, box 74, no. 6).
30. William Urwick, *Biographical Sketches of the Late James Digges La Touche* (London 1868), p. 81.
31. A discussion of Cowper's popularity among the religiously inclined is to be found in Leonore Davidoff and Catherine Hall, *Family Fortunes: Men and Women of the English Middle Class, 1780–1850* (Chicago and London 1987).

32. James Digges La Touche to John Synge, 19 Nov. 1808 (TCD, La Touche–Synge Correspondence, MS 6180/4).
33. William Urwick, *La Touche*, pp. 222–3.
34. *Ibid.* pp. 53–4.
35. The most complete account of the career of John Synge is to be found in P. Clive Williams, 'Pestalozzi John: A study of the life and educational work of John Synge, with special reference to the introduction and development of Pestalozzian ideas in Ireland and England' (unpublished PhD thesis, Trinity College Dublin 1966).
36. Emma Le Fanu, *The Life of the Rev. Charles Edward Herbert Orpen MD* (London 1860). For a personal account of Orpen's European travels and his stay with Pestalozzi see the *Christian Examiner* (Oct. 1828).
37. The purity of the Celtic church and its independence from Rome was a popular theme with supporters of the Reformation in the sixteenth century. See Angus Calder, *Revolutionary Empire: The Rise of the English-Speaking Empires from the Fifteenth Century to the 1780s* (New York 1998), p. 30.
38. Sydney Lee and Leslie Stephen (eds), *Dictionary of National Biography*, vol. XII (London 1885–1901), pp. 1308–9.
39. He makes a brief appearance in English literary history as the young man with whom Jane Austen fell in love in the 1790s, though he eventually married the daughter of a County Wexford yeoman whom he met in Abergavenny in North Wales, where many Wexford Protestants had taken refuge during the Rebellion.
40. Valentine Browne Lawless, *Personal Recollections of the Life and Times of Valentine, Lord Cloncurry* (Dublin 1869), p. 376.
41. Thomas Lefroy, *Memoir of Chief Justice Thomas Lefroy, By His Son* (Dublin 1871); Lee and Stephen (eds), *Dictionary of National Biography*, vol. XI, p. 845.
42. Roger Anstey, *The Atlantic Slave Trade and British Abolition 1760–1810* (London 1975), p. 175.
43. *A Short Account of the Late Mr. Mathias Joyce, Preacher of the Gospel for Thirty Years in Ireland. Written by Himself* (Dublin 1808), p. 9.
44. The correspondence of the Rev. George Hamilton to his wife and daughters affords powerful evidence of the love and affection that characterized evangelical family relations. See George Hamilton to Harriet Hamilton, 20 July 1822 (PRONI, Johnston of Kilmore Papers, MS D.1728/7/18).
45. Charles Edward Orpen to J.H. Pestalozzi, 4 June 1818, and John Synge to J.H. Pestalozzi (1816–1818) Zentralbibliothek, Zurich, Pestalozzi Papers, MS 54 A/272; 55 A/365); Williams, 'Pestalozzi John', pp. 148–54.
46. For an account of the impact of Captain Cook's descriptions of his adventures in the South Atlantic see Kathleen Wilson, 'The island race: Captain Cook, Protestant evangelicalism and the construction of English national identity, 1760–1800' in Claydon and McBride, *Protestantism and National Identity*, pp. 265–90.
47. Martin, *Evangelicals United*, pp. 40–1; D.W. Bebbington, *Evangelicalism in Modern Britain: A History from the 1730s to the 1980s* (London 1989), p. 62.
48. For an evaluation of the attitudes of Dissenting evangelicals to interdenominational cooperation see Deryck W. Lovegrove, 'Unity and Separation: Contrasting elements in the thought and practice of Robert and James Alexander Haldane' in Keith Robbins

(ed.), *Protestant Evangelicalsm: Britain, Ireland, Germany, and America c. 1750–1950, Essays in Honour of W.R. Ward* (Oxford 1990), pp. 153–77.
49. P.R. Thomas, 'The concept of an ecumenical Bible society movement, 1804–1832' (unpublished PhD thesis, University of Lancaster 1980), pp. 5–26.
50. *An Account of the Institution and Proceedings of the Society for Promoting Christian Knowledge and Practice and for Aiding and Assisting Sunday Schools in the Kingdom of Ireland* (Dublin 1788).
51. *An Address to the Proprietors of Irish Estates Residing in Great Britain* (Dublin 1800), p. 2.
52. In a letter to William Wilberforce written in 1799 or 1800, Peter Roe described the feeling he experienced on first reading the *Practical View*, which 'told me more than I ever knew before; brought fully to my conviction the corruption and depravity of my nature, and my need of a redeemer; and proved to me that instead of knowing my duty as a minister of Christ's gospel, I did not know it as a man. It put me on a train of thinking, and to it I may in a great measure attribute any degree of zeal I may possess'. According to his biographer, the letter was left in an unfinished state. Madden, *Peter Roe*, pp. 52–3.
53. Madden, *Peter Roe*, p. 35.
54. Acheson, 'Evangelicals', p. 70; Killen, *Ecclesiastical History*, vol. II, p. 389.
55. Robert Shaw, Carrick-on-Suir, to Josiah Pratt, Secretary, Church Missionary Society, London, 4 April 1802 (CMS Archives, G/AC, 3/2, no. 66).
56. Peter Roe to Josiah Pratt, 16 May 1804 (CMS Archives, G/AC, 3/2, no. 22).
57. Killen, *Ecclesiastical History*, vol. II, p. 390.
58. Peter Roe to Josiah Pratt, 16 May 1804 (CMS Archives, G/AC, 3/2, no. 22).
59. George Carr to Josiah Pratt, 7 Jan. 1805 (CMS Archives, G/AC, 3/3, no. 84).
60. John Owen, *The History of the Origin and First Ten Years of the British and Foreign Bible Society* (London 1816), p. 104.
61. *The Report of the Hibernian Society for the Year 1808, with a list of subscribers and benefactors* (Dublin 1809), p. 7.
62. Acheson, 'Evangelicals', p. 66.
63. *Hints for the Formation and Conducting of Auxiliary Societies and Associations of the Hibernian Bible Society* (Dublin n.d.), p. 2.
64. William Canton, *A History of the British and Foreign Bible Society* (London 1804), p. 113.
65. Brown, *Fathers of the Victorians*, pp. 253–4.
66. *Ibid.*
67. This opinion was by no means unanimous, however. The famous abolitionist Granville Sharp believed that the Emancipation of Catholics would be 'liberty of the sword', and 'The only mode of balancing the superiority of their numbers in Ireland, for the safety of the Irish Protestants, is surely to retain the constitutional limits of power in the hands of Protestants only: but, at the same time it is our duty as Christians to secure to the Romanists the free attainment of equal justice in the King's Courts for the protection of their persons and property; and to treat them also with true Christian benevolence and kindness, as men and brethren, in every other respect except that of restraining their persecuting propensity, a restraint which is equally necessary for their peace, as well as our own.' Granville Sharp to John Jebb, 26 March 1805 (TCD, John Jebb Papers, MS 6396–7/2).

68. *Christian Observer* (April 1814), 240.
69. John Jebb to Charles Brodrick, 26 July 1802 (NLI, Brodrick Papers, MS 8866/1).
70. In 1816, when the tithe question was once again a matter of national debate, Jebb penned a witty epigram in which he drew attention to the hypocrisy of landlords who colluded with the peasantry in opposing the payment of tithe: 'What say the landlords in their grave debate: / "Taxes must be paid for rents are our estate / Taxes are fair, they feed the civil powers / Those persons guard property, and that is ours / But tithes—withhold,—resist them,—put them down / Tithes never brought our Worships half-a-crown." / Landlord and outlaw, thus, at length, proceed / And sordid selfishness their common creed / His worship prompts, and "Moonlight" deals the blow / And tithes, and Church, and pastor are laid low / But mark the strange event of human things / His worship gets the tithe, and "Captain Moonlight" swings.' John Jebb to Charles Brodrick, 12 June 1816 (NLI, Brodrick Papers, MS 8866/5). For an account of Archbishop Brodrick's attitudes as reflected in his personal correspondence see Deborah Jenkins, 'The correspondence of Charles Brodrick (1761–1822), Archbishop of Cashel', *Irish Archives Bulletin* (1979/80), 43–9. Dr Brodrick's wife, Mary, was the daughter of Richard Woodward, Bishop of Cloyne, and his writings reflect many of the preoccupations of his well-known father-in-law.
71. The opinions of Jebb and Brodrick on the role of education in building a Christian society clearly reflect the teaching of Thomas Chalmers, the Scottish theologian and moralist whose influence was in the ascendant during the early years of the century. For an account of Chalmers' life and influence see Stewart J. Brown, *Thomas Chalmers and the Godly Commonwealth in Scotland* (Oxford 1982).
72. R.A. Soloway, *Prelates and People: Ecclesiastical Social Thought in England, 1783–1852* (London 1969), pp. 359–62.
73. D.H. Akenson, *The Irish Education Experiment: The National System of Education in the Nineteenth Century* (London 1970), pp. 20–9.
74. Quoted in *ibid.* p. 31.
75. *Ibid.* p. 32.
76. *Ibid.* p. 61.
77. *Ibid.* pp. 63–74.
78. *An Address to the Proprietors of Irish Estates Residing in Great Britain* (Dublin 1800), pp. 3–4.
79. *Ibid.* pp. 10–11.
80. *Two Reports of the Committee of Education, Appointed by the Association for Discountenancing Vice and Promoting Religion and Virtue, on the Dioceses of Clogher and Kilmore* (Dublin 1800), p. 13.
81. *Report of the Committee of Education, Appointed by the Association for Discountenancing Vice and Promoting the Knowledge and Practice of the Christian Religion* (Dublin 1803), p. 15.
82. *Ibid.* p. 9.
83. One commentator who noted the extraordinary increase of schools throughout Ireland in the early years of the nineteenth century was emphatic in his opinion that material advancement was what lay behind the demand: 'the education of youth is only a secondary object with most parents—many are induced more by custom and necessity to

educate their children, than on account of any moral or scientific advantages that might arise ... the acquisition of gain seems to be the ruling passion of the present day ...' Patrick Carolan, *An Essay on the Present State of Schools in Ireland* (Dublin 1806).
84. *Report of the Committee of Education*, p. 10.
85. *Ibid.* pp. 13–14.
86. James Joseph Sullivan, 'The education of Irish Catholics, 1782–1831' (unpublished PhD thesis, Queen's University, Belfast 1959), pp. 252–7.
87. *First Report of the Commissioners of Irish Education Inquiry* (1825), 400, XII, p. 34.
88. *Ibid.* p. 31.
89. Peter Burrowes to Laurence Parsons, 23 Oct. 1800 (PRONI, Rosse Papers, D/2/11).
90. Shute Barrington to Lord Redesdale, 8 June 1805 (PRONI, Redesdale Papers, T.3030/10/15/c.23).
91. Akenson, *Irish Education Experiment*, p. 77.
92. Quoted in *ibid.* pp. 77–8.
93. Warburton et al., *City of Dublin*, vol II, pp. 852–5.
94. *Ibid.* p. 872.
95. *First Report of the Society for Promoting the Education of the Poor in Ireland* (Dublin 1813), p. 3.
96. *Second Report of the Society for Promoting the Education of the Poor in Ireland* (Dublin 1814), p. 10.
97. Book Sub-Committee, 1815–40 (B.S.1–97). B.S.1 (Church of Ireland College of Education, Kildare Place Archives, box no. 13).
98. *Second Report of the Society for Promoting the Education of the Poor in Ireland* (Dublin 1814), p. 12.
99. *Ibid.* p. 24.
100. Joseph Devonshire Jackson to Henry Monck Mason, 15 March 1815 (CICE/KPSA, CI/101).
101. Joseph Devonshire Jackson to Samuel Bewley, 16 March 1815 (CICE/KPSA, CI/102). Captain Harvey to Henry Monck Mason, 28 March 1815 (CICE/KPSA, CI/103).
102. Akenson, *Irish Education Experiment*, p. 86.

Three: The Mission to the Catholic Population

1. *An Address to the British Public on the Moral and Religious State of Ireland* (London 1805), p. 15.
2. John Jebb to Charles Brodrick, 6 Oct. 1820 (NLI, Brodrick Papers, MS 8866/7).
3. Clarke H. Irwin, *Famous Irish Preachers* (Dublin 1889), p. 28.
4. Hempton, *Methodism and Politics*, p. 121.
5. *Ibid.* p. 120.
6. Charles Graham to Thomas Coke, 11 Sept. 1802 (SOAS/MMSA [Ireland] 1802–25, box 74).
7. Quoted in W.R. Ward, *Religion and Society in England, 1790–1850* (London 1972), p. 118.
8. William Cornwall to the secretary of the Methodist Missionary Society, 26 Dec. 1817 (SOAS/MMSA [Ireland] 1802–25, box 74).

9. James Bell to Joseph Taylor, 29 Sept. 1819 (SOAS/MMSA [Ireland] 1802–25, box 74).
10. William Cornwall to Joseph Taylor, 6 Oct. 1818 (SOAS/MMSA [Ireland] 1818–20, box 74).
11. William Cornwall to Joseph Taylor, 25 Sept. 1819 (SOAS/MMSA [Ireland] 1818–20, box 74).
12. Charles Graham to Thomas Coke, 25 Jan. 1806; William Peacock and John Hamilton to Thomas Coke, 24 March 1806; R. Wilson to J. Taylor, 29 March 1819 (SOAS/MMSA [Ireland] 1802–25, box 74).
13. Mathias Joyce to Thomas Coke, 21 Aug. 1804 (SOAS/MMSA [Ireland] 1802–25, box 74).
14. The family of the duke of Wellington, for example, changed its name from Wesley to Wellesley to avoid association with the great Methodist leader. See R.B. McDowell, *Social Life in Ireland, 1800-45* (Dublin 1957), p. 35.
15. Lawrence Kean to Thomas Coke, 28 Oct. 1802 (SOAS/MMSA [Ireland] 1802–25, box 74).
16. William Hamilton to Adam Averell, July 1806 (SOAS/MMSA [Ireland] 1802–25, box 74).
17. James Bell and William Hamilton to Thomas Coke, 31 Aug. 1804 (SOAS/MMSA [Ireland] 1802–17, box 74).
18. This growth is illustrated in Hempton, 'Methodism in Irish society', 117–42.
19. William Parnell, *An Historical Apology for the Irish Catholics* (Dublin 1807), p. 129.
20. *Draft on Irish Missions for the Report of 1806* (SOAS/MMSA [Ireland] 1802–25, box 74).
21. Hempton, *Methodism and Politics*, pp. 125–42.
22. *Ibid.* p. 127.
23. Madden, *Peter Roe*, p. 127.
24. Motherwell, *Albert Blest*, p. 183; Killen, *Ecclesiastical History*, vol. 1, p. 392.
25. *Report of a Deputation of the London Hibernian Society* (1808), p. 46.
26. *Ibid.* p. 20.
27. *Ibid.*
28. *Ibid.* p.26.
29. Victor Edward Durkacz, *The Decline of the Celtic Languages: A Study of Linguistic and Cultural Conflict in Scotland, Wales, and Ireland from the Reformation to the Twentieth Century* (Edinburgh 1983), pp. 82–5.
30. *Ibid.* pp. 96–153.
31. Charles W.J. Withers, *Gaelic Scotland: The Transformation of a Cultural Region* (London and New York 1988), pp. 151–2.
32. Alexander Haldane, *The Lives of Robert Haldane of Airthrey, and his brother, James Alexander Haldane* (Edinburgh 1855), pp. 104–23.
33. James Godkin, *The Religious History of Ireland, Primitive, Papal, and Protestant, Including the Evangelical Missions, Catholic Agitations, and Church Progress of the Last Half-Century* (London 1873), pp. 233.
34. *Ibid.* p. 83.
35. *Ibid.* p. 195.
36. *Ibid.* p. 182–3.
37. *Sixth Annual Report of the London Hibernian Society* (1812), p. 4.
38. Webster, *London Hibernian Society*, pp. 15–16; Motherwell, *Albert Blest*, p. 225.
39. *Ninth Annual Report of the London Hibernian Society* (1815), p. 5.
40. Motherwell, *Albert Blest*, pp. 245–51.

41. The following observation was made in the annual report of the LHS for 1816: 'It is a remarkable instance of the divine favour that the priests who have been tolerant and friendly towards the society are situated in places where their power is absolute, and where the society has not a single friend to counteract their influence if it had been hostile.' *Tenth Annual Report of the London Hibernian Society* (1816), p. 10.
42. Albert Blest to Charles King O'Hara, 27 Sept. 1814 (NLI, Charles King O'Hara Papers, MS 20,285).
43. John Jebb to Charles Brodrick, 12 March 1814 (NLI, Brodrick Papers, MS 8866/3).
44. For a more in-depth discussion of this subject see Ó Ciosáin, *Print and Popular Culture*, pp. 154–7.
45. John Owen, *History of the British and Foreign Bible Society*, pp. 9–10.
46. Durcacz, *Decline*, p. 119.
47. Christopher Anderson of Edinburgh was a disciple of the Haldane brothers and a prominent member of the Baptist Missionary Society. Brian Stanley, *The History of the Baptist Missionary Society, 1792–1992* (Edinburgh 1992), p. 20.
48. Christopher Anderson, *Memorial on Behalf of the Native Irish with a View to Their Improvement in Moral and Religious Knowledge through the Medium of Their Own Language* (London 1815), pp. 28–34.
49. Daniel Dewar, *Observations on the Character, Customs, and Superstitions of the Irish and on Some of the Causes Which Have Retarded the Moral and Political Improvement of Ireland* (London 1812), p. 25.
50. *Ibid.* p. 34.
51. Ian Douglas Maxwell, 'Civilization or Christianity? The Scottish debate on mission methods, 1750–1835' in Brian Stanley (ed.), *Christian Missions and the Enlightenment* (Grand Rapids, Michigan and Cambridge 2001), pp. 123–40.
52. *Tenth Annual Report of the London Hibernian Society* (1816), pp. 34–5.
53. *First Annual Report of the Baptist Society for the Promotion of the Gospel in Ireland* (1815), p. 10.
54. *Ibid.* p. 37.
55. *Second Annual Report of the Baptist Society for the Promotion of the Gospel in Ireland* (1816), p. 18.
56. *Fourth Annual Report of the Baptist Society for the Promotion of the Gospel in Ireland* (1818), pp. 37–8.
57. Joseph Belcher, *The Baptist Irish Society: Its Origin, History, and Prospects* (London 1845), pp. 25–6.
58. *Sixth Annual Report of the Baptist Society for the Promotion of the Gospel in Ireland* (1820), p. 8.
59. *Seventh Annual Report of the Baptist Society for the Promotion of the Gospel in Ireland* (1821), pp. 101–12.
60. *Sixth Annual Report of the Baptist Society for the Promotion of the Gospel in Ireland* (1820), pp. 4–8.
61. *Fourth Annual Report of the Baptist Society for the Promotion of the Gospel in Ireland* (1818), pp. 11–13.
62. *First Report of the Commissioners of Irish Education Inquiry* (1825), 400, XII, p. 736.

63. As L.M. Cullen has pointed out, the Sligo–Roscommon area, like Carlow and Wexford in the south-east, was a 'shifting frontier' characterized by heavy Protestant settlement. Between about 1780 and 1830 estate owners in this area followed a policy of introducing Protestant tenants, leading to a sharp increase in the Protestant population, and an accompanying rise in agrarian and sectarian outrages. See Cullen, *Modern Ireland*, p. 208.
64. *Christian Observer* (Feb. 1818), 172.
65. *Christian Observer* (1822), appendix, 846.
66. *Christian Observer* (May 1825), 330.
67. *First Report of the Commissioners of Irish Education Inquiry* (1825), 400, XII, p. 70.
68. Akenson, *Irish Education Experiment*, p. 82.
69. William Stewart to Charles Brodrick, 1815 or 1816 (NLI, Brodrick Papers, MS 8869/8).
70. John Jebb believed emphatically that the benevolence of the Church of Ireland clergy was the most effective instrument of moral reform: 'were the clergy placed, not on weaker but on stronger grounds ... their benevolence would have a free and unimpeded channel in which to flow ... and they could be more popular than any other class of society, from the contrast between their generosity, and the hard dealings of lay proprietors, who are too seldom, in an equal degree, liberalized by education and softened by religion. The truth is, I cannot conceive a measure which would be more likely, eventually, to bring over the Roman Catholics to our reformed faith, than strengthening the hands of the clergy. Were this effectively done, could any measure be devised which would make it the interest of the people to settle quietly, the clergyman, instead of waging defensive warfare to protect his rights, would be at full liberty to bend all his power towards conciliation: and it cannot be doubted that conciliation is the best, as it is the only legitimate origin of conversion.' John Jebb to Charles Brodrick, 14 May 1815 (NLI, Brodrick Papers, MS 8866/3).
71. Quoted in Urwick, *James Digges La Touche*, pp. 411–12.
72. *Christian Observer* (Dec. 1814), 845.
73. Robert Daly, *A Sermon Preached at St. Anne's Church in Aid of the Funds of the Sunday Schools Society for Ireland, on Sunday the 28th of February 1819* (Dublin 1819), p. 30.
74. *Tenth Report of the Sunday School Society for Ireland* (1821), p. 11.
75. *Tenth Report of the Sunday School Society for Ireland* (1821), appendix.
76. *First Report of the Commissioners of Irish Education Inquiry* (1825), pp. 62–3.
77. Sullivan, 'Education of Irish Catholics', p. 285.
78. Eva Stoter, '"Grimmige Zeiten": The Influence of Lessing, Herder and the Grimm Brothers on the nationalism of the young Irelanders' in Tadhg Foley and Seán Ryder (eds), *Ideology and Ireland in the Nineteenth Century* (Dublin 1998).
79. Christopher Anderson to the committee of the Irish Society, 6 Nov. 1818 (TCD, Irish Society Proceedings, MS 7644/5). For a discussion of the use of Gaelic script see Ó Ciosáin, *Print and Popular Culture*, pp. 160–2.
80. Tomás Ó hÁilín, 'The Irish Society agus Tadhg Ó Coinnialláin', *Studia Hibernica*, 8 (1968), 68–9.
81. Irish Society Proceedings, 16 Sept. 1819 (TCD, MS 7644), p. 30.
82. *Ninth Report of the Sunday School Society for Ireland* (1819), p. 17.
83. Irish Society Proceedings, 17 March 1819 (TCD, MS 7644), pp. 17–18.

84. Irish Society Proceedings, 23 June 1821 (TCD, MS 7644), p. 85.
85. *First Report of the Commissioners of Irish Education Inquiry* (1825), 400, p. 84.
86. Lefroy, *Memoir of Chief Justice Lefroy*, pp. 89–92.
87. Charles Forster to John Jebb, 9 Oct. 1818 (TCD, John Jebb Papers, MS 6396–7/70).
88. John Jebb to Charles Brodrick, Oct. 1820 (NLI, Brodrick Papers, MS 8866/7).
89. Irish Society Proceedings, 23 June 1818 (TCD, MS 7644), p. 1.
90. Charles Edward Orpen, *The Claims of Millions of Our Fellow Countrymen to Be Taught in Their Own and Only Language—the Irish* (Dublin 1821), pp. 21–3.
91. Hugh Trevor-Roper, 'The invention of tradition: The Highland tradition of Scotland', in Eric Hobsbawm and Terence Ranger (eds) *The Invention of Tradition* (Cambridge 1984), p. 16.
92. Orpen, *Claims of Millions*, p. 9.
93. *Ibid.* p. 11.
94. W.J. McCormack has drawn attention to the similarities between the experiences of religious and national awakening. In raising the question as to why the Irish Literary Revival was called a 'revival', he speculates, 'Is it not in several of its personalities, Yeats, Synge ... O'Grady, and in a varied form, Lady Gregory, the achievement of displaced Irish evangelicals?' See McCormack, *Ascendancy and Tradition*, p. 231. For a further analysis, see Vivien Mercier, 'Victorian evangelicalism and the Anglo–Irish Literary Revival' in Peter Connolly (ed.), *Literature and the Changing Ireland* (Gerrards Cross, Buckinghamshire 1980), pp. 59–101; and Terence Brown, 'The Church of Ireland and the climax of the ages' in Terence Brown (ed.), *Ireland's Literature: Selected Essays* (Mullingar and Totowa, New Jersey 1988), pp. 49–64.
95. Irish Society Proceedings, 22 Oct. 1818 (TCD, MS 7644), p. 3.
96. An account of the career and work of Canon Goodman is provided in an article by Breandán Breathnach, 'Séamus Goodman (1828–96): Bailitheoir cheoil' (James Goodman [1828–96]: Music collector), *Journal of the Kerry Archaeological and Historical Society*, VI, (1973), 152–71.
97. David H. Greene and Edward M. Stephens, *J.M. Synge, 1871–1909* (New York 1989), pp. 28–30.
98. Lefroy, *Memoir of Chief Justice Lefroy*, p. 83.
99. *Fifth Annual Report of the London Hibernian Society* (1811), appendix, p. 26; *First Annual Report of the Baptist Irish Society* (1815), appendix, p. 45; Motherwell, *Albert Blest*, pp. 215–16.
100. *First Annual Report of the Baptist Society for the Promotion of the Gospel in Ireland* (1815), appendix, p. 54.
101. Anderson, *Memorial*, pp. 64–6.
102. Dewar, *Observations*, p. 122.
103. Quoted in Reilly, *Gideon Ouseley*, pp. 203–4.
104. *Fourth Annual Report of the London Hibernian Society* (1810), pp. 17–19.
105. John Jebb to Charles Brodrick, 23 Nov. 1803 (NLI, Brodrick Papers, MS 8866/1).
106. The first mention of this institution occurred in 1809 at the annual meeting of the LHS. It was described as having been established by a Mr Jones and not exclusively connected with any one denomination. Young men were admitted at the age of eighteen and later recommended for situations; in 1809 the LHS undertook to sponsor four candidates

whom it later expected to employ as teachers. *Report of the Committee of the Hibernian Society at the Annual Meeting*, 12 May 1809, pp. 4–5.
107. John Jebb to Charles Brodrick, 23 Oct. 1814 (Brodrick Papers, NLI, MS 8866/3)
108. William Maunsell to William Walker, secretary to the Board of Education, 24 July 1817 (NLI, Dr Michael Quane Papers, MS 17,945).
109. Ó hÁilín, 'The Irish Society agus Tadhg Ó Coinnialláin', pp. 60–78.
110. Quoted in *ibid.* p. 63.
111. Quoted in Sydney Owenson [Lady Morgan], *Patriotic Sketches of Ireland Written in Connaught*, vol. II (Baltimore, Maryland 1809), p. 211.
112. Quoted in *ibid.* p. 206.
113. Thaddeus Connnellan to Charles King O'Hara, 7 July 1834 (NLI, Charles King O'Hara Papers, MS 20,324).

Four: The Politics of Catholic Emancipation

1. John Milner to Daniel Murray, 10 March 1817 (DDA, Troy–Murray Papers, 30/3–105).
2. Quoted in Madden, *Peter Roe*, pp. 229–30.
3. Charles Forster to John Jebb, 9 Oct. 1818 (TCD, John Jebb Papers, MS 6396–7/70).
4. Whelan, *Tree of Liberty*, pp. 133–8.
5. S.J. Connolly, 'The Catholic question, 1801–12', in W.E. Vaughan (ed.), *A New History of Ireland, Volume V: Ireland Under the Union, I: 1801–1870* (Oxford 1989), pp. 241–6.
6. G.I.T. Machin, *The Catholic Question in English Politics, 1820–30* (Oxford 1964), p. 136; John Wolffe, *The Protestant Crusade in Great Britain, 1829–1860* (Oxford 1991), p. 22.
7. Oliver MacDonagh, 'The politicization of the Irish bishops, 1800–1850', *Historical Journal*, XVII, 1 (1975), 39.
8. Bartlett, *Irish Nation*, pp. 250–1; Daire Keogh, 'Catholic responses to the Act of Union' in Daire Keogh and Kevin Whelan (eds), *Acts of Union: The Causes, Contexts and Consequences of the Act of Union* (Dublin 2001), pp. 159–70.
9. Machin, *Catholic Question*, p. 12.
10. MacDonagh, 'Irish bishops', 39. For an account of the political background in which O'Connell launched his campaign against the veto, see Oliver MacDonagh, *O'Connell: The Life of Daniel O'Connell, 1775–1847* (1988–9; London 1991), pp. 92–116.
11. MacDonagh, 'Irish bishops', 38.
12. Machin, *Catholic Question*, p. 15.
13. Quoted in MacDonagh, 'Irish bishops', 40.
14. From a pamphlet on the Quarantotti Rescript (n.p. n.d.) (DDA, Troy–Murray Papers, Green File no. 7, 30/2).
15. R.J. Rodgers, 'James Carlisle, 1784–1854' (unpublished PhD thesis, Queen's University, Belfast 1973), p. 70.
16. John O'Connell (ed.), *The Select Speeches of Daniel O'Connell, M.P.: Edited with Historical Notices, etc., by His Son, John O'Connell*, vol. I (Dublin 1854-5), p. 240.
17. Quoted in Walter Alison Phillips (ed.), *A History of the Church of Ireland from the Earliest Times to the Present Day*, vol. III (London 1933), p. 293.

18. Canton, *History of the BFBS*, p. 27.
19. Owen, *Origin and First Ten Years of the BFBS*, pp. 526–7.
20. Thomas Elrington to Lord Lieutenant, 11 Nov. 1813 (NAI, Calendar of Official Papers, vol. II, 552/389/5).
21. In a report on clerical matters in West Cork, John Jebb reported that there was an increasing demand for bibles, prayer books, and testaments among the parochial clergy: 'The Cork Bible Society has kept itself altogether distinct from the Hibernian. It is managed exclusively by clergy of the establishment, and through them bibles and testaments are quickly distributed to those who want them. The Hibernian Bible Society made a struggle to have it otherwise, but fruitlessly.' John Jebb to Charles Brodrick, 8 March 1814 (NLI, MS 8866/2).
22. Joseph D'Arcy Sirr, *A Memorial of the Honourable and Most Reverend Power le Poer Trench, Last Archbishop of Tuam* (Dublin 1845), p. 44.
23. William Thomas to the secretary of the Baptist Irish Society, 8 June 1820, *Sixth Annual Report of the Baptist Society for the Promotion of the Gospel in Ireland* (1820), appendix, p. 31.
24. Andrew O'Callaghan, *Thoughts on the Tendencies of Bible Societies as affecting the Established Church and Christianity Itself as a 'reasonable service'* (Dublin 1816), pp. 5–17.
25. William Phelan, *The Bible, not the Bible Society: Being an Attempt to Point out that Mode of Disseminating the Scriptures, which Would Most Effectively Conduce to the Security of the Established Church and the Peace of the United Kingdom* (Dublin 1817), pp. 168–71.
26. *Ibid.* p. 14.
27. Desmond Bowen's description of Protestant–Catholic relations in the first two decades of the nineteenth century defies credibility: 'During that period, to a remarkable degree, the Catholic majority people and the minority Protestant ascendancy seemed to be able to tolerate each other. Revolutionary sentiments had been crushed by the savage reprisals following 1798, the Emmet rising had been quickly smothered, and local famines had taken away what little spirit was left in the rapidly increasing rural population. Religious peace existed generally, for, although agrarian secret societies were active in some parts of the country, neither the Catholics nor the Protestants wanted to add to social unrest by raising sectarian issues.' Bowen, *Protestant Crusade*, introduction, p. x. For a more balanced but equally nostalgic account, see Ignatius Murphy, 'Some attitudes to religious freedom and ecumenism in pre-Emancipation Ireland', *Irish Ecclesiastical Record*, vol. cv (Feb. 1966), 93–104.
28. James Warren Doyle, *Letters on a Reunion of the Church of England and Rome* (Dublin 1824).
29. Murphy, 'Religious freedom and ecumenism', 101–3.
30. Eric Richards, *A History of the Highland Clearances: Agrarian Transformations and the Evictions, 1746–1886* (London 1982), p. 29.
31. A good example of Catholic attitudes towards the evangelical mission is provided in a speech by Richard Lalor Sheil delivered at a famous meeting of the Cork Ladies' Auxiliary of the Bible Society in September 1824. Sheil and O'Connell attended the meeting and used the opportunity to pour scorn on the objectives of the voluntary evangelical agencies. Sheil declared that the Irish poor were less in need of bibles than of bread, and that the purveyors of vital religion would be better employed if they

32. While Pius VII was the first pope to warn Catholics against the Bible Society his successor Leo XII (1823–9) issued the famous bull *Ubi Primum* in which he accused the evangelicals of attempting through 'a perverse interpretation of the Gospel of Christ' to turn the Bible into 'a human Gospel, or, what is still worse, into a Gosepel of the Devil'. *The Encyclical Letter of Pope Leo the XII to his venerable brethren, the patriarchs, primates, archbishops, and bishops of the Catholic Church with an English translation of the same. To which are annexed Pastoral Instructions for the R.C. archbishops and bishops, to the clergy and laity of their communion throughout Ireland* (Dublin 1824), p. 16.
33. Quoted in Thomas, 'Ecumenical Bible society', p. 146.
34. Because of the strength of British influence at the Vatican the anti-veto lobby in Ireland had taken great pains to inform papal authorities why the veto would never be acceptable to the Catholics of Ireland: 'It would require the most intimate knowledge of the intricacies and of the various contradictory statements that pervade the history of Ireland at various periods to form an adequate opinion on the value that should be attached to the professions of public functionaries, as well as the faith that should be placed in the authoritative assurances that have been made to the Catholics since the Reformation, which have been invariably violated. The most recent example is proof of the deep-seated conviction which occurred during the proceedings on the legislative union between Great Britain and Ireland. On this occasion *the greater part of the Catholics of Ireland became the dupes of their passive obedience in expectation of their immediate emancipation.* [my emphasis] Punic faith was never more proverbial among the Romans than English faith is with the Irish people. Since the invasion of Ireland in the twelfth century this conviction is exemplified in the Irish language by the term "Sassenagh" [Saxon]. Since the Reformation, and the consequent persecution of Catholics, this epithet of horror is equally applied to a Protestant and an Englishman. In later times any Catholic that had adventured in any act of oppression was included in this national term of reproach; and to complete the climax all Catholics that are suspected to be friendly to the veto are branded as enemies of God and their country.' Edward Hay, Secretary of the Catholic Committee, to Cardinal Litta, 15 Aug. 1817 (reprinted *DEP*, 26 Jan. 1822).
35. In 1817 a correspondent of the Baptist Society reported that 'there are signs that the opposition of the priests will soon be encouraged and stimulated by the highest ecclesiastical authorities'. *Third Annual Report of the Baptist Irish Society* (1817), p. 24.
36. John MacHale, *The Letters of the Most Rev. John MacHale, D.D.*, vol. 1 (Dublin 1888), pp. 6–19.
37. Akenson, *Irish Education Experiment*, p. 90.
38. The following commentary, which appeared in an ultra-Protestant newspaper, perfectly captured the political ideology of religious revivalism in the post-Napoleonic period: 'He who would arrest the march of the Bible Society is attempting to stop the moral machinery of the world and can expect nothing but to be crushed in pieces. The march must proceed. These disciplined and formidable columns which, under the banner of divine truth, are bearing down upon the territories of death have one word of command

from on high, and that word is "Onward" ... May it go onward, continuing to be, and with increasing splendour, the astonishment of the world, as well as the most illustrious monument of British glory.' *The Patriot*, 26 March 1818.
39. 'Thoughts submitted to the Rt. Hon. Charles Grant on the subject of the education of the Irish poor by Lord Fingall and Dr. Troy' (CICE/KPSA, memoranda 1, 1812–28, MI/13).
40. 'Draft of speech made by Mr. Plunket at a meeting held at the Rotunda, 2 February 1821' (*Ibid.* MI/12).
41. 'Draft of speech made by Lord Cloncurry at the Rotunda, February 2nd, 1821' (*Ibid.*).
42. Valentine Browne Lawless, *Personal Recollections of the Life and Times of Valentine, Lord Cloncurry* (Dublin 1869), p. 376.
43. *DEP*, 7 March 1820.
44. Duke of Leinster to Joseph Devonshire Jackson, 3 March 1820 (CICE/KPSA, general correspondence II, 1819–26, CII 1–162, CII/7).
45. Duke of Leinster to Joseph Devonshire Jackson, 3 March 1822 (*Ibid.* CII/47).
46. O'Connell, *Select Speeches*, vol. II, p. 81.
47. Eugene Stock, *The History of the Church Missionary Society: Its Environment, Its Men, and Its Work*, vol. I (London 1899-1916), p. 153.
48. *DEP*, 6 Oct. 1821.
49. Thomas Lewis O'Beirne, *Circular Letter of the Lord Bishop of Meath to the Rural Deans of his Diocese* (Dublin 1821), p. 3.
50. *Ibid.*
51. Even though Bishop Doyle was willing to admit that, on an individual level, the clergymen of the Established Church could be amiable, humane and helpful to their communities, his description of the general body was as harsh as anything that ever came from the pen of O'Connell. See James Warren Doyle, *Letters on the State of Ireland: Addressed by JKL to a Friend in England* (Dublin 1825), pp. 75–7.
52. Information on the ancient Irish Church was most frequently taken from Bede's account of the argument over the dating of Easter, which caused the Irish Church to break with Rome at the Synod of Whitby in 664 AD. 'They [Columba's adherents] followed indeed uncertain rules as to the time of the great festival: since, being so far distant from the rest of the world, no one had brought them the synodal decrees for the observance of Easter. They diligently observed only those works of piety and chastity which they could learn in the prophetical, evangelical, and apostolical writings.' Joseph Belcher, *The Baptist Irish Society: Its Origin, History, and Prospects* (London 1845), p. xv.
53. *DEP*, 19 Dec. 1819; 6 Jan. 1820.
54. *DEP*, 20 Dec. 1819; 6 Jan. 1820.
55. *DEP*, 18 Jan. 1820.
56. Doyle, *Letters on the State of Ireland*, p. 167.
57. Urwick, *La Touche*, p. 404; M. Comerford, *Collections on the Diocese of Kildare and Leighlin*, vol. III (Dublin 1886), pp. 412–13.
58. L.M. Cullen, *An Economic History of Ireland since 1660* (London 1972), p. 103.
59. *DEP*, 11 Jan. 1817; 27 Feb. 1817; 7 March 1817.
60. Power le Poer Trench to Charles King O'Hara, 7 Feb. 1817 (NLI, Charles King O'Hara Papers, MS 20,313–7).

61. William Harty, *An Historic Sketch of the Causes, Progress, Extent and Mortality of the Contagious Fever Epidemic in Ireland during the Years 1817, 1818, and 1819 with Numerous Tables, Official Documnets and Private Communications, Illustrative of Its General History and of the System of Management Adopted for Its Suppression* (Dublin 1820), pp. 117–19.
62. *Ibid.* p. 10.
63. See James S. Donnelly, Jr, 'Pastorini and Captain Rock: Millenarianism and sectarianism in the Rockite movement of 1821–4' in Samuel Clark and James S. Donnelly, Jr (eds), *Irish Peasants: Violence and Political Unrest, 1780–1914* (Madison, Wisconsin 1983), pp. 102–39.
64. Patrick O'Farrell, 'Millenarianism, messianism, and utopianism in Irish history', *Anglo-Irish Studies*, II (1976), 45–68; J.J. Lee, 'The Ribbonmen' in T.D. Williams (ed.), *Secret Societies in Ireland* (Dublin and New York 1973), pp. 26–35.
65. Donnelly, 'Pastorini and Captain Rock', pp. 110–18.
66. Michael Barkun, *Disaster and the Millennium* (New Haven, Connecticut and London 1974), p. 34.
67. The most recent scholarship on the retreat of the Irish language indicates that the ascendancy of English was a direct consequence of the spread of the market economy, and reinforces the belief that the decline of Irish was strongly associated with the rise of the Catholic Church in the late eighteenth century. See Garret Fitzgerald, 'Estimates for baronies of minimum level of Irish-speaking amongst successive decennial cohorts, 1771–1781 to 1861–1871', *Proceedings of the Royal Irish Academy*, 84, 3 (1984); and Seán de Fréine, *The Great Silence: The Study of a Relationship between Language and Nationality* (Cork 1978), especially chapters x and xi.
68. Barkun, *Disaster and the Millennium*, p. 38.
69. *Ibid.* p. 1.
70. Quoted in Donnelly, 'Pastorini and Captain Rock', p. 115.
71. Earl of Rosse to Lord Redesdale, 19 April 1822 (PRONI, Redesdale Papers, T.3031/13/2).
72. Donnelly, 'Pastorini and Captain Rock', p. 114.
73. See Douglas Hyde, *Abhráin atá Leagtha ag an Reachtuire, or Songs Ascribed to Raftery, Being the Fifth Chapter of the Songs of Connaught* (1903; Shannon 1973).
74. Earl of Rosse to Lord Redesdale, 19 April 1822 (PRONI, Redesdale Papers, T3030/13/2).
75. Anonymous (a Dissenter) to the chief secretary, April 1822 (SCP, 2373/10).
76. *DEP,* 15 April 1822.
77. Paul Johnson, *The Birth of the Modern: World Society, 1815–1830* (New York 1991), p. 797.
78. *DEP,* 30 March 1822.
79. The influence of Thomas Chalmers is of profound importance in this context. Chalmers' response to the nightmare of overpopulation was 'moral restraint', which could only be achieved through a reformation of the national character which, in turn, could only be accomplished through universal evangelical Christian education disseminated by the parish churches and schools of a national religious establishment. See Brown, *Thomas Chalmers*, pp. 197–9.
80. A blunt exponent of this position, described as an 'Orange' visitor to Renvyle in County Galway in 1823, informed his hosts of his proposition for tranquilizing Ireland by 'the banishment of all the priests and two-thirds of the population'. *Letters from the Irish*

Highlands of Connemara. By the Blake Family of Renvyle House (1823/4) (London 1825; Clifden 1995), pp. 23–4.
81. Barkun, *Disaster and the Millennium*, p. 77.
82. *Ibid.*
83. In his study of Irish Catholicism before the Famine, S.J. Connolly concludes that 'the triumph of the post-Famine Church was also the victory of one culture over another, and when modern Irish Catholicism came into its inheritance, it did so only by means of the destruction of a rival world'. S.J. Connolly, *Priests and People in Pre-Famine Ireland, 1780–1845* (Dublin 1982), p. 278.
84. Emmet Larkin, 'The devotional revolution in Ireland, 1850–75', *American Historical Review*, LXXVII (1972), 625–52.
85. Thomas McGrath, *Religious Renewal and Reform in the Pastoral Ministry of Bishop James Doyle of Kildare and Leighlin, 1786–1834* (Dublin 1999). For a critique of the Larkin thesis, see Thomas McGrath, 'The Tridentine evolution of modern Irish Catholicism, 1563–1962: A re-examination of the "Devotional Revolution" thesis', *Recusant History*, 20, 4 (Oct. 1999), 512–23.
86. In the case of the Cattle Killing movement in Natal in 1856–7, the links between missionary activity, destructive millenarianism and imperial domination were obvious. When a new and devastating disease known as lung-sickness began to spread among the Xhosa cattle herds in the 1850s, a teenage prophetess educated by Christian missionaries began to preach that if all the cattle, including the healthy ones, were killed that the entire herd would be brought back in a 'born again' state by new people who would save the tribe from the depredations of British colonists. The slaughter made what was an emergency situation into a catastrophe and was exploited by the British governor, Sir George Grey, who used the opportunity to force the native peoples off their lands and into accepting exploitative labour contracts in the mines. See J.B. Peires, *The Dead Will Arise: Nongqawuse and the Great Cattle Killing Movement of 1856–7* (Oxford 1989).

Five: The 'Second Reformation' 1822–7

1. *DEP,* 29 Oct. 1822.
2. *DEP,* 24 Jan. 1824.
3. James Edward Jackson, *Reasons for Withdrawing from the Hibernian Bible Society, Founded on the Public Documents of that Institution* (Dublin 1822), p. 37.
4. In 1822–3 the disturbed condition of counties Cork and Limerick prompted many observers to compare the situation with the Rebellion of 1798. *DEP,* 29 April 1823; D. Woodward to John Jebb, 30 March 1822 (TCD, John Jebb Papers, MS 6396–7/151).
5. *Fifth Annual Report of the Baptist Society for the Promotion of the Gospel in Ireland* (1819), pp. 41–2.
6. An oath found on a suspected Rockite, Denis Egan, captured near Roscrea, County Tipperary, in April 1822, contained the following exchanges: 'What are you? A Christian. Who made you a Christian? St. Peter the Rock. How do you prove yourself a Christian? By being baptized and openly professing and adhering to the Catholic

Church and the sign of the cross until death.' *DEP,* 19 April 1822. Similar references to the Catholic Church as 'the rock' appeared frequently in the rhetoric of Daniel O'Connell as well as in the the oral tradition of the Irish-speaking commnity, as, for example, in the long poem of Anthony Raftery called 'The Catholic Rent': 'But not of blown sand is the foundation of this wall / Christ, as is read, is beneath it, together with Peter / A work that shall not fail and that shall not burst is this Rock / The One-son set it up, who was crucified on earth for us / It was James, no lie, who left Ireland to the English / But we have near home the Revelation, / And I think not far from us is satisfaction'. Hyde, *Abhráin atá Leagtha ag an Reachtuire,* p. 119.

7. The Rev. Mortimer O'Sullivan claimed that bibles were welcomed by people who could not otherwise obtain copies of Pastorini, so that they might study and discuss the book of Revelation, the traditional source of millenarian prophecy. See Donnelly, 'Pastorini and Captain Rock', p. 120. In 1828 a notice posted at the Catholic chapel of Drumkerrin, County Sligo, declared that any Catholic who dealt with Protestants deserved to be beaten with cudgels because Protestants were the locusts mentioned in the book of Revelation. *British Critic* (Jan. 1828), 39.
8. *DEP,* 8 July 1819.
9. Referring to the government's failure to exercise a restraining influence on the virulence of ultra-Protestants in 1823, the *Dublin Evening Post* commented: '... while they permit such mad dogs to run through the streets, who can tell what the consequences will be. We said it before and we repeat it now, that these people are looking for a rebellion in the expectation that it may give them the fling which they exercised in the last—and that it may end in the same way. They forget that there was then a conspiracy, which, when reached at its fountain, was certain to dissolve in ruin to the cause of the conspirators ... In short, times have changed. Conspiracy was the danger then, the danger now is, there is no conspiracy.' *DEP,* 25 Nov. 1823. The influence of a Church of Ireland clergyman, Sir Harcourt Lees, was singled out for its particularly inflammatory character, of which the paper gave the following sample: 'Were the [Catholic] population 10,000,000 I would not value them a rush, for in a week I could raise an army of Protestants in Great Britain and Ireland that would annihilate them even with their Popish Pastors at their head. Therefore, my lads, take care of yourselves; I know how to manage you, if you are not better than Lord Wellesley or the King himself. Political power you shall never have. You are the first fellows I shall make an example of, for depend on it, if I take the field against you it is not nut-cracking but priest-cracking I will be.' *DEP,* 9 Dec. 1823.
10. Donnelly, 'Pastorini and Captain Rock', pp. 127-35.
11. *DEP,* 1 Aug. 1822.
12. *DEP,* 6 July 1822.
13. *DEP,* 31 Oct. 1822.
14. George Ensor, *A Defence of the Irish and the Means of Their Redemption* (Dublin 1825), p. 3.
15. *DEP,* 23 Feb. 1822; 22 Aug. 1822.
16. D. Woodward to John Jebb, 30 March 1822 (TCD, John Jebb Papers, MS 6936/151).
17. In his famous inauguration sermon Archbishop Magee outlined the position of the Church of Ireland in the following terms: 'It will not do ... to content ourselves with exclaiming against what is called *new* light, without endeavouring to extend to our flocks

the benefit of the *old*, to be fearful of an excess of zeal, without any alarm as to the consequence of indifference.' William Magee, *A Charge Delivered at His Primary Visitation in St Patrick's Cathedral, Dublin, on Thursday the 24th of October, 1822* (Dublin 1822), p. 14.

18. The 'Second Reformation' movement as part of the campaign to consolidate a Protestant United Kingdom has been examined by Stewart J. Brown in 'The New Reformation movement in the Church of Ireland, 1801–29' in Stewart J. Brown and David W. Miller (eds.), *Piety and Power in Ireland: Essays in Honour of Emmet Larkin* (Belfast and Notre Dame 2000), pp. 180–208; and Stewart J. Brown, *The National Churches of England, Ireland, and Scotland, 1801–1846* (Oxford 2001).
19. In his inaugural sermon, Bishop Jebb called on the Church of Ireland 'to manfully assert and defend the faith … which, we are persuaded, is the faith of the true Catholic and Apostolic Church—but, to also maintain unity of spirit with brethren of the Church of Rome … to contend, not by reviling or undervaluing, but by being better Christians.' John Jebb, *A Charge Deliverd to the Clergy of the Diocese of Limerick at the Primary Visitation in the Cathedral Church of St. Mary, on Thursday, the 19th of June, 1823* (Dublin 1823).
20. Catholics were present on this occasion out of gratitude for the relief work that Archbishop Trench had engaged in during the famine that swept the western counties in 1822. See chapter 7.
21. W.J. Fitzpatrick, *The Life, Times, and Correspondence of the Right Rev. Dr. Doyle, Bishop of Kildare and Leighlin*, vol 1 (Dublin 1861; 1890), p. 207.
22. According to his biographer, Archbishop Magee had been a lifelong opponent of Catholic claims and had drawn up a petition to oppose the endowment of the Catholic seminary at Maynooth in 1795. A.H. Kenney, *Memoir of the Late Right Rev. William Magee* (Dublin 1842), p. ix.
23. Magee, *A Charge Delivered at his Primary Visitation*, p. 22.
24. Killen, *Ecclesiastical History*, vol. II, pp. 420–1.
25. Fitzpatrick, *Doyle*, vol. I, p. 211.
26. *Ibid.* Doyle's representation of the acuteness of peasant awareness of the tithe problem was borne out by another source. Mortimer O'Sullivan engaged in a conversation with a countryman as to the distinction between tithes and debts: 'I asked him what he meant by debts, if he did not allow tithes to be such; his answer was prompt: "Anything that I get value for, and sure the minister never gave me value for the tithe."' See Mortimer O'Sullivan, *Captain Rock Detected or the Origin and Character of the Recent Disturbances amd the Condition of the South and West of Ireland Considered and Exposed. By a Munster Farmer* (Dublin and Edinburgh 1824), p. 195.
27. Patrick Curtis, *Two Letters Respecting the Horrible Act of Placing a Calf's Head on the Altar of the Chapel of Ardee, and also His Answer to the Protestant Archbishop Magee's Charge Against the Roman Catholic Religion* (Dublin 1822).
28. Charles Simeon to T. Thomason, 26 April 1822. Quoted in Lefroy, *Memoir of Thomas Lefroy*, pp. 94–8.
29. Jackson, *Reasons for Withdrawing from the Hibernian Bible Society*, p. 4.
30. *Seventh Report of the Baptist Society for the Promotion of the Gospel in Ireland* (1821), appendix, p. 19.
31. *Ibid.* p. 21.

32. Doyle, *Letters on the State of Ireland*, pp. 76–7.
33. *Diary of Lady Anne Jocelyn* (unpaginated, NLI, MS 18,430).
34. *Ibid.*
35. Eyre Crowe Evans, *Today in Ireland* (1825; New York and London 1979), p. 14.
36. Lord Farnham, who was, according to W.J. Fitzpatrick, 'in the main a sincere and well-intentioned man, perfectly honest as a politician', was said later in life to have fallen a victim, 'with an immense number of old ladies, to much of the fanatical folly then so prevalent in Ireland'. Fitzpatrick, *Doyle*, vol. II, p. 1.
37. This is the argument advanced by Linda Colley in her study of the formation of British national identity in the late eighteenth and early nineteenth centuries. See in particular her chapter on 'Dominance'. Linda Colley, *Britons: Forging the Nation, 1707–1837* (New Haven, Connecticut and London 1992), pp. 147–93.
38. *Christian Observer* (Feb. 1822), 127.
39. Urwick, *James Digges La Touche*, p. 78.
40. Mícheál McGrath (ed. and trans.), *Cinnlae Amhlaoibh Uí Súilleabháin* (The Diaries of Humphrey O'Sullivan) (London 1936–7), p. 236.
41. The controversial preacher Rev. Robert McGhee remarked of the typical Irish evangelical that 'if he professes to make the gospel the guide of his public principle, whether he be a clergyman or a layman, he is styled as an epithet of singular contempt, a "saint"'. Robert J. McGhee, *Truth and Error Contrasted* (Dublin 1828), p. 303.
42. This should not be confused with the term 'New Light' as used by Irish Presbyterians in the eighteenth century; for the difference between this and the more widespread use of the term in the American colonies see Mark A. Noll, *America's God: From Jonathan Edwards to Abraham Lincoln* (Oxford 2002), p. 98.
43. Crowe Evans, *Today in Ireland*, pp. 21–2.
44. *Ibid.* p. 24.
45. Cullen, *Modern Ireland*, pp. 20–1.
46. F. K. Prochaska, *Women and Philanthropy in Nineteenth-Century England* (Oxford 1980).
47. McDowell, *Social Life in Ireland*, pp. 28–9.
48. *Ibid.*
49. Crowe Evans, *Today in Ireland*, pp. 158–9.
50. *Ibid.* pp. 175–8.
51. *DEP,* 1 June 1824; 4 Sept. 1824.
52. James Roche to Daniel Murray, 12 Oct. 1827 (DDA, Murray Papers, MS 30 [10], no. 2).
53. *Eighth Report of the Baptist Society for the Promotion of the Gospel in Ireland* (1822), p. 12.
54. In the same locality Otway made the following observation about the anti-Protestant tradition in popular culture: 'I may here remark that in almost every religious ruin I have ever visited, the neighbouring people, besides telling you of the original destruction by bloody Bess or cursed Cromwell with his copper nose, always have some more recent instances to narrate of Protestant mischief-doers. The children have got these stories at their fingers' ends: it seems part of a system by these means to preoccupy the minds of the young Roman Catholics with deep and hateful prejudices against their Protestant countrymen …' Caesar Otway, *A Tour in Connaught, Comprising Sketches of Clonmacnoise, Joyce Country, and Achill* (Dublin 1839), p. 308.

55. Crowe Evans, *Today in Ireland*, pp. 159–60.
56. Daniel Murray to Marquis of Lansdowne, 5 Nov. 1827 (DDA, Murray Papers, MS 30 [10], Later File, no. 3).
57. Baptist Wriothesley Noel, *Notes of a Short Tour through the Midland Counties of Ireland in the Summer of 1836, with Observations on the Condition of the Peasantry* (London 1837), p. 103.
58. This was not as uncommon as might have been supposed, and was clearly indicative of the move away from the self-assured confidence of the eighteenth century towards the more rigid polarization of the nineteenth. Among the roster of active evangelical clergymen were offspring of families who had been famous for their championing of the Catholic cause (such as Rev. William Bushe, the nephew of Charles Kendall Bushe), many from families who had recently been Catholic, such as the Rev. Edward Nangle, and others (often the most vehement of all) who had converted from Catholicism, such as the O'Sullivan brothers, Mortimer and Samuel, and the famous propagandist, the Rev. William Phelan.
59. Noel, *Notes of a Short Tour*, p. 103.
60. *The Irish Society: Quarterly Extracts of Correspondence*, no. 16 (1825), pp. 3–4.
61. J.R.R. Wright, 'An evangelical estate *c.* 1800–25: The influence on the Manchester Estate, County Armagh, with particular reference to the moral agencies of W. Loftie and H. Porter' (unpublished PhD thesis, Northern Ireland Polytechnic 1982).
62. 'Since I have returned to England, I have been induced to think that Ireland is blessed in a much greater degree than I thought when I was there. I have made enquiries with regard to the religious state of England since I have been at Hereford, and from what I can collect, the progress towards EVANGELISATION is by no means so rapid here as in Ireland. Preachers of the gospel are not so plentiful, and the schools are not so numerous *in proportion*.' W.H. Krause to Robert H. Inglis, 21 Dec. 1824. Quoted in C.S. Stanford, *Memoir of the Late W.H. Krause, with Selections from his Correspondence* (Dublin 1854), p. 208.
63. *Ibid.* p. 7.
64. *Ibid.* pp. 180–1.
65. T.P. Cunningham, 'The 1826 General Election in Co. Cavan', *Breifne: Journal of Cumann Seanchas Breifne*, II, 2 (1965), 5–46.
66. Stanford, *Krause*, p. 225.
67. *J.K.L.'s Letter to the Rt. Hon. Lord Farnham* (Dublin 1827), p. 4.
68. John Jebb to Robert H. Inglis, 7 April 1827. Quoted in John Charles Forster, *The Life of John Jebb, D.D., Bishop of Limerick, Ardfert, and Aghadoe* (London 1845), pp. 668–9. The more aggressive features of the 'Second Reformation', such as controversial preaching, itinerancy, and the parading of converts, did not meet with the approval of Bishop Jebb. Nevertheless, he considered the conversion of Catholics a most desirable objective and never departed from his lifelong dream that it could be effected through the quiet and steady work of the parochial clergy of the Church of Ireland.
69. *Blackwood's Magazine* (Jan. 1827), 61–73.
70. *Ibid.* May 1827, 575.
71. *Hansard*, 2nd ser., vol. XVII (1826–7), p. 807.

72. George Ensor, *The New Reformation: Letters Showing the Inutility and Exhibiting the Absurdity of What Is Rather Fantastically Termed 'The New Reformation'* (Dublin 1828), p. 26.
73. *Ibid.* p. 8.
74. *Ibid.* p. 37.
75. W.H. Crawford, *Domestic Industry in Ireland: The Experience of the Linen Industry* (Dublin 1972), p. 26.
76. Noel, *Notes of a Short Tour*, pp. 92–3.
77. Ensor, *New Reformation*, p. 37.
78. *Ibid.* pp. 38–9.
79. *Ibid.* p. 53.
80. *British Critic* (Jan. 1828), 49.
81. The correspondence of Lord Farnham for 1831–2 is full of accounts of agrarian crime in County Cavan in the early 1830s. One informant in 1831 described gangs of young men rampaging through the streets on market days attacking any Protestant they could lay hands on. At the Christmas fair in Virginia, Protestants were unable to appear on the streets and had to take refuge overnight with sympathetic Catholics, who had their houses attacked and windows broken as a result. Local Protestants were also out of fear said to be contributing to 'emissaries' who were going through the surrounding townlands collecting funds for O'Connell. John King to Lord Farnham, 10 Jan. 1831 (NLI Farnham Papers, MS 18, 1612/10).
82. *Fifteenth Report of the Irish Society for Promoting the Education of the Native Irish through the Medium of Their Own Language* (1833), p. 7.
83. Noel, *Notes of a Short Tour*, p. 106.
84. Robert Winning to Lord Farnham, 23 July 1830 (NLI, Farnham Papers, MS 18,612/9).
85. Noel, *Notes of a Short Tour*, pp. 95–109.
86. *British Critic* (Jan. 1828), 11.
87. *Ibid.* p. 27.
88. *Ibid.* p. 30.
89. *Hansard*, 2nd ser., vol. XVII (1826–7), p. 809.
90. John Jebb to Robert H. Inglis, 7 April 1827, quoted in Forster, *John Jebb*, p. 680.
91. *Ibid.* p. 672.
92. *Ibid.* pp. 672–7.
93. Connolly, *Priests and People*. See in particular his chapter 'Vile and wicked conspiracies', pp. 219–63, for a thorough treatment of popular anti-clericalism in the eighteenth and early nineteenth centuries.
94. John Jebb to Charles Brodrick, 3 May 1816 (NLI, Brodrick Papers, MS 8866/5).
95. *Ibid.*
96. *DEP,* 13 Nov. 1819.
97. John Jebb to Charles Brodrick, 18 Dec. 1821 (NLI, Brodrick Papers, MS 8866/8). The following resolutions were unanimously adopted at the meeting: 'Resolved: that we altogether disapprove of these secret associations and private meetings, which, in opposition to the laws and to religion, have for some time past unhappily prevailed in different parts of the country.

'Resolved: that we consider it an offence against the laws of God and man to administer and take oaths, which, under the seal of secrecy, have been tendered and still are tendered by designing persons to many of our deluded fellow countrymen.

'Resolved: that we have learned with deep sorrow and hold in utter abhorrence the barbarous atrocities which, in consequence of such oaths and meetings, have been committed in this and in adjoining counties.

'Resolved: that we rejoice in the peace and tranquility hitherto maintained in the parish of Abingdon; and are determined by every means in our power to preserve to ourselves this honourable distinction.'

98. Cullen, *Modern Ireland*, pp. 205–6.
99. Ignatius Murphy, *The Diocese of Killaloe, 1800–50* (Dublin 1992), pp. 100–33. See also Bowen, *Protestant Crusade*, pp. 150–3; and Noel, *Notes of a Short Tour*, pp. 224–9.
100. Forster, *John Jebb*, p. 674.
101. Hyde, *Raftery*, p. 115. It is worth noting that Douglas Hyde, himself the product of a Protestant clerical background, was not at all familiar with the implication of the term 'New Light' and confused it with 'some religious sect' of Scottish origin because he had seen it mentioned in a poem by Robert Burns. Yet the movement for the restoration of the Irish language, in which he played so prominent a role, can trace one of its most visible roots to the Reformation crusade of the earlier part of the century.
102. Noel, *Notes of a Short Tour*, pp. 102–9.
103. *Ibid.* p. 97.
104. *Ibid.* pp. 130–7.
105. Quoted in Acheson, 'Evangelicals', p. 247.
106. On the consequences of one sermon, the Rev. Winning wrote: 'On Sunday last the priest of Ballytrane denounced from the altar the reading of the Irish Scriptures and said the men who were teaching were destroying the country and must be *stopped*. The following night a party of about thirty broke into the houses of the Irish scholars within a circuit of about seven miles between Carrickmacross and Ballybay and beat the poor men with stones in the most shocking manner ... One poor man had not a tooth left; when thrown down they trod them out and drove them down his throat with their iron-shod brogues. Four of the men who have suffered most will not (if they survive) be for months able to earn anything for their families.' Miss Lyster to Mrs Cairns, 4 Jan. 1836 (PRONI, Roden Papers, mic. 147/reel 5, pp. 16–18).
107. *British Critic* (Jan. 1828), 31.
108. In 1828–9 the influence of the Catholic Association was said to be especially strong in the Sligo area, both in pressuring converts to return to the Catholic fold and in heightening political expectations among the common people that the existing order was soon to be overturned. One guileless tenant informed his landlord, obviously a kindly man, that he should not continue to spend money renovating his house 'until the world should be more settled than it is' and other admonitions suggesting how uncertain he considered his landlord's possession to be. *Christian Examiner* (March 1829), 232–3.
109. *Ibid.*
110. The fostering of such an attachment was self-consciously pursued by certain landlords involved in the education enterprise. Consider the case of Richard Smyth of the Ballintray Estate, who made every possible compromise, from employing Catholic

schoolmasters, to permitting the use of the Douay Bible, to inviting the priest to scrutinize what was going on. The reason given for his desire to see the children in attendance, besides the obvious one of education, was that he wanted to become better acquainted with those who were going to be his future tenants: 'I feel it is a natural consequence that, having taken an interest in their improvement as children, I shall be more disposed to regard them with kindness and to promote their happiness and welfare when they grow up into manhood.' Richard Smyth to tenants of Ballintray Estate, 31 May 1827 (CICE/KPSA, General Correspondence III, CIII/17).
111. *British Critic* (Jan. 1828), 38–9.
112. In a debate on the state of Ireland in the House of Commons in 1825, Alexander Dawson described the priests as 'the most mischievous set of men in Ireland. There was no ill-feeling or disturbance they were not the cause of. The Roman Catholic priest causes all the bad feelings between landlord and tenant, and all the evils consequent thereupon.' *DEP,* 19 Feb. 1825.
113. David Thomson and Moyra McGusty (eds), *The Irish Journals of Elizabeth Smith, 1840–50* (Oxford 1980), p. 11.
114. *Ibid.* pp. 11–12.
115. *Blackwood's Magazine* (May 1827), 582.

Six: The Catholic Counter-Attack

1. James Doyle to John Whelan, secretary of the Abbeyleix Rent Committee, printed in *DEP,* 27 Nov. 1824.
2. Ensor, *Defence of the Irish*, p. 24.
3. *DEP,* 4 Dec. 1824, quoted from an editorial in the pro-Orange *Courier.*
4. John Jebb to Robert H. Inglis, 19 Nov. 1824, quoted in Reynolds, *Catholic Emancipation Crisis*, p. 22.
5. Fergus O'Ferrall, *Catholic Emancipation: Daniel O'Connell and the Birth of Irish Democracy, 1820–30* (Dublin 1985), pp. 37–9.
6. Reynolds, *Emancipation Crisis*, pp. 14–16.
7. Thomas A. Kselman, *Miracles and Prophecies in Nineteenth-Century France* (Brunswick, New Jersey 1983), p. 23.
8. Fitzpatrick, *Doyle*, vol. 1, pp. 248–50.
9. Quoted in *ibid.* p. 251.
10. Quoted in *ibid.* pp. 244–5.
11. Quoted in *ibid.* p. 253.
12. As recently as late November 1822, William Conyngham Plunket had claimed that one of Doyle's addresses to his congregation 'would do honour to a Fenelon or Bailey' and hoped it would be circulated and studied in England as an example of the 'liberal and enlightened piety which belongs to a prelate of the Roman Catholic Church'. William Conyngham Plunket to James Doyle, 30 Nov. 1822 (DDA, Murray Papers, Green File II, 1822–3, 30/6/14).
13. *DEP,* 19 Aug. 1823.

Notes to pages 197–201

14. For an account of the Hohenlohe miracles and their impact on denominational relations see Thomas McGrath, *Politics, Interdenominational Relations and Education in the Public Ministry of Bishop James Doyle of Kildare and Leighlin, 1786–1834* (Dublin 1999), pp. 109–15.
15. O'Ferrall, *Catholic Emancipation*, p. 42.
16. William H. Sewell, Jr argues that the rhetoric of Abbé Sieyès' famous pamphlet 'crystallized the resentments of the politically active elite of the Third Estate and charted the political course of the Revolution through the crucial summer of 1789. Moreover, it presaged and prepared the climactic night of 4 August, when the National Assembly abolished the privileges of the aristocracy and the clergy, destroyed the vestiges of feudalism, and established equality of citizens before the law. The night of 4 August was the logical culmination of Sieyès' revolutionary script.' Sewell, *Rhetoric of Bourgeois Revolution*, pp. 64–5.
17. James Warren Doyle, *A Vindication of the Religious and Civil Principles of the Irish Catholics in a Letter Addressed to His Excellency the Marquis Wellesley, K.G.* (Dublin 1823), p. 38.
18. *Ibid.* p. 30.
19. For a complete account and analysis of Doyle's political writings see McGrath, *Politics, Interdenominational Relations and Education*, pp. 1–75.
20. The standard biography of Bishop Doyle is W.J. Fitzpatrick's *The Life, Times, and Correspondence of the Right Rev. Dr. Doyle, Bishop of Kildare and Leighlin* (Dublin 1861; 1890). Despite his status as a giant among contemporaries, Doyle's reputation went into an eclipse in the twentieth century from which it has only recently been rescued by the work of Thomas McGrath.
21. O'Ferrall, *Catholic Emancipation*, pp. 39–49.
22. Quoted in Fitzpatrick, *Doyle*, vol. 1, p. 371.
23. Robert McGhee to Lord Farnham, 28 March 1823 (NLI, Farnham Papers, MS 18,604/1).
24. The customary practice for a Catholic funeral in a Protestant graveyard was thus described by a number of Dublin clergy in 1824: 'the invariable practice until the late unfortunate interruption in St Kevin's was that one of the clergy recited at the grave a form of prayer for the soul of the deceased, that the remaining clergy, if more than one were present, and sometimes the laity, joined in the responses to this prayer, and that during the recital both the Catholic clergy and laity remained with their heads uncovered in a way that would be likely to attract the notice of all present'. *Resolutions Passed by the Dublin Clergy at the Special Meeting Held on March 25th, 1824* (DDA, Troy–Murray Papers, MS 30/8–83).
25. *DEP,* 23 Sept. 1823.
26. *DEP,* 18 Nov. 1823.
27. *DEP,* 24 Jan. 1824.
28. John Jebb to Richard Jebb, 27 Feb. 1824 (TCD, John Jebb Papers, MS 6396–7/179).
29. That it was still a subject of dispute was evidenced in 1828 in a communication from Spring-Rice to Archbishop Murray, who described it as a measure which, 'intended and passed as a relief, has acted unfortunately in an opposite manner and introduced fresh causes of jealousy, strife, and collision'. Thomas Spring-Rice to Daniel Murray, 6 Feb. 1828 (DDA, Murray Papers, MS 30/11–1). See also McGrath, *Politics, Interdenominational Relations and Education*, pp. 119–21.

30. O'Ferrall, *Catholic Emancipation*, p. 21.
31. *Ibid.* pp. 61–5.
32. Hundreds of these letters catalogued in the Murray Papers at the Dublin Diocesan Archives provide an enormous body of information on the state of education in Ireland prior to the setting up of the National Board in 1831, and the disposition of the Catholic clergy at this time.
33. James Roche to Daniel Murray, 27 July 1824 (DDA, Murray Papers MS 30/8–67).
34. *DEP*, 27 April 1824. For an overview of the attitude of the Catholic hierarchy and clergy towards the Kildare Place Society's schools see McGrath, *Politics, Interdenominational Relations and Education*, pp. 157–206.
35. James Doyle to Daniel Murray, 4 Nov. 1824 (DDA, Murray Papers, 30/8/70).
36. The meetings organized for September, October and November of 1824 were sponsored by various branches, associations and ladies' auxiliaries of the HBS, The Sunday School Society for Ireland, the CMS, and the LHS. According to Rev. James Godkin the meetings were deliberately organized for the purpose of drawing the Catholic clergy into a public conflict: 'To these meetings the Roman Catholics of the neighbourhood were "affectionately invited" and their priests were challenged to come forth and defend their system if they dared.' Godkin, *The Religious History of Ireland*, p. 238. The schedule, according to information taken from the *DEP* and the *FJ*, was as follows:

21 Sept.	Cork
21 Sept.	Clonmel
22 Sept.	Dundalk
23 Sept.	Bandon
23 Sept.	Newry
24 Sept.	Drogheda
27 Sept.	Kildare
28 Sept.	Waterford
29 Sept.	Cork
1 Oct.	Clonmel
14 Oct.	Kilkenny
19 Oct.	Loughrea
21 Oct.	Waterford
No date	Ballina
9 Nov.	Carrick-on-Shannon
18 Nov.	Carlow
22/23 Nov.	Easky

37. John Wolffe, *The Protestant Crusade in Great Britain, 1829–1860* (Oxford 1991), p. 34.
38. *DEP*, 14 Sept. 1824.
39. *FJ*, 14 Sept. 1824.
40. *FJ*, 12 Oct. 1824.
41. *FJ*, 15 Oct. 1824.
42. *FJ*, 18 Oct. 1824.
43. *FJ*, 21 Oct. 1824.

44. *FJ*, 24 Oct. 1824.
45. For a full account of the Loughrea meeting by a Protestant sympathizer, see D'Arcy Sirr, *Trench*, pp. 466–71. Details of the proceedings and the motions adopted by the Catholic body are also documented in Hyde, *Raftery*, notes, pp. v–vii.
46. *FJ*, 27 Oct. 1824; 30 Oct. 1824.
47. Hyde, *Raftery*, p. 121.
48. *FJ*, 26 Oct. 1824.
49. *DEP*, 30 Oct. 1824; *FJ*, 1 Nov. 1824.
50. Killen, *Ecclesiastical History*, vol. II, p. 243. See also Bowen, *Protestant Crusade*, p. 104.
51. *DEP*, 6 Nov. 1824; *FJ*, 10 Nov. 1824.
52. *FJ*, 17 Nov. 1824.
53. *FJ*, 24 Nov. 1824.
54. Comerford, *Kildare and Leighlin*, vol. I, p. 132.
55. *DEP*, 24 Nov. 1824.
56. *Christian Observer* (Nov. 1824), 727.
57. Ibid.
58. For the careers of Robert McGhee and Mortimer O'Sullivan, see Bowen, *Protestant Crusade*, pp. 113–23.
59. The books that made Otway's reputation as a travel writer were his *Sketches in Ireland* (Dublin 1827); *Sketches in Erris and Tyrawley* (Dublin 1831); and *A Tour in Connaught, Comprising Sketches of Clonmacnoise, Joyce Country, and Achill* (Dublin 1839).
60. Sir Samuel Ferguson (1810–86), a Belfast-born poet, is chiefly remembered as a nationalist writer, and especially as the author of the patriotic 'Lament for Thomas Davis'. Isaac Butt (1813–79) was a native of County Donegal and is chiefly known as the founder of the Home Rule movement. Because they blended loyalty to the crown with a passionate interest in the literary and cultural heritage of Celtic Ireland, the circle to which Butt and Ferguson belonged in the 1830s and '40s was known as 'Orange Young Ireland'. Lady Gregory put it even more succinctly later in the century when she described Ferguson as a 'Fenian Unionist'. For a discussion of their place in the cultural history of the nineteenth century, see F.S.L. Lyons, *Culture and Anarchy in Ireland, 1890–1939* (Oxford 1979).
61. Benedict Kiely, *Poor Scholar: A Study of the Works and Days of William Carleton, 1794–1869* (Dublin 1972), p. 115.
62. *Ibid.* pp. 73–91.
63. Barbara Hayley, 'Irish periodicals from the Union to the *Nation*', *Anglo-Irish Studies*, II (1976), 88.
64. Quoted in *ibid.* p. 87.
65. John Jebb to Robert H. Inglis, 29 Nov. 1824, quoted in Reynolds, *Emancipation Crisis*, p. 81.
66. In 1825 Bishop Doyle urged his congregation 'to cast from you with horror or contempt all soothsayings, and divinations, and pretended prophecies: they are unworthy of a Christian people, and fit only to be classed with the ravings of itinerant biblemen, or with the productions of some tract society at which we laugh with scorn'. James Warren Doyle, *Pastoral Instructions for the Lent of 1825 Addressed to the Catholic Clergy of*

the *Dioceses of Kildare and Leighlin* (Carlow 1825), p. 19.
67. Quoted in Bowen, *Protestant Crusade*, p. 16.
68. McGrath, *Politics, Interdenominational Relations and Education*, pp. 121–5.
69. The *Dublin Evening Post* recorded that Doyle's letter on the union of the churches fell upon the public ear like the sound of a trumpet, 'coming from an ornament and pillar of the Catholic Church in Ireland, from a Prelate as distinguished for his piety as for his profound erudition—for his Christian humility as for the boldness and energy of his eloquence, it has already caused a sensation as general and as extraordinary as we ever recollect to have witnessed in Dublin'. *DEP,* 22 May 1824.
70. R.F.B. [Fergus] O'Ferrall, 'The growth of political consciousness in Ireland, 1823–47: A study of O'Connellite politics and political education' (unpublished PhD thesis, Trinity College Dublin 1978), pp. 381–401.
71. *DEP,* 28 Sept. 1824.
72. *DEP,* 30 Oct. 1824.
73. Lee and Stephen (eds), *Dictionary of National Biography*, vol. x, pp. 777–81.
74. Fergus O'Ferrall, 'The only lever …? The Catholic priest in Irish politics, 1823–29', *Studies*, LXX, 280 (1981), 308–24.
75. Reynolds, *Emancipation Crisis*, p. 17.
76. Thomas Lloyd to Francis Blackburn, 15 Dec. 1824. *Minutes of Evidence Taken before the Select Committee of the House of Lords Appointed to Inquire into the State of Ireland,* Parliamentary Papers (1825), XIV, 15.
77. James Tandy to Henry Goulburn, 9 Jan. 1825 (NAI/SPO 1825, 2731/1).
78. William Magee to John Jebb, 31 March 1824 (TCD, John Jebb Papers, MS 6396–7/184).
79. I am deeply indebted to Donnelly's 'Pastorini and Captain Rock' for much of this argument.
80. The tradition of the poet as wandering minstrel was still thriving in Connaught at this time. Raftery was not the only 'poet of the people' in the province. His contemporaries Michael MacSweeney of Connemara and Thomas Barret of the Erris peninsula in Mayo were at least as well known and, according to the older people who were Hyde's informants, were better poets than Raftery. All were transitional figures who composed in the traditional idiom but whose themes had to do with contemporary social and political happenings. Much of their work was lost with the decline of the language and the decay of the oral tradition. See Hyde, *Raftery*, p. 15, and Tomás Ó Máille, *Mícheál Mac Suibhne agus Filí an tSléibhe* (Michael Sweeney and the Poets of the Mountain) (Galway 1937).
81. Hyde, *Raftery*, p. 117.
82. *Ibid.* p. 313.
83. With reference to this stanza Hyde asserts that Raftery had in mind the schools of the National Board. This is by no means clear from the Irish text. Raftery died in 1834, only three years after the Board was established. It would appear more likely that he was referring to the schools of the evangelical societies. Hyde's translation of these verses is very loose, and he generally tends to play down the sectarian content, which comes across much more powerfully in the Irish version. For example, the line 'to train up the spy and informer' is used to convey what in the vernacular reads, 'you will betray your-

selves to the breed of Luther'. *Ibid.* p. 23.
84. *Ibid.* p. 115.
85. *Ibid.* p. 123.
86. An advertisement for books recently published by Dublin's chief purveyor of reading material for Catholics had included the *Bull of Leo XII Granting an Extension of the Universal Jubilee, Pastoral Instructions of Catholic Bishop*, the *Douay Bible, The Key of Heaven, The Imitation of Christ, The Poor Man's Catechism, Think Well On't* and *The Devout Life of St. Francis de Sales. DEP,* 25 Feb. 1826.
87. In his pastoral instructions for 1825, Bishop Doyle urged his congregation to purchase and read the religious material on faith and morals available from Richard Coyne of Capel Street, Dublin, or Mr Nolan and Mr Price in Carlow. He charged his clergy to collect money after Mass on Sunday for the purchase of such material, which was distributed to the children of the poor. Doyle, *Pastoral Instructions*, p. 20.
88. Reynolds, *Emancipation Crisis*, p. 67.
89. O'Ferrall, *Catholic Emancipation*, pp. 80–1.
90. For a discussion of the influence of Moore and Cobbett on public opinion in Ireland in 1824–5 see *ibid.* pp. 79–81.
91. McGrath, *Politics, Interdenominational Relations and Education*, pp. 185–7.
92. Doyle, *Letters on the State of Ireland*, p. 152.
93. Thomas Wall, 'Catholic periodicals of the past (2): The Catholic Book Society and the Irish Catholic Magazine', *Irish Ecclesiastical Record*, 5, CI (Jan.–June 1964), 290.
94. Quoted in *ibid.* 291.
95. *Ibid.* 289–95.
96. *Ibid.*
97. *Catholic Penny Magazine* (6 Sept. 1834), 332.
98. Noel, *Notes of a Short Tour*, pp. 22–7.
99. Hayley, 'Irish periodicals', 83.
100. *Ibid.* 101.
101. Thomas Wall, 'Catholic periodicals of the past (1): The *Catholic Penny Magazine*, 1834–5', *Irish Ecclesiastical Record*, 5, CI (Jan.–June 1964), 234–44.
102. *Catholic Penny Magazine* (14 March 1835), 128.
103. *Ibid.* (21 March 1835), 131.
104. Wall, 'Catholic Book Society', 298.
105. Wall, 'Catholic periodicals of the past (6): Duffy's *Irish Catholic Magazine*, 1847–8', *Irish Ecclesiastical Record*, 5, CII (July–Dec. 1964), 98.
106. Hayley, 'Irish periodicals', 93.
107. James Godkin, *The Religious History of Ireland*, pp. 237–8.
108. Bowen, *Protestant Crusade*, pp. 106–7.
109. Quoted in Thomas Wall, 'Catholic periodicals of the past (4): The *Catholic Luminary*, 1840–1,' *Irish Ecclesiastical Record*, 5, CII (July–Dec. 1964), 19.
110. Godkin, *Religious History of Ireland*, p. 239. For a more complete account of the debate, see Bowen, *Protestant Crusade*, p. 107.
111. D'Arcy Sirr, *Trench*, pp. 507–8.
112. *Ibid.* p. 512.

113. *Ibid.* p. 510.
114. Bowen, *Protestant Crusade*, p. 106.
115. Wall, 'Catholic Book Society', 301; D'Arcy Sirr, *Trench*, p. 512. For a complete account of the trial and its implications for denominational relations in the north Leitrim area see Proinnsíos Ó Duigneáin, *The Priest and the Protestant Woman: The Trial of Rev. Thomas Maguire, P.P., Dec. 1827* (Maynooth 1997).
116. *Catholic Penny Magazine* (21 March 1835), 152.
117. Quoted in Wall, 'Catholic Book Society', 301.
118. David Fitzpatrick, 'Class, family, and rural unrest in nineteenth-century Ireland' in P.J. Drudy (ed.), *Ireland: Land, Politics, and People* (Cambridge 1982), pp. 611–12.
119. *Christian Examiner* (June 1829), 442–3.
120. *Christian Examiner* (July 1827), 79; (Dec. 1827), 469.
121. McGrath, *Diaries of Humphrey O'Sullivan*, p. 331.
122. *Christian Examiner* (Dec. 1827), 435.
123. *DEP*, 30 Aug. 1825.
124. Arabella Graves to Dowager Countess Massereene, 25 Sept. 1827 (PRONI, Foster–Massereene Papers D.562/3148).
125. During the period of controversial sermons in Ballymahon, County Longford, in 1827, local Catholics were said to be claiming as converts from Protestantism those who had engaged in mixed marriages, a practice 'so common for many years past and so instrumental to apostasy among the Protestant population'. *Christian Examiner* (July 1827), 79.
126. The career and background of Margaret Anna Cusack are treated at length in a biography by Irene ffrench Eager, *Margaret Anna Cusack: A Biography* (Dublin 1979).
127. No Catholic religious order contributed more, either at home or abroad, to the campaign to save the Catholic poor from falling into the hands of evangelical missionaries than the Mercy Order founded by Catherine McAuley in 1831. By the second half of the nineteenth century its convents and orphanages had spread all over Ireland, Britain, the United States, Canada and Australia. For an account of Catherine McAuley's background and the early years of the Mercy Order see Mary C. Sullivan, *Catherine McAuley and the Tradition of Mercy* (Notre Dame 2000).

Seven: New Directions, 1828–40

1. *The Watchman*, 3 Feb. 1827.
2. M.G. Beresford to Lord Farnham, 9 July 1834 (NLI, Farnham Papers, MS 18,608/10).
3. *Dublin University Magazine* (Oct. 1833).
4. Bartlett, *Irish Nation*, pp. 333–42.
5. Hereward Senior, *Orangeism in Ireland and Britain, 1795–1836* (London 1966), pp. 227–30.
6. Bartlett, *Irish Nation*, p. 342.
7. McGrath, *Politics, Interdenominational Relations and Education*, pp. 152.
8. Hans Hamilton to Lord Farnham, 29 March 1831 (NLI, Farnham Papers, MS 18,612/10); Notebook of Henry Maxwell (NLI, Farnham Papers, MS 3504).
9. Akenson, *Irish Education Experiment*, p. 91.

10. *First Report of the Commissioners of Irish Education Inquiry* (1825), 400, XII, p. 90.
11. *Ibid.* p. 2.
12. Connolly, *Priests and People*, p. 86.
13. *Annual Report of the Hibernian Bible Society* (1831), p. XL.
14. *Annual Report of the Hibernian Bible Society* (1832), appendix III.
15. Noel, *Notes of a Short Tour*, pp. 221–3.
16. D'Arcy Sirr, *Trench*, pp. 2–3.
17. Michael Davitt, *The Fall of Feudalism in Ireland, or the Story of the Land League Revolution* (London and New York 1904), pp. 31–2.
18. A complete account of the Trench family is provided in *A Memoir of the Trench Family, Compiled by Thomas Richard Frederick Cooke-Trench* (Dublin 1896).
19. Bowen, *Protestant Crusade,* pp. 138–9.
20. D'Arcy Sirr, *Trench*, pp. 17–18.
21. *Ibid.* pp. 28–38.
22. *Ibid.* pp. 45–6.
23. Quoted in *ibid.* pp. 46–7.
24. Quoted in *ibid.*
25. Quoted in *ibid.* p. 79.
26. Motherwell, *Albert Blest*, p. 112.
27. Quoted in *ibid.* pp. 82–4.
28. Quoted in *ibid.* p. 92.
29. As early as 1811 Trench had openly sanctioned cooperation with the Dissenters, and he and Archdeacon Digby had since that time enjoyed warm relations with Albert Blest and the LHS. In 1818 the Society printed a circular to refute claims made in the *Christian Guardian* that it was a bigoted organization patronized mainly by Dissenters. (SOAS/MMSA, Methodist Papers [Ireland] box 74, file 2, no. 105).
30. According to S.J. Connolly, the number of Catholics per priest in the Tuam archdiocese in 1834–5 was 4199, compared with 1941 in the more prosperous diocese of Ferns. Poverty and population growth were the main barriers to improvement in Connaught; 'the rate of population growth was faster than in other regions, while at the same time a largely impoverished population were unable to support even the same inadequate rise in clerical numbers which was achieved elsewhere'. Connolly, *Priests and People*, p. 35.
31. Quoted in D'Arcy Sirr, *Trench*, p. 144.
32. *Ibid.* p. 149.
33. Once the threat of famine had passed, much of the money collected by the London Tavern Committee was used to purchase looms and spinning wheels for the peasantry of the west in an attempt to foster the linen industry. What little progress was initially achieved was quickly negated by the dissolution of the Linen Board and the collapse of the domestic linen industry because of the introduction of mechanization. *Ibid.* pp. 151–64.
34. Quoted in D'Arcy Sirr, *Trench*, pp. 152–3.
35. *Ibid.* p. 146.
36. *Ibid.* p. 147.
37. *DEP,* 27 Oct. 1824.
38. Quoted in D'Arcy Sirr, *Trench*, p. 132.

39. Quoted in *ibid.* p. 133.
40. The Rev. Stoney's trials in the Newport area began when he established schools and actively sought the conversion of local Catholics. In addition to the usual denunciations from the altar, he was also the recipient of threatening notices commonly associated with the Whiteboys. An example provided in the Trench biography gives some indication of how he was regarded by at least one belligerent but imaginative representative of the local Catholic community: 'May the devil pull the tongue from root and branch out of your ugly mug. We will leave the devil to punish hypocrite Stoney—amen. Have a care of yourself, or by hell, we will coffin you. You are not fit to be a clergyman over a regiment of monkeys. You are a devil in the shape of a man—all that is wanting is a pair of horns and a tail ... Bad luck to you, Stoney; I am afraid all your prayers won't keep you from hell's fires, when the devil will be laughing with joy to get his brother Stoney, you hypocrite, rascal, scoundrel, swaddler ... We all shakes in our skins when we meet you, you d—d rascal; and I ask you, who wouldn't when they would meet the devil?" Quoted in *ibid.* p. 207.
41. Because of its isolation Connemara became a refuge for Catholics and Protestants fleeing the troubles in the north and later the dragooning of Mayo in 1798. It was notorious as a haven for smugglers because of its indented shoreline and freedom from the forces of law and order. When asked if the King's writ ran in Connemara, Richard Martin was said to have given the reply, 'Egad it does, as fast as any greyhound, if any of my good fellows are after it.' Patricia Kilroy, *The Story of Connemara* (Dublin 1989), p. 71.
42. *Ibid.* pp. 62–76. For an account of the rise of a new elite in the Celtic fringe based on an influx of new money and well-connected matrimonial alliances, see Colley, *Britons*, pp. 158–64.
43. *Ibid.* p. 78; see in particular *Letters from the Irish Highlands of Connemara* for the views of Henry Blake and his wife on Connemara as a tourist venue.
44. For the career of Richard Martin see Shevawn Lynam, *Humanity Dick Martin: 'King of Connemara', 1754–1834* (Dublin 1989); Peter Philips, *Humanity Dick: The Eccentric Member for Galway. The Story of Richard Martin, Animal Rights Pioneer 1754–1834* (Tunbridge Wells, Kent 2003).
45. Kathleen Villiers-Tuthill, *History of Clifden, 1810–1850* (Galway 1981), pp. 11–13.
46. *DEP*, 29 April 1824.
47. Quoted in D'Arcy Sirr, *Trench*, pp. 112.
48. Many Ulster Catholics fled to the western counties in 1796 and 1797. The estate of Lord Altamont, which extended over a vast area of western Mayo between Westport and Louisburgh, was a particular haven for these refugees. Their homeless and destitute condition was a source of grave concern to Lord Altamont, who feared that they would be driven to plunder on this account. W.E.H. Lecky, *A History of Ireland in the Eighteenth Century*, vol. IV (London 1892), p. 140.
49. D'Arcy Sirr, *Trench*, p. 630–6.
50. *Ibid.* pp. 637.
51. *Ibid.* p. 641.
52. *Ibid.* p. 639.
53. Irene Whelan, 'The stigma of souperism' in Cathal Poirteir (ed.), *The Great Irish*

Famine (Thomas Davis Lecture Series, Cork 1995), pp. 135–54; Bowen, *Protestant Crusade*, pp. 215–18.
54. D'Arcy Sirr, *Trench*, p. 645.
55. *Ibid.* p. 643.
56. Lord Farnham's agent, W.H. Krause, for example, in a letter to his sister in 1832, expressed his conviction that the wrath of God had fallen on the Protestants of Ireland because 'popery [is] cherished and encouraged by the rulers of the land' and 'Protestants are emigrating in hundreds, feeling that they have no protection from the government, and that they are not allowed to protect themselves'. Stanford, *Krause*, p. 175.
57. *Dublin University Magazine* (March 1833), 266; (May 1833), 30.
58. *Address and Prospectus of the Protestant Colonisation Society from the Meeting of December 18th, 1829*.
59. *Ibid.*
60. *Dublin University Magazine* (26 Nov. 1829).
61. *Protestant Colonisation Society of Ireland: Transactions ... at a Public Meeting of Subscribers* (Dublin 1832), p. 2.
62. No records beyond the first prospectuses of 1829 and 1832 exist.
63. *DEP*, 26 Jan. 1839. For an account of the Brunswick Clubs see Machin, *Emancipation Crisis*, p. 151.
64. *Protestant Colonisation Society of Ireland: Transactions ... at a Public Meeting of Subscribers* (Dublin 1832), p. 12.
65. *Ibid.* p. 25.
66. *Ibid.* p. 6.
67. J.G. MacWalter, *The Irish Reformation Movement in Its Religious, Social, and Political Aspects* (Dublin 1852), p. 70.
68. Anthony John Preston to Lord Farnham, 30 Nov. 1835 (NLI, Farnham Papers, MS 18,612/27).
69. Acheson, 'Evangelicals', p. 35.
70. Ensor, *New Reformation*, p. 21.
71. *The Watchman*, 25 Nov.; 2 Dec. 1826.
72. Acheson, 'Evangelicals', p. 194.
73. D.P. Thompson, *A Brief Account of the Rise and Progress of the Change in Religious Opinion Now Taking Place in Dingle and the West of the County of Kerry* (Dublin 1846), pp. 7–8.
74. John Jebb to Charles Forster, 17 Nov. 1830 (TCD, John Jebb Papers, MS 6392/22).
75. *Ibid.*
76. *Ibid.* Further details of the life of the Rev. John Goodman of Dingle may be found in Breathnach, 'Séamus Goodman', 154.
77. John Jebb to Charles Forster, 17 Nov. 1830 (TCD, John Jebb Papers, MS 6392/22). According to the official chronicler of the Dingle Mission, the Rev. Gubbins came to the Dingle area in the first instance to assist in famine relief. There is no mention of the involvement of Bishop Jebb in the affair. Thompson, *Brief Account*, pp. 7–9.
78. *Ibid.* p. 69.
79. *Ibid.* p. 10.
80. An account of Charles Gayer's family background and career in Ireland is provided by

Arthur Edward Gayer, *Memoirs of the Family of Gayer* (privately printed, London 1870).
81. Thompson, *Brief Account*, pp. 38–40; Bowen, *Souperism*, pp. 83–4.
82. Thompson, *Brief Account*, p. 29.
83. *Ibid.* pp. 45–6.
84. *Ibid.* p. 27.
85. *Ibid.* pp. 140–4.
86. *Ibid.* p. 36; Bowen, *Souperism*, p. 84.
87. *Ibid.* p. 149.
88. *Ibid.* p. 151.
89. *Ibid.* pp. 85–6.
90. *Ibid.* p. 84.
91. *Ibid.* p. 175.
92. Asenath Nicholson, *Ireland's Welcome to the Stranger, or an Excursion through Ireland in 1844 and 1845 for the Purpose of Personally Investigating the Condition of the Poor* (New York 1847), p. 368.
93. *Ibid.* pp. 369–72.
94. Bowen, *Souperism*, p. 88.
95. Interview with Nuala Ní Dhomhnaill, poet and native of Ventry, County Kerry; Greenwich, Connecticut, 28 Feb. 1993.
96. Henry Wilberforce, *Proselytism in Ireland: The Catholic Defence Association vs. the Irish Church Missions on the Charge of Bribery and Intimidation: A Correspondence between the Rev. A.R.C. Dallas and the Rev. Henry Wilberforce* (London 1852), p. 21.
97. Henry William Wilberforce (1807–73) was the youngest son of William Wilberforce, the famous philanthropist. He had a brilliant career as an undergraduate at Oxford, where he became closely associated with John Henry Newman. Like Newman, he was ordained a clergyman in the Church of England, became involved in the Tractarian movement, and eventually became a Catholic in 1850. In 1852 he became secretary of the Catholic Defence Association, a Dublin organization established to counter the work of Alexander Dallas and the Irish Church Missions and to defend the Catholic cause during the height of the 'No Popery' controversy of the early 1850s. Between 1854 and 1863 he edited the London-based *Catholic Standard*. He spent much of his time in the 1850s in Ireland. He died in Gloucestershire in 1873 and was buried in the Dominican Friary at Woodchester. David Newsome, *The Wilberforces and Henry Manning: The Parting of Friends* (Cambridge, Massachussets 1966), pp. 404–5.
98. Wilberforce, *Proselytism in Ireland*, p. 41.
99. *FJ*, 22 June 1852.
100. Otway, *Tour in Connaught*, pp. 426–7.
101. In an account of the Irish Society's schools in Kingscourt that the Rev. Winning submitted to the *Christian Examiner* in October 1828, it is clear that the Society was already thinking in terms of territorial expansion and expected eventually to extend its system from the Irish Sea to the Atlantic. *Christian Examiner* (Oct. 1828), 306.
102. D'Arcy Sirr, *Trench*, pp. 556–61.
103. Alfred Clayton Thiselton, *A Memorial Sketch of the Life and Labours of Mrs. Henrietta Pendleton, Forty Years Secretary of the Irish Islands and Coasts Society* (Dublin 1895), p. 7.

104. *Ibid.* p. 16.
105. *Ibid.* p. 21.
106. D'Arcy Sirr, *Trench*, p. 598. *Historical Sketches of the Native Irish* was the second of Christopher Anderson's studies of Ireland. One of the outstanding features of the book was its emphasis on the islands and coasts of the west as areas where the English language had made very little impact. Besides stressing the usefulness of Irish in promoting the Protestant religion, Anderson insisted that the national interest would be greatly served by halting its decline, and even suggested the establishment of a model school in Dublin where children could be educated exclusively in Irish.
107. *Seventeenth Annual Report of the Baptist Society for Promoting the Gospel in Ireland* (1831), appendix, p. 48.
108. The Irish Society's report of 1833 mentioned the Achill project as an admirable example of a growing concern to evangelize the inhabitants of the western islands. It also made it clear that it had originated from sources other than the Society. *Fifteenth Report of the Irish Society* (1833), p. 16.
109. *Quarterly Extract of the Irish Society*, 42 (Dublin, 1832), 242–4.
110. Henry Seddall, *Edward Nangle, the Apostle of Achill: A Memoir and A History With an Introduction by the Most Rev. William Conyngham Plunket* (London 1884), pp. 54–62.
111. For a complete account of the Achill Mission, see Irene Whelan, 'Edward Nangle and the Achill Mission, 1834–52' in Raymond Gillespie and Gerard Moran (eds), *A Various Country: Essays in Mayo History, 1500–1900* (Westport 1987), pp. 113–34.
112. Samuel Carter Hall, *Mr S.C. Hall and the Achill Mission: Correspondence between S.C. Hall and Edward Nangle* (Dublin 1844), p. 12.
113. James Johnson, *A Tour in Ireland With Meditations and Reflections* (London 1844), p. 239.
114. Otway, *Tour in Connaught*, p. 413.
115. Nicholson, *Ireland's Welcome*, p. 443.

Conclusion

1. Colley, *Britons*, pp. 11–54.
2. Gertrude Himmelfarb, *On Looking Into the Abyss: Untimely Thoughts on Culture and Society* (New York 1994), pp. 112–3.

Appendix A

1. NLI, Brodrick Papers, MS 8866/1.

Appendix B

1. Quoted in Fitzpatrick, *Doyle*, vol. II, pp. 22–3.

BIBLIOGRAPHY

I. PRIMARY SOURCES
    A. MANUSCRIPTS
    B. NEWSPAPERS AND PERIODICALS
    C. PRINTED SOURCES
    D. PAMPHLETS

II. SECONDARY SOURCES
    A. BOOKS
        1. EIGHTEENTH AND NINETEENTH CENTURY
        2. TWENTIETH CENTURY
    B. ARTICLES
    C. UNPUBLISHED THESES
    D. BIBLIOGRAPHICAL SOURCES

Bibliography

1. Primary Sources

A. MANUSCRIPTS

Westminster College, Cambridge
  The Cheshunt Foundation Papers

Church of Ireland College of Education, Dublin (CICE)
  Kildare Place Society Archives (KPSA)

Dublin Diocesan Archives (DDA)
  Troy-Murray Papers, 1812–23
  Murray Papers, 1823–42

National Archives of Ireland, Dublin (NAI)
  Calendar of Official Papers [Education], 1802; 1810–31
  State of the Country Papers, 1821–31 (SCP)

National Library of Ireland, Dublin (NLI)
  Charles King O'Hara Papers
  Farnham Papers
  Diary of John David La Touche, 1799–1800
  Diary of Lady Anne Jocelyn
  Notebook of Henry Maxwell
  Dr Michael Quane Papers
  Brodrick Papers

Public Record Office of Northern Ireland, Belfast (PRONI)
  Annesley Papers
  Beresford Papers
  Johnston of Kilmore Papers
  Redesdale Papers
  Roden Papers
  Rosse Papers
  Foster Massereene Papers

Representative Church Body, Dublin (RCB)
  Records and Annual Reports of the Sunday School Society for Ireland (1809–1971)
  Proceedings of the Association for Discountenancing Vice and Promoting the Practice of Virtue and Religion

School of Oriental and African Studies, London (SOAS)
  Methodist Missionary Society Archives (MMSA), Methodist Papers (Ireland) boxes 74 and 75

321

Bibliography

Trinity College Dublin (TCD)
>John Jebb Papers
>Annual Reports of the Irish Society for Promoting the Education of the Native Irish through the Medium of Their Own Language
>Irish Society Proceedings, 1818–32
>La Touche–Synge Correspondence, 1808–10
>Francis Kinkead Papers

Zentralbibliothek, Zurich
>Pestalozzi Papers

B. NEWSPAPERS AND PERIODICALS
Blackwood's Magazine
The British Critic and Theological Quarterly
The Catholic Penny Magazine
Christian Examiner and Church of Ireland Magazine
Christian Observer
Dublin Evening Post (DEP)
Dublin University Magazine
Edinburgh Review
Fraser's Magazine
Freeman's Journal (FJ)
The Patriot
The Quarterly Review
The Watchman

C. PRINTED SOURCES
Annual Reports of the Baptist Society for the Promotion of the Gospel in Ireland
Annual Reports of the Hibernian Bible Society
Annual Reports of the Irish Society (Ireland)
Annual Reports of the Irish Society (London)
Annual Reports of the London Hibernian Society
Annual Reports of the Society for Promoting the Education of the Poor in Ireland (Kildare Place Society)
Annual Reports of the Sunday School Society for Ireland
Quarterly Extracts of Correspondence of the Irish Society (Ireland)

Parliamentary Papers
First Report of the Commissioners of Irish Education Inquiry (1825) 400, XII.
Minutes of Evidence Taken before the Select Committee of the House of Lords Appointed to Inquire into the State of Ireland, H.C. 1825 (181), IX, 1.
Hansard's Parliamentary Debates, 2nd ser., vol. XVII (1826–7).

Bibliography

D. PAMPHLETS

Anon. *An Account of the Institution and Proceedings of the Society for Promoting Christian Knowledge and Practice for Aiding and Assisting Sunday Schools i n the Kingdom of Ireland* (Dublin 1788).

Anon. *A Brief Account of the Work of the (Irish) Society During the Past Fifty Years, Extracted from the Annual Report of the Society's Proceedings from the year ending 25 March, 1868* (Dublin 1868).

Anon. *Address of A Christian Philosopher to the Hibernian Society in London for the Diffusion of Religious Knowledge in Ireland* (Dublin 1806).

Anon. *An Address to the British Public on the Moral and Religious State of Ireland* (London 1805).

Anon. *An Address to the Proprietors of Irish Estates Residing in Great Britain* (Dublin 1800).

Anon. *An Account of the Institution and Proceedings of the Society for Promoting Christian Knowledge and Practice and for Aiding and Assisting Sunday Schools in the Kingdom of Ireland* (Dublin 1788).

Anon. *Hints for the Formation and Conducting of Auxiliary Societies and Associations of the Hibernian Bible Society* (Dublin n.d).

Anon. *Hints on the Means of Forming a Plan for Advancing Religious Education, Addressed to the Members of the Association for Discountenancing Vice and Promoting the Practice of Religion and Virtue* (Dublin 1788).

Anon. *The Monstrosities of Methodism: Being an Impartial Examination into the Pretension of our Modern Sectaries, to Prophetic Inspiration, Providential Interferences, and Spiritual Impulse. With a preliminary notice of Dr Walker's New Sect, and the Disputing Society in Stafford Street. By a Curate of the Church of England* (Dublin 1808).

Anon. *Observations on the Consequences of the Excessive Use of Spirituous Liquors and the Ruinous Policy of Permitting Distillation in this Country* (Dublin 1788).

Anon. *Report of the Committee of Education, Appointed by the Association for Discountenancing Vice and Promoting the Knowledge and Practice of the Christian Religion* (Dublin 1803).

Anon. *Two Reports of the Committee of Education, Appointed by the Association for Discountenancing Vice and Promoting Religion and Virtue, on the Dioceses of Clogher and Kilmore* (Dublin 1800).

Carey, William. *An enquiry into the obligations of Christians to use means for the conversion of the heathen* (London 1792).

Carolan, Patrick. *An Essay on the Present State of Schools in Ireland* (Dublin 1806).

Cleland, John. *The Way to Things by Words* (London 1766).

Curtis, Patrick. *Two Letters Respecting the Horrible Act of Placing a Calf's Head on the Altar of the Chapel of Ardee, and also His Answer to the Protestant Archbishop Magee's Charge Against the Roman Catholic Religion* (Dublin 1822).

Daly, Robert. *A Sermon Preached at St. Anne's Church in Aid of the Funds of the Sunday Schools Society for Ireland, on Sunday the 28th of February 1819* (Dublin 1819).

—. *A Sermon Preached at St. Anne's Church, Dublin on Sunday, the 27th of May, 1821, in Aid of the Irish Society* (Dublin 1821).

Dill, Edward. *The Mystery Solved: Or, Ireland's Miseries, the Grand Cause and Cure* (New York 1852).

Doyle, James Warren. *A Vindication of the Religious and Civil Principles of the Irish Catholics in a letter addressed to His Excellency the Marquis Wellesley, K.G.*, 2nd edn (Dublin 1823).
—. *J.K.L.'s Letter to the Rt. Hon. Lord Farnham* (Dublin 1827).
—. *Letters on a Reunion of the Church of England and Rome* (Dublin 1824).
—. *Letters on the State of Ireland: Addressed by JKL to a Friend in England* (Dublin 1825).
—. *Pastoral Instructions for the Lent of 1825 Addressed to the Catholic Clergy of the Dioceses of Kildare and Leighlin* (Carlow 1825).
—. *A Vindication of the Religious and Civil Principles of the Irish Catholics in a Letter Addressed to the Marquis Wellesley by J.K.L.* (Dublin 1823).
Duigenan, Patrick [Theophilus]. *An Address to the Nobility and Gentry of the Church of Ireland as by law established. Explaining the real causes of the commotions and insurrections in the southern parts of the Kingdom respecting tithes* (Dublin 1787).
Duigenan, Patrick. *A Fair Representation of the Present Political State of Ireland* (Dublin 1800).
Ensor, George. *A Defence of the Irish and the Means of Their Redemption* (Dublin 1825).
—. *The New Reformation: Letters Showing the Inutility and Exhibiting the Absurdity of What Is Rather Fantastically Termed 'The New Reformation'* (Dublin 1828).
Harpur, Singleton Rev. *A Sermon against the Excessive Use of Spiritous Liquors* (Dublin 1788).
—. *Observations on the Pernicious Consequences of the Excessive Use of Spirituous Liquors and the Ruinous Policy of Permitting Distillation in this Country* (Dublin 1788).
Jackson, James Edward. *Reasons for Withdrawing from the Hibernian Bible Society, Founded on the Public Documents of That Institution* (Dublin 1822).
Jebb, John, D.D. *A Charge Delivered to the Clergy of the Diocese of Limerick at the Primary Visitation in the Cathedral Church of St. Mary on Thursday, the 19th of June, 1823* (Dublin 1823).
Joyce, Mathias. *A Short Account of the Late Mr. Mathias Joyce, Preacher of the Gospel for Thirty Years in Ireland. Written by Himself* (Dublin 1808).
Knox, Alexander. *Essays on the Political Circumstances of Ireland Written during the Administration of Earl Camden, with an Appendix Containing Thoughts on the Will of the People and a Postscript Now First Published* (Dublin 1799).
Logan, Robert, D.D. and Rev. Robert Winning. *Correspondence between the Rev. Dr. Logan, Roman Catholic Bishop of Meath and the Rev. Robert Winning ... with the Resolutions of one hundred and twenty-five Teachers therein* (Dublin 1827).
McGhee, Robert J. *The Bible, the Rights of Conscience, and the Established Church Vindicated. Being an Answer to the Rev. William Phelan, F.T.C.D.* (Dublin 1817).
—. *Truth and Error Contrasted* (Dublin 1828).
MacHale, John. *Letters of 'Hierophilus' to the English People on the Moral and Political State of Ireland, Demonstrating the Inefficacy Hitherto Applied through the Means of Bible Societies* (London 1822).
Magee, William. *A Charge Delivered at his Primary Visitation in St Patrick's Cathedral, Dublin, on Thursday the 24th of October, 1822* (Dublin 1822).
—. *The Evidence of His Grace, the Archbishop of Dublin, before the Select Committee of the House of Lords on the State of Ireland* (Dublin 1825).
Malcolme, Rev. David. *Letters, Essays and Other Tracts Illustrating the Antiquities of Great Britain and Ireland* (London 1744).
Nangle, Edward. *The Ancient Catholic Faith Defended against Romish Novelties, Being a Reply*

to a Pamphlet Entitled 'Imposture Exposed' and a *Letter Addressed to the Inhabitants of Achill by the Rev. John Keaveney, R.C. Priest* (Dublin 1834).

—. *The Gospel Lever Applied to the Overturning of Romanism (in Six Discourses)* (London 1837).

—. *The Achill Mission and the Present State of Protestantism in Ireland, Being the State of the Rev. E. Nangle at a Meeting of the Protestant Association in Exeter Hall, Dec. 28th, 1838* (London 1839).

O'Beirne, Thomas Lewis. *Circular Letter of the Lord Bishop of Meath to the Rural Deans of his Diocese* (Dublin 1821).

O'Callaghan, Andrew. *Thoughts on the Tendencies of Bible Societies as Affecting the Established Church and Christianity Itself as a 'Reasonable Service'* (Dublin 1816).

O'Sullivan, Mortimer. *Captain Rock Detected, or the Origin and Character of the Recent Disturbances and the Condition of the South and West of Ireland Considered and Exposed* (Dublin and Edinburgh 1824).

—. *A Guide to an Irish Gentleman in His Search for a Religion* (Dublin 1833).

Orpen, Charles Edward. *The Claims of Millions of Our Fellow Countrymen to Be Taught in Their Own and Only Language—the Irish* (Dublin 1821).

Otway, Caesar. *A Lecture on Miracles* (Dublin 1823).

—. *Sketches in Ireland* (Dublin 1827).

—. *Sketches in Erris and Tyrawley* (Dublin 1831).

—. *A Tour in Connaught, Comprising Sketches of Clonmacnoise, Joyce Country, and Achill* (Dublin 1839).

Parnell, William. *An Historical Apology for the Irish Catholics* (Dublin 1807).

Phelan, William. *The Bible, not the Bible Society: Being an attempt to point out that mode of disseminating the Scriptures, which would most effectively conduce to the security of the Established Church and the peace of the United Kingdom* (Dublin 1817).

—. *Evidence of the Rev. William Phelan, B.D, on the State of Ireland, 1825, before the Select Committee of the House of Lords* (Dublin 1825).

Pope Leo XII. *The Encyclical Letter of Pope Leo the XII to his venerable brethren, the patriarchs, primates, archbishops, and bishops of the Catholic Church with an English translation of the same. To which are annexed Pastoral Instructions for the R.C. archbishops and bishops, to the clergy and laity of their communion throughout Ireland* (Dublin 1824).

Protestant Colonisation Society of Ireland: Transactions ... at a Public Meeting of Subscribers (Dublin 1832).

Richardson, John. *A Proposal for the Conversion of the Popish Natives of Ireland to the Established Religion, with the Reasons upon Which It Is Grounded and an Answer to the Objections Made to It* (London 1712).

Sankey, William. *A Brief Sketch of the Various Attempts Which Have Been Made to Diffuse a Knowledge of the Holy Scriptures through the Medium of the Irish Language* (Dublin 1818).

Stokes, Whitley. *Projects for Establishing Internal Peace* (Dublin 1799).

Thorpe, William. *An Address to the Protestants of Great Britain and Ireland on the Subject of Catholic Emancipation, Presenting Facts and Documents Illustrative of the Real Object of the Irish Roman Catholic Leaders* (London 1814).

Trant, Dominic. *Considerations on the Present Disturbances in the Province of Munster, Their Causes, Extent, Probable Consequences, and Remedies* (Dublin 1787).

Bibliography

Vallancey, Charles. *An Essay on the Celtic Language: Showing the Importance of the Iberno-Celtic, or Irish Dialect, to Students in History, Antiquity, and the Greek and Roman Classics* (London 1782).

Woodward, Richard. *The Present State of the Church of Ireland, Containing a Description of Its Precarious Situation and the Consequent Danger to the Public, Recommended to the Serious Consideration of the Friends of the Protestant Interest, to which are Subjoined Some Reflections on the Impractability of a Proper Commutation for Tithes and a General Account of the Origin and Progress of the Insurrection in Munster* (Dublin 1787).

II. Secondary Sources

AI. BOOKS: EIGHTEENTH AND NINETEENTH CENTURY

Anderson, Christopher. *Memorial on Behalf of the Native Irish with a View to Their Improvement in Moral and Religious Knowledge through the Medium of Their Own Language* (London 1815).

—. *Historical Sketches of the Native Irish and Their Descendents, Illustrative of Their Past and Present State with Regard to Literature, Education, and Oral Instruction* (1828; Edinburgh 1830).

Andrews, Thomas. *The Church in Ireland: A Second Chapter of Contemporary History* (London 1869).

Barrow, John. *A Tour through Ireland Around the Sea-Coast Counties in the Autumn of 1833* (London 1836).

Belcher, Joseph. *The Baptist Irish Society: Its Origin, History and Prospects* (London 1845).

Brenan, Rev. M.J. *An Ecclesiastical History of Ireland from the Period of the English Invasion to the Year 1829* (Dublin 1845).

Brooke, Charlotte. *Reliques of Irish Poetry* (1789; Gainesville, Florida 1970).

Burdy, Samuel. *The Life of Philip Skelton* (1792; Oxford 1914).

Canton, William. *A History of the British and Foreign Bible Society* (London 1804).

Cobbett, William. *A history of the Protestant 'Reformation' in England and Ireland showing how that event has impoverished and degraded the main body of the people, in a series of letters* (London 1824).

Comerford, M. *Collections on the Diocese of Kildare and Leighlin*, 3 vols (Dublin 1883–6).

Cooke-Trench, Thomas Richard Frederick. *A Memoir of the Trench Family Compiled by Thomas Richard Fredrick Cooke-Trench* (privately printed, Dublin 1896).

Crookshank, C.H. *History of Methodism in Ireland*, 3 vols (London 1885–8).

Crowe Evans, Eyre. *Today in Ireland* (1825; New York and London 1979).

Curry, John. *Historical Memoirs of the Irish Rebellion in the Year 1641; Extracted from Parliamentary Journals, State Acts, and the Most Eminent Protestant Historians* (London 1758).

D'Alton, John. *The History of Ireland, from the earliest period to the year 1245, when The Annals of Boyle, which are adopted as the running text authority, terminate*, 2 vols (Dublin 1845).

Dewar, Daniel. *Observations on the Character, Customs and Superstitions of the Irish and on Some of the Causes Which Have Retarded the Moral and Political Improvement of Ireland* (London 1812).

Bibliography

Dill, Edward Marcus. *The Mystery Solved: Or Ireland's Miseries, the Grand Cause and Cure* (New York 1852).

Fitzpatrick, W.J. *The Life, Times, and Correspondence of the Right Rev. Dr Doyle, Bishop of Kildare and Leighlin*, 2 vols (Dublin 1861; 1890).

Forster, John Charles. *The Life of John Jebb, D.D., Bishop of Limerick, Ardfert, and Aghadoe*, 2nd edn (London 1845).

Gayer, Arthur Edward. *Memoirs of the Family of Gayer* (privately printed, London 1870).

Godkin, James. *Education in Ireland: Its History, Institutions, Systems, Statistics, and Progress from the Earliest Times to the Present* (London 1862).

—. *Ireland and Her Churches* (London 1867).

—. *The Religious History of Ireland, Primitive, Papal and Protestant, Including the Evangelical Missions, Catholic Agitations, and Church Progress of the Last Half-Century* (London 1873).

Goldsmith, Oliver. *She Stoops to Conquer* (1773; Oxford 1912).

Gregg, Robert Samuel. *Faithful Unto Death: Memorials of the Life of John Gregg, D.D., Bishop of Cork, Cloyne, and Ross, by His Son* (Dublin 1879).

Haldane, Alexander. *The Lives of Robert Haldane of Airthrey, and his brother, James Alexander Haldane* (Edinburgh 1855).

Hall, Samuel Carter. *Mr. S.C. Hall and the Achill Mission: Correspondence between S.C. Hall and Edward Nangle* (Dublin 1844).

Hamilton, Rev. Thomas. *History of the Irish Presbyterian Church* (Edinburgh 1887).

Harty, William. *The Failure of the Reformation in Ireland. Its True Causes Developed in a Petition Addressed to the House of Lords by a Protestant Layman* (Dublin 1837).

—. *An Historic Sketch of the Causes, Progress, Extent and Mortality of the Contagious Fever Epidemic in Ireland during the Years 1817, 1818, and 1819 with Numerous Tables, Official Documnets and Private Communications, Illustrative of Its General History and of the System of Management Adopted for Its Suppression* (Dublin 1820).

Inglis, Henry David. *A Journey Through Ireland During the Spring, Summer, and Autumn of 1834*, 2 vols, 3rd edn (London 1835).

Irwin, C.H. *Famous Irish Preachers* (Dublin 1889).

Johnson, James. *A Tour in Ireland with Meditations and Reflections* (London 1844).

Jones, William. *The Jubilee Memorial of the Religious Tract Society, Containing a Record of Its Origins, Proceedings, and Results* (London 1850).

Kenney, A.H. *Memoir of the Late Right Reverend William Magee, Archbishop of Dublin*, 2 vols (Dublin 1842).

Killen, W.D. *The Ecclesiastical History of Ireland from the Earliest Period to the Present Times*, 3 vols (London 1875).

Law, William. *Serious Call to a Devout and Holy Life* (n.p. 1728).

Lawless, Valentine Browne. *Personal Recollections of the Life and Times of Valentine, Lord Cloncurry* (Dublin 1869).

Lecky, W.E.H. *A History of Ireland in the Eighteenth Century*, 5 vols (London 1892).

Ledwich, Edward. *Antiquities of Ireland* (Dublin 1790).

Le Fanu, Emma. *The Life of the Rev. Charles Edward Herbert Orpen MD* (London 1860).

Le Fanu, Sheridan. *Seventy Years of Irish Life, Being Anecdotes and Reminiscences* (New York 1893).

Lefroy, Thomas. *Memoir of Chief Justice Thomas Lefroy, By His Son* (Dublin 1871).

Letters from the Irish Highlands of Connemara. By the Blake Family of Renvyle House (1823/4) (London 1825; Clifden 1995).

McCullough, William Torrens. *Memoirs of the Right Richard Lalor Sheil*, 2 vols (London 1855).

MacHale, John. *The Letters of the Most Rev. John MacHale, D.D.* (Dublin 1888).

MacWalter, J.G. *The Irish Reformation Movement in Its Religious, Social, and Political Aspects* (Dublin 1852).

Madden, Samuel. *Memoir of the Life of the Late Rev. Peter Roe* (Dublin 1842).

Magee, William. *The Works of William Magee, Archbishop of Dublin*, 2 vols (London 1842).

Malcolme, Rev. David. *Letters, Essays, and Other Tracts Illustrating the Antiquities of Great Britain and Ireland* (London 1744).

Mant, Richard. *History of the Church of Ireland*, 2 vols (London 1840).

Mason, H.J. Monck. *History of the Origin and Progress of the Irish Society* (Dublin 1846).

Moore, Thomas. *Memoirs of Captain Rock, the Celebrated Irish Chieftain; with some Account of His Ancestors, Written by Himself* (London 1824).

Moran, Patrick F. *The Letters of the Rev. James Maher, D.D., Late P.P. of Carlow-Graigue, on Religious Subjects, with a Memoir* (Dublin 1877).

Motherwell, Rev. Maiben C. *A Memoir of the Late Albert Blest, for Many Years Agent and Secretary for Ireland of the London Hibernian Society* (Dublin 1843).

Nicholson, Asenath. *Ireland's Welcome to the Stranger, or an Excursion through Ireland in 1844 and 1845 for the Purpose of Personally Investigating the Condition of the Poor* (New York 1847).

Noel, Baptist Wriothesley. *Notes of a Short Tour through the Midland Counties of Ireland in the Summer of 1836, with Observations on the Condition of the Peasantry* (London 1837).

O'Connell, John. *The Select Speeches of Daniel O'Connell, M.P.: Edited with Historical Notices, etc. by His son, John O'Connell*, 2 vols (Dublin 1854-5).

O'Reilly, Bernard. *John MacHale, Archbishop of Tuam: His Life, Times, and Correspondence*, 2 vols (New York 1890).

O'Sullivan, Mortimer. *Captain Rock Detected, or the Origin and Character of the Recent Disturbances ...* (London 1824).

—. *A Guide to an Irish Gentleman in His Search for a Religion* (Dublin 1833).

Otway, Caesar. *Sketches in Ireland* (Dublin 1827).

—. *Sketches in Erris and Tyrawley* (Dublin 1831).

—. *A Tour in Connaught, Comprising Sketches of Clonmacnoise, Joyce Country, and Achill* (Dublin 1839).

Owen, John. *The History of the Origin and First Ten Years of the British and Foreign Bible Society* (London 1816).

Owenson, Sydney (Lady Morgan). *Patriotic Sketches of Ireland Written in Connaught*, 2 vols (Baltimore, Maryland 1809).

Reilly, William. *Memorial of the Ministerial Life of Gideon Ouseley, Irish Missionary* (New York 1852).

Sankey, William. *A Brief Sketch of Various Attempts Which Have Been Made to Diffuse a Knowledge of the Holy Scriptures through the Medium of the Irish Language* (Dublin 1818).

Seddall, H. *Edward Nangle, the Apostle of Achill: A Memoir and A History With an Introduction by the Most Rev. William Conyngham Plunket* (London 1884).

Seymour, A.C.H. *The Life and Times of Selina, Countess of Huntingdon, by a Member of the*

House of Shirley and Hastings, 2 vols (London 1839).
Sirr, Joseph D'Arcy. *A Memorial of the Honourable and Most Reverend Power le Poer Trench, Last Archbishop of Tuam* (Dublin 1845).
Stanford, Charles Stuart. *Memoir of the Late Rev. W.H. Krause with Selections from his Correspondence* (Dublin 1854).
Stock, Eugene. *The History of the Church Missionary Society: Its Environment, Its Men, and Its Work*, 3 vols (London 1899–1916).
Thompson, D.P. *A Brief Account of the Rise and Progress of the Change in Religious Opinion Now Taking Place in Dingle and the West of the County of Kerry* (London 1847).
Thiselton, Alfred Clayton. *A Memorial Sketch of the Life and Labours of Mrs. Henrietta Pendleton, Forty Years Secretary of the Irish Islands and Coasts Society* (Dublin 1895).
Tyerman, A. *The Life and Times of Wesley*, 3 vols, 2nd edn (London 1870–1).
Urwick, William. *Biographical Sketches of the Late James Digges La Touche, Esq.* (Dublin 1868).
Wilberforce, Henry. *Proselytism in Ireland: The Catholic Defence Association vs. the Irish Church Missions on the Charge of Bribery and Intimidation: A Correspondence between the Rev. A.R.C. Dallas and the Rev. Henry Wilberforce*, 2nd edn (London 1852).
Wilberforce, William. *A practical view of the prevailing religious system of professed Christains in the higher and middle classes of this country contrasted with real Christianity* (London 1797).
Webster, Thomas. *A Brief View of the London Hibernian Society with Extracts of Correspondence* (London 1829).
Warburton, John, Whitelaw, Rev. J. and Walsh, Rev. Robert. *History of the City of Dublin from the Earliest Accounts to the Present Time; containing its annals, antiquities, ecclesiastical history, and charters; its present extent, public buildings, schools, institutions, etc. to which are added, biographical notices of eminent men, and copious appendices of its population, revenue, commerce, and literature*, 2 vols (London 1818).
Wyse, Thomas. *Historical Sketch of the Late Catholic Association of Ireland*, 2 vols (Dublin 1829).

A.2 BOOKS: TWENTIETH AND TWENTY-FIRST CENTURY

Acheson, Alan. *A History of the Church of Ireland, 1691–1996* (Dublin 1997).
Akenson, Donald Harman. *The Irish Education Experiment: The National System of Education in the Nineteenth Century* (London 1970).
—. *The Church of Ireland. Ecclesiastical Reform and Revolution 1800–1885* (New Haven, Connecticut 1971).
Noel Annan et al. *Ideas and Beliefs of the Victorians. An Historic Revaluation of the Victorian Age* (London 1949; New York 1966).
Anstey, Roger. *The Atlantic Slave Trade and British Abolition 1760–1810* (London 1975).
Barkun, Michael. *Disaster and the Millennium* (New Haven, Connecticut and London 1974).
Barnard, Toby. *A New Anatomy of Ireland: The Irish Protestants, 1649–1770* (New Haven, Connecticut and London 2003).
Bartlett, Thomas. *The Fall and Rise of the Irish Nation: The Catholic Question, 1690–1830* (Dublin 1992).
Bebbington, D.W. *Evangelicalism in Modern Britain: A History from the 1730s to the 1980s* (London 1989).

Becker, Carl. *The Heavenly City of the Eighteenth-Century Philosophers* (1932 London; New Haven, Connecticut 1966).
Beckett, J.C. *The Anglo–Irish Tradition* (Belfast 1983).
—. *The Making of Modern Ireland: 1603–1923* (London 1972).
Bowen, Desmond. *History and the Shaping of Irish Protestantism* (New York 1995).
—. *Souperism: Myth or Reality? A Study in Souperism* (Cork 1970).
—. *The Protestant Crusade in Ireland, 1800–70: A Study of Protestant–Catholic Relations between the Act of Union and Disestablishment* (Dublin and Montreal 1978).
Bowen, Elizabeth. *Bowen's Court* (New York 1978).
Boyce, D. George. *Nationalism in Ireland* (Dublin and London 1982).
Bradley, Ian. *The Call to Seriousness: The Evangelical Impact on the Victorians* (London 1976).
Brown, Ford K. *Fathers of the Victorians: The Age of Wilberforce* (Cambridge 1961).
Brown, Stewart J. and Miller, David W. (eds). *Piety and Power in Ireland, 1760–1960: Essays in Honour of Emmet Larkin* (Belfast and Notre Dame 2000).
Brown, Stewart J. *The National Churches of England, Ireland, and Scotland, 1801–1846* (Oxford 2001).
—. *Thomas Chalmers and the Godly Commonwealth in Scotland* (Oxford 1982).
Brown, Terence. *Ireland's Literature: Selected Essays* (Mullingar and Totowa, New Jersey 1988).
Brynn, Edward. *The Church of Ireland in the Age of Catholic Emancipation* (London 1982).
Burke, Peter. *Popular Culture in Early Modern Europe* (New York 1978).
Calder, Angus. *Revolutionary Empire: The Rise of the English-Speaking Empires from the Fifteenth Century to the 1780s* (New York 1998).
Canton, William. *A History of the British and Foreign Bible Society* (London 1904).
Clark, Samuel and Donnelly, James S., Jr (eds). *Irish Peasants: Violence and Political Unrest, 1780–1914* (Madison, Wisconsin 1983).
Claydon, Tony and McBride, Ian (eds). *Protestantism and National Identity: Britain and Ireland, c. 1650–1850* (Cambridge 1998).
Colley, Linda. *Britons: Forging the Nation, 1707–1837* (New Haven and London 1992).
Connolly, Peter (ed.). *Literature and the Changing Ireland* (Gerrards Cross 1980).
Connolly, S.J. *Priests and People in Pre-Famine Ireland, 1780–1845* (Dublin 1982).
—. *Religion, Law and Power: The Making of Protestant Ireland 1660–1760* (Oxford 1995).
Corish, P.J. (ed.). *Radicals, Rebels, and Establishments: Historical Studies XV* (Belfast 1985).
Costello, Nuala. *John MacHale* (Dublin 1939).
Coupland, R. *Wilberforce: A Narrative*, 2nd edn (London 1945).
Crawford, W.H. *Domestic Industry in Ireland: The Experience of the Linen Industry* (Dublin 1972).
Cullen, L.M. *An Economic History of Ireland since 1660* (London 1972).
—. *The Emergence of Modern Ireland, 1600–1900* (Dublin and New York 1981).
d'Alton, Ian. *Protestant Society and Politics in Cork, 1812–1844* (Cork 1980).
Daly, Mary and Dickson, David (eds). *The Origins of Popular Literacy in Ireland* (Dublin 1990).
Davidoff, Leonore and Hall, Catherine. *Family Fortunes: Men and Women of the English Middle Class, 1780–1850* (Chicago and London 1987).
Davitt, Michael. *The Fall of Feudalism in Ireland, or the Story of the Land League Revolution* (London and New York 1904).

de Fréine, Seán. *The Great Silence: The Study of a Relationship between Language and Nationality* (Cork 1978).
de Vere White, Terence. *The Parents of Oscar Wilde* (London 1967).
Dickson, David, *New Foundations: Ireland, 1600–1800* (Dublin 1987).
Dickson, David, and English, Richard (eds). *The Gorgeous Mask: Dublin, 1700–1850* (Dublin 1987).
Drudy, P.J.(ed.). *Ireland: Land, Politics, and People* (Cambridge 1982).
Durkacz, Victor Edward. *The Decline of the Celtic Languages: A Study of Linguistic and Cultural Conflict in Scotland, Wales, and Ireland, from the Reformation to the Twentieth Century* (Edinburgh 1983).
Eager, Irene ffrench. *Margaret Anna Cusack: A Biography* (Dublin 1979).
Elliott, Marianne. *Partners in Revolution. The United Irishmen and France* (New Haven and London 1982).
Foley, Tadhg and Ryder, Seán (eds). *Ideology and Ireland in the Nineteenth Century* (Dublin 1998).
Ford, Alan, McGuire, James and Milne, Kenneth (eds). *As By Law Established: The Church of Ireland Since the Reformation* (Dublin 1995).
Forster, E.M. *Marianne Thornton* (London 1956).
Foster, R.F. *Charles Stewart Parnell: The Man and His Family* (Sussex 1976).
—. *Modern Ireland, 1600–1972* (London 1988).
Fraser, Rebecca. *The Brontës: Charlotte Brontë and Her Family* (London and New York 1988).
Furneaux, R. *William Wilberforce* (London 1974).
Gillespie, Raymond and Moran, Gerald (eds). *A Various Country: Essays in Mayo History, 1500–1900* (Westport 1987).
Gillespie, Raymond and Neely, W.G. (eds). *The Laity and the Church of Ireland, 1000–2000: All Sorts and Conditions* (Dublin 2002).
Greene, David H. and Stephens, Edward M. *J.M. Synge, 1871–1909* (New York 1989).
Haire, Robert. *Wesley's One and Twenty Visits to Ireland* (London 1947).
Harrison, J.F.C. *The Second Coming: Popular Millenarianism, 1780–1850* (London 1979).
Hempton, David and Hill, Myrtle. *Evangelical Protestantism in Ulster Society 1740–1890* (London and New York 1992).
Hempton, David. *Methodism and Politics in British Society, 1750–1850* (London 1984).
—. *Religious and Political Culture in Britain and Ireland: From the Glorious Revolution to the Decline of Empire* (Cambridge 1996).
Hennell, M. *John Venn and the Clapham Sect* (Oxford 1958).
Henriques, Ursula. *Religious Toleration in England, 1787–1833* (London 1961).
Hill, Jacqueline. *From Patriots to Unionists: Dublin Civic Politics and Irish Protestant Patriotism, 1660–1840* (Oxford 1997).
Hilton, Boyd. *The Age of Atonement: The Influence of Evangelicalism on Social and Economic Thought, 1795–1865* (Oxford 1988).
Himmelfarb, Gertrude. *On Looking Into the Abyss: Untimely Thoughts on Culture and Society* (New York 1994).
Hobsbawm, Eric and Ranger, Terence (eds). *The Invention of Tradition* (Cambridge 1984).
Hobsbawm, Eric. *Nations and Nationalism Since 1780: Programme, Myth, Reality*, 2nd edn (Cambridge 1992).

Holmes, Finlay. *The Presbyterian Church in Ireland: A Popular History* (Dublin 2000).
Holmes, Janice. *Religious Revivals in Britain and Ireland, 1859–1905* (Dublin and Portland, Oregon 2000).
Hyde, Douglas. *Abhráin atá Leagtha ag an Reachtuire, or Songs Ascribed to Raftery, Being the Fifth Chapter of the Songs of Connaught* (1903; Shannon 1973).
Johnson, Paul. *The Birth of the Modern: World Society, 1815–1830* (New York 1991).
Johnson, Paul. *A Shopkeeper's Millennium: Society and Revivals in Rochester, New York, 1815–1837* (New York 1985).
Jones, M.G. *Hannah More* (Oxford 1952).
Kavanaugh, Ann C. *John Fitzgibbon, Earl of Clare: Protestant Reaction and English Authority in Late Eighteenth-Century Ireland* (Dublin 1997).
Keogh, Daire. *The French Disease: The Catholic Church and Irish Radicalism, 1790–1800* (Dublin 1993).
Keogh, Daire and Whelan, Kevin (eds). *Acts of Union: The Causes, Contexts and Consequences of the Act of Union* (Dublin 2001).
Kiely, Benedict. *Poor Scholar: A Study of the Works and Days of William Carleton, 1794–1869*, 2nd edn (Dublin 1972).
Kilroy, Patricia. *The Story of Connemara* (Dublin 1989).
Kitson Clark, G. *Churchmen and the Condition of England, 1832–85* (London 1973).
Kselman, Thomas A. *Miracles and Prophecies in Nineteenth-Century France* (Brunswick, New Jersey 1983).
Langton, Edward. *History of the Moravian Church: The Story of the First International Protestant Church* (London 1956).
Leighton, C.D.A. *Catholicism in a Protestant Kingdom: A Study of the Irish Ancien Régime* (Dublin 1994).
Lovegrove, Deryck W. (ed.). *The Rise of the Laity in Evangelical Protestantism* (London and New York 2002).
Lyons, F.S.L. *Culture and Anarchy in Ireland, 1890–1939* (Oxford 1979).
McCormack, W.J. *Ascendancy and Tradition in Anglo–Irish Literary History from 1789 to 1939* (Oxford 1985).
MacDonagh, Oliver. *O'Connell: The Life of Daniel O'Connell, 1775–1847* (1988–9; London 1991).
—. *States of Mind: A Study of Anglo–Irish Conflict, 1780–1980* (London 1983).
McDowell, R.B. *Public Opinion and Government Policy in Ireland, 1801–1846* (London 1952).
—. (ed.). *Social Life in Ireland, 1800–45* (Dublin 1957).
—. *Ireland in the Age of Imperialism and Revolution* (Oxford 1979).
McGrath, Mícheál (ed. and trans.). *Cinnlae Amhlaoibh Uí Súilleabháin* (The Diaries of Humphrey O'Sullivan) (London 1936–7).
McGrath, Thomas. *Politics, Interdenominational Relations and Education in the Public Ministry of Bishop James Doyle of Kildare and Leighlin, 1786–1834* (Dublin 1999).
—. *Religious Renewal and Reform in the Pastoral Ministry of Bishop James Doyle of Kildare and Leighlin, 1786–1834* (Dublin 1999).
Machin, G.I.T. *The Catholic Question in English Politics, 1820–1830* (Oxford 1964).
Martin, Roger H. *Evangelicals United: Ecumenical Stirrings in Pre-Victorian Britain, 1795–1830*

(London and Metuchen, New Jersey 1983).
Mason, J.C.S. *The Moravian Church and the Missionary Awakening in England, 1760–1800* (Woodbridge, Suffolk and Rochester, New York 2001).
Maxwell, Constantia. *Country and Town in Ireland under the Georges* (Dundalk 1949).
—. *Ireland Under the Georges* (London 1957).
Meacham, Standish. *Henry Thornton of Clapham* (London 1964).
Milne, Kenneth. *The Irish Charter Schools, 1730–1830* (Dublin 1997).
Mitford, Eveline Bertha. *Life of Lord Redesdale* (London 1939).
Moody, T. W. and Vaughan, W.E. (eds). *A New History of Ireland: Vol. IV, Eighteenth-Century Ireland, 1691–1800* (Oxford 1986).
Murphy, Ignatius. *The Diocese of Killaloe, 1800–50* (Dublin 1992).
Newman, Gerald. *The Rise of English Nationalism: A Cultural History, 1740–1830* (New York 1987).
Newsome, David. *The Wilberforces and Henry Manning: The Parting of Friends* (Cambridge, Massachussets 1966).
Nolan, William and McGrath, Thomas (eds). *Tipperary: History and Society: Interdisciplinary Essays on the History of an Irish County* (Dublin 1985).
Noll, Mark A. *America's God: From Jonathan Edwards to Abraham Lincoln* (Oxford 2002).
Noll, Mark A., Bebbington, David W. and Rawlik, George A. (eds). *Evangelicalism: Comparative Studies of Popular Protestantism in North America, the British Isles, and Beyond, 1700–1990* (Oxford 1994).
Norman, Edward. *Anti-Catholicism in Victorian Britain* (New York 1968).
O'Brien, Gerard (ed.). *Parliament, Politics, and People: Essays in Eighteenth-Century Irish History* (Dublin 1989).
Ó Ciosáin, Niall. *Print and Popular Culture in Ireland, 1750–1850* (London and New York 1997).
O'Connell, M.R. (ed.). *The Correspondence of Daniel O'Connell*, 8 vols (Dublin 1972–81).
Ó Duigneáin, Proinnsíos. *The Priest and the Protestant Woman: The Trial of Rev. Thomas Maguire, P.P., Dec. 1827* (Maynooth 1997).
O'Faolain, Sean. *King of the Beggars: A Life of Daniel O'Connell* (1938; Dublin 1986).
O'Ferrall, Fergus. *Catholic Emancipation: Daniel O'Connell and the Birth of Irish Democracy, 1820–30* (Dublin 1985).
—. *Daniel O'Connell* (Dublin 1998).
Ó Máille, Tomás. *Mícheál Mac Suibhne agus Filí an tSléibhe* (Michael Sweeney and the Poets of the Mountain) (Galway 1937).
Ó Tuathaigh, Gearóid. *Ireland Before the Famine, 1798–1848* (Dublin 1972).
Orr, J.E. *The Light of Nations: Evangelical Renewal and Advance in the Nineteenth Century* (Exeter 1965).
Peires, J.B. *The Dead Will Arise: Nongqawuse and the Great Cattle Killing Movement of 1856–7* (Oxford 1989).
Perkin, Harold. *The Origins of Modern English Society, 1780–1880* (London 1969).
Philips, Peter. *Humanity Dick. The Eccentric Member for Galway. The Story of Richard Martin, Animal Rights Pioneer 1754–1834* (Tunbridge Wells, Kent 2003).
Philips, Walter Alison (ed.). *A History of the Church of Ireland from the Earliest Times to the Present Day* (London 1933).

Piggin, Stuart. *Making Evangelical Missionaries, 1789–1858: The Social Background, Motives, and Training of British Protestant Missionaries to India* (Abingdon 1984).
Power, Thomas P. *Land, Politics and Society in Eighteenth-Century Tipperary* (Oxford 1997).
Power, Thomas P. and Whelan, Kevin (eds). *Endurance and Emergence: Catholics in Ireland in the Eighteenth Century* (Dublin 1990).
Prochaska, F.K. *Women and Philanthropy in Nineteenth-Century England* (Oxford 1980).
Reynolds, J.A. *The Catholic Emancipation Crisis in Ireland, 1823–29* (New Haven 1954).
Richards, Eric. *A History of the Highland Clearances: Agrarian Transformations and the Evictions, 1746–1886* (London 1982).
Reynolds, James A. *The Catholic Emancipation Crisis in Ireland, 1823–1829* (Westport, Connecticut 1970).
Robbins, Keith (ed.). *Protestant Evangelicalism: Britain, Ireland, Germany and America c. 1750–1950, Essays in Honour of W. R. Ward* (Oxford 1990).
Rosman, Doreen. *Evangelicalism and Culture* (London 1984).
Rupp, Gordon. *Religion in England, 1698–1791* (Oxford 1986).
Schlenther, Boyd Stanley. *Queen of the Methodists: The Countess of Huntingdon and the Eighteenth-Century Crisis of Faith* (Durham 1997).
Senior, Hereward. *Orangeism in Ireland and Britain, 1795–1836* (London 1966).
Sewell, William H., Jr. *A Rhetoric of Bourgeois Revolution: The Abbé Sieyès and What is the Third Estate* (Durham, North Carolina 1994).
Smyth, Jim (ed.). *Revolution, Counter-Revolution and Union: Ireland in the 1790s* (Cambridge 2000).
Soloway, R.A. *Prelates and People: Ecclesiastical Social Thought in England, 1783–1852* (London 1969).
Stanley, Brian (ed.). *Christian Missions and the Enlightenment* (Grand Rapids, Michigan and Cambridge 2001).
—. *The History of the Baptist Missionary Society, 1792–1992* (Edinburgh 1992).
Stewart, A.T.Q. *The Narrow Ground: Aspects of Ulster 1609–1969* (London 1977).
Sullivan, Mary C. *Catherine McAuley and the Tradition of Mercy* (Notre Dame 2000).
Thomson, David and McGusty, Moyra (eds). *The Irish Journals of Elizabeth Smith, 1840–50* (Oxford 1980).
Thompson, E.P. *The Making of the English Working Class* (New York 1966).
Thuente, Mary Helen. *The Harp Re-Strung: The United Irishmen and the Rise of Irish Literary Nationalism* (Syracuse, New York 2001).
Thrupp, Sylvia (ed.) *Millennial Dreams in Action. Studies in Revolutionary Religious Movements* (New York 1970).
Vaughan, W.E. (ed.). *A New History of Ireland, Volume V: Ireland Under the Union I: 1801–1870* (Oxford 1990).
Villiers-Tuthill, Kathleen. *History of Clifden, 1810–1850* (Galway 1981).
Ward, W.R. *The Protestant Evangelical Awakening* (Cambridge 1992).
—. *Religion and Society in England, 1790–1850* (London 1972).
Welch, Edwin. *Spiritual Pilgrim: A Reassessment of the Life of the Countess of Huntingdom* (Cardiff 1995).
Whelan, Kevin. *The Tree of Liberty: Radicalism, Catholicism and the Construction of Irish Identity, 1760–1830* (Notre Dame and Cork 1996).

Williams, T.D. (ed.). *Secret Societies in Ireland* (Dublin and New York 1973).
Withers, Charles J. *Gaelic Scotland: The Transformation of a Cultural Region* (London and New York 1988).
Wolffe, John. *The Protestant Crusade in Great Britain, 1829–1860* (Oxford 1991).

B. ARTICLES

Berman, David. 'David Hume on the 1641 rebellion in Ireland', *Studies*, XV (1976), 101–12.
Breathnach, Breandán. 'Séamus Goodman (1828–96): Bailitheoir cheoil' (James Goodman [1828–86], Music collector), *Journal of the Kerry Archaeological and Historical Society*, VI (1973), 152–71.
Bric, Maurice. 'The Rightboy movement, 1785–88', *Past and Present*, 100 (Aug. 1983), 100–23.
Cahill, Gilbert A. 'Irish Catholicism and English Toryism', *Review of Politics*, 19 (Jan. 1957), 62–76.
Corish, P.J. 'The Catholic community in the nineteenth century', *Archivium Hibernicum*, XXXVIII (1983), 26–33.
Crawford, Michael J. 'Origins of the eighteenth-century evangelical revival: England and New England compared', *Journal of British Studies*, 26, 4 (Oct. 1987), 361–97.
Cullen, L.M. 'The hidden Ireland: A re-assessment', *Studia Hibernica*, 9 (1969), 7–47.
Cunningham, T.P. 'The 1826 General Election in Co. Cavan', *Breifne: Journal of Cumann Seanchas Breifne*, II, 2 (1965), 5–46.
Curtin, Nancy. 'The transformation of the United Irishmen into a mass-based organization', 1794–6, *Irish Historical Studies*, 24, 96 (Nov. 1985), 463–92.
Donnelly, James S., Jr, 'The Rightboy movement', *Studia Hibernica*, 17/18 (1977–8), 120–202.
—. 'The Whiteboy movement, 1761–5', *Irish Historical Studies*, 21, 81 (March 1978), 20–54.
—. 'A contemporary account of the Rightboy movement: The John Barter Bennett manuscript', *Journal of the Cork Archaeological and Historical Society*, LXXXVIII, 247 (1983), 1–50.
Fitzgerald, Garrett. 'Estimates for baronies of minimum level of Irish-speaking amongst successive decennial cohorts, 1771–1781 to 1861–1871', *Proceedings of the Royal Irish Academy*, 84, 3 (1984).
Hayley, Barbara. 'Irish periodicals from the Union to the *Nation*', *Anglo-Irish Studies*, II (1976), 83–108.
Hempton, David. 'The Methodist crusade in Ireland', *Irish Historical Studies*, 31, 85 (March 1980), 33–48.
—. 'Methodism in Irish society, 1770–1830', *Transactions of the Royal Historical Society*, 5, 36 (1986), 117–42.
—. 'Gideon Ouseley: Rural revivalist, 1791–1839', *Studies in Church History*, 25 (1989), 203–14.
Hill, Jacqueline. 'Popery and Protestantism, civil and religious liberty: The disputed lessons of Irish history, 1690–1812', *Past and Present*, 118 (Feb. 1988), 96–129.
—. 'National festivals, the state, and Protestant ascendancy in Ireland, 1790–1829, *Irish Historical Studies*, 24, 93 (1984) 30–51.
Jenkins, Deborah. 'The correspondence of Charles Brodrick (1761–1822), Archbishop of Cashel', *Irish Archives Bulletin* (1979–80), 43–9.
Jupp, Peter. 'Irish parliamentary elections and the influence of the Catholic vote, 1801–20',

Historical Journal, 10, 2 (1967), 183–96.

Kelly, James. 'The context and cause of Thomas Orde's Plan of Education in 1787', *Irish Journal of Education*, XX, 1 (1986), 3–26.

—. 'Interdenominational relations and religious toleration in late eighteenth-century Ireland: The "Paper War" of 1786–88', *Eighteenth-Century Ireland*, 3 (1988), 39–67.

—. 'Relations between the Protestant Church of Ireland and the Presbyterian Church in late eighteenth-century Ireland', *Éire–Ireland*, XXIII, 3 (Fall 1988), 38–56.

Kiernan, V. 'Evangelicalism and the French Revolution', *Past and Present*, 1 (Feb. 1952), 44–56.

Kincheloe, J.L. Jr. 'European roots of evangelical revivalism: Methodist transmission of the pietistic socio-religious tradition', *Methodist History*, 18 (July 1980), 262–71.

Larkin, Emmet. 'The devotional revolution in Ireland, 1850–75', *American Historical Review*, LXXVII (1972), 625–52.

Lebow, Ned. 'British historians and Irish history', *Éire–Ireland*, VIII (1973), 3–38.

Love, Walter D. 'Charles O'Conor of Belnagare and Thomas Leland's "philosophical" history of Ireland', *Irish Historical Studies*, 13, 49 (March 1962), 1–22.

McCartney, Donal. 'The writing of history in Ireland, 1800–1830', *Irish Historical Studies*, 10, 40 (Sept. 1957), 347–62.

MacDonagh, Oliver. 'The politicization of the Irish bishops, 1800–1850', *Historical Journal*, XVII, 1 (1975), 37–53.

McGrath, Thomas. 'The Tridentine evolution of modern Irish Catholicism, 1563–1962: A re-examination of the "Devotional Revolution" thesis', *Recusant History*, 20, 4 (Oct. 1999), 512–23.

McNamee, Brian. 'The Second Reformation in Ireland', *Irish Theological Quarterly*, 33 (1969), 46–9.

Miller, David W. 'Irish Catholicism and the Great Famine', *Journal of Social History*, 8 (1975), 81–198.

—. 'Presbyterianism and "modernization" in Ulster', *Past and Present*, 80 (1978), 66–90.

Milne, Kenneth. 'Irish Charter Schools', *Irish Journal of Education*, VIII, 1 (1974), 3–29.

Murphy, Ignatius. 'Some attitudes to religious freedom and ecumenism in pre-Emancipation Ireland', *Irish Ecclesiastical Record*, 105 (1966), 93–104.

Murphy, John A. 'The Support of the Catholic clergy in Ireland, 1750–1850' in J.L. McCracken (ed.), *Historical Studies*, vol. V (London 1965), 103–21.

Ó hÁilín, Tomás. 'The Irish Society agus Tadhg Ó Coinnialláin' (The Irish Society and Thady Connellan), *Studia Hibernica*, 8 (1968), 60–78.

O'Brien, Susan. 'A transatlantic community of saints: The Great Awakening and the first evangelical network, 1735–55', *American Historical Review*, 91, 4 (Oct. 1986), 811–32.

O'Farrell, Patrick. 'Millenarianism, messianism, and utopianism in Irish history', *Anglo–Irish Studies*, 2 (1976), 45–67.

O'Ferrall, Fergus. '"The Only Lever …?": The Catholic Priest in Irish Politics', *Studies*, LXX, 280 (1981), 308–24.

Pinnington, John. 'The Church of Ireland's apologetic position in the years before Disestablishment', *Irish Ecclesiastical Record*, 108 (1967), 303–25.

Thuente, Mary Helen. 'Poetry and song of the United Irishmen', *Irish Literary Supplement*, 2, 1 (Spring 1992).

Vance, Norman. 'Celts, Carthaginians, and constitutions: Anglo–Irish literary relations, 1780–1820', *Irish Historical Studies*, 22, 85 (1973), 3–28.
Wall, Maureen. 'The rise of a Catholic middle class in eighteenth-century Ireland', *Irish Historical Studies*, 11, 42 (Sept. 1958), 91–115.
Wall, Thomas. 'Catholic periodicals of the past (1): The *Catholic Penny Magazine*, 1834–5', *Irish Ecclesiastical Record*, 5, CI (Jan.–June 1964), 234–44.
—. 'Catholic periodicals of the past (2): The Catholic Book Society and the *Irish Catholic Magazine*', *Irish Ecclesiastical Record*, 5, CI (Jan.–June 1964), 289–303.
—. 'Catholic periodicals of the past (3): Philip Barron's *Ancient Ireland*, 1835', *Irish Ecclesiastical Record,* 5, CI (Jan.–June 1964), 375–88.
—. 'Catholic periodicals of the past (4): The *Catholic Luminary*, 1840–41', *Irish Ecclesiastical Record*, 5, CII (July–Dec. 1964), 17–27.
—. 'Catholic periodicals of the past (5): Duffy's *Irish Catholic Magazine*, 1847–1848', *Irish Ecclesiastical Record,* 5, CII (July–Dec. 1964), 86–100.
—. 'Catholic periodicals of the past (6): Duffy's *Irish Catholic Magazine*, 1847–1848, part II', *Irish Ecclesiastical Record*, 5, CII (July–Dec. 1964), 129–47.
Ward, Robert and Coogan Ward, Catherine. 'The Catholic pamphlets of Charles O'Connor', *Studies*, LXVIII (1979), 259–64.
Ward, W.R. 'The relations of Enlightenment and religious revival in central Europe and in the English-speaking studies in Church history', *Subsidia*, 2 (1979), 281–305.
—. 'Power and piety: The origins of religious revival in the early eighteenth century', *Bulletin of the John Rylands Library of Manchester*, 63, 1 (1980), 231–52.
Whyte, J.H. 'The influence of the Catholic clergy on elections in nineteenth-century Ireland', *English Historical Review*, 75 (1960), 239–59.
—. 'Landlord influences at elections in Ireland, 1760–1885', *English Historical Review*, 85 (1965), 740–60.

C. UNPUBLISHED THESES

Acheson, Alan R. 'The evangelicals in the Church of Ireland, 1784–1859' (PhD thesis, Queen's University, Belfast 1967).
Binns, June R. 'A history of Methodism in Ireland from Wesley's death in 1791 to the re-union of Primitives and Wesleyans in 1878' (MA thesis, Queen's University, Belfast 1960).
Brown, Dorothy. 'Selina, Countess of Huntingdon: Leader of the first Dissenting Methodists' (MA thesis, Southern Methodist University 1986).
Clayton, Helen R. 'Societies formed to educate the poor in Ireland in the late eighteenth and early nineteenth centuries' (MLitt thesis, Trinity College Dublin 1981).
Hanna, S.G. 'The origin and nature of the Gracehill Moravian settlement 1764–1855, with special reference to the work of John Cennick in Ireland, 1746–1755' (MA thesis, Queen's University, Belfast 1964).
Hehir, Irene M. 'New Lights and old enemies: The "Second Reformation" and the Catholics of Ireland, 1800–1835' (MA thesis, University of Wisconsin–Madison 1983).
Hill, Myrtle. 'Evangelicalism and the churches in Ulster Society, 1750–1850' (PhD thesis, Queen's University, Belfast 1987).

Jamieson, J. 'The influence of the Reverend Henry Cooke on the political life of Ulster' (MA thesis, Queen's University, Belfast 1980).
Knickerbocker, Driss Richard. 'The popular religious tract in England, 1790–1830' (PhD thesis, Oxford University 1981).
Liechty, Joseph. 'Irish evangelicalism, Trinity College Dublin, and the mission of the Church of Ireland at the end of the eighteenth century' (PhD thesis, St Patrick's College, Maynooth 1987).
Martin, R.H. 'The pan-evangelical impulse in Britain 1790–1830: With special reference to four London societies' (PhD thesis, Oxford University 1974).
Ó Canáinn, Seán. 'Relations between the Catholic Church and the State with regard to education in Ireland, 1795–1825' (MEd thesis, Trinity College Dublin 1979).
O'Ferral, R.F.B. [Fergus]. 'The growth of political consciousness in Ireland, 1823–1847: A study of O'Connellite politics and political education' (PhD thesis, Trinity College Dublin 1978).
Rodgers, R.J. 'James Carlisle, 1784–1854', (PhD thesis, Queen's University, Belfast 1973).
Sullivan, James Joseph. 'The education of Irish Catholics, 1782–1831' (PhD thesis, Queen's University, Belfast 1959).
Thomas, P.R. 'The concept of an ecumenical Bible society movement, 1804–1832' (PhD thesis, University of Lancaster 1980).
Williams, P. Clive. 'Pestalozzi John: A study of the life and educational work of John Synge, with special reference to the introduction and development of Pestalozzian ideas in Ireland and England' (PhD thesis, Trinity College Dublin 1966).
Wright, J.R.R. 'An evangelical estate *c.* 1800–1825: The influence on the Manchester Estate, County Armagh, with particular reference to the moral agencies of W. Loftie and H. Porter' (PhD thesis, Northern Ireland Polytechnic 1982).

D. BIBLIOGRAPHICAL SOURCES

Boylan, Henry. *A Dictionary of Irish Biography* (Dublin 1978).
Burke, John. *A General and Heraldic Dictionary of the Peerage and Baronetage of the British Empire*, 3rd edn (London 1829).
Burtchaell, George James and Sadleir, Thomas Ulick. *Alumni Dublienses: A Register of the Sudents, Graduates, and Provosts of Trinity College in the University of Dublin* (Dublin 1935).
Cokayne, George Edward. *The Complete Peerage of England, Scotland, Ireland, Great Britain and the United Kingdom, Extant, Extinct, or Dormant*, Vicary Gibbs (ed.), 5 vols (London 1910–21).
Crone, John A. *A Concise Dictionary of Irish Biography* (Dublin 1937).
Lee, Sydney and Stephen, Leslie (eds). *The Dictionary of National Biography ... From the Earliest Times to 1900*, 22 vols (London 1885–1901).

Index

Abbeyleix 63
Acheson, Alan 19
Achill 254, 260, 262-5
Act of Union 49-50, 53, 80, 125, 126, 157
Adams, Dr Neason 264
ADV 55-7, 70, 75, 77-80, 93, 107, 108, 112, 114, 121, 130
agrarian protest 25-33, 48, 142, 184, 270
Allan, Joseph 92
Allen, Rev. James 263
America
 and Native Americans 150
 war of independence 26-7
Anderson, Dr Christopher 100-2, 103, 111, 112, 116, 119
 Historical Sketches of the Native Irish 262
Annesley, Lady Lucy 173
Anstey, Roger 66
anti-Catholicism 92, 115, 117, 133, 164, 170, 227, 271
 and Catholic counter-attack 192-230
 and Dr William Magee's sermon 155-6
 element of evangelical world view 129
 from ultra-Protestant press 139, 153-4
anti-Protestantism 142, 146, 153, 171, 213
Armagh 138, 180

Arminianism 11
Askeaton 183-7
Association for Discounte-nancing Vice *see* ADV
Aughkeely 253
Averell, Adam 254

Ballina 88-9, 263
Bandon 155
Baptists 69, 92-107, 118-19, 131, 170, 228, 263
 Baptist Society for the Promotion of the Gospel in Ireland 93, 100, 103-4, 153, 162
Baring, Sir Thomas 113
Barkun, Michael 145, 149
Battersby, William Joseph 221-2, 223, 224
Becker, Carl 22
Bell, James 89, 91
Belzunce, bishop of Marseilles 242
Bennett, John Barter 29-31, 32-3, 34-6
Beresford, M.G. 231
Beresford, Rev. Dr John George, Protestant primate of Ireland 138
Bethesda Chapel, Dublin 17-19, 47, 60-1, 174
Bewley, Samuel 81-2
BFBS 69-70, 71-3, 84, 100, 113, 133, 138, 224

Bible
 and Bible societies 69-70, 71-3, 92, 114, 130-41, 160, 204-9, 229
 and Bible War 174, 204-10, 214, 225, 268-9
 crisis 130-41
 distribution of bibles and tracts 72-3, 107, 153
 Douay version 140, 222
 and education 79-80, 89, 134-7
 and evangelicalism 14, 58, 68
 in Irish 111, 119, 172, 248
 reading without note or comment 134-9, 223, 234, 269
 as supreme source of moral authority 129
 see also scriptures
Blackwood's Magazine 177, 191
Blake, Henry 247-8
Blake, Martha Louisa 248-9
Blake, Rev. Michael 200
Blasket Islands 257, 259
Blest, Albert 9, 10, 11, 94, 96-7, 98, 121, 240
Bogue, David 94
Boulter, Rev. Hugh, Protestant archbishop of Armagh 76
Bowen, Desmond 270

Bowen, Elizabeth 51, 161
Boyle 240
Bradley, Ian 16, 17
Brasbie, Fr 257-8
Bristol, earl of 73-4
British Critic 180, 182, 186, 190
British and Foreign Bible Society *see* BFBS
Brodrick, Charles, archbishop of Cashel 75, 85, 90
Brooke, Charlotte 2, 42-3, 115
  Reliques of Irish Poetry 42
Brooke, Henry 38-9, 41, 42
Brown, Terence 117
Browne, Rev. Denis 254
Brunswick Clubs 232, 253
burial controversy 200-1
Burke, Edmund 39, 199
Burke, Richard 48
Burrowes, Peter 80, 193
Butler, Hubert 167-8
Butt, Isaac 211, 212
Butterworth, Joseph 92

Calvinists 10-12, 60
Camden, Earl 49, 238
Canning 127, 177
Carey, William 69
Carleton, William 121, 211-12
Carlisle, Rev. James 128
Carlow 208
Carmelite order 97
Carr, Rev. George 72
Carrick-on-Shannon 207-8
Castleisland 78-9
Castlewellan 89
Catholic Association 175, 193-4, 196, 199, 200-4, 208, 214, 269-70
  and Catholic rent 215-16, 218, 232
  in London 221
  and New Catholic Association 232
Catholic Book Society 221-3
Catholic Church
  attitude to Pastorini

  prophecies 143
  condemnation of Reformation movement 189-91
  counter-attack 192-230, 272
  missionaries in Scotland 96
  opposition of clergy to evangelicalism 89, 94, 118, 131, 149
  opposition of clergy to Protestant schools 107, 183, 189
  respect for other beliefs 131-3
  response to Archbishop Magee 156-7
  response to criticism 140-1
  theological pamphlets 219
Catholic Committee 127
Catholic Defence Association 260
Catholic Directory 222
Catholic Emancipation 37, 39, 47-50, 74, 80, 92, 106, 123, 144, 268-9
  and the clergy 127-9, 143, 149-51
  debated at Bible Society meetings 204
  granted 233-4, 271
  politics of 124-51, 175-7, 180, 193, 196-7, 209-10, 214, 232-3
  and Protestant fears 153, 155, 175-6, 178
  and rejection of Catholic relief bill 127-8
  and Rome 127-8
Catholic Penny Magazine, The 223, 227
Catholic Relief Act 232-3
Catholic Society of Ireland 221
Catholics
  education of 76-9, 97, 109, 118, 149
  hostility to proselytizing schools 77

  increase in population 95
  middle class & gentry 23-5
  mission to 85-123
  political consciousness of 95
Cavan 107, 172-82
Celtic Church 65, 139
Celtic revival 23, 43, 64-5, 111, 117
Cennick, Rev. John 5-6, 267
Charlemont, earl of 40
Charles, Rev. Thomas 94, 96, 100, 101, 103
Charter Schools *see* education
Cheap Book Society 82
China 150
cholera 256, 262
Christian Examiner and Church of Ireland Magazine 210-13, 223-4, 228
Christian Observer 71, 73, 74, 105-6, 164, 209-10
Church of England 13, 18, 138, 139
Church of Ireland 8, 10, 45, 139
  attitude of clergy to Irish language 99
  attitude to Methodists 91
  disestablishment 213, 233
  evangelical wing 12-14, 17, 55, 59, 74-5, 90, 93, 108-18, 129-30, 162, 236
  mission to Catholic Irish 92-3
  Present State of the Church of Ireland, The 33
  religious revival in 53-62
  see also Protestants; tithes to Established Church
Church Missionary Society 69
Church Temporalities Act 233-4
City of London Bible Auxiliary 210
Clapham Sect 13, 18, 53, 56,

340

62-3, 69-70, 165, 204
  attitude to Catholic
    Emancipation 74
Clare 89, 90, 103, 104
Clarkson, Thomas 57
Clifden 248-51
Clifford, Lieutenant 257
Cloncurry, Lord 65, 134, 135-6
CMS 71-2, 73, 130, 224
Cobbett, William 178
  History of the Protestant Reformation 219-20
Coke, Dr Thomas 87, 90, 91-2
Colley, Linda 27
colonialism 17, 20, 266-7
  and imperialism 147
  and view of the native Irish 38, 40
Colthurst, Sir John Conway 29-30, 31, 32, 36
Congregationalists 93, 96, 105, 228
Congress of Vienna 133
Connaught 100-1, 104, 119
Connellan, Thaddeus 121-2
Connemara 89, 248-51
Connolly, S.J. 20, 235
conversions
  and controversy 172-87, 254, 259
  of priests 188-9
  and return to Catholic faith 180, 260
  and social conflict 180-1, 187-91, 250-1, 258
  and social hierarchy 264-5
Conway, W.F. 193, 202
Cork 64
  Bible Society 130, 205
  Farmers' Club 29, 30, 36
Cornwall, William 88
Cornwallis, Lord 238
Costelloe, Fr O'Brien 185
Courier, The 192
Coyne, Richard 222, 225
Crolly, Dr William, bishop of Down and Connor 222

Cullen, Paul Cardinal 150
cultural revival 19-37, 37-8, 42
Curry, John 38, 40-1
Curtis, Dr Patrick 156
Cusack, Margaret Anna 229-30

Dallas, Alexander 250
d'Alton, Ian 50
Daly, Fr Peter 206
Daly, Rev. Robert 112, 115, 116, 172, 177, 208, 210, 263
Darby, John Nelson 64
D'Arcy, Hyacinth 250-1
D'Arcy, John 248, 250
D'Arcy, Robert 207
Davis, Thomas 64
Davitt, Michael 238
de Vesci, Viscount 63
debates 224-30
Defenders 48
Delany, Daniel, Catholic bishop of Kildare 46
Denny, Lady Arabella 13
Dewar, Rev. Daniel 100, 102, 112, 119
Digby, Rev. William 130, 240, 248
Dillon, Michael 239-40
Dingle 254-60
Dissenters 92-107
Donegal town 91
Donnelly, James S. 28
Downpatrick 227
Doyle, James Warren, bishop of Kildare and Leighlin 132-3, 139-40, 163, 186, 214, 217, 222, 272
  background 198-9
  letters and pamphlets 192, 194-6, 197-9, 202, 220-1
  and Prince Hohenlohe 193-204
  response to Archbishop Magee 156-7, 159-60, 269
  response to Lord Farnham 175-6, 178-9

Drennan, Dr William 45, 155
Dublin 20
  Bethesda Chapel 17-19, 47, 60-1
  philanthropists 13, 81-2
  school for poor children 82
  York Street Chapel 96
Dublin Evening Mail 206
Dublin Evening Post 136-7, 152, 154, 155-6, 158-9, 169, 185, 199, 202
  on anti-Catholic attacks 214-15
  Bishop Doyle's letter in 202
  on Connemara 248
  editor 193, 202
  on education 203
  on Fr Tom Maguire 226
  on Protestant Colonisation Society 253
  on Trench 245
Dublin Society 22
Dublin University Magazine 211-12, 231, 252
Duigenan, Patrick 34-6, 39
Durham, bishop of 80-1

Easky 207
East India Company 69, 96
economic crisis 26, 123, 141-2, 153, 168, 179, 268
ecumenism 10, 132
Edinburgh Gaelic School Society 103
Edinburgh Society for Promoting the Education of the Poor in Ireland 113
education
  Baptist schools 104-5, 131
  and the Bible 79-80, 89, 134-8
  board of 81
  of Catholics 76-84, 97, 109, 118, 141, 149, 194, 201-3, 234-5, 268, 271
  Charter Schools 21-2, 45-6, 77, 135

of the deaf and dumb 64
discriminatory against
  poor and females 259
in hedge-schools 78-9,
  83, 94
in the Irish language 98-
  104, 112-13, 122, 257
KPS 63, 65, 80-1, 83-4, 93,
  100, 103-4, 107, 113, 134-
  7, 201
land donated for schools
  130-1
LHS schools 97-107, 120
and moral reform 50, 56
Pestalozzi method 63
and proselytism 134, 235
reform of system 45-6,
  234-5
by religious orders 97,
  259-60, 272
schools in Achill 264
state support for 76
statutory commission of
  inquiry on 81
teachers 83, 97-8, 120-1,
  131, 181, 189
Ellis, Rev. Brabazon 249,
  250-1
Elphin 240-1
Elrington, Charles, bishop
  of Meath 55
Elrington, Thomas, bishop
  of Ferns and Leighlin 130
emigration 271-2
Emmett, Robert 125
English Catholic Board 127
English language, adoption
  of 144
Enlightenment 19-20, 22,
  42, 67, 68, 112
and educational reform
  45-6, 76
German 4
and Protestant
  intellectuals 39-40
Scottish 69, 94
Enniscorthy 155
Ennismore, Lord 169

Ensor, George 156, 178-80,
  192, 254
Established Church Home
  Mission Society 236
evangelicalism 5, 10-11, 17,
  46-7, 67, 165, 235-6, 266
aimed at Catholics 74-5,
  103, 140, 267
and the Bible 14, 58, 68
in Church of Ireland 6,
  12-14, 55, 59, 74-5, 90, 236
cooperation between
  churches 62
in Dublin 162
and good works 59
Independent 59, 74, 86,
  93, 94, 111, 118, 158
Low Church 16
Methodist 86-7, 111
and new economic order
  149
and new Reformation
  movement 139-40
opposition of Catholic
  clergy 131
overlap between religion
  and politics 177-8
and political conservatism
  265, 270-1
popular response to 118-23
propaganda 170, 176
Rev. John Richardson's
  proposals 21
role of women 163-4, 167-8
social and political aims
  62
in west 238-51
Evans, Eyre Crowe, *Old and
  New Light* 163-6, 168-9, 171

famine 149-50, 242-6, 254,
  265, 271
and cholera 256, 262
and emigration 260
relief 242-6, 262-3
and souperism 250, 256
and typhus epidemic 142,
  144

Farnham Estate, Co. Cavan
  107, 172-5
Farnham, Lord 172-6, 178,
  181, 188, 200, 232, 253
Ferguson, Samuel 211
Fingal, Lord 125, 135
Finney, Charles Grandison 15
Fitzgibbon, John 32
Fitzherbert, Alleyne 77
Fitzpatrick, Jeremiah 45
Fitzpatrick, W.J. 158
Fitzwilliam, Earl 49
Fontana, Cardinal, in Rome
  114, 133-4, 140
foreign missions 71-2, 73,
  86-7, 93, 96, 129-30, 267
Catholic 272
George Ensor's comments
  178-9
Forster, Rev. Charles 114, 124
Forster, Rev. Mark Anthony
  249, 251
Foster, Leslie 182
Freeman's Journal 193, 204-
  8, 260
French Revolution 15-16,
  50, 52, 68, 69
Fuller, Rev. Andrew 103

Gaelic Ireland 37-8, 42
Gardiner, Anne 238
Gayer, Rev. Charles 256,
  258-60
General Evangelical Society
  96
George III 55, 155
George IV 155
Godkin, Rev. James 225
Goodman, Canon James 117
Goodman, Rev. John 255
Goodman, Rev. Thomas
  Chute 255-8
Gordon, Captain James
  Edward 204-8
Goulburn, Henry 216
Grace, Archdeacon Thomas
  243
Graham, Charles 87-8, 254

Index

Graiguenamanagh 233
Grant, Charles 74, 135, 155, 268
Grattan, Henry 127, 155
Gregg, Rev. John 254
Gubbins, George 256-8
Guinness, Arthur 81
Guinness family 13, 19
Guthrie, John 206-7, 215

Habsburg Empire 126
Haldane, James and Robert 10, 96
Hall, Samuel Carter 264
Hamilton, Dr Hugh 58
Hamilton, Hans 57-8, 234
Hamilton, William 90, 91
Harpur, Rev. Singleton 55
Harty, William 142
Hastings, Selina *see* Huntingdon, countess of
Hastings, Warren 69
Hayes, Sir Edmund 253
Hayley, Barbara 213, 223
HBS 52, 61, 63, 72-3, 93, 130, 138, 146, 161, 167
   distribution of auxiliaries 236
   Ladies' Auxiliary, Cork 205
   hedge schools 78-9, 83, 94, 120-1
Hely-Hutchinson, John, provost of Trinity College Dublin 77
Hempton, David 6, 17, 87
Henry VIII 143
Herrnhut settlement 3-4
Hibernian Bible Society *see* HBS
Hibernian Church Missionary Society 65
Hibernian Society for Establishing Schools and Circulating the Holy Scriptures in Ireland 97
Hierophilus letters 134, 202
Hill, Jacqueline 39, 41, 44
Hill, Myrtle 6

Hill, Rowland II 96-7
Himmelfarb, Gertrude 273
Hobart's Relief Act 48
Hohenlohe, Prince 193-204
   miraculous cures 194, 196-7
Home Mission Society 254
Howard, Theodosia, Viscountess Powerscourt 63-4, 167
Hughes, Rev. Thomas 94
Hume, David 40-1
Huntingdon, countess of 2, 11, 17
   Connexion 8-9, 10, 11, 12, 47, 96
Hutchinson, Sir James 45-6
Hutton, Alderman Henry 13, 96-7

Iberno-Celtic Society 64, 111, 115
Incorporated Society in Dublin for Promoting English Protestant Schools in Ireland 21
Independent churches 59, 74, 86, 93, 94, 96, 111, 118, 158, 267
India 147
Inglis, Sir Robert H. 183
Irish Auxiliary to the Jews Society 65
Irish Catholic Magazine 223
Irish Catholic Magazine of Entertaining Knowledge 223-4
Irish Catholic Society for the Diffusion of Useful Knowledge 221
Irish Church Missions 260
Irish language 64-5, 98-104, 111-12, 115-17, 119, 122, 190
   in Dingle 255, 257, 260
   Methodist mission in 8, 87-92, 105, 254
   teaching scriptures in 261
Irish parliament 26-7

Irish Society 65, 93, 100, 112, 114-16, 190, 235, 248-9, 257-8, 261-2
   Connaught Auxiliary 261
   in Kingscourt 172-4, 181
   Ladies' Auxiliary 262
Islands and Coasts Society 262

Jackson, James Edward 152, 161-2
Jackson, Joseph Devonshire 137
Jacobite rising 39
Jebb, Rev. John, bishop of Limerick 52, 75, 108, 158, 183-7, 217, 245
   on anti-Protestant ballads 213
   on burial controversy 201
   on Catholic Emancipation 193, 271
   on Dingle 255-6
   on education 120-1
   on evangelicalism 176-7
   on the Irish language 99
   on proselytism 85, 114
Jefferies, Arabella 32
Jocelyn, Lady Anne 163
Jocelyn, Viscount *see* Lord Roden
Johnson, Paul 15, 17, 147-8
Joyce, Mathias 90

Kean, Lawrence 90
Keating, William Power 238
Kelly, Dr Oliver, Catholic archbishop of Tuam 45, 132, 140
Kiely, Benedict 212
Kiernan, V. 14-15, 17
Kildare, Co. 116, 253
Kildare Place Society *see* KPS
Kildimo 121
Kilkenny 58-9, 206
Killen, W.D. 159
Kingscourt 172-82, 188, 235, 237, 258, 261

343

schools on the estate 173
Kinsale 229
Knox, Alexander 49
KPS 63, 65, 80, 81, 83-4,
    103-4, 107, 113, 234-5
  accused of proselytism
    134-7, 202-3, 269
  and education in Irish
    schools 183, 248-9
Krause, Rev. William 174-5

La Touche family 13, 19, 61
La Touche, James Digges
    60-2, 63, 90, 111
La Touche, John David 61,
    72, 90
La Touche, Lady Emily 240
La Touche, Robert 240
La Touche, William George
    Digges 63
landlords 98-9, 130-1, 148-9,
    161-72, 190-1
  pressuring tenants to
    attend Protestant
    schools 169-72
Lansdowne, Lord 171
Larkin, Emmet 150
Le Fanu, Sheridan 212
Ledwich, Rev. Edward 44
Lees, Sir Harcourt 147, 160
Lefroy, Anthony 65
Lefroy, Thomas Langlois
    65, 114, 115, 118, 134, 232
Leinster, duke of 136-7
Leland, Rev. Thomas,
    History 40-1
Lever, Charles 212
LHS 10, 92-107, 112, 122, 235,
    248, 249
  distribution of schools 105
  non-interference with
    pupil's religion 106
  occupations of school
    supervisors 106
Liechty, Joseph 47
Limerick, Co. 145
literacy 96-102, 122, 260, 269
Locke, John 198

London Hibernian Society
    see LHS
London Missionary Society
    93-4
London Tavern Committee
    243
Lord Lieutenant's Fund 105
Lorton family 240-1
Lorton, Lord 115, 130, 148-
    9, 162, 167, 241
Lough Derg 119-20, 182,
    211-12
Loughrea 206-7
Louis XIV 38

McBride, Ian 46
McCarthy, Rev. Isaac
    103-4, 162
McCauley, Catherine 230
McCormack, W.J. 37
MacDonagh, Oliver 44, 126
McDonnell, Eneas 221
McDowell, Dr Benjamin 60
McDowell, R.B. 13
McGhee, Rev. Robert 200,
    210, 227, 241
McGrath, Thomas 150
MacHale, Rev. Dr John
    133-4, 136, 153, 156, 202,
    263, 269
McKenna, Theobald 126, 157
McQuigg, James 87
Macartney, Sir George 40
Magdalen Asylum 13
Magee, Dr William,
    archbishop of Dublin 19,
    55, 129, 139, 216-17, 229
  and militant Protestantism
    153-60
  sermon in St Patrick's
    Cathedral 155-9, 175,
    193, 269-70
Maguire, Fr Tom 214, 225-7
Mahon, Catherine
    Hartland 257
Maiben, Andrew 9-10
Mangan, James Clarence
    212

Mant, Dr, bishop 114, 201
marriages between evangel-
    ical families 166-7
Martin, Richard 247-8
Massereene, dowager
    Countess 228
Mathew, Thomas 24
Mathias, Rev. Benjamin
    William 18, 60-1, 72
Maunsell, Rev. William 121
Maxwell, Henry 234
Maxwell, John James *see*
    Farnham, Lord
Mayo 88-9, 90, 103, 118, 249
Mead, Henry 9
Methodists 4-7, 16-18, 47,
    59, 61, 67, 183, 267
  Calvinistic 10-12, 96
  evangelical 86-7, 111
  mission to Irish-speaking
    population 8, 87-92,
    105, 254
  in Ulster 8
Midlands 104-5
millenarianism 141-51, 162
Mills, Samuel 94
Milner, John 124
Moira, Lady 9, 11, 13
Moll Flanders 201
Molyneux, William 38
Monck Mason, Henry
    Joseph 64-6, 111-12, 117,
    122, 172, 261, 263
Montesquieu 135
Moore, Thomas 64, 111
  Memoir of Captain Rock
    220
moral ascendancy 161-72
moral reform 16, 45, 50,
    52-84
Moravian refugees 3-6
More, Hannah 55, 56, 68
Morgan, Lady, *Patriotic
    Sketches* 121-2
Moriarty, Thomas 258
Morning Herald 226
Mosse, Bartholomew 12
Motherwell, Maiben 240

Index

Moylough, east Galway 154
Mulcahy, Fr James 169
Munster 24, 28, 30-2
Murphy, Dr, bishop of Cork 205-6
Murray, Dr Daniel, Catholic archbishop of Dublin 170, 171-2, 196, 203, 213-14
Murray, Rev. Daniel 183-4, 187
Murroe 185

Nangle, Rev. Edward 249, 251, 260-4
Napoleon 74, 91, 129, 133, 141, 153
Nash, Rev. 254
Natal 150
National Board of Education 107, 234
nationalism 43
New York 15
Newman, Gerald 15-16, 43
Nicholson, Asenath 259, 264-5
Noel, Baptist Wriothesley 181, 187, 188, 204-8, 222, 236-7, 262
Nolan, Fr 188-9
Nolan, Fr Edward 208
Nonconformists 62, 69, 106
North, John Henry 201-2

O'Beirne, Dr Thomas Lewis, bishop of Meath 57, 138
O'Brien, Lady 131
O'Brien, Susan 3
O'Brien, William Smith 215
O'Callaghan, Andrew 131
O'Connell, Daniel 65, 84, 126-30, 132-7, 149, 153, 177, 198, 233
and Catholic Association 194, 199, 214-17, 219-20, 232, 269
counsel for Fr Tom

Maguire 226-7
elected in Co. Clare 232
in *Freeman's Journal* 204, 207
speeches 204, 205
O'Connor, Dr, of Castleknock 55
O'Conor, Charles 38-9, 40-1, 199
Ó Criomthain, Tomás 260
O'Donnell, Sir Richard 263
O'Halloran, Sylvester 38
O'Hara, Charles King 98
O'Leary, Fr Arthur 33, 34-5
O'Shaughnessy, Rev. James, bishop of Killaloe 203
Ó Suilleabháin, Eoin Ruadh 217
O'Sullivan, Humphrey 165, 228
O'Sullivan, Rev. Mortimer 210
OCA 57-9, 71-2, 74
Orange Order 49, 53, 65, 92, 146-7, 154-6, 166, 224
allegation against Fr Tom Maguire 226-7
anti-Catholic agitation 196, 200, 232-3, 269
Orde, Thomas 45-6, 77, 79
Ormond, Lord 206
Orpen, Charles Edward 64, 67, 115-17
Ossory Clerical Association *see* OCA
Otway, Rev. Caesar 170, 210-13, 260, 264
Ouseley, Gideon 8, 87, 88, 90, 92, 119, 267
Oxford Movement 260

Palatine settlers 7-8, 186
Parnell, Sir John 48
Parnell, Thomas 263
Parnell, William 91
Pastorini prophecies 143-6, 149, 153, 213, 216, 218
Patrician Brothers 141

Patrick, Saint 139
Patriot parliament 77
patriotic view of Irish history 39
Peckwell, Henry 11-12
Peel, Robert 154, 219
penal laws 21, 27, 31, 80, 159
Pendleton, Henrietta 261-2
Pendleton, Rev. E.C. 262
Perkin, Harold 14, 17, 53
Pestalozzi, Heinrich 63, 64, 67
Phelan, Rev. William 131
philanthropy 2, 12-13, 81-2, 83
Pidgeon, Rev. Edward 58
Piggin, Stuart 15
Pitt, Prime Minister 50, 125
Pius VII, Pope 133-4
Plunket, William Conyngham 135, 155, 157, 178, 230
Plymouth Brethren 64
Poland 133
Pope, Alexander 242
Pope, Rev. Richard 205, 206, 208, 225
poverty 21, 103, 120, 141-2, 179-82
Power, Thomas P. 21
Powerscourt 110
Powerscourt family 63, 162
Powerscourt, Lord 114
Pratt, Josiah 71, 73
preachers, itinerant 5-7, 8, 10-12, 59, 103, 104, 118, 131, 153
confrontation with Catholic clergy 204-9
and the landed classes 161
Presbyterians 7, 8, 24, 36, 60, 96, 106, 228
and anti-tithe movement 45
attacked by Magee 159
and burial controversy 201
links with Scotland and America 27-8
Mary's Abbey 13
in Ulster 109

345

and Unitarian beliefs 106
Proclamation Society for the
  Suppression of Vice 55-6
propaganda, and counter-
  propaganda 209-24, 229,
  271
proselytism 134-7, 139, 140,
  141, 169-70, 202-3, 218, 223,
  235, 264
Protestants
  and anti-Protestantism
    146, 153, 171, 213
  ascendancy 33, 36, 50, 54,
    65, 80, 125, 268
  colonies 251-65
  emigration of 251-2
  fear of Catholicism 24-5,
    37, 54
  as 'foreign oppressors' 19
  liberal 155, 157, 215
  missionary movement 69
  political culture of 50
  see also Church of Ireland;
    ultra-Protestants
Prussia 83
Puritanism 6, 14, 17, 21

Quakers 81-2
Quarantotti, Dr 127, 155
Quarry, Rev. John 64

Raczynski, Archbishop 133
Raftery, Anthony 207,
  217-19, 239
Rawson, T.J. 116
rebellion of 1641 26, 40
Rebellion of 1798 49, 53, 71,
  80, 87, 109, 125, 238
Redesdale, Lord 80, 125, 145
Reformation 139, 266
  'Second' 107, 152-91, 220,
    228, 233, 245, 247, 251,
    254, 257-8
religious revival, and inter-
  national awakening 3-19
Religious Tract and Book
  Society 93, 108, 263
Religious Tract Society 69

Reliques of Irish Poetry 42
revolutionary democracy in
  America and Europe 36-7
Reynolds, J.A. 215-16, 219
Ribbon organization 188
Richardson, Rev. John 21
Rightboys 28, 30, 31-5, 45
Robertson, William 40
Roche, Fr James 203
Rock, Captain 142-3, 153
Rockite Movement 142-3,
  146, 153, 154, 157, 184
Roden, Lord 115, 232
Rodens of Co. Down 162
Roe, Rev. Peter 57-60, 70-2,
  74, 93, 124, 206
Rogers, Rev. Edmund 103
Romantic movement 14, 42
Rome 27, 133
Roscommon 162
Rosse, earl of 145, 147
Rousseau 67-8
Rowan, Rev. Arthur B. 254
Royal Irish Academy 42, 65
Russell, Thomas 45, 173

Sackville Institute, Dublin,
  debate between Maguire
  and Pope 226
St George, Matthew 207
St Kevin's Churchyard,
  Dublin 200
Sankey, William 112-13
Saxony, Court of 4
schools *see* education
Scotland 78, 93, 95-7, 98,
  100, 102-3, 113
  Gaelic language and
    culture 115-16, 122
  oppression of poor by
    landowners 132
scriptures
  individual interpretation
    of 96
  readers 104
Scripture Readers' Society
  65, 93, 114, 172, 190, 235,
  254 *see also* Bible

translation into vernacular
  languages 93
Scully, Denis 126, 157
sectarian conflict 109, 132,
  134, 138, 141, 153, 160, 170,
  187-8
  at Bible Society meetings
    205
  in Cavan 181, 187-8
  in Dingle 258
  in Mayo 249, 262-3
  and millenarianism 141-51
  in print 209
  and rift between religions
    137, 271-2
  and ultra-Protestants 154-5
  and violence 154
  sermons and debates 224-30
Seymour, Rev. Charles 241,
  246-9
Shannon, Lord 29
Shaw Mason, William 115
Shaw, Rev. Robert 57-8, 71,
  206
Sheehy, Fr Nicholas 25-6
Sheil, Richard Lalor 194,
  196, 205, 229
Shirley, Rev. Walter 9
Shopkeeper's Letters 29
Simeon, Rev. Charles 19, 161
Singer, Rev. Joseph 210
Sirr, Joseph D'Arcy 239,
  249, 261
Sisters of Mercy 230
Sligo 9-10, 96-7, 98, 103,
  119, 190
Smith, Elizabeth 11
Smith, Rev. Sydney 178
Smyth, Edward 17
Smyth, William 17
Society for the Education of
  the Poor in Ireland 81-2
Society of Friends 81-2
Society for the Irish Church
  Missions 250
Society for Promoting
  Christian Knowledge 108
Southey, Robert 64

Southwell, Robert 175
Staunton, Michael 193
Steelboys 34
Stewart, William, archbishop of Armagh 108
Stokes, Whitley 54, 101, 115, 116
Stoney, Rev. William 229, 247, 249
Stopford, Rev. Joseph 57
Sunday Schools 68, 81-2, 90, 92, 109-11, 120, 249
  Catholic 110-11, 141
  in the Irish language 113
  number of 110
  Sunday School societies 61, 63, 65, 90, 93, 100, 103, 108-10, 113
Swift, Jonathan 2, 5, 12, 21
Synge, John 61, 63-4, 67
Synge, John Millington 117

teachers 83, 97-8, 120-1, 131, 181, 189
Teignmouth, Lord 113
Temple, Sir John 26
Thomas, Rev. Anthony 249
Thompson, David 257
Thompson, E.P. 14-15
Thompson, Mrs D.P. 256, 257-8
Tighe, Rev. Thomas 57, 60
Tipperary 24-6
tithes to Established Church 25, 160
  and anti-tithe movement 28-30, 33-4, 45, 47, 157, 184-5, 198, 218, 233
  and campaign against Catholic priests' dues 31, 33
Tollymore 163
Trant, Dominic 30, 36
Trench, Charles 239
Trench, Dr Power le Poer 115, 130, 142, 158, 206-7, 226
  background 238-42
  and evangelical movement in west 238-51, 254, 261
  sermon in Tuam 246
  work in famine relief 242-6
Trevelyan, Charles 271
Trevor-Roper, Hugh 116
Trimmer, Sarah 56
Trinity College Dublin 13, 18, 35, 54
  role in Church of Ireland revival 19, 45, 47, 55, 57, 60-1, 63, 66
  study of Irish language in 65, 117, 261
Troy, John, archbishop of Dublin 126, 135
typhus epidemic 142, 144
Tyrone 180

Ullathorne, Bishop 226
Ulster 27-8, 34, 49, 109, 110, 120, 166, 174
  religious division in 209, 232
ultra-Protestants 139, 147, 172, 175, 177, 232, 270
  anti-Catholic agitation by 200
  propaganda 153-5, 174, 199, 220
United Irishmen 43, 48, 49, 54, 111, 155
Urwick, Rev. William 62, 63, 165, 207

Ventry, Lord 256-8
Ventry, mission station 258
Volunteer movement 27, 41

Wales 78, 94-8, 100, 102, 122, 132, 139
Walker, Joseph Cooper, *Bardic Remains* 43
Wall, Thomas 223-4, 226
Wallace, A.F.C. 144
Walmesley, Charles, *A General History of the Christian Church* 143
Walsh, bishop of Waterford 140
war between Britain and France 48, 50
Warburton et al., *City of Dublin* 52
Watchman, The 231, 254
Waterford 206, 214
Wellington, duke of 232
Wesley, Charles 4-7, 267
Wesley, John 4-12, 18, 67
Wesleyan Missionary Committee 87
Westmeath, Co. 236, 237, 256
Whelan, Kevin 21, 24
Whiteboys 25-6, 30
  and Gentlemen Whiteboys 29, 31, 32, 33, 34-6, 45
Whitefield, George 8, 11, 267
Wilberforce, Henry 260
Wilberforce, William 55, 68, 70, 113, 155, 268
  address to London Auxiliary of Irish Society 148
  and the Clapham Sect 13, 53, 56, 63, 74, 165
  and CMS campaign 130
Winning, Rev. Robert 173, 175, 181, 188
Wolfe Tone, Theobald 33
Wood, Rev., tutor to Prince George 253
Woodward, Dr Richard, bishop of Cloyne and Ross 33-7, 45, 47, 54, 90, 125, 175, 269
Woodward family 157

Yeats, William Butler 212
York Street Chapel 96
Youghal 110
Young Ireland movement 64, 212

Zinzendorf, Count Nicholas 3-5, 10